'Fresh, with an appealing analysis o[...]
and challenges of today's economy [...]
broad: it looks at a new way to conceptualize the corporation
and at how this new corporation fits in a potentially new
institutional order in the future... Practitioners and academics
alike will find intriguing insights in the book, and will enjoy the
case vignettes drawn from multiple industries and cultures.'

'Zadek is to CSR what Madonna is to pop music.'

'Eschewing the hype and romanticism that characterizes much of the
debate on Corporate Social Responsibility, *The Civil Corporation* is still the
best and most balanced account of this emerging global movement. Simon
Zadek takes us on a wonderfully illuminating tour of Capitalism's present
and possible futures. If you are looking for a guide to this all-important
journey, then take this book along with you.'

'Corporations can only be as civil as we – including the governments we
elect – choose to be. In *The Civil Corporation*, Simon Zadek spotlights the
enabling social, economic and political contexts for corporate citizenship.
A benchmark book.'

'After I read Simon Zadek's *The Civil Corporation* in 2001, I made it
compulsory reading for my course in management education at the
College of Europe. It was and remains an outstanding contribution to the
emerging societal–institutional theory of the firm.

He has achieved this by clearly identifying three levels ("Generations")
of questions and hypotheses for research about the changing role of
business in society from an evolutionary perspective.

The framework Zadek proposed for "Civil Regulation" serves as the
platform for action in reshaping the relationships between government,
business and civil society. His newly conceived of "Fourth Generation"
in this revised edition – although still in its early phases of development
– may open up a new agenda on the leadership role of the corporation in
driving progressive societal change.'

'What sets this book apart is its dispassionate analysis of the current state of corporate aspirations and behaviour. [Zadek] is able, in an engaging and accessible style, to develop a new understanding of corporate responsibility through the creation of the "civil corporation".'

Andrew Wilson, Director, Ashridge Management School

'Fresh and thoughtful look at the societal role of 21st century business, as the focus shifts to sustainable development, corporate citizenship and the new civil governance exemplified by the UN's Global Compact.'

Future Survey

'Simon Zadek offers the rare perspective of someone who has worked on a global basis with a variety of corporations, governmental bodies and civil society organizations. The result is a thoughtful and thought-provoking contribution to the increasingly important and inter-related topics of corporate citizenship and global governance.'

Jane Nelson, Director, CSR Initiative,
Center for Government and Business, Harvard University
(also Director, International Business Leaders Forum)

'A bold manifesto for the future.'

Eurobusiness

'After more than a decade of work with many of the biggest firms and most innovative institutions of our new era, Simon Zadek has done us all a service by condensing his wisdom into this deeply insightful and deftly written book. *The Civil Corporation* offers not only a fascinating description of cutting-edge controversies but also a clear pathway toward the new relationships and new forms of accountability that a sustainable economy will require.'

Bob Massie, Founding Chair, Global Reporting Initiative

'The future depends on our ability to manage corporate ambition within a sustainable social and environmental framework. Simon Zadek's book is a huge contribution to understanding the mechanics of how this problem might be successfully addressed. His "sceptical optimism" is the spirit of the age.'

Ian Hargreaves, Professor of Journalism, Cardiff University,
and former Editor, New Statesman and the Independent

'[Zadek] tackles the complex problems facing corporations today and creates an academic source from which further discussions of these crucial matters can take shape. *The Civil Corporation* lays the groundwork that will help drive corporations to develop viable business strategies and practices that can enable businesses to address the aspirations underpinning sustainable development.'

Soundview Executive Book Summaries

'In his latest book, Simon Zadek provides a macro-, yet comprehensive, analysis of the growth of the corporate social responsibility movement. In *The Civil Corporation: The New Economy of Corporate Citizenship* his knowledge, experience and passion are obvious. Dr Zadek lures the reader through the book with vivid examples that both support and contradict his own thinking.'

www.socialfunds.com

'Zadek should be commended... His description of how the debate developed is clear and fair-minded. His analyses are acute.'

Community Affairs Briefing

The Civil Corporation

Simon Zadek

London and Sterling, VA

Revised edition first published by Earthscan in the UK and USA in 2007

First edition 2001

ISBN: 978-1-84407-431-0

Typeset by JS Typesetting Ltd, Porthcawl, Mid Glamorgan
Printed and bound in the UK by Cromwell Press, Trowbridge
Cover design by Susanne Harris

For a full list of publications please contact:

Earthscan
8–12 Camden High Street
London, NW1 0JH, UK
Tel: +44 (0)20 7387 8558
Fax: +44 (0)20 7387 8998
Email: earthinfo@earthscan.co.uk
Web: **www.earthscan.co.uk**

22883 Quicksilver Drive, Sterling, VA 20166-2012, USA

Earthscan publishes in association with the International Institute for
Environment and Development

A catalogue record for this book is available from the British Library

Library of Congress Cataloging-in-Publication Data

Zadek, Simon.
    The civil corporation : the new economy of corporate citizenship /
Simon Zadek. — Rev. ed.
        p. cm.
    Includes bibliographical references and index.
    ISBN-13: 978-1-84407-431-0 (pbk. : alk. paper)
    ISBN-10: 1-84407-431-5 (pbk. : alk. paper)
  1. Social responsibility of business. I. Title.
    HD60.Z33 2007
    174'.4—dc22

                                2007006300

The paper used for this book is FSC-certified and
totally chlorine-free. FSC (the Forest Stewardship
Council) is an international network to promote
responsible management of the world's forests.

Mixed Sources
Product group from well-managed
forests and other controlled sources
www.fsc.org Cert no. TT-TOC-2082
© 1996 Forest Stewardship Council

Contents

List of Figures and Boxes   *viii*
Preface   *x*
List of Acronyms and Abbreviations   *xiii*

Introduction: Beyond the Mainstream   1

Part 1 The New Economy of Corporate Citizenship

1   Can Corporations Be Civil?   29
2   Opening Minds   42
3   Ethical Futures   51
4   Breaking the Trust Barrier   63
5   Civil Regulation   76
6   Framing the Business Case   90
7   The Future of the Civil Regulators   102
8   The New Civil Governance   115

Part 2 The Civil Corporation

9   Foundations of Sustainability   131
10 Sustainability as the Art of the Possible   148
11 Civil Learning   162

Part 3 Building the Civil Corporation

12 Building Civil Corporations   179
13 How Much is Enough?   184
14 Useful Measures   196
15 Conversational Corporations   219
16 Professionalizing Credibility   232

Part 4 Conclusions

17 How Civil Can Corporations Be?   245

Notes   252
Bibliography   269
Index   280

List of Figures and Boxes

FIGURES

0.1	Generations of Corporate Responsibility	11
0.2	Determining What Counts	16
0.3	Pathways to Extensive Accountability	19
0.4	Collaborative Governance: Shifting Roles	21
3.1	Ethical Trade Futures?	60
4.1	Level of Confidence in Different Organizations in the UK	70
5.1	Civil Regulation in Action	80
5.2	Civil Regulation in Theory	81
5.3	Business is not Paying Enough Attention to its Social Responsibilities	83
5.4	Manufacturer Brand	85
5.5	Retailer Brand	85
5.6	Divergent Market Responses	87
5.7	The Goyder Effect	88
5.8	The Korten Effect	89
6.1	The Four-level Business Case	90
7.1	NGO Approaches to Changing the World	106
8.1	Complementary or Competing Governance Hierarchies?	121
9.1	Triple Bottom Line: What Does It Mean?	133
9.2	Metaphoric Visualization	137
9.3	Literal Visualization	138
9.4	Cognitive Visualization	138
9.5	Economics as Means Not Ends	141
10.1	Hierarchy of Opportunities, Investment and Risks	157
10.2	Linking Tactics and Strategy	158
10.3	Hierarchy of Influence	159
11.1	The Data–Knowledge Continuum	169
11.2	Civil Learning Cycle	171
13.1	Evolving Boundaries: the Case of Labour Standards	192
14.1	How Labels Work	202
14.2	Mediating Indicators	211
15.1	Participation Ladder	224

BOXES

2.1	Possible Core Standards	44
2.2	Six Possible Reasons Why Things Don't Change	46
5.1	Why Companies Do The Right Thing	77
5.2	Consumers' Caring *Can* Count	86
6.1	The Traditional Business Case for Employing Disabled People	91
6.2	Socially Responsible Investment Counts – a Bit	94
6.3	Innovation through Partnership	96
6.4	Corporate Citizenship and Risk Management	97
6.5	Corporate Citizenship's Three Generations	98
6.6	Citizenship Challenges and Pathways	100
6.7	Citizenship Pathways and Business Case Levels	101
7.1	The Growing Size of the NGO Community	105
7.2	Engaging Dilemmas	107
8.1	Reasons for Evolving Global Policy Networks	118
8.2	Civil Society Challenges the UN Global Compact	119
9.1	Talking About Sustainability	132
9.2	GRI Perspectives on the Elements of Sustainable Development	136
9.3	The Natural Step's System Conditions	142
9.4	SIGMA's Five Capital Model	143
9.5	Weak and Strong Sustainability	146
10.1	Debunking the Sustainable Enterprise	149
10.2	Uncomfortable Trade-offs, Incomparable Valuations	150
10.3	SAM's View of BMW's Strategic Opportunities and Risks	155
10.4	SAM's View of Teijin Ltd's Strategic Opportunities and Risks	156
11.1	The Knowledge Dividend	170
12.1	Getting the Balance Between the Yogi and the Commissar	182
13.1	Conversations about Boundaries	185
13.2	Characterizing Organization	187
13.3	Evolution of GRI Standard	193
14.1	Which Non-financial Measures do Investors Value Most?	200
14.2	Criteria for Effective Social Labels	204
14.3	Traidcraft on 'Fairness'	210
14.4	GRI Spheres of Reporting	214
14.5	Measuring the Living Wage	215
15.1	The Body Shop's Formal Stakeholder Dialogue	220
15.2	What is Stakeholder Dialogue?	223
16.1	Panel Members Make Their Choices	236
17.1	Some of the CIA's View of the World in 2015	248

Preface

The Civil Corporation synthesizes and presents the thoughts and conclusions emerging from two decades' work and efforts of myself and others in encouraging corporations to deliver more social and environmental 'goods', and fewer 'bads'. Since the early 1990s, this field of endeavour has exploded with ideas, experiments, civil campaigns and new organizations. For some, this is at best a sign of early spring after the very frosty 1980s and at worst a light autumnal breeze. This book proposes that corporate citizenship is, or could be, more than some short-term allergic, inter-generational reaction to chillier times.

This ferment of activities around the role of business in society has created its own special brand of chaos. Divergent, and often conflicting, preconceived views based on partial and inappropriately extrapolated facts are proving pervasive, as much within as between people and organizations. Chaos does provide opportunities for innovation in addressing both new and very old problems. However, it also carries the danger that the really big fish slip away in the ensuing confusion. The big fish in this instance concerns the question of how much corporations can and should be expected to actively contribute to the provision of social and environmental goods, and the terms on which this contribution should and can be realized.

This book seeks to provide some answers to this knotty and yet critically important question. It goes without saying that my answers are partial, contingent, and may prove totally wrong. The world is changing as we describe it, so to claim otherwise would be just plain silly. It is nevertheless critical that this question be addressed because of its importance for public policy, corporate strategy, the evolution of civil activism and – without being melodramatic – our individual and common futures.

It was suggested to me by some generous readers of early drafts of the manuscript that this had the makings of not one but two books. The first half, it was argued, offers what could be a self-contained analysis of the emergence and current state of corporate citizenship. The second half of the book provides an assessment of, and guidance on, *how* corporations can most effectively contribute to sustainable development. I thought long and hard about this, and eventually chose to remain on my chosen path of producing a single book. The main reason for this was certainly not any love of long books, and I hope that those with limited time will not have to flick past too many pages to find the bits they really want to read. I chose to keep it all together because there seemed to be a need in the realm of corporate citizenship to offer a framework for thinking about *both* the broader changes in the external environment, and how corporations could best learn and so change internally to meet its emerging challenges and opportunities.

This book has evolved over several years, undoubtedly both profiting and suffering as a result. Because of this extended gestation, bits of the argument have been produced in various publications that I have authored, co-authored and otherwise contributed to, notably: *The Materiality Report: Aligning Strategy, Performance and Reporting* (with Maya Forstater, Chris Tuppen, Debbie Evans, Alan Knight and Maria Sillanpää; AccountAbility, 2006); *Responsible Competitiveness: Reshaping Global Markets Through Responsible Business Practices* (with Peter Raynard, Cristiano Oliviero, Edna do Nascimento and Rafael Tello; AccountAbility, 2005); *Mainstreaming Responsible Investment* (with Mira Merme and Richard Samans; World Economic Forum in association with AccountAbility, 2005); *Adding Values: The Economics of Sustainable Business* (with Chris Tuppen; BT, 2000); *Building Corporate Accountability* (with Peter Pruzan and Richard Evans; Earthscan, 1997); *Conversations With Disbelievers: Persuading Companies to Increase Their Social Engagement* (with John Weiser; Brody and Weiser, 2000); *Ethical Trade Futures* (New Economics Foundation, 2000); *The New Economy of Corporate Citizenship* (with Niels Hojengard and Peter Raynard; The Copenhagen Centre, 2000); *Partnership Alchemy* (with Jane Nelson; The Copenhagen Centre, 1999); and *Unlocking Potential: The New Business Case for Disability* (with Susan Scott-Parker; Employers' Forum on Disability, 2000). Those with a passion for this book's less recent foundations may want to look at my dusty doctoral thesis, published as *An Economics of Utopia: The Democratisation of Utopia* (Avebury, 1993) and *Value-Based Organisation* (New Economics Foundation, 1994).

Most authors owe thanks to all sorts of people, mostly alive and occasionally dead, who have contributed to their particular treasured volume. My acknowledgements, similarly, range far and wide. First is my thanks to those with whom I have worked on elements of this book through the above publications, particularly Richard Evans, Niels Hojengard, Alex McGillivray, Susan Scott-Parker, Jane Nelson, Sasha Radovich, Peter Raynard, Peter Pruzan, Chris Tuppen and John Weiser. The second set of co-conspirators are others whom I have also had the privilege to work with and draw lessons from, particularly Gavin Andersson, Jutta Blauert, Mike Edwards, Maria Eitel, Georg Kell, David Korten, Maria Sillanpää, Vernon Jennings, David Vidal, David Wheeler and Lynda Yanz. Then must come my salute and thanks to other 'usual suspects' from whose thinking and experience I have shamelessly borrowed throughout the book, including David Logan, Mark Goyder, Mark Wade and John Elkington.

The role of two further groups of people in crafting this book cannot remain invisible. The first is that indispensable group of patient and loving people who pick you up when you are down, and then helpfully trip you up with mesmerizing challenges. Thanks on this basis to Mira Merme and

Lisa Curtis, whose insightful and occasionally painful comments never failed to find their just target. Particular thanks are also due to Ed Mayo, Director of the New Economics Foundation, erstwhile colleague and indefatigable believer in this book as it continued to break even the most pessimistic deadlines; my caring and sharing supporter, Jonathan Sinclair Wilson from Earthscan; and Philippe Puyo-Tschanz.

Finally my thanks to those whose support has minimized the pain in writing this book. Thanks particularly to Stephan Schmidheiny and his colleague Lloyd Timberlake. Thanks also to Finn Junge-Jensen, President of the Copenhagen Business School, and his colleagues, for welcoming me as a Visiting Professor during 2000 and so helping to create the space for the book to be completed; and to the whole team at AccountAbility for putting up with my endless, and work-distracting drafts of the revised edition.

Simon Zadek
London
1 March 2007

Acronyms and Abbreviations

AI	Amnesty International
AMRC	Asia Monitoring Resource Centre
API	American Petroleum Institute
BAA	British Airport Authority
BAe	British Aerospace
BAT	British American Tobacco
BMW	Bayerische Motoren Werke
BP	British Petroleum
BRT	Business Roundtable
BSR	Business for Social Responsibility
BT	British Telecommunications
CBI	Confederation of British Industry
CEO	chief executive officer
CEPAA	Council of Economic Priorities Accreditation Agency
CERES	Coalition of Environmentally Responsible Economies
CIA	Central Intelligence Agency
COP	Corporate Europe Observatory
CVG	Corporación Venezolana de Guayana
CTE	Committee on Trade and Environment
DJSI	Dow Jones Sustainability Index
DTI	Department of Trade and Industry (UK)
DIY	do it yourself
EMAS	Eco-Management and Audit Scheme
ENDS	Environmental Data Services
ETI	Ethical Trading Initiative
EVA	economic value added
EU	European Union
FAO	Food and Agriculture Organization
FLA	Fair Labor Association (US)
FTF	Fairtrade Foundation
FT	*Financial Times*
GATT	General Agreement on Tariffs and Trade
GCC	Global Climate Coalition
GM	General Motors
GMO	genetically modified organism
GNP	gross national product
GDP	gross domestic product
GRI	Global Reporting Initiative

G7	group of the seven most industrialized countries
HDI	Human Development Index
HSE	Health, Safety and Environment
HPI	Human Poverty Index
IBFAN	International Baby Food Action Network
IBLF	International Business Leaders Forum
ICFTU	International Confederation of Free Trade Unions
IDS	Institute of Development Studies
ILRF	International Labor Rights Fund
IPPR	Institute for Public Policy Research
ISEA	Institute of Social and Ethical AccountAbility
ISO	International Organization for Standardization
IMF	International Monetary Fund
ILO	International Labour Organization
ITGWU	International Textiles and Garments Workers Union
MAI	Multilateral Agreement on Investment
M&S	Marks & Spencer
NEF	New Economics Foundation
NGO	non-governmental organization
OPS	Overleg Platform Stedelijk Vernieuwing (The Netherlands)
OECD	Organisation for Economic Co-operation and Development
PPP	purchasing power parity
R&D	research and development
RIIA	Royal Institute of International Affairs
SAI	Social Accountability International
SAM	Sustainability Asset Management
S&P 500	Standards and Poor's 500 Index
SIF	Social Investment Forum
SIGMA	Sustainability Integrated Guidelines for Management
SMART	Specific, Measurable, Actionable, Relevant and Timely
TCC	The Copenhagen Centre
TINA	there is no alternative
TOES	The Other Economic Summit
UBS	Union of Bank of Switzerland
UN	United Nations
UNEP	United Nations Environment Programme
UNDHR	UN Declaration of Human Rights
UNCTAD	United Nations Conference on Trade And Development
UNRISD	United Nations Research Institute for Social Development
USCIB	United States Council for International Business
WBCSD	World Business Council for Sustainable Development
WDM	World Development Movement
WHO	World Health Organization
WTO	World Trade Organization
WWF	World Wide Fund for Nature
WWI	Worldwatch Institute
Y2K	year 2000

Beyond the Mainstream

The Civil Corporation is firmly grounded in the future. It envisages the implications of today's practices being tomorrow's history. Its empirical focus is the practice of corporate responsibility, but its deeper concern is in what this contemporary phenomenon might presage for the business of business. It carries, in short, the DNA of far more sweeping societal changes that will alter both the very nature of business and its place in emerging governance arrangements.

At stake is the very heartland of how we organize our affairs, the relationship between the markets through which we create material wealth, and the politics through which we mediate diverse and often divergent interests. Nobel Prize-winning economist Milton Friedman felt at ease encouraging businesses to 'be responsible' by making as much money as possible because he envisaged economies disciplined by governments that were more or less accountable to the people. Friedman built on Adam Smith's comparatively advantage-seeking businesses, who were similarly conceived of as being subject to the rules and norms established through a liberally debated political realm, described eloquently in his *Theory of Moral Sentiments*.[1] The *Financial Times'* Associate Editor and Chief Economics Commentator, Martin Wolf, more recently pinpointed the nub of this classical view in arguing that 'markets are not accountability mechanisms, they exist within a broader institutional landscape that establishes the basis on which market actors should and can be held to account.'[2]

The Civil Corporation asserts that this classical separation of roles is no longer a tenable lens with which to understand the changing world around us. It argues that our traditional view of business as legalized poacher responsible to financial capital, and of the state as paternalistic gamekeeper accountable to the people, not only fails to describe what *is*, but is way off the mark in mapping what is likely to be in the future. Moreover, although activists, business leaders and politicians alike might wish otherwise, the classic differences and associated roles of these players no longer reflect how we would re-organize the rules of the game given some reasonable debate and choice in the matter.

The corporate responsibility movement is where new arrangements governing the relationship between market players and politics in its broadest sense are being invented, tested and institutionalized. *The Civil Corporation* is suggestive of this deeper, changing landscape. In so doing, it pushes the stakes beyond the more limited agenda of seeking to make business more responsible within some modified rules of the existing game. It provides a 'beta version' of the organization of business in a very changed society. Such organizations will have more autonomy by virtue of their scale, transnationality and evolving legitimacy to be at the table where major public policies are debated and decided upon, and their involvement in the roles and responsibilities of collaborative governance.[3] Yet, simultaneously, they will have less scope for independent action, by virtue of this very fact of their embeddedness in mutual 'accountability compacts' that provide pathways to secure the gains of private enterprise in return for being party to delivering much-needed public goods.[4] *The Civil Corporation*, and later work, suggests that these extended accountabilities will arise not through a collective epiphany, but through the result of a sequence of traditional business responses that will add up to far more than the sum of their parts.[5]

Such developments have profound implications for our understanding of business, and its practice and impact. Extending accountabilities of business place it and the state increasingly on a par with each other in key respects. We see a convergence in their legitimacies, despite their very different historical foundations – one in security, mediation and political representation, and the other through their production of material needs and returns to finance capital. Such a convergence is accelerated by several factors, including: the declining legitimacy of traditional electoral routes to the politics of representation; the emerging political empowerment of citizens through their roles in markets, notably as owners of capital; and the growing prevalence and visibility of complex partnerships involving public and private actors tasked to deliver public, and indeed private, goods.

Such a vista, in practice, may unlock extraordinary potential and provide the foundations for overcoming today's dead-end stalemates on major issues such as climate change, water scarcity, underlying poverty and civil unrest. Or else it may turn out to be a virulent dystopia, a symptom of the problem with little or nothing to offer for solving the dilemmas of our time. Corporatization of public policy is what many activists see as the problem, certainly not the solution. From this view, a creeping legitimization of businesses' role in highly sensitive areas of public policy from education through to energy security is equally seen as far from helpful. And growing involvement in business activities by the governments of newly emerging economic and political powerhouses, notably in China and Russia, is feared for its broader geopolitical consequences.

To view the corporate responsibility movement as a key (if not *the* key) to tilting us towards the brighter end of this menu may seem unreasonable to many. After all, however enthusiastic one might be about current trends in corporate responsibility, the effectiveness of many of its prototypical components, smuggled into reality under the guise of an agenda for incremental improvement, remain unproven. It is unclear at best, for example, whether multi-stakeholder initiatives can effectively unlock public policy stalemates by providing resource and direction to overcome business or national-level first-mover disadvantages and free-riders intent on avoiding or undercutting standards. Moreover, although societal expectations have in many respects served progressive interests over the last decade, this is certainly not a historical given. Social and environmental pressures could just as easily, if not more easily, invert the impact of this driver, encouraging xenophobia and the exercise of available power to secure resources and security. Most of all, can we envisage the forces that have driven corporate responsibility thus far to power such an amplification of its scope and impact as to be significant in the broader landscape of our global affairs in this coming century?

Yet that is exactly what is argued in *The Civil Corporation*: that corporate responsibility is a critical arena where both tomorrow's business models and practices, and the next generation of broader accountability innovations, will be invented, tested and contested. Failure not just to rein in business's misdemeanours, but to re-empower it with a broader set of rights and responsibilities, will leave old political systems in place, degenerating liberalism at best, or at worst a new era of authoritarian states acting in the dual cause of security and economic development. Success, on the other hand, will rewrite the rules of economy and business and with it the nature of citizens' participation and the place of the state.

The Civil Corporation is clear about which outcome seems preferable, but argues strongly that where we end up depends on us. Historical tendencies, like genetic dispositions, provide the backdrop to ensuing events. It all depends, in short, on what we do with what we've got. It offers, without apology, a blend of observation, prediction and advocacy. Its 'sceptical optimism' does not allow for unfounded speculation, senseless idealization or dead-end cynicism. It provides a cocktail of real events, tenuous conclusions and predictions, and an overlay of a normative sensibility towards preferred directions. It is, at its heart, a grounded imagination about the world we can and should create, one out of many and by no means the favourite in the race.

This opening essay explores some of *The Civil Corporation's* propositions five years on since the first edition of the book was published. It is not an assessment as such. We are not far enough down the road to really know the fate of the experiments and innovations it describes. But much has happened in the intervening period, a lot of which does validate the book's main thrust. In fact, there is little in the book that is not as relevant today as when originally penned, if not more so. Also there is new research to draw on, including some undertaken by myself with friends, colleagues and collaborators, which has drilled further into some issues and perspectives only lightly sketched in the book.

FROM AVANT-GARDE TO OLD GUARD

Five years have passed since publishing *The Civil Corporation*, and more or less a decade since it first became a work in progress. The world evolves, but paradoxically. Much has changed, while everything has also remained dramatically the same.

The Civil Corporation was first published in early 2001. It was a product of the 1990s, reflecting the zeitgeist of a post-communist, post-Thatcher/ Reagan era. Most of all, this meant a stoic acceptance of the need to innovate for the public good from within a globalization process driven by a cocktail of heady vision, and narrow vested political and economic interests. It was a period of being awed at the pace of globalization, the penetration of the practice of privatization, the cult of commerce and the associated messages from business and political leaders alike that business was, almost by definition, good. There seemed few structural limits to the corporate community's emergent power to define its own world and us within it. A global civil society was inventing itself as history's counter-point to those forces that governments seemed unable or unwilling any longer to manage for the public good. An emerging cacophony of civil voices demanded that business must be *made to be* good if it was to secure the legitimacy of its heightened economic and political muscle.

The world of 'business in society', or 'corporate responsibility', has matured beyond most expectations. Hundreds of thousands of businesses have embraced, to a greater or lesser degree, the need to better measure and manage their social and environmental footprints. Innovative experiments of the 1990s have become lore and legend, catalysing an explosion of initiatives addressing many of the very Cinderella issues previously deemed taboo by mainstream business. The Body Shop produced the world's first serious, externally audited sustainability report ('The Values Report') in early 1996, when the Global Reporting Initiative was barely a thought, let alone the main game in sustainability reporting standards. Shell, BP and Rio (then British Petroleum and Rio Tinto) broke new ground in 1997 in adopting human rights policies at a flamboyant event at Chatham House. Today, witness the emerging consensus that the UN should lend its name to a (voluntary) international agreement on how business should handle human rights issues as they arise in relation to their products and process. Social auditing has passed from being a campaigning weapon to becoming a billion dollar business, complete with assurance standards produced not only by innovators such as AccountAbility[6] and Social Accountability International (SA8000), but by the heartland of professional conservatism, the International Auditing and Assurance Standards Board.

There has been amazing progress. No business sector has remained untouched, and some have been deeply impacted, by corporate responsibility perspectives, actions and outcomes. Drug pricing for pharmaceuticals; social and environmental criteria for investors; digital exclusion for information and communications companies; chemicals and genetically modified organisms for the agricultural sector; slave labour for chocolate producers; obesity for food companies; and carbon emissions for the cement (and every other) industry. The list is endless, and growing literally every day, in its breadth of issues and coverage of the business community. The drivers for these changes, fundamentally, remain the same, but they too have evolved in strength and impact. Consumers, perhaps most of all, have grown enormously in their sophistication and orientation. A decade ago, it was common wisdom that 'ethical consumers' were a strictly niche phenomenon lodged somewhere between income classifications B and C2 (the rich – A, that is – remaining in the main aloof from such matters, and lower income groups – D and E – not having the discretionary purchasing power to move beyond financial value for money).

These characterizations remain important signals, but have meanwhile become unhelpful caricatures of consumer behaviour on the ground. *What Assures Consumers?*, prepared by AccountAbility and the UK-based National Consumer Council, has been one of a steady stream of reports highlighting the steady extension of the ethical consumer movement beyond its historical niche.[7] And this extension has also very much been geographical. Today, institutional intermediaries through which corporate responsibility emerged during the 1990s, such as Business for Social Responsibility, the Global Compact, SustainAbility and the World Business Council for Sustainable Development, are almost as active from Shanghai to Calcutta as they were in the early days from California to Berlin.

All in all, if the aim for those in the vanguard over the last decade was to embed social and environmental issues into codified practices for the mainstream business community, they should be quite satisfied that this task has been well advanced.

CHALLENGING SUCCESS

Transiting from the avant-garde to the old guard means the scaling up and mainstreaming of practice. But this does not in itself mean, or guarantee, success. Understanding progress in this more normative sense requires a more probing enquiry as to what has really been achieved and what were the aims in the first place. There is, however, no widely accepted framework for analysing success. In fact, few advocates of corporate responsibility have set out a concrete vision of success, preferring rather to specify shorter-term achievable targets like 'greater transparency' or 'code adoption'. To call for a 'more responsible role for business in society' is all well and good, but hardly provides either sparkling vision or ideology, or a basis for applying SMART (Specific, Measurable, Actionable, Relevant and Timely) metrics to assess progress.

The previous section does suggest that some real successes have been achieved. Real workers' lives have improved; access to life-saving drugs has increased for people and nations who could not pay the commercial going rate; investments in dams and roads are made in ways more sensitive to community interests and the environment; and those that trade, buy and wear diamonds have less blood on their hands than ever before. These examples illustrate substantial developments that have impacted positively on millions of people's lives, and which cannot be shrugged off through caveat, objection or cynicism.

But just as these developments are real enough, expectations have in other respects been dashed. Since publishing the first edition of *The Civil Corporation*, iconic First Generation corporate responsibility leaders have fallen under the hammer, most symbolically Ben & Jerry's to Unilever and The Body Shop to its erstwhile, less-than-ethics-conscious rival, L'Oréal. The movement of such independently spirited businesses to becoming owned, classic brands was not merely a matter of profit-taking by smart founder–entrepreneurs. Sadly, moreover, these were not cases of masterfully planned, mainstreaming of the sustainability agenda 'through the back door' of the corporate community. Both were ultimately instances of poorly managed businesses unable to cope with maturing markets and, arguably, and most significantly, signs of the limits of ethical markets in the face of rapacious, attention-deficit consumerism.

Second Generation business leaders have also stumbled. Ford Motor Corporation, while seeking to position itself as the auto industry's inspired eco-castle of sustainability, in practice got stuck making out-dated, oversized, gas-guzzling cars. The company's precipitous loss of market share and lack of effective leadership in bringing carbon-light vehicles to market sadly demonstrated the consequences of a noble vision (in this case that of William Ford Jr.) being out of touch with ground-level performance. BP's acquisition strategy during the 1990s took it from being a second-class oil company to a first-class energy company. The Beyond Petroleum vision was, and perhaps still is, core to its long-term strategy, and provided inspiration and leverage for a community of activists seeking to mainstream public debate and action around both climate change and corruption. But BP found itself struggling with the far tougher execution challenge of integrating its acquisitions and delivering more efficient processes and ever-expanding financial returns.[8]

And we looked to Europe, notably the UK, to maintain its historical leadership role in internalizing social and environmental costs into business practices. After all, the UK government provided the world with its first 'Minister for Corporate Social Responsibility' and, at the time of publication of *The Civil Corporation*, was poised to break new ground in embedding social and environmental disclosure requirements into its revised Company Law. But the new-found political voice of corporate responsibility was subsequently downgraded to a junior minister, effect-ively moonlighting the field as an extra-curricular activity. UK Company Law became a battleground, largely strewn with the dead and wounded of the corporate responsibility movement, as the traditional rump of the British business community successfully impressed their displeasure about the proposed enhanced accountability on a nervous New Labour government. And to crown a less-than-satisfactory journey from its newly elected heights of 1997, the UK government, having championed the Organisation for Economic Co-operation and Development (OECD) Convention on Foreign Corrupt Practices and the ensuing fight against corruption, foreclosed on its own police force's investigation into alleged murky dealings between BAE Systems and its US$20 billion client, the Saudi government.

The state of working conditions in the global supply chains of the apparel and textiles, footwear and sports good sectors is in many ways the litmus test of progress. This issue in this sector was more than any other the heartland of corporate responsibility during its take-off stage in the 1990s. The anti-Nike campaign was the jewel of the anti-globalization movement, outranking the longer-lasting but somehow deflated baby milk campaign targeted at Nestlé. And progress was made: numerous multi-stakeholder initiatives, such as the Ethical Trading Initiative, the Fair Labor Association and Social Accountability International, followed hot on the heels of aggressive campaigning and delivered widespread adoption by European and North American premium brands of codes based on core International Labour Organization (ILO) conventions. Even Wal-Mart, the proverbial 'elephant in the bedroom' of this and other sectors, eventually embraced the principles of responsibility for working conditions in its vast global supply chains.

Progress has been made, but the disappointments have been all too visible and deeply troubling. An early casualty was the Global Alliance for Workers and Communities, closed down in 2004 after its main sponsors, the International Youth Foundation, Nike, Gap and the World Bank, accepted that the initiative had failed to gain traction among the business, activist or development communities.[9] Far more disturbing was the effective collapse in 2006 of the much-vaunted Atlanta Agreement to secure 'child-free' stitching of leather footballs in Sialkot, Pakistan. This turn of events was startling to many, if only because of the high-profile engagement of many international organizations, notably the ILO and Save the Children's Fund, as well as the international labour movement, in both brokering and implementing the deal. Perhaps exactly because multi-stakeholder standards initiatives were first developed around labour issues in the apparel and textiles sector, these initiatives have been the first to come under close scrutiny regarding their performance. And the jury is at best still out. The Ethical Trading Initiative (ETI), for example, a much-used case in *The Civil Corporation* because of my early insider knowledge as the founding Chair, has been the subject of a polite, very critical evaluation undertaken by the prestigious Institute of Development Studies.[10] Campaigners War on Want have attacked the ETI as 'part of the problem', arguing that businesses are using their memberships of the initiative to protect them against criticism and so avoid implementing much-needed changes in the ways in which their business practices impact on workers lives.

Success over the last decade must at least in part be measured against the interests of business. Business engagement in the corporate responsibility agenda was, and remains, for most companies, a matter of risk management. I return to this issue below. During the 1990s, this translated into the far more comfortable, if somewhat disingenuous, language of 'trust'. Business wanted to be trusted, employing enthusiastic people to make products and deliver services to willing customers without unnecessary and costly interference by governments or others who might see fit, and be able, to upset the business of business. Trust was the business solution to a world where effective compliance and sustainable arms-length market relationships were costly to secure.

Set against this benchmark, there is little evidence that corporate responsibility has succeeded. Business is *still* not trusted, despite a decade of appealing to peoples' better nature, according to GlobeScan and other pollsters. People remain outraged by business profits, chief executives' remuneration, and the extraordinarily large bonuses paid to the youthful fund managers who we foolishly rely on for the stewardship of our life savings. And at least some of this outrage seems validated by the evidence that many business models are dependent for their success on irresponsible behaviour. Corruption is unquestionably the practical and symbolic crux of the problem of irresponsibility. Not only is it illegal, but it also plays a pernicious role in degrading the integrity and effectiveness of our public servants and institutions, as well as private commercial enterprises. Transparency International's Bribe Payers Index covers perceptions of business from 30 countries. The 2006 results show a considerable propensity for multinationals of all nationalities to bribe when operating outside of their home countries, with even those perceived as least corrupt (Switzerland, for example) scoring considerably below the maximum potential, and the worst offenders – Russia, India and China – scoring on average well below half the total possible score.

But then, no one ever said that the realignment of business's responsibilities in society was going to be easy. Old ways are deeply embedded in the fabric of markets and the psychology of those who create and lead them. The state of the investment community epitomizes the entrenchment of such old ways. The evidence indicates that business leaders systematically abandon prospective financial returns in favour of winning immediate beauty contests whose judges are financial analysts and fund managers focused more on their Christmas bonus than the interests of the owners of the capital that they are stewarding.[11] To be frank, the prospects for enabling businesses to pursue long-term strategies for value creation, let alone of us taking a sustainable development pathway, are pretty dim unless we can change these investors' short-termism.

The imperative of an agenda for realignment towards responsibility, accountability and sustainable development is not, it must be stressed, just for business. Even those focused exclusively on corporate accountability see the growing need to reform the basis on which the business of government is undertaken. This is obvious when it comes to corruption – in Nigeria alone an estimated US$400 billion in oil revenues since the 1960s has been stolen by politicians and civil servants. But much-needed reforms need to go further than halting these practices. Much of government is no longer fit for the purpose of either delivering public services and infrastructure, or stewarding on the public's behalf their delivery by business. The success of Al Gore's *An Inconvenient Truth* is probably as much due to its implicit indictment of our political leaders as it is due to its eloquent restatement of the resulting impending climate change catastrophe.[12] Anger over Halliburton's profiting from post-invasion activities in Iraq have given way to despair and fury over the far broader implications of failure of US- and UK-backed policies towards the region and the underlying issues. More mundanely, if also more pervasively, the troubled history of public–private partnerships as an often-failed means of enhancing the 'public good' has arguably been rooted more in the inadequacies of public institutions than in the to-be-expected will and ability of their businesses to take commercial advantage of weak and incompetent partners.[13]

The Civil Corporation's underlying frame of reference is summed up in its very first sentence: 'the role of business in society is the 21st century's most important and contentious public policy issue'. Events over the past decade challenge this all-embracing assertion. In one sense it remains almost by definition true, since the role of business in the process of wealth creation makes its behaviour so pivotal in determining many social and environmental outcomes. But whether business, even 'big' business, will be the locus, let alone the driver, of change in the coming decades is less certain given the emerging, broader political landscape.

Opinion polls repeatedly highlight deteriorating confidence in politics, and indeed the practice of politics. One survey of political attitudes in Latin America in 2006, published by Latinobarómetro, reported that barely more than one half of respondents across Latin America (58 per cent) agreed that 'democracy was the best system of government'. This figure fell to 46 per cent for the continent's largest nation, Brazil, which is just emerging from a national presidential contest where the successful candidate, Luiz Inácio Lula da Silva, has made much of his efforts to encourage responsible business practices. But the survey provides worse news still. Affirmative scores as high as 35 per cent, in the case of Guatemala, were registered in answering the question 'are there circumstances when an authoritarian government can be preferable to a democratic one?'.

The 21st century provides the historical stage where China, India and an energy-rich, resurgent Russia will take an increasingly critical role in shaping the global marketplace for ideas and profits. Indignation over the social and environmental shortfalls of Western extractive companies will, and probably should, pale into insignificance in the face of 'race-to-the-bottom' 'conditionless' loans, and business ventures by China into Africa and Latin America in pursuit of natural resources. Hard-won progress grounded in new initiatives like the Equator Principles and the Extractive Industries Transparency Initiative are under threat by the growing importance of Chinese and other investors across Africa and Latin America who are shunning these initiatives in favour of competitive (and highly successful) tactics that offer finance, expertise and markets free of social and environmental conditions.

Multinationals that have, through force of circumstances, taken leadership roles in driving forward responsible business practices find themselves challenged by new or resurgent actors. This is most obvious in, but not confined to, the energy sector. Shell, with their mould-breaking experiences in the 1990s linked to their disposal of the Brent Spa oil platform and their much-disputed track record in the Niger Delta, is now the victim of Russia's nationalistic energy policies, stripped of their controlling interest in the massive Sakhalin gas pipeline project because of alleged environmental failures. Today's global energy majors are dwarfed by the scale of emerging national energy players that, in an age of globalization, are extending their global economic and political reach well beyond their national boundaries.

And of course there is climate change, which is important both because of the associated potential down-side risks and because of its 'paradigmatic' place in the sustainability agenda. Climate change, by most accounts, will impact quite simply on everything, affecting every product, process, business model, political system and individual's life, and often profoundly so. It is the most disturbing case of a 'public good' that, despite Mr Stern's seductive reminder of a potential US$500 billion market, remains under-delivered because of the perceived first-mover disadvantages to any country or region really seeking to curb its emissions. Climate change presents us with a classic collective action problem, where self-evident 'market failure' is reinforced rather than overcome in equal measure by the politics of development (why should emerging nations curb themselves at their point of take-off, especially when developed economies refused to first take serious leadership?) and short-termism in electoral democracies (why should democratically elected governments damage their electoral prospects in exchange for uncertain and widely shared gains long into the future?).

THE SECOND GENERATION: STRATEGY

Civil corporations embrace a broader accountability for their actions and, in so doing, contribute to addressing societal needs and challenges in ways that could also deliver economic value and success. But existing win–win scenarios are unlikely to cover all market failures, the full spectrum of opportunities that, once realized, will deliver under-provided, and much-needed, public goods. That is, how far can we expect changing business models and performance, responding to market dynamics, to underpin the solutions to our pressing social and environmental problems? And since such circumstances and opportunities are created rather than discovered, what actions need to be taken, not only by business but by non-market players, to catalyse further, and systemically more significant, scenarios for civil corporations to prosper?

The Civil Corporation describes (in Chapter 6) three generations of corporate responsibility: compliance and risk management *(First Generation)*, strategy and innovation *(Second Generation)*, and transforming markets *(Third Generation)*. This taxonomy, while (or perhaps because) it's so simple, has proved to be both durable and useful. At the time of writing, there was little to see on the empirical – as opposed to the rhetorical - landscape beyond the First Generation. But the intervening period has seen interesting and important developments, both in practice and theory.

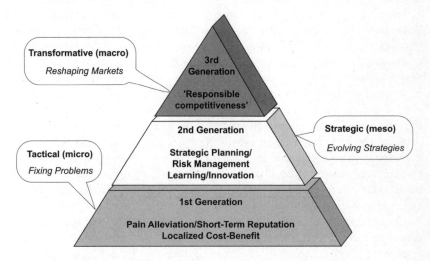

Figure 0.1 *Generations of Corporate Responsibility*

At a practical level, there are now simply far more cases of the Second Generation in practice. The level of sugar and salt content in food is no longer just a matter of taste, just as the energy rating of domestic household goods or a car's fuel consumption has become far more than a 'nice-to-have'. Drug pricing has become a global moral debate, just as workers' conditions have become key issues in the market for everything from coffee to T-shirts to wine to bananas. And there are a new, more mainstream and, therefore, influential set of 'leadership converts' along these pathways to economic success. GE's Chief Executive, Jeff Immelt, for example, has made much of the company's hard-headed Ecoimagination strategy, arguing that:

> There is an alignment between the world's most pressing needs and the areas of our most aggressive investment. As the world's need for cleaner, efficient

forms of energy grows, we are creating new technology and building new capacity to meet those needs. As sources of clean water become scarce, our filtration and desalination technologies expand supplies.[14]

Witness also the trendsetting Richard Branson in his commitment at one of the Clinton Global Initiative New York spectacles to invest an estimated US$3 billion of Virgin's profits into technology ventures to combat, and profit from, climate change. Such leaders have understood that their markets are undergoing fundamental change because of far-reaching systemic shifts, notably – but by no means exclusively – linked to climate change and energy security. A decade ago, raising the topics of obesity, climate change or 'the fortune at the bottom of the pyramid' would have drawn a blank face from all but the most prescient of fortune-tellers. Today, no self-respecting boardroom buzz is without one or all of them.

The Second Generation of corporate responsibility is about how to turn issues into new products and processes, underpinned by focused strategies for exploiting emerging markets, or creating new markets. At times this involves hardcore technological innovation. But more often than not the need is for 'soft innovation' to appreciate the implications of societal changes for tomorrow's markets. But stepwise change of this kind requires that a business can undergo broader, systemic innovation in how it thinks and, crucially, in how it learns. Today's cosmopolitan consumers and high-value employees are networked globally. They increasingly assess their purchasing habits and employment choices on the basis of information channelled to them through an array of non-traditional communication pathways, from relatively stable sources such as environmental and human rights groups and their faith communities, through to increasingly anarchic blog-using vigilante groups bent on revealing the latest corporate and political scandals. In this context, classical approaches to gathering market intelligence simply fail. A conservative Christian is as likely to agree with Al Gore's position on climate change as a committed Muslim is likely to favour Iran's nuclear ambitions while wearing Nike shoes, listening through an iPod and drinking Red Bull. And these choice-conscious individuals are by no means confined to the shores of Europe and North America. In India, comparable concerns are closer to home and often expressed at scale, as Monsanto discovered to its cost amid the wreckage of its strategy to advance the sales of its genetically modified seeds across Asia, and as Coca-Cola has experienced in the form of mass riots linked to the drawing off of water by one of its Indian bottling plants.

Learning differently rather than just learning about different things is at the heart of *The Civil Corporation's* very definition as being 'civil':

> Judging and ultimately guiding corporate performance requires an ex-
> amination of whether a business is *doing what it can do* given its range of
> external options and internal competencies. Internally, this concerns the
> formal, explicit policies and processes, organizational cultures and values,

and patterns of leadership. Externally, this is a question of the multitude
of business drivers, from direct, short-term market pressures through to
longer-term strategic challenges and opportunities.

A business's contribution to sustainable development therefore needs to
be understood in terms of its viable options and what it makes of them.
Internal and external factors together create a spectrum of possibilities at
any point in time that defines a corporation's practical scope for making
decisions between viable choices. Whether and how a corporation acts
within its degrees of freedom must be the test of responsibility, and indeed
the basis on which management decisions are framed. These are the
fundamentals of the *civil corporation*.

'Logging' possible issues is only the starting point in working out which
ones will count in tomorrow's markets. Labour standards in global textiles
and apparel supply chains are undoubtedly important to workers, and
may be an in-your-face reputational issue to today's premium brand
businesses. But it is another matter to accurately predict whether they
might be a truly material factor to tomorrow's business success and, if
so, in what ways. Al Gore is surely illuminating stark and convincing
evidence that climate change will profoundly impact our lives. But does
that mean that Rick Murray, Swiss Re's Chief Claims Strategist, is right
in asserting with an advanced, turn-of-the-Millennium business mindset,
that 'we do not want customers that do not understand the impact of
climate change on their business'?[15] Or are some issues important to some,
but nevertheless immaterial to traditional business performance?

Many companies are learning the tough lesson that reputational
problems are often the thin edge of the wedge for a business suffering the
consequences of deeper strategic malaise. Wal-Mart's campaign-resistant
strategy was based on the company's long-held view that, in effect, legal
compliance was tolerable, but going the extra mile beyond the law was
failing their shareholders and undermining their business model. Anti-
Wal-Mart campaigns were founded on moral, not business, principles, and
have carried no torch whatsoever for business imperatives or shareholder
interests. But the studied view of growing numbers of the company's
investors is that the company's strategy of depressing labour costs to
maintain price leadership in the face of productivity rates consistently
lower than those of its rivals is not durable.

Google's decision to accept censorship as an entry ticket to China's
lucrative market has so far done little more than disappoint their many
supporters, who had taken the company's 'do no evil' motto as more than
a slogan. Yet Google may live to regret its China decision insofar as its
underlying business model will require global communities to entrust the
company with their most intimate details. The New York-based campaign
group Human Rights Watch, for example, has asserted that many web
firms have become complicit in politically repressive activities. Calling
the policies of Yahoo!, Google and Microsoft 'arbitrary, opaque and
unaccountable', they have challenged these companies' future business

models in arguing that 'it was ironic that companies whose existence depends on freedom of information and expression have taken on the role of censor, even in cases where the Chinese government makes no specific demands for them to do so.'[16]

The magic is to be able to work out which of the many issues are (or could be made to be) material to a business's strategy and underlying performance. The concept of 'materiality' in financial auditing and reporting should carry considerable weight in this regard. It concerns:

> The magnitude of an omission or misstatement of accounting information that, in the light of surrounding circumstances, makes it probable that the judgement of a reasonable person relying on the information would have been changed or influenced by the omission or misstatement.[17]

This should mean that if Rick Murray from Swiss Re is quite right, a business's approach to climate change would be material and need to be 'accounted for' in financial terms, attested to by the auditor. Of course, the translation from business acumen to accounting rarely happens in practice. The notion of materiality has become degraded in the face of the very short-term interests of investors described above, reducing what is important to stuff that hits the heavily discounted analysis of the bottom line within a quarter or two.

The second half of *The Civil Corporation* places considerable weight on the role of new measures of responsibility. On 23 March 2005, the BP Texas City refinery experienced a catastrophic process accident. It was one of the most serious US workplace disasters of the past two decades, resulting in 15 deaths and more than 170 injuries. In the aftermath of the accident, BP followed the recommendation of the US Chemical Safety and Hazard Investigation Board and formed an independent panel, chaired by James Baker, to conduct a thorough review of the company's corporate safety culture, safety management systems and corporate safety oversight at its US refineries. The resulting report, published on 15 January 2007, was damning of many aspects of BP's operations. Notable were its conclusions on the topic of measurement:

> BP primarily used injury rates to measure process safety performance at its US refineries before the Texas City accident. Although BP was not alone in this practice, BP's reliance on injury rates significantly hindered its perception of process risk. BP tracked some metrics relevant to process safety at its US refineries. Apparently, however, BP did not understand or accept what this data indicated about the risk of a major accident or the overall performance of its process safety management systems. As a result, BP's corporate safety management system for its US refineries does not effectively measure and monitor process safety performance.[18]

BP arguably failed to listen, learn or respond to people on the ground who understood the problems and risks. It is therefore not a 'soft' thing to emphasize, as does all of AccountAbility's standards and metrics work, in particular, the ways in which appropriate metrics are selected and the importance of involving stakeholders in that process. Stakeholders, it is argued, have both knowledge relevant to the decision about what counts and implicit rights to be involved given their stake in the outcome. What counts in such a process is framed by three criteria: business policies and imperatives; stakeholder concerns; and societal norms. This three-level framework for determining what is material and so should be reported on has weathered reasonably well, but it is nevertheless under-specified. It helps, certainly, but fails to provide sufficient guidance to either the business or its stakeholders in prioritizing directions, actions and the associated metrics.

There has been much progress in the development of such metrics since 2001. Most visible has been the continued blossoming of standards initiatives. A lingua franca is beginning to converge around a small number of standards, notably the Global Reporting Initiative's so-called G3 Sustainability Reporting Guidelines and AccountAbility's AA1000 Assurance Standard. Both, individually and together, provide clearer guidance on the selection, use and validation of metrics. Both build on the commitment to stakeholder involvement in selecting metrics, for the G3 in particular, through the inclusive manner in which the proposed metrics included in the standard have been chosen and developed. Both advocate stakeholder engagement as a means of improving the quality of metrics and their productive application.

But beyond these specific, branded performance metrics and frameworks has emerged a body of work that has gone further in redefining materiality and the basis on which material issues could, and arguably should, be determined.[19] At the heart of this work is an attempt to re-establish 'materiality' as the critical organizing principle for identifying, measuring, managing and also, of course, reporting on and judging how smart a business is in understanding and moving to take advantage of its shifting context. New approaches to materiality therefore provide the core of an emerging management accounting framework for building civil corporations. This work is contentious in that it has arguably tipped the balance in selecting issues, and so metrics, towards those that are more likely to lie at the heart of the business's future value-creation process. That is, stakeholder concerns may well be important, but might through this route be deemed immaterial to the business. This route might therefore have a restraining effect on stakeholders' voices in the materiality determination process and reduce the representation of their concerns in the final reckoning of what is really taken into account. At the same time, it encourages companies to focus on those non-financial aspects of their footprint that they are most likely to impact through changes in their underlying business model.

But all this is just the start for Second Generation companies. The really hard job comes once a business has identified what is likely to be material. Then they have to work out how to respond more effectively. It

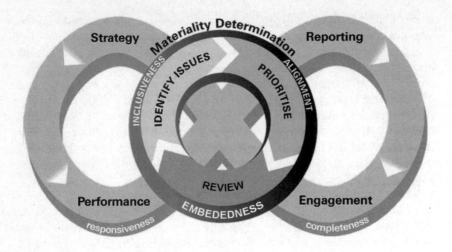

Figure 0.2 *Determining What Counts*

Source: Forstater et al (2006)

is an extraordinary fact that, despite having at their disposal some of the best brains on the planet and more resources than any other community on Earth, businesses monotonously repeat past errors, both their own and those of their peers and competitors. There is a consistent pattern of denial by businesses that any newly emerging issue is their fault, their concern or their responsibility. McDonald's, Nestlé, and Cargill are just three cases among many – but, after all, three of the world's great food companies by *almost* any measure – that have ably demonstrated this pattern. Furthermore, knowing how to respond is hard enough in itself, but also not enough for success. Coca-Cola, facing riots in India and legal challenges elsewhere, has concluded that it has to take leadership on the issue of water, just as BP has on the topics of climate change and corruption, or like Nike and Gap eventually have over labour standards. Such leadership certainly has to leverage the company's existing competencies – such as its global communications reach, distribution infrastructure and financial strength. But Coca-Cola will clearly have to complement these strengths with other, currently weak or absent, competencies, building alliances with non-traditional partners, perhaps including competitors, and certainly including erstwhile foes. Ian Davis, McKinsey's Managing Director, was not merely musing when he placed an article in *The Economist* arguing that 'corporate social responsibility', in his view a distracting misnomer, is where some of the new strategic drivers are being brewed inside and outside of the business community. His core message was, 'this is important, this is hard, and you will need the likes of us', a perfectly legitimate market signal from the world's most important outsourced collection of strategic competencies.[20]

Businesses are not built for (even successful) issue management, and are rarely rewarded for it. Their performance is based, and ultimately judged, on their ability to interpret societal needs into products and services that they make accessible to those who want them. Moreover, the most important contribution of business to social and environmental challenges will be in *what they do* in achieving success rather than *what they avoid doing*. To achieve this, businesses will need to align strategies and performance management to emerging social and environmental constraints and opportunities. That is, it is in the Second Generation that we begin to see the civil corporation come into its own, reinventing itself and its basis of engagement with others to meet the needs of existing markets, and create new ones.

THE THIRD GENERATION: RESPONSIBLE COMPETITIVENESS

'When I speak about civil society', Kofi Annan, until recently UN Secretary General, observed, 'I don't mean only non-governmental organizations, though they are a very important part of it. I also mean universities, foundations, labour unions and – yes – *private corporations*'.[21]

Civil society is a complex mosaic of purposive collective endeavours in pursuit of diverse, and at times conflicting, perceived 'public goods'. *The Civil Corporation*, like Mr Annan, proposed the unthinkable: that commercial enterprises could be 'civil' in this sense. For many, including some of my closest friends and allies, this placed the text beyond the pale, at best confirming me as well meaning but misguided. For others, this was a pointless, 'theoretical' debate. Even some of the strongest advocates for transforming business preferred business to stick to making money subject to appropriate constraints, rather than seeking to reinvent (or perhaps reconstitute) their reasons for being.

Much of contemporary corporate responsibility has been framed by the so-called 'business case'. At its most straightforward, this is about the pragmatic need to convince businesses that it is in their narrow institutional interest to improve their social and environmental performance, even (or at times especially) where relevant legislation was absent or unenforced. This 'business case' dimension to the thinking behind, and practice of, corporate responsibility has been the single most important mainstreaming driver. It has allowed for unholy alliances across a spectrum of players, from the advocates of a Friedmanite 'do it for the money' approach to business, to those with a more radical change agenda.

Much of the 'business case' debate, however, although understandable, has been misguided. The view that there is a stable relationship between, say, adhering to human rights and profitability is, to be frank, foolish. A study by Booz Allen Hamilton, *Smart Spenders: The Global Innovation 1000*, suggests there isn't even a statistically stable relationship between R&D

spending and profitability.[22] Most would agree that the much-vaunted positive impact of good corporate governance on business success is seriously over-rated, or else poorly specified and understood. There are many factors that mediate the relationships between context, drivers, enablers and performance. Put simply, some businesses will work out how to make money from, say, improved environmental performance, while others will go bust in trying.

The definitive conclusion that there is no business case *per se* edges both the analyst and practitioner towards a more meaningful framework for understanding the conditions under which doing good can be good for business, and how this can be best understood in terms of the assertion of 'civility'. This theme has preoccupied me subsequent to the publication of *The Civil Corporation*, largely because it seemed to be the pivotal challenge implicit in the Third Generation of corporate responsibility. The results of this work to date were initially published in a *Harvard Business Review* article in December 2004, 'Paths to corporate responsibility', and subsequently in a Harvard Working Paper entitled 'The logic of collaborative governance: Corporate responsibility, accountability and the social contract' and a co-authored AccountAbility publication, *Responsible Competitiveness: Reshaping Global Markets Through Responsible Business Practices.*[23]

In particular, these papers attempted to be more helpful in operationalizing the notion of the 'civil' by linking it not so much to *purpose* as to the theoretically well-grounded distinction between *intensive* and *extensive* accountability, exploring how these can evolve over time. Businesses are traditionally understood to be 'intensively' accountable: focused principally on one group of stakeholders, the owners of capital or their representatives. Civil society organizations, on the other hand, like public institutions, are conventionally seen to be more 'extensively' accountable, that is to a wider range of stakeholders. Businesses classically rationalize their embrace of a wider responsibility through the 'business case' narrative that in effect says 'financial returns are increased by being more responsible to wider society and the environment'. Over time, we observe in many instances a business's response to a maturing issue evolving from one of denial or compliance, through to more sophisticated responses involving not only product and process innovation but often collective initiatives involving both competitors and non-market actors. That is, their intensive accountability mandate to shareholders is enacted through a more extensive accountability. In this way, a business's *de jure* intensive accountability becomes increasingly to resemble, in practice or *de facto* terms, extensive accountability. The AccountAbility report in particular provides an ad hoc body of evidence that this Third Generation is to be observed in practice, not only conceptualized in theory. More recently this has been further supplemented by a regional report covering the competitiveness of three European sectors: finance; information and communication technology; and pharmaceuticals.[24]

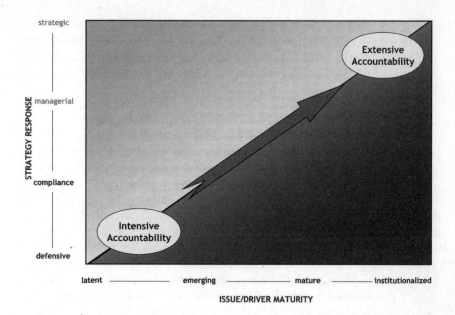

Figure 0.3 *Pathways to Extensive Accountability*

Source: Zadek (2004, 2007)

Viewing the 'civil' through this more developed accountability lens connects directly back to *The Civil Corporation*'s attempt to set out the broader political ramifications of this vibrant renegotiation process of the role of business in society. The thrust of this argument was best summarized (Chapter 1) as follows:

> ...corporate citizenship *can* become a significant route for overcoming global poverty, inequality and environmental insecurity. This requires that it evolves to a point where business becomes active in promoting and institutionalizing new governance frameworks that effectively secure civil market behaviour, globally. Leading civil corporations will therefore be those that go beyond getting their own house in order, and actively engage in promoting governance frameworks that enable the wider business community to address, effectively and without contradiction, the aspirations underpinning sustainable development.

This perspective first surfaced in an earlier piece, *Ethical Trade Futures*, published by the New Economics Foundation in 2000.[25] This slim pamphlet was the result of three years' work with leading labour activists exploring some of the longer-term, often unintended, ramifications of their campaigning around working conditions in global supply chains, particularly in the related textiles and apparel and footwear sectors.

Among the many fascinating insights gained during this work, the one that stood out was the conclusion that activists were increasingly finding themselves in the paradoxical position of encouraging corporations to lobby governments, often democratically elected, to be more progressive in their handling of social and environmental issues.

The Civil Corporation imagined such developments but had, frankly, little data to use to illustrate, let alone demonstrate, its point. But times have changed. In May 2005, for example, the Chief Executives of 13 major corporations wrote to then-UK Prime Minister Tony Blair professing concern over the government's handling of climate change. Unusually, the Corporate Leaders Group on Climate Change – made up of ABN Amro, AWG, BAA, BP, Cisco Systems, F&C Asset Management, HSBC, John Lewis Partnership, Johnson Matthey, Scottish Power, Shell, Standard Chartered Bank and Sun Microsystems – were not asking for less regulation, and indeed their position might imply more rules governing the ways in which climate change impacted markets and the business community. Even more unusual was that they had broken away from the position of the UK's main business association, the Confederation of British Industries, which, supported by the government's own Department of Trade and Industry and the Prime Minister himself, was arguing for the government to let the market respond freely to climate change.

Similar developments can be seen across many issues, sectors and geographies. At the time of writing *The Civil Corporation*, factory-level, code and audit-focused collaborative initiatives like the Ethical Trading Initiative (ETI) and the Fair Labor Association (FLA) were a new phenomenon. Today, we see the next generation of collaborative initiatives emerging, focused more on public policy and governance. The MFA Forum, for example, was formed in late 2004 by a coalition of businesses, civil society and labour organizations, and public institutions, along with many of the First Generation initiatives like the ETI and FLA. The MFA Forum, hosted and convened by AccountAbility, was created to address the threat to workers and economies of specific developing countries posed by the ending of the Multi Fibre Arrangements (MFA). Important in this context was that the Forum was established to build country-level, not company-level, initiatives, involving governments, international public institutions and business associations, as well as individual private businesses. Furthermore, its members' focus was on macro-conditions that impacted factory-level outcomes, rather than the specifics of worker conditions in particular factories. Crucially, this meant a particular focus on how best to promote the competitiveness of apparel and textiles sectors facing intensified competition in a post-MFA world, notably from China. Thus, more or less for the first time, we see civil society organizations joining with business in an appreciation of, and direct effort to impact, competitiveness conditions. So, for example, many of the apparel companies and activists involved in the MFA Forum have joined together in lobbying the US government (successfully, as it turned out) to extend the Africa Growth and Opportunity Act and thereby secure, at least in the short to medium term, the industry in countries like Lesotho that are highly dependent on their textiles and apparel exports to the US markets for sustained employment and economic growth.

This Third Generation, then, is about reshaping markets such that they systematically reward responsible business practices and penalize the converse. Market leaders are important in edging us into these markets, but considerably more is needed for this generation of developments to mature. Alliances involving businesses and civil society organizations are key in evolving non-statutory standards that can engage a second tier of companies. But we also see here the statutory role of the state becoming once again significant in this stage. In some areas, market dynamics consistently reward first movers, and collaborative rule-setting can bring along the rest. In other instances, first-mover disadvantages are more significant, and collaboration outside of the rule of law cannot tame a fragmented or aggressive market. Here we see businesses advocating firmer statutory action as an integral element of their competitive strategy.

THE FOURTH GENERATION

The Civil Corporation provides a window onto a phenomenon that appears incrementalist but, on second glance, turns out to involve risky venturing in the redesign of our basic institutions and how they are governed. Looked

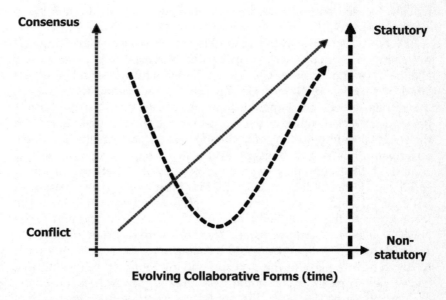

Figure 0.4 *Collaborative Governance: Shifting Roles*

at through the first lens, it describes ways to conclude a comfortable accommodation by business of a set of more or less universal values that encourage greater equity and sound environmental management. From this end of the telescope, the project is grounded on a bed of rights cooked up by a liberally minded, global elite. It is what most people mean and see when they talk about corporate responsibility, even among the most radical activists. But through the second, more speculative lens, the project looks a lot scarier. Here we see a largely unplanned and generally chaotic dismantling of distinct public and private spheres, and the distinction between them. Predicted through this end of the telescope is their reconfiguration into a new generation of institutions that blend their traditionally separated legitimacies, accountabilities and actions.

This is far from the liberal dream for the majority who, in the main, long for strong, autonomous governments, democratically elected by knowledgeable, thoughtful and engaged citizens – in fact, in their minds, people much like themselves. But it is equally a far cry from the business imagination, which on the one hand demands less regulation and seeks to weaken the state, but on the other hand ultimately depends entirely on governments able and willing to set rules, enforce property rights and mostly allow for a level playing field. And the spectre of an unbundling of traditional, well-defined roles and responsibilities is little less than a nightmare for most civil society organizations. It is perhaps a bitter irony that most are deeply conservative in being unwilling to consider radical institutional innovations. As one Brazilian civil society leader exclaimed in a discussion about the role of business in society, 'I do not want to see business take on a truly wider role in society; I would rather that it remains focused on profit-making, and that governments do their job in regulating them'.[26]

NGOs are also conservative in thinking about their own evolving role in society. In February 2002, I participated in a meeting on civil society and the UN at the Pocantico Conference Center of the Rockefeller Brothers Fund in Tarrytown, New York. The workshop, organized as part of the Secretary-General's Panel of Eminent Persons on UN–Civil Society Relationships, also known as the Cardoso Panel, was designed to explore the governance implications of multi-stakeholder partnerships for global governance.[27] During the meeting I presented a paper proposing several scenarios built around the key proposition that civil society organizations could evolve their roles with the UN into positions of structural power, with well-defined decision-making rights and responsibilities. The feedback from the assembled civil society leaders was clear and to the point. As one participant explained, 'Our role is to lobby, to influence, to shape thinking. These roles would be compromised by your proposals for us to have a place at the decision-making table.' In proposing that civil society organizations should have greater power, this and others participants agreed, I clearly did not fully appreciate the importance of protecting the historic their role.

The Civil Corporation's imagined future is, however, one of stronger governance, quite different to a libertarianism more often associated with the political empowerment of business. Envisioned is a collaborative approach to governance involving blended institutions engaged in business and matters of public concern underpinned by powerful new accountability mechanisms and processes. Equally, this is no argument for a more corporatist, paternalistic governance. Rather, it argues the case for democratic renewal based on revised terms of reference for, and access to, decision-making across all major institutions, notably the state and business. 'Stakeholder engagement', after all, is a vibrant experimental zone for new models of citizens' participation beyond, and in some instances instead of, traditional electoral pathways.

The jury, of course, remains out until the future becomes part of our history. It is in the nature of predictions involving such dramatically different options that we cannot know in advance which will prevail. Historians may well cast their eyes over this period and reflect on the corporate responsibility movement as a momentary, romantic, but ultimately dead-end hangover from a very troubling 20th century. After all, this would not be the first social movement that had its fiery moment, only to find itself absorbed by a conservative mainstream, or else overrun by history's subsequent twists and turns.

Alternatively, historians may look back on this period and conclude that the endless tactical back-and-forth campaigning and business responses during this period delivered a Fourth Generation of corporate responsibility, beyond tactics and risk management (First Generation), beyond new business strategies (Second Generation), and even beyond the collaborative approaches underpinning responsible competitiveness (Third Generation). This Fourth Generation would go beyond a reshaping of the role of business in society to inventing a new politics. This scenario would involve a very different relationship between markets and public governance. Today's experience of public–private or multi-stakeholder partnerships would have evolved into new and more stable institutions involved in both the creation of material wealth and the stewardship of the public interest. These institutions would form the heartland of our reinvention of global governance, and so also national and local governance, as ad hoc, issue-based compacts mature and create longer-term connectivity with each other.

Above all, this Fourth Generation would have to involve dramatic innovations in accountability, new means for civilizing power. Today's experiments in corporate responsibility would contribute to the foundations of these innovations, stretching or extending classical accountabilities and reconfiguring traditional institutional specializations through the learnings built on current experiences in public–private or multi-stakeholder partnerships. The essential DNA of this new accountability would, however, depend on the evolution of the heartland of today's experiments in stakeholder engagement, which would need to provide new pathways for citizens to participate in decisions that impact their lives.

Paradigms – the foundations and boundaries of how we think things work – change when repeated attempts to interpret our experience and base our decision-making on conventional wisdoms no longer deliver the goods. Thomas Kuhn, in his ground-breaking 1962 book *The Structure of Scientific Revolutions*, argued that science is not a steady, cumulative acquisition of knowledge, but a series of peaceful interludes punctuated by intellectually violent revolutions.[28] As the evidence grows that one way of looking at the world is inaccurate and unhelpful, new thinking emerges. That the world is not flat and does not sit in the middle of the universe, or that humans evolved from apes, are but two of the thought-shattering realizations that have, for many, if not most of us, changed our understanding of ourselves and our relationship with everything around us.

Revolutions in thinking are a strange breed of social upheaval. They are always disruptive, but often establish new people, thinking and practices alongside remnants, often deeply embedded, of the very systems that they seek to overthrow. Kuhnian scientific revolutions are just like this, typically allowing for new ways of thinking to co-exist (often for a long time) alongside very conventional wisdoms, before the tension between the two eventually overturns elements of the latter. The architects and proponents of the endangered conventional wisdoms, defending their turf, and often their fame and fortunes, generally first try to suppress and then co-opt the new thinking into their world view, seeking to create the appearance, for as long as possible, that all is well in the ways in which they see the world. Until recently, the threat of climate change has been dismissed by most politicians and business people as exaggerated or simply non-existent. Climatic data were explained away as deliberately distorted, melting ice caps considered natural variation. Then, almost mystically, the conventional wisdom shifts and climate change triggered by human activities becomes the new truth, often eloquently articulated by the very same people and institutions who had hitherto held back the tides of change.

The Civil Corporation describes, and indeed exists on, the cusp of a Kuhnian revolution in our understanding of the practice of business and governance. Business leaders are at pains to say that 'we do corporate responsibility because it is good for business, for our financial bottom line'. Indeed, one might say that they are legally obliged to do just that, given today's understanding of the fiduciary duties of managers of publicly listed companies. Yet in the same breath, increasingly, such leaders argue that their businesses are key actors in society in addressing such pervasive challenges as global poverty and climate change. Here, the lens is reversed, and business becomes a vehicle to other, broader ends than profit-seeking. These two lenses may, and do, seem perfectly rational and consistent to someone rooted in today's business (and indeed broader) paradigm of how we see the world around us. We feel secure when evoking the so-called 'business case' for acting responsibly, particularly when we work for business and need to actually deliver to the bottom line.

But step back for a moment and imagine being from some other place in space or time – a time traveller if you like from some (perhaps not too distant) future moment. What sense would you make from a studied reading of our way of seeing, and so describing, the contemporary phenomenon of business? Would not the juxtaposition of the two competing paradigms about business in society seem unnecessarily and perversely convoluted? Surely as a self-respecting, presumably well-trained, time traveller you would ask, no doubt politely, 'why are you so hell-bent on insisting that businesses' purposes must to be so narrow, when it is so clear that they are central in addressing far wider challenges?'.

Actually, the time traveller's state of bemusement is much closer to our own daily experience than most of us would admit. A modest level of schizophrenia comes with living in a world as connected, complex and confusing as ours. After a hard day's work, most of us return to the heart of our families and reflect on the too-often ugly acts that have taken place in the name of business and personal economic success. In our more private moments, as our neighbours and relations are made redundant after years of dedicated service, and nameless hedge funds trade the shares of hard-built businesses for momentary gain, we wonder if business really has to be done this way. But it's tough to be sane in a pretty crazy world. Let's be frank: most of us reflect on such matters in the privacy of our living rooms, among families and friends, and then return the next day to the fray, more or less refreshed, if not enlightened.

A successful transition to a Fourth Generation of corporate responsibility would involve a move from the cusp to the heart of a paradigm shift in the place of business in society. The *de facto* extension of business accountabilities advanced in the Second and Third Generations would be acknowledged and legitimized through a *de jure* shift in the accountability of business. This means, ultimately, a shift in the purpose of business. Such a shift would be expressed through changes in the laws governing their fiduciary responsibilities, the compass used to focus decision-making by those vested with the authority to govern. By extension, it would imply a dramatic change in who was at the table in making such decisions, in terms of both interests and competencies. Such changes, in fact, would simply consolidate the new practices of production, wealth creation and governance that had evolved from within today's world. They would recognize and support the transition enabled by the emergence of civil corporations towards the ultimate aim of a more civil society.

Part 1

The New Economy of Corporate Citizenship

CHAPTER 1

Can Corporations be Civil?

Many of Britain's best-known companies are already redefining the traditional roles of the corporation. They are recognizing that every customer is part of the community and that social responsibility is not an optional extra.

Rt Hon Tony Blair MP, British Prime Minister[1]

If business is so powerful, and is now doing so much good; why is so much wrong in the world?

Oded Grajew, President, Instituto Ethos[2]

The role of business in society is the 21st century's most important and contentious public policy issue. Business is increasingly moulding societal values and norms, and defining public policy and practice, as well as being the dominant route through which economic and financial wealth is created. How business is done will underpin how local and global communities of the future address social and environmental visions and imperatives. This is true whatever one believes to be critical in creating a just and sustainable world. Economic welfare, peace and security, global warming, human and animal welfare – to name just a few – are and will continue to be deeply informed by business in practice.

Our views of business today hang in the balance. On one hand, business is in the limelight of increasingly concerned public scrutiny. The popular media carries daily fresh allegations of its misdemeanours. An outpouring of books, pamphlets, films and conferences challenge and debate its social and environmental performance. Grass-roots, anti-corporate demonstrations adorn the streets outside city offices, and regularly surround meetings of the world's leaders and major international institutions. On the other hand, recent years have seen the emergence of the philosophy and practice of 'corporate citizenship'. Corporations have sought under this umbrella to gain broader trust and legitimacy through visibly enhancing their non-financial performance. Today, the focus is shifting from philanthropy to the impact of core business activities across the broad spectrum of social, environmental and economic dimensions represented by the vision of sustainable development.

Surprisingly little has been said about where this critical debate and practice might lead us in the future. Activists leading the assault on corporate power and influence have in the main remained entrenched in their negative critique. Few have mapped out credible alternatives for generating and distributing sufficient economic wealth to provide a decent quality of life for a growing world population. Similarly, few advocates of corporate citizenship have addressed the challenge of whether or how such approaches are likely to deliver adequate social and environmental gains to reverse the underlying pattern of growing levels of poverty, inequality and environmental insecurity.

In addressing the *why*, the *how*, and the *so what* of corporate citizenship, this book seeks to establish what should and can realistically be expected from the business community in addressing the imperatives and aspirations underpinning sustainable development. It goes on to address whether and how these expectations can in practice be realized. It seeks to achieve this by exploring:

- contemporary forms of corporate citizenship emerging from the dynamics of the New Economy;
- new patterns of civil governance underlying emerging partnerships between business, governments and private non-profit organizations;
- the scope for engagement, learning and advocacy which corporations have in maximizing their contribution to sustainable development; and
- under what conditions corporate citizenship can play a significant role in addressing the darkest sides of unsustainable development.

GLOBAL BALANCE SHEET

Much happened in the last century. As a species we became taller, faster and stronger. We learnt how to dominate our natural environment – and to appreciate its ability to strike back. We experienced terrifying excesses of nationalism and racism – and matched this with expressions of universal values such as those underpinning the vision of the United Nations (UN). Democracy, at least the elective version, came into its own in the 20th century, building from the revolutions of the 19th century to South Africa's liberation struggle.

But the most pervasive outcome of the last hundred years has been the incredible growth of economic wealth and the associated level of material consumption. Certainly, the technological revolutions of the 18th and 19th centuries marked the onset of a rapid acceleration in the income and wealth of a small but significant minority in Europe and North America. But it was during the 20th century that this acceleration took on quantum proportions. The global economy at the turn of the millennium was driven by annual expenditure on consumption of almost US$30 trillion, a doubling in just 25 years.[3] By the turn of the 20th century, a billion or so people were experiencing extraordinary material standards of living. Average incomes across this group rose at least six-fold between 1900 and 2000.[4]

Economic growth has unquestionably delivered real gains. Few could quibble about the improvements in most of the better-known indicators of human development, such as personal health, literacy and longevity, for enormous numbers of people. As the United Nations *Human Development Report 1999* concluded:

> People in many countries live a much longer and healthier life than just two decades ago. In 31 of the 174 countries included in the Human Development Index (HDI), life expectancy has increased by more than a fifth since 1975... Between 1975 and 1997 most countries made substantial progress in human development, reducing their shortfall from the maximum possible value of the HDI. Of the 79 countries for which HDI trends between 1975 and 1997 are available, 54 made up more than 20 per cent of their shortfall, 31 more than 30 per cent and 19 more than 40 per cent.[5]

The United Nations *Human Development Report 2000*, similarly, highlights that:

> The achievement of human potential reached unprecedented heights in the 20th century... Worldwide, 46 countries, with more than a billion people, have achieved high human development... In developing countries during the past three decades, life expectancy increased by ten years... adult literacy increased by half... and the infant mortality rate declined by more than two fifths.[6]

Well-documented facts are equally clear on the negative side of the equation. Nearly one in three of the world's workforce is unemployed,[7] 1.2 billion people live on less than US$1 a day,[8] and 840 million people go hungry each day.[9] The world's 225 richest individuals have a combined wealth of over US$1 trillion, equal to the annual income of the world's poorest 47 per cent – about 2.5 billion people. A further 100 million in the so-called developed world are relatively impoverished.

Over the same period, the state of the natural environment has worsened. The climate has noticeably changed, half the world's original forest cover has disappeared, and overall the capacity of the Earth's ecosystems is estimated to be degrading at about 3 per cent a year.[10] The growth in consumption has been underpinned by a mushrooming in the use of natural resources, and in the levels of waste and emissions; a quintupling of fossil fuel use since 1950; and a doubling of the use of fresh water since 1960. As the ecologist and writer Paul Hawken poetically notes about the US economy, 'For every 100 pounds of product we manufacture... we create at least 3200 pounds of waste'.[11]

Consumption patterns of the materially well-off have taken on proportions that would be comic if they were not equally tragic. The UN points out that Europe and the US spend almost US$13 billion annually on perfume, and almost US$18 billion on pet food; Europeans annually spend more than US$50 billion on cigarettes, and Japanese business runs up an annual entertainment account of almost US\$35 billion.[12] Against this must be compared the profile of consumption of the typical household in a developing country, where about 80 per cent of income goes on buying basic foodstuff. Equally it compares with the annual cost of only US\$40 billion, according to the UN, that it would take to achieve universal access to all basic services; such as basic education, water and sanitation.[13]

Confusing Causalities

Facts abound, but what do they mean? Is the heady consumption of wealthier citizens a constraining factor to development for others – the zero-sum view that the wealth of the few condemns many to poverty? Or is such profligate consumption the salvation of those currently in poverty? Many argue, after all, that what is needed is for those without enough to emulate, catch up and join the party. Sakiko Fukuda-Parr, Director of the UN Human Development Office, captures perhaps the middle path between these views when she argues that:

> It is not a matter of more or less consumption. I cannot agree with the hair-shirt view that less consumption will make the world a better place. The issue is what kind of consumption – of ensuring that consumption is not environmentally destructive, and that it challenges poverty and inequality.[14]

Such diversity of opinion feeds through, naturally, to contested views about the role of economic growth in promoting human development and environmental security. As the UN, amongst many, reminds us:

> *The link between economic prosperity and human development is neither automatic nor obvious.* Two countries with similar income per capita can have very different HDI values; countries with similar HDI values can have very different income levels. Of the 174 countries, 92 rank higher on the HDI than on gross domestic product (GDP) per capita (purchasing power parity, PPP\$), suggesting that these countries have been effective in converting income into human development. But for 77 countries the HDI rank is lower than the GDP per capita (PPP\$) rank. These countries have been less successful in translating economic prosperity into better lives for people.[15]

Our understanding of what-causes-what is not obviously enhanced through increased volumes of data. The economically wealthiest countries certainly offer up the most comprehensive data imaginable, but the results continue to confound us. Economic competitiveness, we are often told, is the foundation of long-term societal success. But we know, equally, that economic competitiveness does not always yield the promised social dividends. For example, the Republic of Ireland, US, and UK figure in the top ten competitive nations,[16] according to Jeffrey Sachs and the World Economic Forum. But this efficient club of three turns out to be the same group identified by the UN as having the highest levels of poverty and inequality among industrialized nations.

> Among the 17 industrialized countries included in the HPI-2 [measure of human poverty], Sweden has the lowest human poverty, with 7 per cent, followed by The Netherlands and Germany, with 8.3 per cent and 10.4 per cent. The industrialized countries with the highest poverty according to the HPI-2 are the United States (16.5 per cent), Ireland (15.3 per cent) and the United Kingdom (15.1 per cent).[17]

Tramline Debate

The most confusing facts of all concern the contested contributions of business, particularly the corporate community, to the positive and negative sides of last century's overall accounts. The corporate community is vast and rapidly growing. Of the 100 largest 'economies' in the world today, 51 are corporations.[18] The top 200 corporations have sales equivalent to one quarter of the world's total economic activity.[19] General Motors has annual sales equivalent to the GDP of Denmark, and the annual income of Sears Roebuck is comparable to the total annual income of over 100 million Bangladeshis.[20] There has been a 12-fold increase in world trade since 1945, dominated by a small number of global corporations. This trade now accounts for about 20 per cent of measured, global economic income. The 1990s witnessed a massive growth in the pattern of international capital flows to developing countries. In 1990, public sources accounted for more than half of the international money flowing to developing countries. By 1995, 77 per cent came from private sources.[21] The volume of foreign direct investment nearly quadrupled over the same period, jumping to US$96 billion by 1995.[22] Foreign direct investment increased by 27 per cent in just one year, 1997.[23]

With so large a footprint, one might expect that corporations' contribution to the global accounts would be utterly obvious. Far from it. Indeed, the facts have underpinned a largely polarized debate about the contribution of the corporate community. Facts abound, but they seem inadequate to the task of building a common view as to whether corporations are at the leading edge of positive change, or irreducibly part of the problem. This polarization is plain to see in the veritable outpouring of publications about the future of the corporation, backed by conferences, workshops, Internet-based debates, counselling-based 'confrontations', and every other possible form of interaction. Every possible statistic, anecdote and mystical vision has been fashioned to demonstrate that corporations are good, bad or just plain ugly.

Debate on the future roles of the corporation is guaranteed to bring out people's most extreme and often bunkered views. The tramline nature of the debate is not surprising. Stories, even those that make ample use of facts, are written for specific audiences. They need to be understood in terms of how they seek to persuade and influence. This is certainly true in the area of corporate citizenship. Some people's words and deeds are meat and bread to corporate audiences, but stick in the throats of those who campaign against the World Trade Organization (WTO) or Monsanto. Similarly, the views of those who target the would-be activist as audience are in the main dismissed by those charged with the practical challenges of navigating these corporations into the future.

Paul Hawken and Amory and L Hunter Lovins describe this debate as being made up of the pro-marketers ('blues'), the believers in socialism ('reds'), and those who see the world in terms of ecosystems ('greens'). They encourage us to become 'whites' – essentially synthesists who do not 'entirely oppose or agree with any of the other three views, and are optimistic in adopting a path of 'integration, reform, respect, and reliance'.[24] Hawken and the Lovinses are astute in the caricatures they paint. But it is not clear that the 'rational way' must be for the 'whites' to lead the charge of real change, as they suggest. The paths of those with opposing views about the corporate community do of course cross and at times even converge. Increasingly, innovative partnerships and processes are generated at these unlikely intersections. However, these interactions have also stimulated new generations of opponents, often disappointed and embittered by their sense of a lack of real progress in addressing underlying social and environmental challenges. The increasingly vehement public demonstrations against the WTO, the World Bank (WB), and the many other symbols of the so-called Washington Consensus,[25] more than anything reveal the accumulated frustration following a decade of tentative engagement. Lynda Yanz, co-organizer of the Canadian-based Label Behind the Label coalition sums up this frustration:

> The view 'from the ground' on codes is so very different from what it looks like when you're zooming in from the international angle. The worlds are so different... Almost every group we're working with has a different beef with one or more of the Northern-based campaigns or initiatives we're working with.[26]

Oded Grajew, a Brazilian businessman and President of Brazil's leading business association for social responsibility, Instituto Ethos, similarly and even more starkly summed up the underlying confusion and frustration in a question tabled at an annual conference of the business network, Business for Social Responsibility: 'If business is so powerful, and is now doing so much good; why is so much wrong.'[27]

Debate about the corporate community brings out in people the worst of either evangelical optimism or narrow cynicism. And there is no shortage of fuel to feed either habit. There are ample cases of corporate misconduct with bad and sometimes catastrophic social or environmental consequences. When yet *another* case of under-aged workers is uncovered in Nike's supply chains, it only serves for many to reinforce a deep sense of cynical anger and frustration. Similarly, there are many examples where corporations *have* 'done the right thing'. With hundreds of high-profile branded corporations and tens of thousands of less-known multinationals, there is more than ample scope for digging-up and exhibiting examples that seek to 'prove' one view or the other.

The tramline character of the debate is therefore understandable. It is unsurprising that polarities are hard to overcome when people have such different world views, experiences and information, and often an undisclosed cocktail of anger and disappointment, confusion or just simple ignorance. Objectively, the stakes are high, and historical outcomes have for many been less than satisfactory. It is foolish to dismiss what appears to the 'balanced observer' as extremism of one sort or another that merely needs to be 'flushed from the system' for rationality to prevail. The confrontational features of the current debate cannot be eroded by a 'middle path' that neither appreciates nor engages a fuller spectrum of views and interests. Neither can they be marginalized by repeated demonstration, however convincing, that some companies can indeed behave in better ways in increasingly competitive markets. No side will emerge victorious by either inductive or deductive proof that there is 'only one way to go'. A deeper process is needed that will deliver on three fronts. First, the myths about corporate behaviour – both good and bad – need to be revealed and dismissed. Second, there is a need to identify the varied and often opposing possible pathways that this implies for corporate social and environmental performance and impact. Third, is a need to make a considered judgement of what can be expected from different strategies, and in all honesty what cannot.

THE NEW ECONOMY OF CORPORATE CITIZENSHIP

Corporate citizenship has emerged in its contemporary forms within the context of the emerging New Economy. The New Economy embraces far more than its exotic variants of (now largely defunct) dot.coms, and extends beyond the communities of wealthy over-consumers and business-2-business Internet relationships. It is, as the 'first great philosopher of cyberspace', Manuel Castells, points out, a social revolution that implies radical changes in the nature of the institutions of the state and business, and redefines the roles of the citizen, both individually and collectively.[28] The New Economy is characterized by the acceleration of every aspect of social life; the collapse of geographical distance as a basis for defining and sustaining difference; and the growing significance of knowledge and innovation as the primary source of business competition and economic value. As such, the New Economy impacts on the livelihoods of Mexican and Indian farmers, just as it shifts the terms on which wealthy New Yorkers consume to secure their self-esteem.

Corporate citizenship is about business taking greater account of its social and environmental – as well as its financial – footprints. The last decade has certainly witnessed a renaissance in corporate citizenship. However, it would be foolish to assume that this has been underpinned by a widespread moral 'road to Damascus' or evolution in human consciousness. Although individuals' values, vision and moral commitments are often enabling factors, corporate citizenship as an institutional phenomenon is essentially an outcrop of the New Economy. Success in the New Economy is as much about a corporation's ability to build a sense of shared values with key stakeholders as it is about the technical quality of products and services. Corporations that achieve this will extract the maximum premium for their branded, lifestyle products, get the best employees on terms that secure their committed labour to the business, and most effectively offset criticism from increasingly globalized networks of non-governmental organizations (NGOs). Accounting for broader societal and environmental outcomes *from this perspective* is merely another way of expressing Milton Friedman's proposition that corporations will and should focus on maximizing financial performance, if necessary by engaging more effectively with stakeholders that can make or break the business.

Understanding corporate citizenship as emerging from underlying structural shifts in the economy does not, unfortunately, mean that the New Economy necessarily creates good companies. Corporate citizenship is not the same as *good* corporate citizenship. Taking stakeholders into account does not automatically translate into 'doing good things' for people and the planet. Just as the New Economy opens opportunities for businesses to strengthen their competitive position by positively addressing social and environmental aspects of their performance, so too does it offer ample scope for businesses to externalize social and environmental costs. Economic globalization offers profitable pathways for businesses to behave unethically, to drive down labour standards, to minimize their tax contributions, and to exert undue influence over governments anxious to attract their investments. Different stakeholders, after all, have very different 'social' interests. The need must therefore be to identify and enhance the drivers of corporations' more progressive engagement in the vision of sustainable development.

THE CIVIL CORPORATION

The aspiration of sustainable development leads many people to talk of the need to create 'sustainable business'. While understandable, this imaginative leap creates more confusion than good. Social, environmental and economic gains and losses arising from particular business processes cannot simply be added up. We do not know, for example, whether an additional four weeks of employee training, minus a dozen or so trees, plus a ton of profit, add up to more or less sustainable development. We cannot in all honesty predict the contribution of energy and other resource intensive corporations to the cause of sustainable development, given the complexity of their direct and indirect impacts over time. In fact, we do not and probably cannot know enough about the system to understand in this sense the relationship between the activities of one organization and the whole system.

There is little point in blaming pigs for not being able to fly. Similarly, there is little point in condemning an organization for something beyond its control. Microsoft did not, after all, invent computers, and can hardly be entirely blamed for their costs or congratulated for their many benefits. Similarly, there is little point in blaming Nestlé for the impact on the South African economy of a collapse in gold prices, South African Breweries for the level of HIV/AIDS across the African continent, or Credit Swiss First Boston for the state of Britain's railways. Judging and ultimately guiding corporate performance requires an examination of whether a business is *doing what it can do* given its range of external options and internal competencies. Internally, this concerns the formal, explicit policies and processes, organizational cultures and values, and patterns of leadership. Externally, this is a question of the multitude of business drivers, from direct, short-term market pressures through to longer-term strategic challenges and opportunities.

A business's contribution to sustainable development therefore needs to be understood in terms of its viable options and what it makes of them. Internal and external factors together create a spectrum of possibilities at any point in time – that define a corporation's practical scope for making decisions between viable choices. Whether and how a corporation acts within its degrees of freedom must be the test of responsibility, and indeed the basis on which management decisions are framed. These are the fundamentals of the *civil corporation*. A corporation that is said to be civil is understood here as one that takes full advantage of opportunities for learning and action in building social and environmental objectives into its core business by effectively developing its internal values and competencies. This formulation provides a sound basis for grounding our expectations of business, and how strategy can be conceived and developed, to address the aspirations and challenges underlying sustainable development.

CIVIL GOVERNANCE

The emergence of NGOs acting as *civil regulators* of corporations through public campaigning and other forms of pressure is one of the notable features of the last decade. More than any other body of institutions, NGOs have driven the process of popular education and political and economic mobilization around social and environmental issues. As with the corporate community, NGOs' increased visibility and influence is itself a manifestation of the New Economy, which brings with it associated opportunities and risks. In their civil regulatory role, NGOs have engaged with increasing intimacy with their target, the corporate community. In so doing, they have increased their knowledge of the business process and how to influence it through personal relationships, the development of management and accountability tools, and by otherwise impacting directly on the markets within which business operates.

This increased level of intimacy has, however, also provided a basis through which business has been able to penetrate more deeply into the NGO community. This in turn has provided them with leverage over future NGO activities, and indeed the very shape of future generations of NGOs. In so doing, they are increasingly influencing, and sometimes effectively undermining, new challenges and opportunities emerging from the NGO community. At the same time, some are thereby deepening their knowledge of civil society processes as a basis for enhancing their ability to respond positively to social and environmental challenges in commercially viable ways. In practice both tendencies are, and will continue to be, in play, the balance depending on many factors. It is significant, however, that the continued effectiveness of NGOs in challenging business behaviour is unlikely to be secured by seeking to sustain their separation from the corporate community. Rather, the shift from a challenge-based phase of civil regulation into more intimate, binding relationships between NGOs and corporations will necessitate a more complex set of strategies and tactics on the part of NGOs if their effectiveness as a driver for progressive change is to be sustained.

It is in this context that civil partnerships have emerged as a vehicle through which new frameworks of rules have been negotiated within which the corporate community might operate in a more legitimate and, hopefully, progressive manner. Civil partnerships are far more than a 'more effective form of delivery'. They are evolving, organic governance structures and processes that go beyond elements of the cut-and-thrust forms of civil regulation into more institutionalized rule-based frameworks. Some of these frameworks may eventually find their way on to the statute books of national governments or international institutions. In some instances this can be with the active blessing of elements of the corporate community seeking, for example, to level the playing field or to re-externalize costs into strengthened public sector institutions. Other rule frameworks, however, will remain outside the statutory realm, overseen by increasingly sophisticated partnership arrangements. Corporate codes of conduct created through and overseen by multi-sector partnerships are an early manifestation of these developments. More generally, companies are increasingly seeking to stabilize their commitments and risks by nurturing partnerships that involve human rights and development NGOs.

This is the essence of the *new civil governance*, which lies at the heart of the New Economy of corporate citizenship. It comprises processes through which rules are built around and within markets in relation to which corporations find themselves subject. These rules are negotiated and overseen by a spectrum of institutional arrangements and processes ranging from public scrutiny and debate through to partnerships and more traditional statutory structures. These different elements have certainly always existed in some form. What is new is that there is no longer a de facto (or for many even an aspirational) pecking order that places statutory rules as higher, more legitimate, or more effective governance instruments. Furthermore, there is no longer a presumption that different rule systems will be stable, well bounded, or even consistent with each other. The new civil governance is most of all marked by an acceptance of partial and temporary rule systems co-existing in an often dynamic relationship, overseen by diverse players and institutional arrangements with complex and often unstable bases of legitimacy and effectiveness.

CIVIL NAVIGATION

The civil corporation needs to understand what nuts and bolts will help it to identify 'best thinking' from the often confused reality of divergent, contested views. It will need to be able to assess and influence its degrees of freedom within what are generally high-risk, complex, dynamic market environments. Perhaps most of all, it needs to be able to manage its relationships with key stakeholders in ways that support learning and change without unnecessarily risking commercial disaster that would bring misfortune to many of these stakeholders.

There are no magic bullets that will create civil corporations. There are no standard systems that substitute for real-life, messy solutions made up of cocktails of unusual leadership, coincidence and luck, and really hard work. But the effective systematization of such cocktails is, nevertheless, a critical ingredient of longer-term success, both in developmental and in commercial terms. Many systems aimed at aligning core business strategies and processes with elements of social and environmental aims and outcomes have emerged in the last ten years. Equally prolific has been the outpouring of books and reports either advocating their development and use, highlighting their irrelevance, or predicting their imminent demise. For most, and most of all for business, it is all rather confusing, and indeed increasingly irritating. In fairness it must be said that 'it is early days', which both explains and in a sense justifies the chaos. After all, it is barely 15 years since environmental management systems began to be taken (and so developed) seriously by mainstream business. However, these 'early days' are taking their toll in terms of rising concerns and cynicism by stakeholders both external to, and within, the corporate community.

There is a need for tools that enable corporations to be civil across the practical dimensions of, for example, information and knowledge management; engagement, dialogue and communication; decision making and governance; and performance assessment. This is not a matter of turning over a clean sheet of paper and starting the design process all over again. Existing tools for organizational learning provide many elements of the kit that is needed. At the same time, this is not a matter of pursuing a cut-and-paste approach. There is a need to go back to basics to understand what are the possible uses of existing tools and what adjustments need to be made to their design and operation. There are, furthermore, notable gaps where new tools need to be developed or at least existing ones substantially upgraded.

The application of best thinking to the development of tools is itself a dynamic process in every sense of the word. Our understanding of sustainable development itself changes over time. What is a priority today may not be the most critical issue in a decade, or even tomorrow. The manner in which priorities are made will also change, both for societies and for corporations. For example, child labour is not a new phenomenon, yet today it is a far more critical issue for global corporations than it was just a few years ago. Similarly, the rights of indigenous people to set the terms of access to natural resources has become far more significant for oil and mining companies than ever before. Today, the notion of a global living wage may seem implausible. In years to come it could well be the reality for workers and business alike.

It is too early to say which standards, guidelines, systems, procedures and practices will turn out to make most sense for any one company, let alone for the wider business community, and society at large. It is unclear, for example, whether the more daunting 'The Natural Step' will prevail over the pragmatic ISO14000 series, or whether the labour code and monitoring standard, SA8000, will prove to do the job compared with alternative approaches that embrace wider dialogue and engagement. How this will all, moreover, fit into tools like the Balanced Scorecard or Total Quality Management is entirely unclear. Indeed, we do not know if these latter tools will even survive the coming years. And it is in any case a complete mystery how such approaches – all designed for relatively stable manufacturing systems – will fare in the New Economy where the social and environmental footprints of dominant corporations are less clearly defined.

Effective *civil navigation* lies at the heart of making the most out of the opportunities afforded by the New Economy of corporate citizenship for enhancing social and environmental benefits and minimizing associated costs. This is true for individual corporations, but is also the case for the system as a whole. The trick, however, is not to place all one's bets on a particular approach. Better at this stage is to look for the underlying principles needed to guide the evolution of appropriate approaches in the future. This is the aim of the book's third and final section, which identifies and explores the fundamental principles underlying four particular dimensions of corporate behaviour:

(1) *Setting boundaries* of learning, accountability and responsiveness.
(2) *Building engagement* that forms the basis for learning.
(3) *Creating measures* that validate and make knowledge effective, and so form the basis for decision-making and actions.
(4) *Institutionalizing trust* in ways that create a virtuous circle of practice and further engagement with stakeholders.

IS BEING CIVIL ENOUGH?

Corporations can be civil. But can they and will they be civil enough? Can even the most enlightened business improve its social and environmental performance sufficiently to reach universally accepted standards while remaining a viable business? It would be fair to say that not a single major corporation has achieved this to date across the bulk of its social and environmental footprint. Furthermore, even if some could achieve this by virtue of their visionary leadership and powerful market position, would they remain worthy but isolated examples within what is otherwise a swamp of poor social and environmental performers? Finally and most importantly, will all these developments add up to a coherent response to the question of what roles good corporate citizenship will play in addressing the really big social and environmental challenges of both today's and tomorrow's world?

The cases drawn on throughout this book highlight just how much individual corporations acting alone can achieve. But these cases, and the accompanying analysis, also suggest that even the strongest and most progressive corporations, acting alone, will rarely be able to sustain *significantly* enhanced social and environmental performance for extended periods of time. Another way of looking at this is that if such corporations are not emulated by their competitors, it means either that the corporation has failed to achieve any competitive advantage through its good practices, or that its competitive advantage exists only within a restricted market niche that has high barriers to entry and does not threaten the broader market (and so will not have extended impact). From this perspective, corporate citizenship based on leadership practices that are not institutionalized beyond the individual corporation is unlikely to make a major contribution to achieving a sustainable development path.

But corporate citizenship *can* become a significant route for overcoming global poverty, inequality and environmental insecurity. This requires that it evolves to a point where business becomes active in promoting and institutionalizing new governance frameworks that effectively secure civil market behaviour, globally. Leading civil corporations will therefore be those that go beyond getting their own house in order, and actively engage in promoting governance frameworks that enable the wider business community to address, effectively and without contradiction, the aspirations underpinning sustainable development.

CHAPTER 2

Opening Minds[1]

Perplexity, the outcome of a situation for which we cannot recognize a precedent, has kept us in a dead-end alley and barred the road to imaginative, novel and bold solutions.

Manfred Max-Neef[2]

The world in the 21st century, like the world in any other century, will be what we want it to be. Ideas, political convictions, cogent arguments, faith, hope and charity (or their opposites): these will shape the future.[3]

GETTING OFF THE TRAMLINES

South African Breweries produces an annual Corporate Citizenship Report,[4] as does its gambling and leisure group subsidiary, Southern Sun.[5] But no amount of proof of good deeds, contented employees, or even happy consumers would convince someone who was fundamentally against the consumption of alcohol or gambling that this company was a good corporate citizen. Ericsson, a world leader in mobile communications, has recently formed a partnership with the UN to contribute its institutional competencies and hardware to UN disaster relief initiatives. But for those who are absolutely opposed to the arms industry, Ericsson is essentially a blacklisted company. The same holds true for characteristics of businesses beyond their products and services. Premier Oil has a human rights policy, but this does not appease activists who advocate boycotting any company operating in Myanmar. Nike has a labour code of conduct based on the International Labour Organization (ILO) core conventions, and one of the world's largest cadres of private labour inspectors. But this counts for little to those who see the key issue as being the demonstrably inadequate wages paid to workers employed in global supply chains. The annual *Financial Times* (FT) survey to determine the world's most respected companies found that fund managers deemed the most socially responsible companies to include McDonald's (5th), Philip Morris (11th) and Starbucks (15th). These companies may indeed do laudable things. But they are all serious under-performers according to many of those concerned with treatment of employees, animal rights, environmental protection, health and the situation of small coffee producers in developing countries.[6]

'Good business' means different things to different people. The US-based business network, Business for Social Responsibility (BSR), understands social responsibility as where a corporation 'operates in a manner that meets or exceeds the ethical, legal, commercial and public expectations that society has of business'.[7] David Logan, Director of the Corporate Citizenship Company, defines corporate citizenship more expansively and yet neutrally as concerning the 'total impact of business on society'.[8] Definitions abound. Those who see private ownership as the root driver of all that is good or bad about business take this as their starting point. Radical localizers like Colin Hines are opposed to both codes of conduct and fair trade between community producers and ethical traders, even if both can deliver demonstrable benefits to workers and small-scale producers.[9] Those, like Naomi Klein, concerned with the homogenizing impact of global brands, decry any ethical dimension to corporate reputation as merely reinforcing the problem.[10] Campaigning organizations like the World Development Movement (WDM) and trade union confederations such as the International Confederation of Free Trade Unions (ICFTU) take the core internationally agreed conventions, such as those set out in Box 2.1, as the critical benchmarks for defining what is good behaviour.

There is little point in calling for consensus about what is 'good'. Many factors, both old and new, will continue to reinforce often radically different perspectives. Actually, there is much to be said for a diversity of views. But such differences should not and need not perpetuate a tramline debate about what we should expect from the corporate community, and how best to realize it. Tramline debates are rarely about difference per se, but more often concern people's difficulty in reflecting on their positions, and adjusting them in the light of experience and the potential for change. Tramline debate also rarely underpins real change, since it tends to embed intransigence or simple inertia. For this reason, tramline characteristics of the current debate about the role of business in society need to be overcome for progress to be made.

CONFUSING INNOVATION

The early to middle phase of the evolution and diffusion of most innovations is characterized by a profusion of different and often conflicting approaches, language, standards, institutions and processes. Symptomatic of this phase is that increasing numbers of people know that they want 'it', but are rarely clear about exactly what it is and how to find it. At the same time, growing numbers of people want to supply the increasing demand, but are not yet really up to the task of delivering consistent quality.

This is exactly the situation for the field of corporate citizenship. Indeed, this is *so* true that it is hard in many instances to distinguish success from failure. What appears to some to be 'progress' appears to others as 'failure'. Does a new monitoring report by Reebok represent 'good but not good enough', or does it 'mark another weakening of resolve of those

Box 2.1 *Possible Core Standards*[11]

Basic human rights: The Universal Declaration of Human Rights: Articles 3 and 5 and Preamble. The UN Code of Conduct for Law Enforcement Officials

Working conditions: ILO Conventions 29, 87, 98, 155, 105 and 138. ILO Tripartite Declaration 34, 33 and ILO Tripartite Declaration 37

Equality: ILO Conventions 100 and 111

Consumer protection: UN Guidelines for Consumer Protection; World Health Organization (WHO) Codes on breast milk substitutes and on promoting pharmaceuticals, Food and Agriculture Organization (FAO) convention on pesticides, Food standards of Codex Alimentarius

Environment: Rio Declaration, Agenda 21, Conventions on Climate Change, Biodiversity and the Law of the Sea, the Basle agreement, the Montreal Protocol, the Rotterdam Convention

Local communities: ILO Convention 169 on Indigenous and Tribal Peoples 7, 14, 15, 16, 20

Business practices: United Nations Conference on Trade and Development (UNCTAD) Rules for the Control of Restrictive Business Practices (D 1-4)

Sovereignty and development strategies: UN Charter of Economic Rights and Duties of States, Articles 1 & 2. ILO Tripartite Declaration of Principles concerning Enterprises and Social Policy 10, 19, 20

who play ball'?[12] Is the Global Alliance for Workers and Communities, a partnership involving Nike, Gap, the World Bank and the International Youth Foundation, a progressive innovation or, as its critics argue, a cynical public relations ploy?[13] When representatives from US business and the international trade union movement agree with each other that labour standards are a matter for the ILO, is this cause for celebration, or the perverse end-game of a failed approach?[14] When the accountants KPMG launch a world-wide 'sustainability advisory service', is this a sign that the non-profits have successfully created a 'market for change', or is this a sign that a professionalization path has set in that will not deliver the goods?[15] Are we witnessing an extraordinary step forward when many of the world's largest corporations commit themselves to upholding the nine human and labour rights and environmental protection principles defined under Kofi Annan's Global Compact, or are we seeing the final gasps of an ailing UN body that can only secure its future by mortgaging its independence?

How can one distinguish success from failure? The answer lies partly in ensuring a strong empirical orientation towards the analysis. But this alone is not enough. As the earlier profile of the Global Balance Sheet highlighted, data are inevitably incomplete, and generally contested. Most data are sadly inadequate in helping us to map the chains of cause-and-effect that would help us to understand how the present creates the future. In fact, data do not help unless they are set within a reasonably clear framework that reflects how one sees the world. Conversations do not work when these frameworks remain as shadowy, unacknowledged bases for difference. The field of corporate citizenship is marked by groups' differing views as to what the data mean, and which data count, for what, and for whom. Radical differences in the way people involved in labour standards issues see the world, rather than the empirical details, largely explain the strongly contested views over the meaning of, for example, particular company initiatives. For some, the aim of codes initiatives is to improve the lot of specific workers in particular factories or farms. This essentially 'welfarist' approach implies performance measures focused on whether the situation of specific workers has materially improved. Others, equally concerned about workers' situations, see the extension of their rights to organize and negotiate collectively as the key aim. From this latter perspective, welfare improvements remain important, but institutional issues underpin assessments of effectiveness, for example the effect of codes of conduct on the strength of independent trade unions. Indeed, from this perspective, welfarist-type improvements dilute the pressure to organize and so are seen by some as being against workers' long-term interests.

People and institutions with these varied perspectives do increasingly sit together and discuss everything from the scope for shared values to what are the appropriate metrics for assessing compliance with health and safety standards. But it is small wonder that they find it hard to reach agreement. It is not so much the data that they are disagreeing about (although this may also be the case), but rather what constitutes meaningful progress, and what does not.

WHY DOESN'T SOMEONE DO SOMETHING?

We are told that unless we reduce our levels of material consumption, we are likely to destroy the very ecological systems that we need to survive. Gro Harlem Brundtland's stern warning rings clear: we would need ten worlds, not one, to satisfy all of our needs if 7 billion people were to consume as much energy and resources as we do in the West today. Detailed work at the Wuppertal Institute shows that we need to reduce our energy use by up to 90 per cent in order to get back towards a sustainable development path – the so-called Factor Ten proposition. In today's publicity conscious world, even the US government's Central Intelligence Agency (CIA) offers us dire warnings of the dangers to come through the combined effects of population growth, water shortages and poverty.[16]

We are faced with major, potentially fatal, problems; we know about it, and yet very little is done to address it. Why? Actually, we are so accustomed to off-the-shelf assumptions that things will *not* happen that we rarely give the question serious thought. When we do, it is customary to explain the really serious failures to act by pointing to the constraining effects of individual and institutional interests. The problems of poverty, inequality and environmental degradation are from this perspective a result of decisions by undemocratic institutions, corrupt despots and ignorant individuals. Personal responsibility clearly plays a part, but 'there is after all little that one person can do'.

Suppose we step back for a moment from the troubling magnitude of these problems and focus instead on a lesser, although also very important, issue. Authoritative evidence suggests that as many as 11,000 people worldwide die each day from smoking-related illnesses.[17] We are overwhelmed with evidence of how this happens, and with well-meaning and now increasingly commercialized suggestions as to how to kick the habit. Why then do people continue to smoke cigarettes despite the overwhelming evidence that it significantly increases their chances of dying both prematurely and with considerable pain to them and their loved ones? Box 2.2 offers six possible reasons.

Box 2.2 *Six Possible Reasons Why Things Don't Change*

1 People Want to Die
2 Selfishness = Inertia
3 Optimism + Factor 4 = Inaction
4 Certainty + Uncertainty = Inertia
5 Certainty + Prisoner's Dilemma = Inertia
6 Concern + Understanding > Action

Proposition 1: People Want to Die. Smoking cigarettes is a bit like the problem of unsustainable development – we know it is bad for us, we know it may sink us in the end, but we just keep on going. From this perspective, the problem of smoking might be restated as, 'How can we stop people doing things that appear to be bad for them?' A super-rationalist proposition might be that people 'smoke to kill themselves for selfish reasons'. This argument is patently absurd, save possibly for a very small number of people. It seems similarly absurd to posit that people are, for example, consciously consuming in an unsustainable manner in order to bring an end to their lives.

Proposition 2: Selfishness = Inertia. Over-consumption is partly about so-called 'negative externalities'. In our example of cigarette smoking, this would be equivalent to the habit mainly affecting other people's health (eg passive smoking). In this situation, in order to stop, the smoker would need to care more about those people, or to have to take them into account for some legal or other reason. This seems at first glance to be a far more difficult problem than trying to get people to care for themselves, particularly since most negative externalities are borne by people our unreconstructed smoker-consumer will never know.

This is similar to the challenge of sustainable development, where according to one environmental economist, Robert Costanza, the value of global ecosystems services to humanity that are effectively not being costed into our market equation is as much as US$33 trillion per year, equivalent in magnitude to total measured Global Product.[18] The problem is that no one has to pay this bill in the short term – or at least no one with real power – so few people seem to care. Indeed, the 'seventh generation' model implicit in the broader view of sustainable development highlights the fact that most of the people we are being asked to care about do not even exist yet.

We might state this simply as, 'How can we stop people doing things that appear to be bad for other people about whom they seem to care too little?'

Proposition 3: Optimism + Factor 4 = Inaction. People perhaps continue to smoke because they do not believe in the evidence. If this is the case, trying to 'make them care' misses the point entirely, as does any attempt to make them act on their selfish interests to stay alive.

For cigarettes, this is equivalent to the argument either that the evidence that smoking kills is wrong, or that a solution will arise within a relevant time period that will make acting on the current apparent dangers unnecessary. For sustainable development, this view is well-rooted in the idea that technological solutions will massively reduce the output-to-energy use ratios that currently dominate industrial economies. Amory Lovins and others lend credence to this view. In his work on automobiles, he concludes that 'only 1 per cent of the gasoline moves you to your destination', and has designed a 'hypercar' and many other technological pathways that offer massive output to energy use gains. Using existing technology, he argues, we could achieve a four-fold increase in energy-efficiency – the so-called Factor Four proposition.[19]

Lovins clearly seeks to demonstrate that there are ready solutions, and that we should act to take advantage of them. He is the quintessential enemy of passivity caused by ignorance. Yet an equally plausible argument is that the development and purveying of such helpful solutions has the perverse effect of undermining the sense of urgency in seeking higher-level, system-wide changes that some consider necessary in addressing the challenges of sustainable development.

Proposition 4: Certainty + Uncertainty = Inertia. The smoker, faced with irrefutable evidence that smoking will kill, might say, 'But if I stop smoking, something else will kill me instead.' The long list of possible, known sources of premature death lends some credence to this argument, as do those sources that are often 'discovered' long after the damage has been done. How often have those living in a major city heard the smoker argue, 'what is the point of stopping smoking since urban pollution must be just as bad'?

This faint whiff of fatalism or perhaps even nihilism certainly has its place in the arena of sustainable development. Public opinion surveys often confirm people's views that they believe that the world is falling apart and that there is nothing that they can do about it. The challenge is 'just too great', since even if we fix one of the problems, something else will get us in the end.

Proposition 5: Certainty + Prisoner's Dilemma = Inertia. Of course this is not merely a problem of uncertainty but of the difficulty of collective action. Most of us know about the classic case of the 'Prisoner's Dilemma'. This is a mathematical exercise that demonstrates that two (or more) individuals can make the best possible choice for each if they collaborate, but may make poor choices if they do not know what the other person is going to do. For example, we need to jointly decide not to throw litter on the ground; otherwise few people will put rubbish in the dustbin even if they all hate experiencing it on the streets.

This is related to the negative externalities argument in another form, where what the person means is 'why should I do something when it is unlikely to help me?' Similarly, it is related to the 'free-rider' argument, where society does not make me pay for the particular mess that I make.

Proposition 6: Concern + Understanding > Action. But is what appears as nihilism or fatalism so easily explained through an 'economic rationality' type argument? Public opinion surveys about corporate ethics tend to find the following pattern of results consistently emerging:

- People think companies should behave better than they do.
- People think it is unlikely that they will behave better than they currently do.
- The reason is that people believe that 'there is no alternative' (TINA) to the current way in which things are organized.

We need to understand why people do not act despite a very real sense of concern. If we believe that this phenomenon arises because they are selfish and see no reason for change, we can approach the matter from a behaviourist perspective, for example pricing up those items that we think should be conserved, and wait for people to 'start caring'. But we do not do this in practice, at least nothing like to the degree that would make a difference. Petrol prices continue to be low enough to put the private car within the reach of an increasing number of people across the world. Indeed, higher petrol prices have most recently brought the citizens of Europe on to the streets in one of the region's largest concerted acts of civil disobedience. Electricity and gas prices make it uneconomic to insulate our homes within a time horizon that we choose to take into account. The absurdly low cost of plane tickets allows untold millions to travel thousands of miles for a quick business meeting, a shopping spree, a dose of sun, or maybe just a spot of lunch. One analysis of the 'ecological footprint' of the products we consume indicated that the footprint of a newspaper is equivalent to 10 per cent of an individual's daily allowable ecological consumption.[20] Yet there is no suggestion in the mainstream market for products or ideas that newspapers should be priced on that basis.

FACTOR X

Each of us holds in our minds, and uses, fragments of diverse models of how the world works. We apply these fragments simultaneously despite their, often very apparent, contradictions. The semblance of any coherence in our lives is rarely underpinned by high levels of consistency in our views, decisions or actions. People and communities, similarly, block change for many reasons. Indeed, they will often resist the language and ideas of change until there is simply no choice. Showing people that Factor Four (improved energy efficiency based on existing technology) is a real possibility, or that Factor Ten (what will make Europe play a sustainable role in the world's ecological systems) is a real need, rarely makes change happen, at least not on its own. Having insight into how to make it happen also does not always do the job. We know only too clearly how community-based development finance mechanisms, enterprises, trading systems and currencies can help to reverse the decline of local communities.[21] We know that a small tax on all international financial movements (the 'Tobin tax') might reduce unhealthy financial speculation and generate an international tax base. We understand in practice how different approaches to developing health delivery can enhance the health of people and simultaneously reduce costs. We understand all of these things. But this knowledge makes very little difference to what happens without a sense of how to get there from the here and now, the essence of Ernst Bloch's 'concrete utopia'.[22]

Moving from an understanding of sustainable development to becoming an agent for making it happen requires that we overcome what the Chilean politician and ecological economist, Manfred Max-Neef, describes as a 'state of perplexity'.[23]

Perplexity, the outcome of a situation for which we cannot recognize a precedent, has kept us in a dead-end alley and barred the road to imaginative, novel and bold solutions.

We are indeed in a 'state of perplexity' about the corporate community. The ways in which it has wielded its growing size and power, and to what ends, leave much to be desired. Yet it has an extraordinary ability to bring economic prosperity to those communities that need it most, and to forge or at least apply the technologies that are most likely to offset our destructive impact on the environment. Most of all, the corporate community exists. Its pervasive influence makes it very unlikely that it will be dispersed by even its most committed enemies. It cannot and will not be wished away. Transformation is clearly the real option. But this requires insight and vision if it is to be more than an attempt to tame and constrain. Actually, we do not want less or more of the corporate community, as it is often presented. What is needed is something quite different: a corporate community that is enabled to enact our best thinking on how to create the conditions for sustainable development. This is the essence of the civil corporation.

CHAPTER 3

Ethical Futures

This new frictionless economy will produce an unparalleled rise in living standards and human potential for all of society's members.

Tom Cavenagh, Conference Board[1]

In this age of triumphant commercialism, technology – with science as its handmaiden – is delivering a series of almost magical inventions that are the most phenomenally lucrative ever seen. We are aggressively pursuing the promises of these new technologies within the now unchallenged system of global capitalism and its manifold financial incentives and competitive pressures.

Bill Joy, Co-founder of Sun Microsystems[2]

ENTER THE NEW ECONOMY

Visions of the New Economy evoke a spectrum of evangelical, sceptical and worried cynical responses.[3] For some it is a source of hope, delivering a safe natural environment secured through 'e-materialization', progressive work opportunities complete with family and community synergies, and a democratic renaissance based on technology-enabled, direct citizen participation. For others, it spells out greater insecurity for all, the collapse of geographical communities, the loss of privacy in the personal domain and an acceleration of problematic global investment, trading patterns and unsustainable material consumption.

There are many definitions of the New Economy on offer. Most are polemical and carry underlying and unexpressed normative presumptions. Few offer even an accurate description of current events, let alone useful analysis for predicting the future. Narrow, media-friendly descriptions place the Internet and the dot.com phenomenon at stage centre. Broader views describe the New Economy as no less than a complete socio-economic revolution. There are equally diverse views on the balance of costs and benefits of the New Economy. The Indian grass-roots intellectual, John Samuels, argues that the 'delusions of development, wealth and participation [features of the New Economy] they create will not effectively change the ground realities of inequality, mistrust, social paranoia and moral degeneration'.[4] Tom Cavenagh of the Conference Board sums up the views of New Economy enthusiasts in arguing that 'barriers will fall, productivity will soar... and this new frictionless economy will produce an unparalleled rise in living standards and human potential for all of society's members'.[5]

Most definitions, however, share the sense of impending dramatic and pervasive change. Jim Wolfensen, President of the World Bank, describes the New Economy as: 'shorthand for nothing less than a revolution in the way business works, economic wealth is generated, societies are organized, and individuals exist within them'.[6] As the 'first great philosopher of cyberspace', Professor Manuel Castells, concludes, the New Economy implies radical changes in the nature of the institutions of the state and business, and redefines the roles of the citizen, both individually and collectively – for example, as employee, consumer, investor, parent and voter.[7] Such change is not just a matter for the post-industrial citizen, despite the public focus on the consumerist face of the dot.com bubble. Samuels is right in challenging what will be the impact of the New Economy on 'ground realities'. However, there is no doubt that there *will* be an impact on the lives of the people he describes, from the small Mexican coffee producer to the Indian subsistence farmer and diamond and gold miners of Southern Africa. The New Economy embraces the globalizing process underpinned by technological developments that will alter the terms on which every community will derive its livelihood and experience life on a daily basis.

The New Economy is marked by three underlying dynamics. The first is the *speed of change*. As Wim Duisenburg, the President of the European Central Bank (ECB), explains, 'What appears to be meant by the New Economy is that the speed limits of the economy have increased.'[8] The accuracy of Moore's Law, that the processing power of silicon chips will double every 18 months, is testimony to this rapid acceleration.[9] But this characteristic is not purely a technological phenomenon. In business, there has been an acceleration, for example, in the product innovation cycle, in the pace of change of brand recognition, and in share trading velocity.[10] In the personal and broader social spheres, similarly, there have been extra-ordinary increases in the speed of how communities evolve, and the pace and nature of development of visual and verbal language. This acceleration is of course not geographically, culturally or in any other way uniform. We all straddle the past and present as if we were virtual time travellers and so face the challenge of understanding and integrating the old with the new.[11] The accelerating speed of change therefore exacerbates and opens new social fractures, posing new challenges for those seeking to create bridges of understanding, empathy and support between different communities and individuals.

The second characteristic of the New Economy is the increased importance of *knowledge, innovation and communication*. Knowledge is the asset and basis upon which the performance of companies in the New Economy will be understood. Economic wealth is located increasingly at higher points in the business life cycle, towards the image and social meaning of the product rather than its production. As *Business Week* concluded, 'The turn of the millennium is a turn from hamburgers to software. Software is an idea; hamburger is a cow'.[12] A notable feature of the knowledge economy is the growing importance of intangible assets, such as intellectual capital, skills, research and development (R&D), brands, relationships and reputation. Tobin's so-called 'q' measures the ratio of the market value of a company to its book value. In 1996, for the UK stock market as a whole, q stood at 1.3, while for knowledge-based stock, such as Zeneca, it was 6. In the US, the average was 1.5, while for Microsoft it was 15.[13] Intangible assets are king in the New Economy. Interbrand estimates that one-quarter of the world's total financial wealth is tied up in a single part of a company's intangible assets, *brand value*.[14]

The third characteristic of the New Economy is *shifting proximity*. As an Organisation for Economic Co-operation and Development (OECD) report puts it, 'The "death of distance" that is intrinsic to information networking is probably the most important economic force shaping society at the dawn of the 21st century.'[15] Tele-working across time zones will be the future norm for working successfully in the New Economy, whether one is a high-paid knowledge-worker or a low-paid telephonist answering customer queries from across the world. Tele-working in the UK, for example, is predicted to underpin the work patterns of 50 per cent of the UK working population by 2010, a dramatic increase over 1999, when only 1 million people worked in this way.[16] Shifting proximity puts 'diversity' at centre stage. The workspace increasingly reflects the extraordinary breadth of communities from which expertise is being drawn, whether disabled, Christian fundamentalist, or the aged. As one commentator puts it, 'Mighty is the Mongrel'. Increased proximity can therefore, but need not, increase people's empathy for the plight of others, a point I will return to below.

The New Economy is fundamentally an organizational revolution. This has a deep impact on how business is conducted. We are in practice seeing the most radical shift in how commerce is organized since the 19th century industrial engineer Frederick Winslow Taylor introduced the time-and-motion mechanics of *scientific management* into our management vocabulary and daily practice. The impact of the three characteristics of the New Economy manifests itself in the downsizing and flattening of the main part of most corporations, and the dispersal of their core functions into market networks (through, for example, franchising and out-sourcing).

Equally, the New Economy affects how values are moulded and play out in practice. For business, this is where the significance of Tobin's q becomes apparent. A company that is able to build trust and integrity into its key relationships thereby lowers the cost of establishing and maintaining increasingly complex networks of suppliers, franchisees and agents, physically dispersed staff. As Mark Casson argues, the most important link between business ethics and financial performance is the impact of a culture of trust on the reduced need to 'police' business relationships.[17] Such a company is able more effectively to handle multiple levels of actual and potential regulators, from the local town council to the WTO. A stakeholder-based company is one that in many respects is most fit to take advantage of the technological and regulatory changes that underpin and enable the globalization of effective production and distribution.

Values are therefore integral to the organizational dynamics of the New Economy. Its underlying characteristics alter the basis on which values are shaped and applied. Yet the New Economy is essentially amoral. It does not define which values get played out in practice. Like all social and indeed most ecological phenomena, it is what you make of them that counts. This brings us to the phenomenon of corporate citizenship. Corporate citizenship is about businesses taking account of their total impact on society and the natural environment. Successful companies in the New Economy will engage effectively with key stakeholders in the markets for goods and services, finance, labour and political patronage. Corporate citizenship implies a strategy that moves from short-term transaction towards relationships that seek to capture stakeholders' loyalty by ever-more surgical interventions that align profitable opportunities with their social identities and underlying values. In this sense, *corporate citizenship is an outcrop of the New Economy.*

Corporate citizenship may prove to be a progressive outcome of the New Economy. Taking greater account of stakeholders' interests will deliver social goods in so far as people may care more as a result of the dynamics of the New Economy. This may indeed be the case because of:

(a) *increased information and knowledge* driven by the technological and organizational change;
(b) *alignment of caring with core lifestyle decisions*; choosing ethical brands is an expression of increased consumer choice;
(c) *increased empathy for the troubles of others* on the part of those with market power because of increased fears about the prospects for their, and their family's and friends', own sources of income and overall security.

But taking stakeholders into account does not automatically translate into 'doing good things'. People's fear of insecure lifestyles feeds many forms of discriminatory behaviour. Enhanced mass communication can breed populist antagonism towards refugees, the unemployed, disabled people, and other disadvantaged groups. Surgically differentiated consumer markets offer opportunities for branding based on less-than-ethical factors in people's desires and self-image. With e-commerce, the balance of information between purchaser and seller is reversed; the purchaser hands over personal information in order to buy, without knowing much about the company they are purchasing from.[18] For the online advertising agency DoubleClick, taking close account of people's revealed preferences meant that it wanted to sell data correlating people's records of visits to websites with their names and addresses.[19] What may, for example, seem like a website providing information on parenting turns out to endorse Polaroid pictures as a good way of promoting self-esteem in children.[20] Dietary control food stuffs, home security systems, small weapons and bottled water are some of the fastest growing consumer product areas. They are all fed by social and environmental fractures, yet none seeks in any way to 'fix' the problems they reflect and profit from.

The New Economy offers many opportunities for businesses to behave unethically, to drive down labour standards, to minimize their tax contributions, to exert undue influence over governments anxious to attract their investments and the job opportunities they bring with them. Similarly, the New Economy offers ample scope for businesses to market ethical products, and can enable companies to demonstrate their ethical credentials to protect and strengthen their brand, reputation and overall licence to operate. From these perspectives, corporate citizenship – a company's acquisition of, and response to, in-depth information about people's values, fantasies and interests – does not in itself guarantee any particular behaviour or outcome.

CITIZENSHIP CULTURES

Good corporate citizenship comes in many shapes and forms all over the world. The continental European tradition, for example, has historically led in addressing social exclusion through labour market interventions. US corporations have proved innovative in forging new ways of working in communities in distress, and in some sectors also have the cutting edge experience in handling labour standards in global supply chains. South Africa can be looked to for its recent leadership in driving black empowerment through the financial, rather than only the labour markets. And of course particular corporations from around the world offer celebrated cases of good corporate citizenship, such as Tata and Excel in India, South African Breweries in South Africa, the Ayala Corporation in the Philippines, and Globo in Brazil. One only has to look at the corporations that were represented at the launch of the UN Global Compact in New York in July 2000 – including Aracruz Celulose from Brazil, the Esquel Group from Hong Kong, and Eskom from South Africa, as well as many from continental Europe – to see the many facets of corporate citizenship.[21]

The emerging, dominant forms of global corporate citizenship are, however, deeply influenced by Anglo-American (US or UK) practice. Fourteen out of fifteen of the world's most socially responsible corporations are either from the UK or the US, according to a recent *Financial Times* (FT) survey of 800 international business leaders.[22] A recent benchmark study of global corporations' social and environmental public reporting sponsored by the United Nations Environment Programme (UNEP) placed 15 Anglo-American corporations in the global top 25. Five out of the top ten market corporate leaders, identified by the Swiss-based group Sustainability Asset Management as having practices most consistent with its understanding of sustainable development, are from the UK or the US.[24]

There are many reasons for this. First and foremost is that US corporations in particular are strong or dominant in many sectors, notably energy, chemicals, healthcare, retail and consumer goods, food and beverages and information technology. The same FT survey asked leading fund managers which companies they most respected, both in terms of their current performance and in terms of their expectations five years from now. In both cases, no fewer than 13 out of 15 corporations named were Anglo-American.[25] Obviously, these figures, and the basis on which they have been collected, are influenced by the international hegemony of the English language. But this hegemony is, fairly or not, merely a reflection of the fact that the Anglo-American corporation and approach to corporate practices, including corporate citizenship, dominates the global marketplace.

The underlying nature of the Anglo-American business model, as well as its growing international importance, also helps us to understand why it has generated what can usefully be seen as its mirror image, good corporate citizenship. It is not a coincidence that 'socially responsible investment' has emerged most strongly in the US and the UK. It is at least in part a reaction against the infamous short-termism of their respective financial markets. Moves towards measurement and transparency about social and environmental performance, similarly, draw on the Anglo-American focus on transparency as a source of accountability, and the associated models of corporate governance.

The Anglo-American corporate model is not, however, homogeneous. Corporate citizenship certainly has many manifestations in the US. However, the British approach has in the last decade proved to be globally far more influential, certainly well beyond its contemporary national economic or political power. The UK pursues an unwieldy blend of US traditions, with its unfettered markets and privatized provision, and the European tradition of social partnership. During the 1980s, of course, the UK approach leant more towards the US model than ever before, driving down the welfare floor and opening up financial markets. Sadly for the UK, this was accompanied by a rapid climb in poverty and inequality, and an equally precipitous fall in health and education standards. Indeed, this legacy of the 1980s led Heinrich von Pierer, the Chief Executive of Siemens, to conclude, 'The UK has lost its social cohesion... You may call me a social romantic, but I do not believe that financial markets should play such a strong role.'[26]

British leadership in corporate citizenship is a more attractive and productive legacy of the 1980s. The UK today is characterized more than anything else by a search for a renewed social contract that effectively bridges the UK's muddled traditions and delivers both economic vigour and the benefits of European-style cohesion. British companies, and indeed non-British companies with a strong presence in the UK markets, have sought to claw back some of the legitimacy that they lost or failed to gain during the aggressive period of privatization and the accompanying social dislocations. Their social indicators and reports, in this light, are as much a conversation with the public about the shape of a new social contract as they are robust performance measures, as discussed in later chapters.

European companies often view the British experience of corporate citizenship with barely disguised disdain. They point to the perceived strengths of, for example, their co-determination, centralist and consensual models of both national and business-level governance and declare, 'We have always practised corporate citizenship – the UK is merely catching up in an inevitably ad hoc, individualistic manner.' But the traditional European social partnership tradition is under pressure at home and abroad. The institutional arrangements that underpin it are increasingly sclerotic, creating rigidities that pose real dangers in a period where adaptability lies at the heart of economic success. The strongest indication of the rise of UK (as opposed to US) styles of corporate citizenship within the European business community perhaps lies in the activities surrounding their non-European operations. For example, Suez may indeed adopt a classically French approach within its domestic borders, but finds that the Anglo model of more open-ended stakeholder engagement, including working closely with NGOs, is the order of the day when it comes to, for example, water management contracts in Latin America.

A further source of the UK's strength in the field of corporate citizenship is its (some would say) over-abundant endowment of what are probably the world's most powerful set of development, environmental and human rights organizations. Multinational NGOs like Amnesty and Oxfam represent merely the tip of a powerful cocktail of pressure groups that top the charts of every UK public opinion poll when it comes to matters of trust. This, largely benign, element of the UK's colonial legacy has proved a vital force in many campaigns aimed at the corporate sector, historically for example against Nestlé, and more recently against Monsanto, Shell and many others. UK companies have, as a result, become among the world's most sophisticated operators when it comes to dealing with NGOs and related social and environmental issues. Furthermore, this history of confrontation has spawned a huge infrastructure of researchers and consultants of every conceivable shape or form to advise business, and also NGOs and governments, on how best to engage with each other in reaching pragmatic bases for moving on.

This is certainly not a profound analysis of the nature of Anglo-American or specifically British approaches to corporate citizenship. Suffice to say, perhaps, that it is widely seen to be world class, and that there are well-grounded reasons for supporting this view. This does *not* mean that Anglo-American companies necessarily have better social and environmental performance, although both the FT survey and the UNEP-sponsored global reporting benchmarking study suggest that in some sectors this may be the case. What it does suggest is that the Anglo-American styles of corporate citizenship are likely to inform the approaches adopted by many other corporations in the coming years. In some respects this is already happening. The Global Reporting Initiative (GRI), for example, adopted by increasing numbers of corporations across Europe and also now in Asia, emerges from a typical Anglo-American emphasis on metrics and transparency as a key foundation and driver of accountability and performance. The evolution of the UN Global Compact, similarly, has been particularly influenced by a small group of largely UK and US corporations. The most extensive business networks in the field of corporate citizenship remain Business for Social Responsibility (BSR) based in San Francisco, and the International Business Leaders Forum (IBLF) based in London. BSR's approach has informed the development of comparable networks across Central and Latin America. In the same way, it is a small group of Anglo-American corporations that have taken real leadership in the evolution of the newly re-branded pan-European business network, CSR Europe.

Corporate citizenship is *not* an Anglo-American phenomenon. However, the Anglo-American experience is deeply informing those contemporary approaches to corporate citizenship that are emerging as leading global practices, and in turn embedding themselves in some of the evolving standards in the field.

CONTINGENT FUTURES

The way in which corporate citizenship plays itself out in the New Economy depends on how a company seeks, and successfully gains, competitive advantage through its integration into core business strategy. Companies such as BP and Shell, Unilever, Ford, and even smaller players like The Body Shop and the Co-operative Bank in the UK, are relatively dominant in their respective markets or the niches they have created. In pursuing strategies that embrace aspects of good corporate citizenship, these corporations have sought to enhance or stabilize their market positions, products' price premium, or their ability to recruit the best in the 'war for talent'. At the same time, they have sought to avoid being at a cost-disadvantage (where additional costs are involved) through the adoption of good social and environmental practices, often by pressuring 'follower' competitors to imitate their approaches.

Such a virtuous circle need not necessarily work. Wal-Mart's entry into the UK market though its purchase of Asda, for example, will intensify price-based competition between food retailers in what has to date been a relatively lifestyle conscious, food retail market. Wal-Mart's alliance with

AOL Warner to promote ShopSmart Ltd, a British website focused on the provision of price comparisons, is just one example of its attempt to raise the prominence of price as the principal competitive factor in British (and indeed global) food retailing. Wal-Mart is well placed to dominate such a market because of its enormous economies of scale in procurement and distribution, and its lengthy experience in the US market in pursuing such a strategy. Such a shift will almost certainly reduce the importance of 'ethics' in the strategy mix for its competitors, such as those companies associated with the UK-based Ethical Trading Initiative (ETI). This in turn could well undermine progress by UK supermarket chains in, for example, improving labour standards in their global supply chains.

A further possibility is that companies that can sustain a strategy that embraces aspects of good corporate citizenship do not prove to be strong enough in their respective markets to pressure other companies to follow suit. In this situation, companies that have embraced good corporate citizenship will effectively be ghettoized within the confines of those markets that can sustain higher social and environmental performance, whether because of the resulting increase in employee productivity, improved customer loyalty, or more responsive and positive government action.

Good corporate citizenship practices by particular businesses can therefore have one or more of three possible effects. They can create citizenship micro-climates where one of a small number of businesses can survive and indeed prosper. They can be squeezed out of the market through the ability of other businesses to take advantage of, for example, any cost disadvantages created for those companies seeking to 'do good'. Finally, they can lead to shifts in the underlying conditions of the market that extend the take-up of the particular good practices. These three pathways are summarized in Figure 3.1,[27] and described further below.

Oasis. This is what best describes most of the the current 'best practice' situations. A significant but small group of companies have taken up the challenge of aligning their business strategy and operations to the imperatives of, and opportunities associated with, sustainable development. This group, together with some NGOs and governments, are pushing for positive social and environmental change in the context of business needs and performance. However, the bulk of the business community, and many parts of civil society, are either not aware of the possibilities of being part of this process, or have actively chosen not to engage.

Desert. There is the possibility that over time the desert will encroach on the oasis, where corporate citizenship has for some time sustained a competitive edge in a market niche. This encroachment could happen for many reasons, including short termism in the financial community and public cynicism, resulting in responsible corporate behaviour

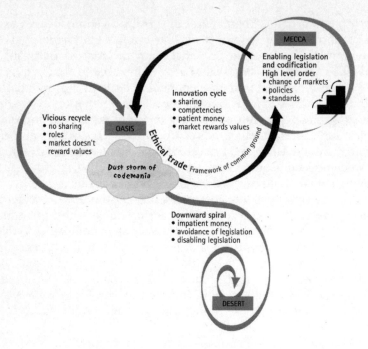

Figure 3.1 *Ethical Trade Futures?*

being neither adequately recognized nor rewarded. Along this pathway, therefore, there is an erosion of the 'win–win' areas where they existed, preventing businesses in a competitive environment from moving along a sustainable development path.

Mecca. Mecca is not an endpoint but a pathway of positive change. Leading companies achieve competitive advantage by evolving innovative and effective business strategies that deliver greater social and environmental accountability, and associated behaviour and outcomes. Their success encourages other companies to move in similar, or at least compatible, directions. In some instances, regulation is effective in encouraging these other market players to follow in the steps of corporate innovators rather than adopting business strategies that could undermine the gains achieved through the latter's activities across the economic, social and environmental spheres.

These three pathways offer ways of thinking about how current trends have played, or may play, themselves out. The Body Shop, for example, succeeded for a long time in constructing a safe and profitable Oasis, and has gone some way down the Mecca pathway by shifting the market for mid-price ranged body care products in its handling of animal testing. More recently, however, the company has found itself on the borderline between Oasis and Desert as competitors encroach, having for example taken on board (and so reduced the distinguishing edge of) its environmental and animal testing features, while being more competitive in other ways. The Body Shop's experimentation with social auditing, discussed in more detail in later chapters, also placed them at the vanguard of a movement sweeping through increasing swathes of the business community. In this instance, however, the corporate citizenship innovation did not yield to an Oasis or Mecca-like competitive edge, and the company made few if any significant competitive business gains through the practice as a result.

The three pathways may co-exist within a particular sector, or even across different parts of a single business. Leading, high-profile energy and mining companies are increasingly endorsing approaches to site development that take explicit account of human rights issues. These companies are market leaders, and over time will in all likelihood drive large parts of their respective markets towards higher human rights standards. A classic Mecca pathway is being carved out in this sphere of the sector's activities and performance. At the same time, some of the same companies are entering into joint ventures with companies that have not embraced similar standards, even aspirationally. BP's small (2 per cent) stake in the Chinese state-owned oil corporation is a case in point. Similarly, energy companies have very different approaches towards global warming. In this instance, the leadership model that has – even falteringly – begun to work in the sphere of human rights, has manifestly failed to date in driving the sector.

ETHICAL FUTURES?

This and the previous chapter have sought to frame the exploration of what we might usefully expect from the corporate community, and how best to realize these expectations. Effectively addressing the question requires us to make explicit the underlying presumptions about what is going on and what the future might hold. Technological optimists will tend not to see the need for major institutional change, and will rarely challenge the key role to be played by business in moving along the Mecca route. Those focused on environmental limits are usually more despairing of the current institutional arrangements, and see the need for more active government intervention in levelling the playing field down to environmentally more sustainable pathways. The anti-corporate movement sees the Desert as the most likely long-term pathway if corporations continue to be as powerful as they are today. Mecca for them generally embraces an agenda of localization, which means dismantling, or at the very least constraining the global ambitions of, the multinational business community.

Value differences do play a role in framing these and other variations, but actually less than is commonly presumed. One is hard pushed to find a corporate manager who thinks that human rights is a 'bad idea', or that environmental security is for the birds. Similarly, most people who have joined the ranks of the anti-business movement are essentially products of both globalization and the corporate world. Yet they find themselves frustrated by their inability to find an effective voice that challenges the manifest problems of which they are both a part and dependent on. Value differences do exist, of course. But more prevalent are different assumptions about how best to realize visions of desirable outcomes.

Corporate citizenship may indeed be a necessary outcrop of the New Economy. But its form, scope and impact are contingent. In some cases, this may result in the delivery of products at the cheapest possible price to the fussiest consumers – certainly a version of 'being good' to many. In other instances, the values promoted will cover a wider range of factors and points of interest, for example in the areas of the environment, animal rights, and human rights, that effectively do the job of securing the loyalty of key stakeholders. What this tells us is that markets, even those dominated by corporations responsive to short-term financial imperatives, can go either way when it comes to the challenges and aspirations underpinning sustainable development. It is simply mistaken to argue that these markets are inherently and unchangeably biased against broader and longer-term interests and concerns. There clearly are business models that will tend to produce the social and environmental goods, and those that militate against such outcomes. It is in this context that I turn in the next three chapters to explore some of the intricacies of the business case for corporate citizenship.

CHAPTER 4

Breaking the Trust Barrier

Would you trust your doctor if a plaque on the wall of the waiting room declared his mission as being to 'maximize profit'. Of course not... Profitability in fact flows from the client believing that they share with the doctor a common purpose that is not about business.

Professor John Kay, Said Business School[1]

FALLEN ANGELS

Levi Strauss was the first global corporation to adopt a code covering labour standards in its global supply chain, its so-called Terms of Engagement. For several years during the early 1990s the company was seen as a leader in this – and indeed other – areas of 'ethical behaviour'. As codes became more prevalent, however, so did the calls for proof that the company's deeds were as grand as its words. Levi Strauss resisted, arguing that to follow this route would be to suggest that it was being ethical *in order* to enhance its reputation rather than because being so was simply the 'right thing to do'. As Alan Christie, a senior Levi Strauss executive, concluded at a meeting hosted by the European Commission on codes of conduct and social labels, 'Our brand is our label.'[2]

In 1997, President Clinton's administration supported Nike, Reebok, Sarah Lee, Liz Claiborne and other US apparel and footwear retailers in launching the Apparel Industry Partnership (AIP) with a view to developing an agreed code and approach to monitoring and certifiable external verification. Levi Strauss, among others, declined to join. Its stated view at the time was that the adoption of policed, external standards was not consistent with its own policy and approach to engaging with suppliers and dealing with issues in a sensitive, developmental manner.

Across the Atlantic in the UK, another famous retailer, Marks & Spencer (M&S), was also following an independent course. M&S had built up a fabulous high street reputation over several decades as the 'retailer that the public trusts'. Good quality, mid-range apparel and food products combined with a long-standing dedication to superb customer service endowed the company's brand with an unrivalled level of trust with the consuming public. The pressure through the first part of the 1990s on companies to open their books with regard to social policy and practices did not initially impact on M&S, even though its competitors in both apparel and food retail were having to cope with ever-more aggressive and well-informed public campaigns. Then in 1998 the British television production company, Granada, screened at peak-viewing time a documentary that revealed the presence of child labour in M&S's supply chains, specifically in the factory of a Moroccan supplier. M&S sued Granada, and succeeded in winning a lengthy libel case. Interestingly, the case was won not on the argument that there was no child labour, the presence of which was not in dispute. M&S argued successfully that the libel was rooted in the documentary's erroneous claim that the company should have known about, and taken responsibility for, the use of child labour in their supplier's factory even though they were buying through an agent.

The Ethical Trading Initiative (ETI) was launched in the UK in 1998 with government support and a string of leading retailers as its founding members working with development and human rights NGOs and the international trade union movement. As the UK Secretary of State for International Development, Clare Short, explained at the launch of the ETI:

> The next stop is to agree how best to ensure that companies are effectively monitoring practice against these codes. This will require an agreed approach to monitoring and independent verification that will ensure the right quality of information, involve labour organizations and NGOs, and ultimately give the public the confidence they want that companies have put their houses in order.[3]

M&S declined to join the ETI, citing its preference to develop its own approach rooted in its historic tradition of building long-term relationships with its suppliers and customers.

As the 1990s unfolded, companies in the textiles industry came under increased public scrutiny. One by one, the larger, high-value brand companies yielded to pressure and adopted a variety of routes that committed them both to broadly similar codes of conduct and also to the principle of external verification. In 1997, Levi Strauss joined with Oxfam (UK) in testing out an NGO-led monitoring and engagement initiative with one of its suppliers in the Dominican Republic. A leading Dominican Republic feminist activist, Magaly Pineda, led the initiative. Respected internationally, she attested to the values-led commitment by Levi Strauss, and the effectiveness of an engagement strategy in bringing real improvements to workers' lives.[4] The results of this initiative were finally published in late 1998, signalling the company's gradual shift towards monitoring and external verification.[5]

Levi Strauss underwent other changes during the course of 1999. Its decision to close a string of its US and European production facilities was central. Citing the precipitous downturn in sales of its prime product, blue jeans, the company ended its long-standing tradition of maximizing in-market sourcing, and also of being able to effectively protect the livelihoods of its workforce through difficult times. In so doing, Levi Strauss was alleged to have reversed another long-standing commitment not to produce in China in the light of the country's poor human rights record. This high-profile policy position had actually long been misunderstood. The company had never 'pulled out' of China, as earlier headlines suggested, but rather had decided not to expand its China-based production. The closure of North American and European plants, Levi Strauss argued, did not signal a shift of production into China. Furthermore, the company stressed, it did not mean an underlying move away from high-cost, unionized labour to the use of low-cost, largely non-unionized labour in Asia and Latin America. Despite these public statements, however, few believed that the future would see a re-growth of apparel production for Levi Strauss in the high-cost areas of North America or Western Europe.

In mid-1999, Levi Strauss took the plunge and joined the AIP, by then renamed the Fair Labor Association (FLA). In so doing, it abandoned its long-standing resistance to external verification by accredited auditors, the single most important feature of the FLA model. More or less at the same time, the company joined the ETI in the UK. While not designed to be a standards body, membership required a commitment to external verification and public reporting. Together, these acts completed the shift in the company's underlying philosophy and approach to dealing with ethics, behaviour and reputation.

The last two years of the millennium were a nightmare for M&S. It suffered a collapse in sales and profitability, and experienced unsightly and counterproductive Board in-fighting, as well as a rapid and unruly turnover of its senior management. In an effort to stem the financial crisis, the company reversed its long-standing tradition of extensive UK-sourcing. It chose to unceremoniously walk away from British suppliers with which it had worked for decades, creating unemployment and public outrage from businesses and workers alike. During this painful process, it managed to use up much of the social capital it had built up over many decades in an effort to achieve much-needed gains in financial performance. In mid-1999, M&S reversed its publicly held position and joined the ETI.

These experiences of Levi Strauss and M&S in many ways reflect the dynamics of the New Economy set out in the previous chapter. Both companies reached what may prove to be the peak of their reputations in the early 1990s. Both were associated with a high standard of ethics in their business behaviour, and were as a result applauded by key stakeholders, including employees and the trade union movement. Both, in short, were trusted to 'do the right thing'. Equally, they failed to correctly judge their respective shifting business environments in both their product markets and in the spheres of production. Both lost massive market share and found themselves in deep financial trouble. Both companies made major and fairly rapid shifts in their sourcing strategies in an effort to increase flexibility and cut costs while they sought to rebuild their position in their product markets.

Both were, in short, 'fallen angels', having to break relationships and commitments built up over decades. Their reputations lost their historic sense of 'untouchability', and the ethics of their behaviour became a legitimate target for debate. In this context, both companies saw the writing on the wall. It was no longer possible to stand above the all-too-public fray into which their competitors had fallen. Both saw fit to join the various initiatives that until then they had held themselves apart from, such as the FLA and the ETI. In doing so, both companies signalled their recognition that they had entered a new phase in their corporate histories where credibility would need to be based on their ability and willingness to prove their good behaviour. For both companies, the era of bottomless trust had come to a precipitous and painful end.

THE 'SHOW ME' MYTH

It is customary to speak today of the 'show me' or even the 'prove it' world. This is apparently counterpoised to some attractive past time where relationships were built on implicit trust. Nowadays, it is claimed, we have all become learned empiricists, basing our judgements on the facts, and nothing but the facts.

But the 'show me' metaphor does not really describe how we form our impressions about whether companies or indeed any other institutions are behaving in an acceptable manner. Consider our varied approaches to awarding faith in institutions. We demand proof of Rio Tinto's claims to be environmentally responsible in its mining operations throughout the world, but take it as given that Save the Children Fund's activities are as green as they should be. One public opinion poll after another confirms that the public trusts essentially undemocratic NGOs more than they do any other institutions, including the governments they elect. Although we remorselessly scrutinize the personal activities of our national political leaders, we do not even enquire into the name of Oxfam's current Chief Executive, let alone David Bryer's personal habits and predilections. The legal responsibilities for public reporting are far greater for publicly listed companies and governments than they are for NGOs. Yet we distrust the former and continue to voluntarily shower the latter with our hard-earned money and scarce time.

Indeed, we seem at times to make decisions about which institutions we trust *despite* available information. It turned out that Greenpeace was quite simply wrong in its public pronouncements about the environmental consequences of Shell's proposal to sink the redundant Brent Spar oil platform to the bottom of the North Sea. But this has done little to reduce Greenpeace's or other NGOs' public credibility in challenging, for example, Monsanto over genetically modified agricultural and food products, BP over its planned intrusion into the Alaskan wilds, or Premier Oil's human rights record in Burma. Customers and other stakeholders were surprised, perhaps sad, when the small, British fair trade company, Traidcraft, revealed in its first published social report that only a small percentage of the sales price of a typical product that it sold went to those community producers for whom the company purported to exist and trade.[6] Indeed, inventory storage charges turned out to be far greater than the proportion received by those who made the products. This fact did little, however, to dissuade the company's customers from buying its relatively high-priced crafts and textiles.

Corporate social and environmental performance in the New Economy depends on what people really think about business, and what is actually important to them. These will be major determinants of which of the three pathways described in the previous chapter proves dominant. This in turn depends on how people – as consumers, employees, investors and voters – get and judge information about the corporate community. We may think, or like to think, that this means that we live in a 'global goldfish bowl'. But if this delightful metaphor is meant to imply that we spend our precious time studying the facts and nothing but the facts, it is simply wrong.

PEOPLE TRUST PEOPLE

People do not trust the business community, just as they increasingly distrust the other large institutions that dominate the skylines of their day-to-day work and play. Yet they neither form nor respond to this distrust by basing their opinions about corporations on a systematic exploration of the facts, as the 'show me' metaphor about today's society would have us believe. Instead, they form their views by looking to the attitudes of those people who they trust, believe in, or admire.

When the British fair trade chocolate company, the Day Chocolate Company, launched its first product, Divine, it used the comedian and writer, Ben Elton, to promote it through a series of fast-moving 10-second television commercials. Ben Elton had never advertised a product in his life, visibly and vocally opposed as he says he is to all manner of ventures that push things on the unsuspecting punter. Equally, however, he has a reputation for avoiding the more pious end of 'doing the right thing'. These two dimensions of his character and reputation made him the perfect person to advertise a product that positioned itself as unique in being both fair and very tasty.

Michael Jordan's role in promoting Nike products is probably the most famous case of personality driven marketing, as Walter LaFeber documents in his book, *Michael Jordan and the New Global Capitalism*. Jordan was not simply the best basketball player the world had ever known. By combining his own skills and ambition with the emerging telecommunications revolution and the power of corporate sponsorship, he rose to become viewed as the symbol of American dynamism and, at least for some time, virtue. LaFeber reports: 'In mid-1998, *Fortune* magazine estimated that Jordan had at least a US$10 billion [positive] impact on the US economy. About half, or US$5.2 billion, the article suggested, benefited Nike.'[7] Not surprisingly, perhaps, Nike's founder and CEO, Phil Knight, concluded that Michael Jordan is the greatest endorser of the 20th century.[8]

Companies that have begun to publish reports covering their social and environmental performance have sought to build their credibility through the inclusion of well-respected people. The British commercial bank, NatWest, included the views of the environmentalist and Director of Forum for the Future, Sir Jonathon Porritt CBE, and Rabbi Julia Neuberger. The latter explained her role as follows:

> My role as social policy adviser to NatWest has enabled me to witness at close quarters their efforts to make their community and wider public policy interests integral to the work of the organization.[9]

The importance of the shift from belief in institutions to a reliance on the word of individuals should not really be surprising in this messy, complex world. The economist will tell us that this approach is 'transactionally efficient' in that it can dramatically reduce the cost of searching for and analysing information on which to make decisions. The social psychologist, on the other hand, will perhaps stress that this reinforces the view that choice is largely informed by one's social identity. Others would view the critical role of the individual as the purveyor of trust as arising because of the collapse of institutionalized ideologies.

In appearing in NatWest's Social Review, Porritt and Neuberger lend our trust in them to the company, and thereby enhance its reputation in our eyes. Our trust that they would not lie about a company with which they are willing to be associated strengthens our confidence in NatWest. It adds a human face to what is essentially a perfectly normal commercial financial institution. But NatWest does *not* gain our trust as a result, although we might loosely and inaccurately talk about 'our trust in them'. Trust cannot be traded so readily. Were Porritt to publicly denounce the company tomorrow and explain to our satisfaction how he had been duped into believing that they were behaving responsibly, our trust in his ethics would lead us to join him in rejecting NatWest's intimate overtures.

INSTITUTIONALIZED TRUST

Trust is usually something that exists between people, distinguishing it from reputation. But some people acquire an institutionalized reputation that looks like trust. A few people will have actually spent time with Jonathon Porritt during his time as founder and director of Friends of the Earth, and now as Director of Forum for the Future. Some will actually know him through their personal and professional networks and activities. For these people, trusting Jonathon can be understood in the conventional sense that I have alluded to above. But this direct personal connection does not exist for the vast majority of people who see Jonathon's face on the pages of the NatWest Social Review. For most people, he is an institutionalized phenomenon, as would be a politician, a member of a royal family, or some other celebrity. The trust that he elicits from the reader of the NatWest report is not based on their personal knowledge of him, but on a construction of his public persona that is comparable, although not the same as, the way reputation is built for institutions. This is of course the same for Ben Elton and Michael Jordan. We talk about them, read gossip about them as if they were our neighbours, and in so doing act as if we know them as individuals. We feign a knowledge and experience of their whole personalities and so construct some semblance of an intimate link with them. When they do odd things, as in Michael Jordan's well-publicized gambling and other foibles, or Ben Elton's relationship with the newly elected President George W Bush, we forgive or condemn them as if they were our friends and lovers. But actually, we do not really know them at all.

Anita Roddick and Ben Cohen, co-founders of The Body Shop and Ben & Jerry's respectively, are quintessential examples of how, at least for some time, to create an apparently seamless integration of institutionalized trust and reputation. Both not only symbolized their company, but *were* the company in the eyes of those who either liked or hated their flamboyant moralizing and its intimate link for many years to extraordinary business and personal financial success. Richard Branson and the Virgin group of companies is a later version of the same phenomenon. He has built his brand on the back of a personal cult that he has painstakingly developed over many years. Indeed, his success has been such that he won by a considerable margin a British media-led 'scam poll' in 1999 to identify who the public would like most as their next king or queen. Branson has distanced himself from the 'sixties ethics' promulgated by Roddick and Cohen. Indeed, he has kept clear of taking any public stance on any environmental and human rights issues. But Branson has essentially played on the same social sensibility, positioning himself as the amateur eccentric 'David' against the gigantic, suited 'Goliaths' of modern times; in this case the major branded multinationals.

The trust that these three personalities have built up has paid off amply in business terms, although interestingly this trust has declined for all three in recent times. Both The Body Shop and Ben & Jerry's came under public attack in the mid-1990s for allegedly misleading their customers and the wider public in their claims for 'purer-than-pure' environmental and fair trade performance. Despite a sustained media campaign against the two companies, particularly The Body Shop, in both Europe and North America, their key stakeholders remained loyal. Richard Branson's Virgin Train ventures in the UK have badly under-performed, leaving tens of thousands of daily commuters in very expensive discomfort. Yet the brand continues to flourish, not least on the back of the much-publicized 'personal commitment' by Branson himself to 'get it right'.

TRUSTING INSTITUTIONS

So trust is in people, institutionalized trust is in celebrities, and organizations have reputations. But not all reputations are alike. This is not just a matter of some having high and others having low reputations. Neither is it only a case of some organizations being trusted for different things, say for their good products as opposed to their good treatment of their employees. There are qualitative differences in how people place their faith in institutions, and we need to understand a little more about how and why.

The most obvious example of this is the radically different way in which the public places trust in NGOs as compared with businesses. NGOs have many of the same imperatives as businesses. They have to stick to the law (more or less), survive financially, and compete for attention and funds in an increasingly cut-throat market for foundation grants, membership fees, donations and government and business support. Many of them are in the business of selling products and services, increasingly through non-charitable trading arms that nevertheless benefit from tax-exempt status. Just like the middle and upper ranks of the corporate community, they are staffed by normal people, although in the main with a bias towards higher education and middle-class backgrounds. Indeed, with the growth in their business activities, increasing numbers of people at senior levels

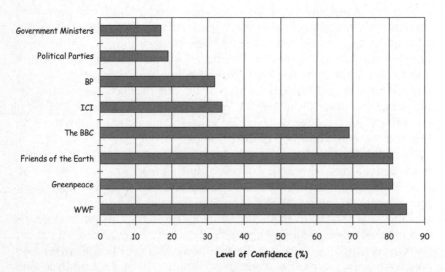

Figure 4.1 *Level of Confidence in Different Organizations in the UK*

have had experience in the business community, and are drawn in exactly because of associated skills and networks. Are NGOs, then, just another class of organization with reputations to make, lend or burn?

Companies such as Shell International, in seeking to build their credibility, almost always turn first to representatives of NGOs for 'lent trust'. One of its recent public reports on its social, economic and environmental performance has no fewer than six personal testimonies from external opinion leaders. Each testimony offered a balanced blend of positive endorsement of Shell's recent progress and carefully worded cautionary encouragement about the need to do more in the future. This is well illustrated by the statement included in the report by Judy Kuszewski, then Director of Corporate Programs at the Coalition of Environmentally Responsible Economies (CERES) with special responsibility for the Global Reporting Initiative (GRI):

> The environmental performance information shows that gains have been made in a number of areas of impact for Shell...

> ...Shell's commitment to renewables, while noteworthy, continues to be relatively small, and Shell will need to expand these areas significantly in order to achieve the historic transition to a hydrogen economy it envisions.

> In an industry which lacks many leaders, the gains Shell makes toward sustainability have enormous impact on their own, as well as power to influence the Group's peers fundamentally.[10]

Another good example comes from Will Day, the Chief Executive of Care International (UK), who says in the Shell Report 1999:

> When the first Shell Report was published, we were surprised to find ourselves agreeing with much of what was written. However, our enthusiasm was tempered with a healthy and traditional dose of NGO scepticism.[11]

The growing significance of NGOs lending their reputation to businesses has not even required individual faces. General Motors' high-profile support of the GRI, and more recently the Global Sullivan Principles, will certainly have delivered reputational gains to the company. These gains have not been of a public nature such as for Nike in the case of Michael Jordan, but gains in their reputation among the cadre of professional opinion leaders who influence what the media says and writes, and also the evolution of public policy. The British food retail chain, Sainsbury's, gained reputationally when Oxfam (UK) added a carefully worded, positive statement at the beginning of the company's annual report congratulating it for moving forward in the area of labour standards in its global supply chains. The company similarly gained when it joined, and in many ways helped to create, the ETI, also interestingly in close collaboration with Oxfam (UK). BP, Rio Tinto and Shell International have all benefited from the positive support (albeit, not endorsement) they received from the Amnesty Business Group for their respective referencing of the UN Declaration of Human Rights in their respective revised core business principles.

NGOs have the closest to what one might call 'institutional trust'. This is not because they are fronted by famous people, although this is a reinforcing technique used by some NGOs. It is because NGOs build their legitimacy by projecting a sense of non-financial purpose, and purport to represent the best interests of the wider community. They build a sense of shared values with external and often distant stakeholders. This is rarely through engagement and dialogue; after all, few of Human Rights Watch's many supporters have ever been to one of their events, let alone engaged with the NGO in a serious discussion about policy or performance. NGOs are able to mobilize and sustain a sense of shared trust by resembling, in their active view and engagement in the world, that part of people's visions of, or desire about, themselves about which they feel most proud. People are overwhelmingly against governments that regularly abuse human rights. But few are personally willing to take the time, spend the money, and possibly place themselves at risk in mobilizing against them. Every person would wish to see starving people given food, and therefore want to support an Oxfam or ActionAid that will express in practical ways this inner vision of what is right and wrong in the world. People trust NGOs because – or as long as – they are able to express a part of themselves that is not otherwise adequately experienced in their day-to-day lives.

Mostly, then, supporters' inner engagement with NGOs' objectives and actions (as they perceive them) is deeply rooted, and forms the basis for a very special kind of organizational reputation. This distinguishes NGOs from most businesses, and in particular from larger businesses that have no obvious and long-standing root in the community. It is not that Nike is not about people's dreams; arguably its roughly US$500 million annual marketing budget certainly aims to associate Nike's Swoosh with no less than people's fantasies, hopes and aspirations. Shell, similarly, aims to build a reputation for addressing the aspirations of us all to improve human well-being and environmental security. But so far, the moves by companies to take the moral high-ground have actually met with fairly limited success. Their reputations can and do in many cases improve, certainly. People continue to buy – or perhaps resume buying – their products and services. Some even know the names of those companies that opinion leaders publicly endorse as being better than the rest. However, corporations remain, fundamentally, untrusted.

DANGEROUS AFFAIRS

Borrowing trust can be a dangerous affair, both for the lender and the borrower. Andrew Young, the former US Ambassador to the UN, acted as consultant to Nike in reviewing labour standards in a number of its suppliers' factories. He concluded in his published report that there was no evidence of systematic abuse of workers' rights, and that in the main the factories were 'clean, organized, adequately ventilated and well-lit'. Both Young and Nike must have regretted this ringing, high-profile, public endorsement when labour rights activists successfully discredited Young's approach, arguing that it was superficial, producing damning evidence that workers' rights in some Nike suppliers were being repeatedly abused.[12] John Elkington, one of the pre-eminent corporate advisers on sustainable development, writer, and founder and Chair of the consultancy SustainAbility Ltd, has long risked the wrath of NGOs by working with some of the world's most controversial pharmaceutical, chemicals and energy companies. In early 1999, however, he resigned from his retainer relationship with Monsanto, citing a collapse in his belief in the company's willingness to engage in meaningful dialogue or change.

Organizations in the trust-lending business have also found themselves the subject of criticism. During the time that I worked for the NGO think-tank, the New Economics Foundation (NEF), the organization found itself hounded by the journalist, Jon Entine, for its association with The Body Shop and subsequently Ben & Jerry's. The Amnesty Business Group arm of Amnesty UK has been criticized for its implicit endorsement of Rio Tinto and Shell's new business principles. Christian Aid and the WDM have been challenged for their involvement in the ETI. Even the San Francisco-based anti-corporate campaigning organization, Global Exchange, usually on the serving end of such attacks, found itself targeted by erstwhile allies for offering a very limited public support for Nike's decision to encourage increased wages in some of their supplier factories.

These challenges to individuals and organizations, while varied in tone, have all more or less focused on the same issues: independence, competency and method. The Maquila Solidarity Network Canada admirably summarizes these concerns in a memo in April 1999 to leading labour rights activists working on codes and their implementation:

> While many labour rights advocates, such as Charlie Kernaghan of the US National Labor Committee, are absolutely opposed to private sector involvement in monitoring of codes of conduct, some labour leaders, such as Neil Kearney, are generally supportive of the SA8000 model and feel that the proper role for NGOs and unions is to consult with the professional social auditors and be prepared to challenge unjustified certifications, rather than to engage directly in monitoring.

> While we and other labour rights advocacy groups would acknowledge that in most Southern countries human rights, women's and religious groups do not currently have the capacity to monitor or audit the thousands of supplier factories producing for Northern apparel companies, we are increasingly uncomfortable with the emerging model in which large private sector social auditing firms with little or no human rights experience or commitment

to workers' rights are becoming the primary judges of whether codes of conduct are being adhered to.

Even with proper training, we question whether Northern private sector auditors, who will inevitably be seen as company representatives, will have sufficient trust of Southern workers to receive their full story. While private sector auditors may be able to adequately evaluate supplier compliance with measurable standards, such as air quality, we are sceptical about their ability to judge violations of workers' right to organize or other less objectively measurable standards.[13]

Although focused exclusively on monitoring and verifying adherence to labour standards, the memo is equally relevant to other aspects of corporate social and environmental accountability. One dimension of this is clearly the issue of the financial relationship between the external person or body and the organization being assessed. In offering a personal commentary in NatWest's Social Review, Jonathon Porritt, for example, was also acting as a paid Environmental Policy Adviser. When Andrew Wilson from Ashridge College signed off BT's first Social Report as external verifier, he was doing so as a paid consultant. Professor Kirk Hanson's (Stanford University) 'show all' Social Assessment of The Body Shop, published in 1996 following the damaging public allegations of corporate misconduct and deception, was undertaken in his capacity as hired assessor, as was Paul Hawken's role as external assessor for Ben & Jerry's over the same period. Similarly, when the author signed off an external review of The Novo Group's Environmental and Social Report, he did so having worked in a paid capacity with the company as social accountability adviser for almost three years.

The matter of competencies is also a moot point across the full spectrum of corporate performance subjected to external assessment, review or verification. Rabbi Julia Neuberger, as Social Policy Adviser to NatWest, offers the following in her 'personal commentary' in the company's Social Review:

A good example of [the company's integration of public policy interests into its business] is the secondary schools programme, Face 2 Face With Finance, which seeks to deliver a clear benefit to both the business, in reputation terms, and young people.[14]

Rabbi Neuberger is quite correct in applauding NatWest's Face 2 Face With Finance programme, which has since won wider public recognition through the UK's Business in the Community Annual Awards. What is not clear, however, is whether the Rabbi is well placed to offer what in effect is a public endorsement of the company's social policies and practice based on what is essentially a philanthropic initiative. The same applies in the case of Nobel Prize winner Archbishop Desmond Tutu's effective endorsement of one of the world's largest insurers, Winterthur International, or Nelson

Mandela's appearance in a global advertising campaign for the hotel chain, Hilton International. I will return again to the specific matter of external verification in a later chapter.

TRUST PUZZLES

A corporation's long-term competitive advantage in the New Economy is rarely a function of technical quality, price or availability. These are the most basic entry conditions to the market, the *sine qua non*, beyond which a meaningful differentiating edge needs to be built. Sustainable competitive advantage is based on the quality of relationships with key stakeholders. Without sufficient trust, productive knowledge is withheld, competencies denied, repeat customers fade into the background, and much-needed flexibility of statutory bodies is not forthcoming.

Trust is a word of the times. Everybody talks about it, and everyone wants it because of all the real benefits that can accrue as a result of its acquisition. But trust is a complicated and volatile substance. Corporations rarely have much of it, at least when it comes to their wider role in society. They can lose apparently deeply rooted reputations by misunderstanding the ebb and flows of the New Economy, by failing, for example, to secure the safety of stakeholder relationships through the mismanagement and the fallout of financial crisis. Acquiring trust from a low base is a messy business. It increasingly requires forming new relationships with those who have more, particularly the NGOs and others who can swing public opinion. Indeed, building trust for many corporations has in practice required adjustments to their response to the contemporary phenomenon of *civil regulation*, to which we can now turn.

CHAPTER 5

Civil Regulation

> GAP sales are down and executives are quitting, or moving on to
> 'spend time with family'. Of course, there was no mention of our
> campaign (the protests, the letters, the teach-ins) to expose GAP
> Inc's sweatshop abuses and how we may have had something to do
> with GAP's losses. We should [nevertheless] see this as a victory
> and take credit for the disorientation that we have caused this
> company.[1]

> (Whilst)... not investigated in a scientific way... the negative
> press referring to specific incidents is not proved to have a long-
> term negative effect on the price of the company's shares.[2]

FRIEDMAN COMES OF AGE

Today, the corporate citizenship test is being applied to more and more parts of the business. As corporate citizenship becomes increasingly significant in terms of policy commitments and practices, there are growing calls for proof from all stakeholders — customers, employees, suppliers, governments, communities, and indeed, shareholders. Shareholders, of course, want to know what are its financial bottom-line effects. But other stakeholders are also increasingly concerned about the business case, rightly seeing this as a measure of the viability of corporate citizenship. Even the most anti-business lobby realizes that virtuous but uncompetitive companies will not stay the course. The business case, in short, counts.[3]

At its crudest level, the proposition states that 'being good is good for financial performance'. It suggests that social and environmental gains can deliver financial benefits by producing, for example, business-relevant reputational, productivity and efficiency effects.[4] The win–win proposition is certainly evocative. It suggests that the corporate community will produce social and environmental dividends through its successful long-term pursuit of profit. It evokes a sense of ethics into what increasingly appears at best an amoral evolution in global, market capitalism. Indeed, it suggests a *necessary* convergence of financial success with societal good – a domesticated Darwinism at its very best.

Milton Friedman famously stated that the sole responsibility of business was to maximize financial returns to shareholders.[5] Corporate citizenship has been taken as a challenge to this assertion and associated practices.

Box 5.1 *Why Companies Do The Right Thing*

The company's commitment is in part a matter of reinforcing their positive reputation to the general public and the various layers of government with which they regularly interact given the nature of their business.[6]

Suez

If we are the leading corporate citizen, it will do several things for us. It will create an image for Ford that is different from others, and in a cluttered and crowded marketplace in which differentiation is hard to obtain. If we achieve this we will attract better employees and the highest calibre of people out of universities. They're going to want to come work for a company like Ford.[7]

William Clay Ford Jr, Ford Motor Company

It is our belief that this commitment to environmental protection, social progress, and shared economic benefit will give us preferred access to gold projects around the world, thus ensuring our continued success and growth.[8]

Placer Dome

To deny that our neighbours have a genuine stake in the company is to deny not only the reality of their lives, but also their ability to obstruct, delay and even stop the growth of our airports.[9]

Sir John Egan, *BAA plc*

We believe that our commitment to contribute to sustainable development holds the key to our long-term business success. . . Society is still exploring exactly how to put sustainable development into practice but it is clear that we are on a journey and not aiming at a known end-point. For Shell this journey is part of our transformation to become 'top performer' of first choice.[10]

Shell International

We recognize that we will have to be sensitive in our development of retail units in the cities, taking greater account of the diversity of our client base and employees. These are the factors that will define our success in achieving future growth.[11]

Ahold

Concern is sometimes expressed that 'corporate social responsibility' has no clear business benefits and could destroy shareholder value by diverting resources from core commercial activities. . . However, the WBCSD supports the view that a coherent CSR strategy based on sound ethics and core values offers clear business benefits.[12]

World Business Council for Sustainable Development

Alice Tepper-Marlin, the President of the Council on Economic Priorities, in reflecting on a decade over which corporate citizenship emerged as a major field of activity, concluded: 'Milton Friedman, the prime advocate of the position that the responsibility of business is exclusively to maximize profit for shareholders, has lost the debate.'[13]

Actually, the reverse may be closer to the truth. The 'profits-with-principles' argument underlying the traditional corporate citizenship proposition is more a sophisticated restatement, than a refutation, of Friedman's position. Friedman always said that businesses should comply not only with the law but also with the norms and expectations of the societies within which they operate. From this perspective, the win–win proposition more or less restates this in saying that business should address new social norms embodied in the idea of corporate citizenship and through this can maximize long-term financial performance.

The win–win proposition is as provocative as it is evocative. David Korten argues that 'real ethics' costs real money, that is, there is a trade-off between profits and principles. For this reason, he continues, truly ethical companies are necessarily pushed out of a competitive market.[14] For Korten and other critics of corporate behaviour, the win–win proposition is at best a muddle by well-meaning individuals, and at worst a well-orchestrated deception that covers up the underlying growth of corporate power.

The win–win proposition lies at the heart of the confusion over the role and impact of business in society, as highlighted in the first chapter's discussion of the Global Balance Sheet and the Tramline Debate. The view that there need be no trade-off between financial profitability and being responsible to society and the planet is, plainly, a nonsense if it is argued to be always and everywhere correct. It is easy to identify cases of business behaviour that are immensely profitable and cannot even with a stretch be argued as 'ethical'. Destructive drugs (legal or otherwise), child prostitution, laundering funds stolen by politicians, and weapons of war designed to maim or kill civilians all come to mind as relatively uncontentious examples. More disputed examples of questionable business practice adorn our newspapers on a daily basis, ranging from animal testing in the development of cosmetics and the use of genetically modified organisms through to, for some, products and services that offer protection against pregnancy. In practice, 'sharp' and immensely profitable dealings exist in all spheres of business.

Advocates of corporate citizenship circumvent these stark examples by arguing that such irresponsible companies will not survive in the long run. Mark Goyder, Director of the UK-based Centre for Tomorrow's Company, is such an advocate. He asserts that tomorrow's successful companies will necessarily be those that are 'inclusive' in the way they deal with their stakeholders.[15] The others, he argues, just won't make it. But even someone so committed to the win–win proposition acknowledges that 'being responsive to key stakeholders' does not mean *all* stakeholders, and almost certainly does not mean those most in need who have little or no power to impact on the business. The win–win proposition clearly emphasizes the need for business to take into account those stakeholders that can affect the financial bottom line. This is quite different from the more difficult question of the responsibility of business to solve pervasive social and environmental problems. After all, would companies like Liz Claiborne, Adidas and even Levi Strauss have addressed the issue of child labour and other dimensions of labour standards in its global supply chains had these worker-stakeholders not been 'lent power' by campaigning organizations that threatened to disrupt the company's reputation in its principal markets.[16]

The cruder representations of the profits-with-principles proposition come dangerously close to being tautological or an untestable belief. Empirical testing must ultimately allow it to be confirmed or refuted, and more importantly determine under what conditions the proposition may be true. The empirical dilemmas are many. It is certainly difficult to generalize from company to company, sector to sector, and country to country. Nike and Levi both experienced significant falls in earnings during the late 1990s. Yet they have almost diametrically opposite corporate citizenship reputations. Over the same period, Nike was subjected to a long-running worldwide campaign by NGOs for its alleged failure to secure the appropriate treatment of labour in its global supply chain. Levi, on the other hand, was consistently celebrated for its social responsibility programmes, winning for example the coveted Corporate Conscience award from the New York-based Council on Economic Priorities (CEP).

The same disjuncture between financial and corporate citizenship performance can be observed in the energy sector. Shell under-performed financially throughout the late 1990s compared with its main sector competitors, BP and Exxon (now ExxonMobil). However, it would be a misreading of the evidence to attribute this to its miscalculation over Brent Spar, or to its alleged malpractice in Nigeria. Similarly, Shell's poor financial performance over that period cannot convincingly be attributed to the fact that at the same time it became a leader in 'triple bottom line' reporting. Equally for BP, there is no obvious reason why its short-term, measured financial success should have anything directly to do with the company's progressive and much-noted decision to exit the Global Climate Coalition.[17]

The lack of any simple connection between financial, and social and environmental performance, can be further observed in the fate of the two 'ethical business' icons emerging from the 1960s, Ben & Jerry's and The Body Shop. Both showed more than healthy financial results for many years, building strong positions in profitable niche markets based in large part on perceptions of their social and environmental performance as part of their customer offering. More recently, however, both have fared poorly in financial terms, despite maintaining a strong social and environmental performance.[18]

Doing good clearly does not guarantee financial success over any reasonable timeframe, just as being less-than-ethical does not guarantee financial disaster. Understanding the relationship, if any, between financial and other measures of performance clearly requires a more in-depth exploration of the business drivers underlying corporate citizenship.

CIVIL REGULATION IN THEORY

The most visible driver that translates social and environmental 'goods' into positive market signals and related financial gains is *civil regulation*.[19] Corporations are increasingly under pressure from NGOs and other organizations to drive enhanced social and environmental performance standards through the business process. This includes elements within

Figure 5.1 *Civil Regulation in Action*

their own organizational and legal boundaries – for example in relation to their own staff – and increasingly down global production chains and up towards and indeed beyond the point of consumption. These pressures come in the form of activist campaigning which aims to damage companies' market performance by undermining their reputation.[20]

Civil regulations in the main involve collective processes, albeit often through loose forms of social organization. They are the manifestations of essentially political acts that can affect business performance through their influence on market conditions. In their early stages, civil regulations are quintessentially organic and often volatile systems of rules. Indeed, they can best be understood as non-statutory regulatory frameworks governing corporate affairs. They lie between the formal structures of public (statutory) regulation, and market signals generated by more conventional individual and collective preferences underpinned by the use and exchange value of goods and services. How this early stage of civil regulation transforms into more stable rule frameworks is returned to in later chapters.

There have been several celebrated international cases of civil regulation in the last two decades. Probably the longest-lasting campaign has been against the Swiss food giant, Nestlé, for its alleged approach to marketing baby milk substitutes in developing countries.[21] In terms of human tragedy caused by a single event, the case of Union Carbide in Bhopal, India, has probably spawned the most significant and longest-running campaign. In recent times, one of the most celebrated cases has been the campaign against Shell, first against its attempts to dispose of the Brent Spar oil platform in the North Sea, and then for events surrounding its massive operations in Nigeria. Of equal significance has been the campaign against McDonald's. In France and India this has focused centrally on the company's alleged role in undermining cultural traditions embedded within food and eating

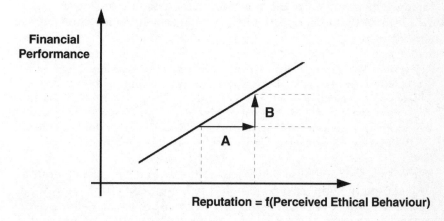

Figure 5.2 *Civil Regulation in Theory*

habits. Elsewhere, and in the case of the celebrated court case, the issues have revolved more around environmental and animal rights issues. The anti-Nike campaign, probably the most vociferous, widespread and extended campaign against any single company in recent decades, has come to symbolize the essence of the movement against globalization and multinationals. Finally, although in no way exhaustively, has been the largely European campaign against Monsanto in the late 1990s, the company most visibly involved in the promotion of agricultural processes and products involving genetically modified organisms.

The thinking behind civil regulation is that the reputation of companies can be damaged by civil action to a degree that will affect their business performance. This relationship is characterized in its most simple form in Figure 5.2.[22] As the company's ethical behaviour as perceived by key stakeholders improves, so does its financial performance, and vice versa (an increase/reduction in reputation of the amount 'A' based on perceived ethical behaviour leads to an increase/decrease in financial performance of the amount 'B'). There are various reasons why this might be the case. Staff may be more motivated when the company for which they work is not the subject of public criticism. Governments may be more at ease in granting planning permission, renewing operating licences, or choosing not to pass constraining public legislation. Customers, particularly for retail companies, will buy their products, and investors are less nervous. In simple terms, the steeper the line in Figure 5.2, the greater the financial gains from increasing perceived ethical behaviour, and vice versa.

THE PEOPLE SPEAK OUT

Show-stopping campaigns like those against Nike, Monsanto and Shell – as well as many others of lesser fame – have all basically had this relationship in mind: 'Hit them till it hurts, and then they will change for the better.' Certainly many of the more radical campaigning and development NGOs think that it works. An email announcement on the anti-GAP list serve declared:

> Business Week reported that over the last year GAP sales are down and executives are quitting, or moving on to 'spend time with family'. Of course, there was no mention of our campaign (the protests, the letters, the teach-ins) to expose GAP Inc's sweatshop abuses and how we may have had something to do with GAP's losses. We should see this as a victory and take credit for the disorientation that we have caused this company.

The significance of the cut-and-thrust element of civil regulation appears to be strongly supported by opinion polls of people's views who, as consumers, employees and voters, are the final arbiters in defining what is and is not acceptable business behaviour.[23] The results of the May 1999 Millennium Poll on consumer expectations of corporate social responsibility were significant. The poll was conducted by Environics International in collaboration with the IBLF and The Conference Board. It covered 23 countries on six continents, a total of 25,000 interviews. The survey found that, across the globe, roughly two in three consumers want companies to go beyond their historic role of making a profit and obeying laws, and in particular want business to contribute more to achieving broader societal goals. Over one in five consumers reported actually, and almost as many again have considered, rewarding or punishing companies in the previous year, based on their perceived social and environmental performance.[24]

These findings are broadly confirmed in many other studies. An opinion poll on public attitudes in Europe towards business was conducted on behalf of CSR Europe in the last quarter of 2000.[25] The findings are consistent across Europe.

(1) Over half of Europeans surveyed in 12 countries considered that business does not pay enough attention to its social responsibilities.

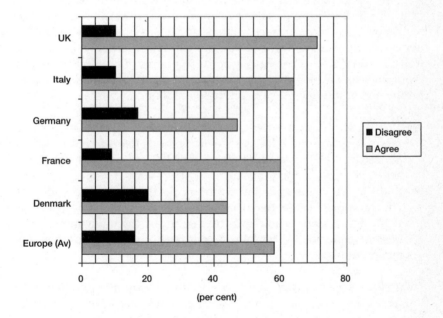

Figure 5.3 *Business is not Paying Enough Attention to its Social Responsibilities*

(2) Over one-quarter of those surveyed said that they had engaged in one or other activity in the previous six months that either introduced ethics into actual consumer purchase decisions or else made such views known by other means.

As part of the Millennium Poll, The Conference Board surveyed 1000 Americans in 1999. Of these, 42 per cent said that they held companies completely or partially responsible for helping to solve social problems like crime, poverty and lack of education. Fully one-third said that companies should focus on setting higher ethical standards, going beyond what is required by law, and actively helping to build a better society for all. The Conference Board, similarly, found that consumers stated their willingness to back up their expectations with action. Forty-six per cent of respondents said that they had made a purchase decision, or spoken out, in favour of a company because of a positive perception of its social responsibility. Forty-nine per cent of respondents said that they had decided not to purchase a product or service from a company, or had spoken critically of a company, because it did not meet their standard for being a socially responsible company.[26]

Fleishman Hillard, similarly, in a 1999 survey of about 4000 Europeans aged 15 or older, found that 86 per cent would be more likely to purchase a product from a company 'engaged in activities to help improve society'.[27] A recent report on ethical consumerism in the UK commissioned by The Co-operative Bank found that increasing numbers of citizens as consumers both expected more from corporations, and felt as consumers and holders of pension funds that they could do more to effect corporate behaviour.[28] Cone Inc. conducted a convincing study in partnership with Roper-Starch Worldwide that explored the impact of cause-related activities on customer loyalty and brand image.[29] The study found that:

- Nearly two-thirds of Americans, approximately 130 million consumers, report they would be likely to switch brands (66 per cent in 1993, 65 per cent in 1998) or retailers (62 per cent 1993, 61 per cent 1998) to one associated with a good cause.
- Eight in ten Americans have a more positive image of companies who support a cause they care about (84 per cent 1993, 83 per cent 1998). Education, crime and the quality of the environment were designated as the top social concerns for business to address in local communities.

Finally, for the more technically minded, a study purporting to show a clear link between aspects of good corporate citizenship, consumer behaviour and reputation was undertaken by Walker Information as part of the Council on Foundations report on corporate citizenship.[30] This study used survey data to develop correlation coefficients between reputation, brand loyalty, economic value and its definition of 'societal value'. The latter included treatment of employees, caring about the environment, strong ethics and financial stability.

Walker Information published results for two companies, a manufacturer and a retailer. The results for the manufacturer (Figure 5.4) showed that a 1-unit increase in Societal Value led to a 0.27-unit increase in Company

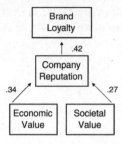

Figure 5.4 *Manufacturer Brand*

Reputation. A 1-unit increase in Economic Value led to a 0.34-unit increase in Company Reputation. A 1-unit increase in Company Reputation led to a 0.42 unit increase in Brand Loyalty. The results for the retailer (Figure 5.5) showed that a 1-unit increase in Societal Value led to a 0.55-unit increase in Company Reputation. A 1-unit increase in Economic Value led to a 0.27-unit increase in Company Reputation. A 1-unit increase in Company Reputation led to a 0.32 unit increase in Brand Loyalty.

MONEY TALK

Financial performance, and so also share prices, can be vulnerable to public outcry. There is considerable evidence that share prices can be affected when the issue concerns the direct health and welfare of the consumer. The cases of Perrier and Coca-Cola come to mind, both of which suffered financially through consumer reaction to concerns over contaminated product. The high-profile crisis faced by Monsanto is also a case in point. The financial significance of the public actions against genetically modified organisms only took hold where the campaign's focus shifted from the plight of subsistence farmers in developing countries to consumer health (the 'Frankenstein foods' campaign). There can also be observed financial effects when very specialized issues become

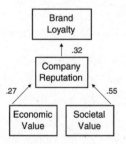

Figure 5.5 *Retailer Brand*

entwined in national consciousness, such as animal rights issues in the UK. Public disquiet at stories of animal abuse at Huntingdon Life Sciences Laboratories has in the past demonstrably depressed the company's share value, and indeed more recently has been associated with doubts over its continued existence.[31]

Box 5.2 *Consumers' Caring Can Count*

Electrolux was faced from the late 1980s with concerted action from Greenpeace and other environmental non-profit organizations over the damaging effects of CFCs on the world's climate and in particular on depletion of high-level ozone. Initially the company spent considerable resources seeking to demonstrate their 'innocence'. By the early 1990s, civil pressure had begun to affect sales as customers increasingly sought CFC-free products. Eventually, concluded the company's environmental manager: 'When the stock price depended on our ability to come up with CFC-free refrigerators, of course, managers considered the issue important.'[32]

The case of Electrolux is repeated daily across the world in a myriad of different ways. Political action creates a perceived business risk – in this case through the potential for reduced sales.

But there is a slight hitch to this apparent statistical demonstration of people power. The more generalized argument that corporate citizenship is good for business because of the impact of civil regulation, although enticing, is simply not true in its crudest form. Even the very high profile civil campaigns against the likes of Shell, Nestlé and Nike have had little or no demonstrable effect on share prices or dividends. One unpublished study investigating the connection between market value, social/ethical performance and negative press in cases of Nike, Nestlé and Shell concluded:

> (Whilst)... not investigated in a scientific way... The examples show that the negative press referring to specific incidents is not proved to have a long-term negative effect on the price of the company's shares.[33]

The available evidence is that, with few exceptions, the media-effective attacks on these companies' reputations caused no significant, sustained impact on their share prices. As Michael Hopkins, summing up his own attempt to map corporate social and environmental responsibility against financial performance, concludes:

> ...the company that did worst in [my social responsibility] rankings – News International – actually had the largest share price rise. Clearly, the public's purchasing of shares is still not greatly affected, as yet, by the companies' level of social responsibility.[34]

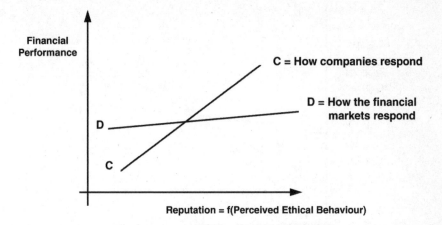

Figure 5.6 *Divergent Market Responses*

For those readers with a predilection for graphs (particularly the economists among you), I have supported the remainder of this section with a series of graphical representations that builds on the basic visualization of civil regulation set out in Figure 5.2. So Figure 5.6 suggests that while many companies respond to civil regulation *as if* it is a powerful financial driver (shown by the steep curve, CC), the financial markets respond in a manner that suggests that they are far less concerned that perceived ethical behaviour impacts on the financial bottom line (shown by the flatter curve, DD).

The Goyder Effect

So, the apparent paradox is that companies often respond *as if* civil regulation really counts, whereas the financial markets rarely seem to really care. There are a number of possible explanations for this. The first is that companies respond to the pressures of civil regulation because they (think they) know better than the financial markets in predicting long-term performance. Thus, the more horizontal, flatter line (F1F1 in Figure 5.7) indicates the lack of responsiveness by the financial markets given their preoccupation with short-term returns. The steeper curve (EE), on the other hand, reflects companies' longer-term view of the critical relationship.

If the companies are correct, the response curve of the financial markets will eventually swivel towards a steeper slope to reflect new information about financial performance.[35] This would be the view that 'being good is good for business (in the long term)'. We might call this the 'Goyder Effect' in recognition of the key roles played by Mark Goyder and before him his father, George Goyder, in setting out and promoting the argument for 'inclusivity' as a pre-condition for a long-term successful business strategy.[36]

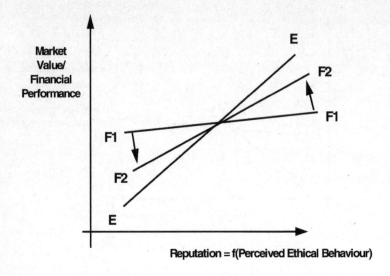

Figure 5.7 *The Goyder Effect*

The 'Korten Effect'

The alternative view is that companies are systematically over-estimating the financial significance of reputational losses through perceptions of ethical misdemeanours, and vice versa. There are several possible reasons for such over-estimation. Important here is that this growth has not been matched by tools and procedures for fully understanding how such intangibles develop and can best be managed. As reported by Susan Fry Bovet in *PR Week,* only 25 per cent of companies with revenues above US$500 million have formal systems for measuring reputation, an issue we will return to in the chapters on method later in the book.[37] This has given considerable influence within companies to 'reputation teams' dedicated to the protection of brand values, a key element of intangible assets. These teams may overrate the importance of ethics-based reputational value, both as a means of minimizing risk for their companies, and in some cases as a means of enhancing their own importance within the organization. As a reputation manager from a major UK multinational commented, 'The harder the NGOs come at us, the easier my job gets.'

If the financial implications of reputational gains or losses are indeed not (as) significant as often construed, then the financial markets will eventually trade down companies which over-respond to civil regulation. Eventually, following the Desert pathway described in the previous chapter, global corporate citizenship will be squeezed out of companies wishing to survive. We might call this the 'Korten Effect', in recognition of David Korten's forceful critique of corporate citizenship.[38] In graphical terms, this can be represented as companies' response curves swivelling

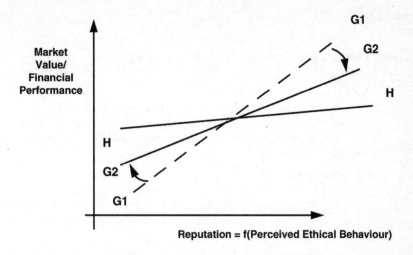

Figure 5.8 *The Korten Effect*

from their highly responsive, steep slope to a flatter, less responsive, state, as set out in Figure 5.8.

BEYOND CIVIL REGULATION?

Civil regulation is a fickle driver of good corporate citizenship. Clearly people care, and some act with their feet in their roles as consumers, investors, employees and voters. But the investment community does not in the main take this either as a serious threat or opportunity, at least to date. The fact that some high-profile companies are responding *as if* civil regulation is important to their financial futures can clearly be read in different ways, the most marked distinctions hopefully captured in the descriptions of the Korten and Goyder Effects. Of course the fact that market leaders do respond in this way may in some instances in itself create futures where good corporate citizenship counts. The unknown is how much, how robust, and to what effect.

What is clear is that the sheer force of people's stated concerns is not in itself sufficient to drive companies to better practices. Equally clear is that the companies that do act as if good citizenship is an important ingredient of success have increasingly articulated strong business cases that go well beyond the cruder cut-and-thrust of pressure-based civil regulation. It is to these business cases that we now turn.

CHAPTER 6

Framing the Business Case

At their most eloquent, proponents of neoliberalism sound as if they are doing poor people, the environment, and everybody else a tremendous service as they enact policies on behalf of the wealthy few.

Noam Chomsky[1]

You know you are doing the right thing when you get the key organizations to do the right thing at the right time for the wrong reason.

Tom Friedman, New York Times[2]

UNPACKING THE BUSINESS CASE

There is no single business case for corporate citizenship. Equally, there is no single route to demonstrating its significance as an actual or potential driver of business behaviour. To understand the business dynamics of corporate citizenship, the 'business case' must be unpacked into its interrelated, component parts. The business case can be usefully broken down into four broad (and interrelated) categories, summarized below.

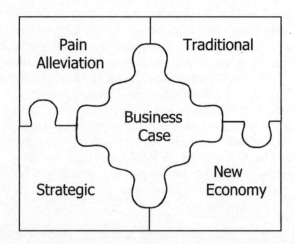

Figure 6.1 *The Four-level Business Case*

Defence (or pain alleviation) This is essentially the business case underpinning the dynamics discussed in the last chapter on civil regulation. Companies defend themselves against media-friendly pressure from non-profit campaigners, governments and international agencies, and employees and other direct stakeholders (including shareholders).

Traditional Business Case (or cost-benefit) This generally involves specific activities where there are associated tangible actual or potential financial gains. This often involves actual and potential employees, for example building greater diversity, quality of workplace, and linkages to home life. It also can involve targeted actions to gain specific contracts (eg affirmative action contracts), planning permission (eg for retail units), or resource management and exploitation rights (eg water utilities, energy and mining operations). Box 6.1, for example, summarizes key aspects of the traditional business case for employing disabled people.

Box 6.1 *The Traditional Business Case for Employing Disabled People*[3]

- Disabled people are as productive and as reliable as any other employees

- In living their day-to-day lives many disabled people develop transferable problem-solving skills that are invaluable in the workplace

- Disabled people in work tend to have better attendance records, stay with employers longer and have fewer accidents at work. Most do not require adjustments at work

- Government support is often available should workplace adjustments be needed to enable business to realize the potential of disabled people

- Employers report enhanced staff morale and team development when they are seen to be good employers of people with disabilities

- Organizations accessible to disabled customers will be more accessible and appealing to all consumers and stakeholders

Strategic Business Case The heart of the strategic business case is that it only includes those elements of corporate citizenship that shift the business as a whole in a significant new direction. At this level, therefore, corporate citizenship becomes an integral element of the company's broader strategic approach to long-term business performance. This may involve fundamental shifts, for example, by energy companies like BP and Shell away from non-renewable towards renewable resources, or by retail product suppliers like Interface away from product sales to service rentals. It may also involve investment in a wider global role for the business, for example in public policy or the promotion of human rights and other elements of an emerging global framework for business. Unlike the traditional business case (and more like the defensive business case), the strategic dimensions of corporate citizenship cannot easily be subjected to standard financial cost-benefit analysis. They are part of a broad pattern of investments being made by the business that build on each other and together create potential financial gains.

New Economy Business Case (or learning, innovation and risk management) The fourth level concerns the capacity of the business to learn, innovate and effectively manage risk in an increasingly dynamic, complex business environment. This includes how corporate citizenship can be a means of acquiring and acting on high-quality information about stakeholder interests that are likely in the future to translate into market signals, how to build new competencies in and around the business, and how to understand and respond to new forms of risk.

These four levels are of course not completely distinct, and can evolve into each other. Often what ends as a strategic issue and corporate approach starts as a marginal issue with a small philanthropic response. Novo Nordisk has for many years delivered dietary training to insulin users to minimize their need to use their own products, to reduce costs to public health systems, and so to become their preferred suppliers.[4] More recently, however, access to health care has become a more visible public policy issue, particularly in developing countries. It is increasingly understood that access to health care will be a crucial issue in the years to come, and companies' responses to this issue will be significant in defining their broader reputation and licence to operate. Novo Nordisk, while maintaining its market-aligned philanthropic programmes, has responded to this by engaging in public policy debate, for example, by chairing the relevant committee at the WTO, and working through the World Business Council for Sustainable Development (WBCSD).

The same issue, furthermore, can route into different companies through different levels of the business case. For example, companies like Texaco and Ford Motor Corporation have been publicly condemned over alleged racism. Both have announced large remediation programmes, good examples of the defensive business case. However, in the case of Shell, moves to increase the level of diversity at senior management levels were taken in recognition of the positive effect of greater diversity for the company's understanding of risks and opportunities: the New Economy business case. The South African insurance company, Hollard Insurance, sees its major market growth area as the emerging black middle class. Its investment in employee diversity is a recognition of the long-term importance of these markets, and how best to get at them: the strategic business case. DuPont has for many years been seen as a leader in employee diversity strategies and programmes. Core to their reasoning has been that it enhances overall employee motivation and so brings distinct productivity gains to the company: the traditional business case.

The significance of these different levels of the business case for our understanding and promotion of corporate citizenship is that:

- businesses operate at differing levels depending for example on sector, business-specific experience, and leadership and vision;
- the part of the business that is interested in corporate citizenship is fundamentally linked to which level of business case is being considered;
- different stakeholders, for example shareholders as opposed to employees or government, have differing levels of understanding and interest across these levels; and
- approaches to analysis and measurement differ radically between levels.

THE SHAREHOLDER'S VIEWPOINT

At the launch in September 1999 of the Dow Jones Sustainability Index, *The Economist* magazine argued in uncharacteristically bullish manner: 'Companies with an eye on their triple bottom line – economic, environmental, and social sustainability – outperform their less fastidious peers on the stock market.'[5] Numerous studies have explored this relationship, for example:

- A study by Graves and Waddock of long-term share price movements of the values-led companies first examined by Collins and Porras in *Built to Last* concluded that they outperformed the average by almost 11.6 per cent.[6]
- A study by Towers and Perrin found that a selected group of 25 companies that they identified as excelling in their stakeholder relationships – 'stakeholder superstars' – outperformed the S&P 500 (Standards and Poor's Index) by more than 100 per cent over a 15-year period to 1999.

These results are not, however, as straightforward and compelling as they might seem. The difference in performance of these funds can be argued to be primarily due to different industry 'bets' implicit in the social screening process. Studies suggest that if the Domini Social 400 Index, for example, were reweighted so that it matched the S&P 500's macro-economic and industry exposures, it would have performed essentially the same as the S&P 500 during the study period. And that is not all. Graves and Waddock found evidence that, statistically, excellent financial performance causes better social performance, and the converse – that better social performance causes better financial performance. Better financial performance in one

Box 6.2 *Socially Responsible Investment Counts – a Bit*

Investment funds that contain social and environmental screens have until recently been an oddity that most companies and fund managers have happily ignored. Recently, however, the growth of these funds and their wider influence is making such behaviour less sustainable. The US-based Social Investment Forum estimates that taking social screening and shareholder activism together, there were US$1497 billion in screened portfolios in 1999, up from US$529 billion in 1997 – approximately 9 per cent of the US$16.3 trillion in investment assets under professional management in the US in 1999.[7] As important is that these funds are shifting rapidly from a negative screening approach – essentially excluding the 'bads' from their portfolios – to an activist shareholder approach that variously offers public challenges and private advise to companies that they target for improved social and environmental performance. Screened funds are rapidly becoming a force to be reckoned with because of the leverage they can create well beyond the nominal and still relatively small share they make up of the market.

year was a good predictor of better social performance in the following year, and better social performance in one year was a good predictor of better financial performance in the following year.

Good behaviour does not necessarily mean good news for a company's share price, despite the growth of socially responsible investment. That makes the different levels of the business case all the more important, since only some elements will be taken into account by shareholders with a primary interest in potential earnings. In practice, these shareholders will be concerned with the:

- *defensive* business rationale of corporate citizenship where business performance is seriously threatened;
- *traditional* business case where corporate citizenship can deliver significant cost-savings or enhancements of efficiency;
- *strategic* business rationale where corporate citizenship is clearly aligned and relevant to business strategy; and
- *New Economy* business rationale where corporate citizenship is an indicator of, and support to, the company's ability to acquire and handle new market information, and so effectively adapt its organizational competencies and adjust its offering of products and services.

Shareholders care about good corporate citizenship when it is a sign that the company is likely to perform well financially. This means that good corporate citizenship needs to be read by shareholders as a surrogate for something that, as shareholders, they *do* care about. This argument was offered by Reto Ringger, the President of Sustainability Asset Management, in his explanation of the thinking behind the Dow Jones Sustainability Index:

> It is our thesis that companies which are better managed environmentally, indicate more sophisticated management throughout the company... And good management is the single most important factor in corporate profitability, growth, and future earnings.[8]

This thesis is attractive. It suggests that tomorrow's most successful companies will be those who pursue such strategies *because* they have the best management. Furthermore, it suggests that demonstrably good corporate citizenship offers outcome-based lead (ie with predictive value) measures for the financial markets to identify companies with good management.

Although attractive, this apparently neat solution is certainly not conclusive. After all, the last chapter highlighted the fact that it is certainly possible to be profitable (over the time period in which shareholders are generally interested) without being 'a good corporate citizen'. What makes more sense of Ringger's proposition is that good corporate citizenship will only really pay if it is part of a clear business strategy. Levi Strauss has a long tradition of corporate citizenship, and has led the way over the decades in developing and implementing 'good practice' approaches to dealing with its own employees and people employed in its global supply chains. Nike, on the other hand, is seen as having a poor record of dealing particularly with the latter, only improving its practices when placed under the public spotlight. Yet both companies have suffered major setbacks in their financial fortunes in recent years. The British telecommunications giant, BT, has for many years been seen as a leader in corporate citizenship, as has the retailer, Sainsbury's. Yet both companies have lost market share and experienced relatively weak financial performance. Business alignment of corporate citizenship clearly counts.

RISK, LEARNING AND INNOVATION

Strategy varies from business to business. However, there is common ground underlying strategic approaches between companies and indeed sectors. Key is that successful businesses in the future will be those that are able to effectively innovate their process, products and services on a continuous basis.[9] As Professor Manuel Castells argues, 'In an economic system where innovation is critical, the organizational ability to increase its sources from all forms of knowledge becomes the foundation of the innovative firm.'[10]

Such innovation will at its core have dynamic and resilient relationships between the company and its key stakeholders. These 'future facts', increasingly acknowledged by business leaders, public policy makers and other 'thought leaders', are driving the development, for example, of

Box 6.3 *Innovation through Partnership*

B&Q is the UK's largest DIY retail chain. It is establishing 300 partnerships nationwide between stores and local disability groups to develop its training on disability awareness and improve its service provision for disabled people. It has also established national partnerships with disability organizations. The programmes address the specific needs of local disabled residents by establishing bespoke relationships between local staff and local disabled groups.

Through the creation of long-term and sustainable relationships B&Q is improving its wider customer care competencies on the basis that, '*If we get it right for disabled people, then we can get it right for most people.*' Many relationships also offer local disabled people with the opportunity to gain skills, for example through work experience or mock job interviews. B&Q has improved its sales to disabled people and has increased overall employee satisfaction, retention and productivity rates. Local disabled people are able to shop in stores that meet their needs as well as benefiting from personal development opportunities.

businesses' knowledge systems, stakeholder relationship management, human resource development, and communications.

Corporate citizenship is a critical linkage in the innovation and learning pathway because:

- it is relationship-focused and cuts through the redundant distinction between internal and external stakeholders;
- it builds a learning model with non-traditional sources of knowledge such as non-profit organizations which existing knowledge management frameworks do not accommodate or even recognize; and
- it is partly driven by social and environmental aims, which are in themselves motivating and so can create a self-generating dynamic.

Corporate citizenship can, in short, be an excellent basis for learning and innovation.

Learning and innovation can also be understood in terms of the effective risk management that is increasingly important to successful business. The staggering growth in the level of dynamic complexity of the business environment has secured risk management as one of the fastest growing business services, particularly for larger companies. There is, of course, the constant danger of being shown to have acted irresponsibly in social and environmental terms, particularly for companies sporting high-value retail brands. But this is only the most visible tip of the iceberg, as the previous discussion has already highlighted. The increasing geographic,

Box 6.4 *Corporate Citizenship and Risk Management*

- *Managing short-term risk* by acquiring critical, high quality information through dialogue
- Acquiring critical information about *future societal so market trends*
- Reaching *greater consensus* with stakeholders
- *Influencing views and behaviour* of both stakeholders and the company in ways that enable performance improvements

cultural and legal spread of corporations raise disturbing challenges as to the locus of responsibility and liability for parts of the business process over which the corporate core may have little direct control or even oversight.

Traditional tools are proving inadequate to the task of managing risk in this chaotic business context. Most are functionally specific, covering for example product safety or employees' health and safety. They fail as a result to handle the dynamic interplay of risk across stakeholder groups. The alleged poor performance of Shell in Nigeria, for example, impacted deeply on employee recruitment, government relations in many countries, and retail customer loyalty. Furthermore, many tools focus particularly on legal compliance, and fail to effectively penetrate the interplay between the legal environment and the management of intangible assets. Most risk management tools are oriented to predicting and handling traditional sources of risk, such as product defects and macro political risk. Few are able to handle the new generation of risks, such as child labour, which are often sourced in little known civil society organizations and rooted in the interests of stakeholders that have historically had little or no leverage over the business. Corporate citizenship:

- offers a route for building more flexible and sensitive risk management systems and processes.
- raises awareness and capacities of people to respond to diverse and unfamiliar patterns of social change.
- brings risk-related information into, and sensitizes, the business on a cross-functional basis.
- is a means of influencing stakeholders and thereby shifting the underlying foundations of risk rather than only working on how best to respond to it.

It is perhaps not surprising therefore that the services associated with social and environmental performance provided by the largest consultancies are often located within their risk management divisions.

THIRD GENERATION FUTURES

Suspicions towards corporate citizenship lie partly in its association with such differing visions, behaviour and outcomes across companies, communities and over time. The British retailer, Tesco, has been applauded for its highly successful programme of donating computers to schools. Yet this sits uneasily under the same rubric of 'corporate citizenship' as Littlewoods's leadership in addressing labour standards in global supply chains, Waitrose's approach to common ownership as part of the John Lewis Partnership, or Iceland's high-profile stance in the market-sensitive campaign against genetically modified organisms.

Such diversity becomes all the more problematic when it appears to be present within a single company. Ford Motor Corporation has sought to take a leadership role within the automobile sector in using the principles of sustainable development to frame its business strategy. But it remains unclear how this squares with alleged racism within the company's facilities at Dagenham in the UK, or its approach to the recent revelations over apparent fatal weaknesses in the alchemy of their SUV vehicles and Firestone tyres. As Billy Tauzin, House Commerce Sub-Committee Chairman, put it, 'You can't tell me someone at Firestone or Ford didn't know they had serious problems... long before the body count started to rise.'[11] Similarly, it is unclear how best to respond to the progressive, philanthropic overtures of Philip Morris and British American Tobacco when their underlying business models require the continued promotion of cigarette consumption, the impacts of which have been discussed in an earlier chapter.

Despite such diversity, the contemporary evolution of corporate citizenship, or at least the Anglo-American variant that is proving increasingly influential, does have a broader, underlying pattern. This can usefully be summarized in terms of three generations, each differently framing

Box 6.5 *Corporate Citizenship's Three Generations*

First Generation
Can corporations be responsible in ways that do not detract from, and may add commercial value to, their business?

Second Generation
Are more responsible companies likely to prosper in the future?

Third Generation
Is corporate citizenship likely to make a significant contribution to addressing the growing levels of poverty, exclusion and environmental degradation?

the challenge of corporate citizenship.[12] The **First Generation** framed the question, '*Can corporations be responsible in ways that do not detract from, and may add commercial value to, their business?*' Businesses in this generational phase in the main take corporate citizenship as being equivalent to philanthropy with little or no link to the basic success model, essentially the early stages of corporate community involvement. This generation also marks the rise of corporate citizenship as a route to pain alleviation, the lowest level of the business case.

The answer to the First Generation turned out to be a measured 'yes'. Philanthropic costs are generally too low to count against commercial success. At times, better still, they yield limited but worthwhile financial benefits through positive general reputational effects in both product and labour markets. Corporate citizenship as an integral element of a communication strategy to combat public criticism was also proving more effective than the more traditional denials of culpability (or even responsibility) adopted by, for example, Nestlé, in at least the early stages of its handling of the long-running issue of baby milk marketing.

The **Second Generation** of corporate responsibility raised the question of whether '*responsible companies are more likely to prosper in the future*'. This question took the debate beyond the short-term frame of simple cost-benefit analysis and pain alleviation. Rather, it posed the challenge of whether corporate citizenship could underpin or at the very least be an integral part of a business's long-term strategy for success.

The response to the Second Generation challenge seems to be a qualified 'maybe'. Here are the proclaimed strategies and emerging practices of companies like BP in 'moving beyond petroleum', Interface in renting rather than selling their product, and Novo Nordisk in embracing the fundamental right to health as one key element of its business model for developing and delivering insulin products to diabetics.

That brings us to the more daunting **Third Generation** question of whether corporate citizenship '*is likely to be significant in addressing growing levels of poverty, exclusion and environmental degradation*'. To what extent, for example, will the responsible behaviour of the world's largest purveyor of alcoholic beverages, Diageo, *actually* reduce the level of alcoholism and the associated abuse, crime, violence and death? Will the results of Ford embracing sustainable development make a *significant difference* to the growing environmental and health problems caused by automobile-related pollution?

The simple answer to the Third Generation challenge is that current, essentially voluntary approaches by individual companies to corporate citizenship will *alone* not contribute significantly to resolving deeply rooted social and environmental problems. Take the very important and bitterly contested issue of labour standards in global supply chains. If companies like GAP, Levi and Nike all effectively implement an agreed labour code of conduct throughout their supply chains, it might *directly* benefit perhaps 10 to 20 million workers. This is a painfully paltry number set against the 1.2 billion people living in absolute poverty. That does not make such initiatives wrong or bad – just limited. Something else needs to happen for even major changes in the behaviour and performance of leadership to make a significant difference in addressing social and environmental problems.

STATE OF THE BUSINESS CASE

These generational challenges can be mapped against the different pathways and levels of the business case. All three pathways can involve businesses doing good things and ensuring that they are not as a result placed at a competitive disadvantage. Both the Oasis and Mecca pathways allow for companies that build corporate citizenship into their core business strategies. But it is only in the Mecca pathway that leadership companies succeed in shifting the values and operational characteristics of the markets within which they operate sufficiently for good citizenship to become part of how the broader business community does business.

Box 6.6 *Citizenship Challenges and Pathways*

Generational Questions	*Desert*	*Oasis*	*Mecca*
Can corporations be responsible in ways that enhance their business?	Yes	Yes	Yes
Are more responsible companies likely to prosper in the future?	No	Yes	Yes
Are leadership-based, voluntary approaches to responsibility enough in addressing the growing levels of poverty, exclusion and environmental degradation?	No	No	Yes

The ethical futures map is as relevant for a single company as it is in describing the bigger picture. A company seeking to build corporate citizenship into its core business strategy needs to consider, for example, whether its approach will establish a significantly higher cost base than its competitors, at least in the short term, which will need to be offset by longer-term gains in brand equity, customer loyalty, innovations in product offering and delivery. Similarly a single company needs to predict whether price-based competition from other market players is likely to erode brand equity gains from corporate citizenship, whether in the market for products and services, the labour market, or indeed

Box 6.7 *Citizenship Pathways and Business Case Levels*

Business Case	Desert	Oasis	Mecca
Defensive (Pain Alleviation)	Yes	Yes	No
Traditional (Cost-Benefit)	Yes	Yes	Yes
Strategic	No	Yes	Yes
New Economy (Learning and Innovation)	No	Yes	Yes

the financial markets. There is little doubt, for example, that the effective implementation of codes of conduct covering labour standards in global supply chains significantly increases the cost base in labour-intensive industries such as apparel and footwear, certainly in the short term. This makes it easier for premium brands like Nike and Reebok to implement such codes, since they are less vulnerable to price-based competition than players operating at the lower end of these markets.

The business case for good corporate citizenship is clearly multi-layered. The evidence suggests that it is possible to make financial gains through being good, particularly through its impact on employee recruitment, retention and productivity, customer loyalty and a positive public policy environment. However, it is equally possible to do all sorts of good things and see no financial gains or, worse, suffer financial losses as a result of taking one's eye off the critical elements of business success. Securing a place in the first rather than the second scenario requires that a company embraces good corporate citizenship as an integral element of core business strategy, rather than an ad hoc add-on.

The third generational challenge, taken together with the Oasis scenario, raises a further dilemma in examining the business case. Together they highlight that it is possible to 'do well by doing good' without really doing very much in relation to the actual social and environmental challenges and vision that are embodied in our projection of sustainable development. 'Viable well-doing' is clearly an inadequate way of thinking about sustainable development. It is therefore necessary to be far clearer about the limits of good corporate citizenship, and to be able to assess whether any particular company has reached the limits of what it can achieve and contribute. We will return to this in the next section.

CHAPTER 7

The Future of the Civil Regulators

Business should challenge the NGO community to practise what they preach - if Washington and Corporate America don't move decisively, NGOs could dominate public opinion on global trade and finance.

Jeffrey Garten, Dean of Yale Management School[1]

We should use the increasing scrutiny of NGOs as a tool to strengthen our performance, including those who wish we were not here.

John Jennings, Chairman of Shell Transport and Trading

PENETRATING THE NON-PROFIT MYSTERY

For much of the 1990s, the NGO community was largely a mystery to most businesses. It rarely spoke with one voice where a deal was being sought by one or other business. Yet it seemed to cohere across radically different agendas when the potential for damage to business was greatest. It proved to have an almost unintelligible set of norms that tripped up even the most studious and diplomatic business person. Most significant, perhaps, was that it had an entirely unclear pattern of accountability.

With considerable pain and investment of time and money, parts of the business community have begun to overcome much of its costly ignorance. Those companies most in the firing line of hard-hitting civil regulatory thrusts have not, surprisingly, invested most. With good or poor grace, they have accepted that NGOs are part of the business landscape, and that they would do best in learning from them, and thereby also hopefully getting them onside. As John Jennings, Chairman of Shell Transport and Trading, spelt out in 1997, shortly after the onset of the trend-setting barrage against them: 'We should use the increasing scrutiny of NGOs as a tool to strengthen our performance, including those who wish we were not here.'[2]

But this penetration of the NGO community increasingly extends beyond those businesses most directly at risk. Other companies – perhaps counting their luck at having avoided public humiliation – are making the investment to understand more fully what is going on, and how they should best respond. As the *Financial Times* noted in an article about the new, soft-spoken, Australian Chairman of Coca-Cola, Douglas Daft: 'Significantly, there does not yet appear to be an anti-Coca-Cola website, and it will be a measure of Mr Daft's success in moulding Coca-Cola's brand image if there ever is one.'[3]

The mystery of the NGO community is gradually being dispelled. Business has begun to treat this encounter as they would any other challenge; information acquisition, pattern recognition and prediction, strategy development, and building competencies and action. Of course the same is also true the other way around. The NGO community is gaining a clearer understanding of how the business community actually functions, how decisions are made within particular companies, and how best to create the conditions for change. Some NGOs, particularly the high profile, global variants, have faced the same institutional imperative as business in seeking to regularize their relationships with the business community. Underlying the noisy campaigning there is, in reality, a normalization process taking place in the relationship between these NGOs and much of the business community. It is this process that is the subject of this and the next chapter as we conclude our exploration of the external environment of the civil corporation.

CIVIL REGULATION COMES OF AGE

Civil regulation perhaps finally came of age when *The Economist* reflected on the failure in Seattle in November 1999 to initiate a new round of trade liberalization negotiations under the auspices of the WTO.

> As politicians pore over the disarray in Seattle, they might look to citizens groups for advice. The non-governmental organizations (NGOs) that descended on Seattle were a model of everything the trade negotiators were not. They were well organized. They built unusual coalitions... they had a clear agenda to derail the talks. And they were masterly users of the media...
>
> ...In short, citizens groups are increasingly powerful at the corporate, national and international levels. How they have become so, and what this means, are questions that urgently need to be addressed. Are citizens groups, as many of their supporters claim, the first steps towards an international civil society (whatever that might be)? Or do they represent a dangerous shift of power to unelected and unaccountable special-interest groups?[4]

The article's tone clearly challenged the legitimacy of these NGOs. To reinforce this point (and taking a leaf from those NGOs that it decried), the cover of *The Economist* carried a picture of a poorly clad Asian child under the banner headline, 'The Real Losers from Seattle'. In its presentation of this story, *The Economist* was certainly conservative, perhaps reactionary, and arguably hypocritical. However, the article highlights some awkward yet well-grounded questions, including:

- *Who* are these non-profit organizations?
- *Whom* do they represent and on what basis?
- *Whose* interest, by implication, do they seek to marginalize?
- Ultimately, *what* are the direct effects and longer-term implications of the rising influence of these organizations?

These are questions that have been raised by people from within the NGO community. Most recently, for example, Michael Edwards in a pamphlet published by the UK-based think-tank, the Foreign Policy Centre, has challenged the legitimacy and accountability of the NGO community, particularly those engaged in international development.[5] 'The challenge for NGOs,' Edwards argues, 'is to show that they can put into practice the [accountability] principles that they campaign for in others.'[6]

Unfortunately, there has been a relatively weak response to such insider-critiques from those NGOs that might have led in forging new patterns of accountability to underpin their enormously enlarged role and the associated risks and responsibilities. A report on NGO standards prepared by Hugo Slim at Oxford Brookes University, for example, highlighted the relative lack of progress across the NGO community in building more robust mechanisms for accountability and transparency.[7] This inadequate response from within the NGO community to the accountability challenge has given space to outsider-critiques to make increasingly public attacks on the NGO community, often in ways that do not discriminate between the poor performers and leading edge good practice.

ENGAGING DILEMMAS

NGOs have developed three interrelated approaches to influencing the corporate community:

(1) The most traditional manner is *public pressure*, the classic campaigning organization. In Europe, the Clean Cloths Campaign illustrates this style most directly, as does work of the WDM in the UK. Internationally, probably the best known in this category is the Baby Milk Campaign against Nestlé and other companies marketing breast milk substitute products.

(2) The second form of engagement is *competency based*. These are the NGOs that work with companies on the basis of their technical competencies. This is usually the most private form of engagement. Examples of this in the UK would be the work of the Fairtrade Foundation with Sainsbury's and other supermarkets.

Box 7.1 *The Growing Size of the NGO Community*

The Numbers The Yearbook of International Organizations puts the number of international NGOs at more than 26,000 today, up from 6000 in 1990. A recent article in *World Watch*, the bi-monthly magazine of the Worldwatch Institute, suggested that the US alone has about 2 million NGOs, 70 per cent of which are less than 30 years old. India has about 1 million grass-roots groups. Another estimate suggests that more than 100,000 sprang up in Eastern Europe between 1988 and 1995 alone. Membership growth has been impressive across many groups, but particularly for environmental NGOs. The World Wide Fund for Nature (WWF), for instance, now has around 5 million members, up from 570,000 in 1985. The Sierra Club now boasts 572,000 members, up from 181,000 in 1980.

The Economics The measured financial income flows through the 'third sector' of most developed countries amount to anything up to 3–5 per cent of GDP. This percentage can surely be multiplied by several times if the wealth of voluntary labour and other non-financial contributions are taken into account. The voluntary sector is, as Peter Drucker points out, the most rapidly growing area of most mature economies as we enter the new millennium.[8]

The Influence Beyond size, NGOs are more influential than ever in both public policy circles and in moving corporate behaviour. Since the Rio Summit it has become increasingly the norm that NGOs are visible and active participants in policy debate alongside governments, business, and the trade union movement. Opinion polls repeatedly confirm that the public believes NGOs when it comes to ethical issues. One recently completed by the global public relations company, Edelman, concluded that NGOs are twice as trusted to 'do what is right' as compared with government, media or corporations. In the same survey, nearly two-thirds of respondents said that corporations only care about profits, while well over half say that NGOs 'represent values I believe in'.[9] A survey of public opinions of who they trust in the particular field of biotechnology revealed a far more marked tendency towards believing NGOs.

---

(3) The third form of engagement is *legitimizing*, where NGOs work with companies with the express intention of conferring on, or denying, them a degree of legitimacy in return for demonstrated performance achievements or improvements in agreed areas.

Poacher and Gamekeeper Intertwined

More recently, there has been an increased incidence of NGOs engaging directly with corporations in seeking to improve corporate social and environmental performance. NGOs working in this way have been integral

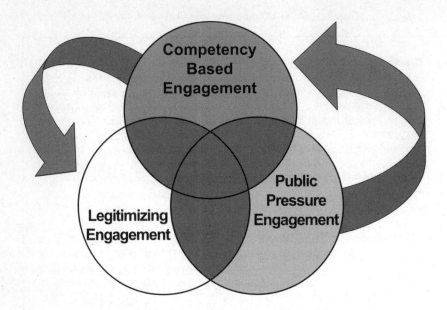

Figure 7.1 *NGO Approaches to Changing the World*

in the creation of the new language of corporate citizenship, such as ethical trade, social auditing, partnership, stakeholder dialogue and codes of conduct. This close-up engagement between NGOs and the business community has been dubbed the 'dolphin' strategy by John Elkington and others in their assessment of varied NGO approaches to dealing with corporate responsibility issues.[10]

The dolphin strategy has become more prevalent across many aspects of the relationship between NGOs and business. This has not been an exclusive tactic. It is in fact increasingly the norm that NGOs will campaign publicly, often adopting the tried and tested negative-confrontational style, *and at the same time* engage with elements of the business community in a more 'business-friendly' manner. The Fairtrade Foundation (FTF) in the UK, for example, has undertaken extensive, long-term consultancies to assist major food retailers in drawing 'fair trade' into their business processes. At the same time, FTF is a labelling institution, and therefore finds itself certifying the social qualities of products that are produced or marketed through often the same companies. FTF was created, and is governed, by the major UK-based development NGOs. This includes NGOs that are actively and very publicly campaigning around corporate accountability issues, which often cover the same product areas and indeed the companies that FTF covers in either their consultancy activities, their labelling certification role, or both. This is, indeed, vertical integration at its best.

Taking this one stage further, the NGOs that oversee FTF's work also often engage directly with the same companies that FTF works with. Oxfam, for example, contributed to the introduction in an annual report of the British food retailer, Sainsbury's. Oxfam agreed after some soul-searching to offer through this route a carefully nuanced endorsement of the company's performance, if only through association. The company's (now former) Chief Executive, Dino Adriano, also sits on Oxfam's Board. To complicate the matter still further, Oxfam is increasing its own trading activities, and is currently seeking to build a strong sub-brand of fair trade products that will be sold through major outlets, including Sainsbury's.

A growing number of multilateral partnerships are emerging, involving NGOs, business, and in some instances trade unions and governments. These partnerships will be considered in more depth in the next chapter. Of relevance here, however, is the added level of intertwined relationships between NGOs and companies that these partnerships involve. The ETI in the UK, for example, has a board comprising three representatives from the corporate membership, three from the NGOs, and three from the trade union movement. The two organizations sitting at board level that have been most significant in making the ETI happen are, once again, Oxfam and Sainsbury's.

Box 7.2 *Engaging Dilemmas*

'Old allies who have entered into negotiations are now sworn to secrecy, our relationship and communication with them has changed.'
'It seems as if our Northern "partners" have found a new way to raise money on the back of our problems – by becoming part of the problem.'
'Once we get into negotiations with companies, how can we continue to be an effective watchdog?'

There is no suggestion here of any inappropriate dealings on the part of the organizations described. The examples of Oxfam, Sainsbury's and the FTF simply illustrate an underlying pattern where poachers and game-keepers have become increasingly intertwined. Indeed, it is no longer possible (if it ever really was) to ensure the absence of *structural* conflicts of interests. These structural conflicts of interest make it understandable that many of those outside the insider-circles are increasingly voicing concern about the nature of these relationships. The Asia Monitoring Resource Centre (AMRC) in Hong Kong is one of the few NGOs based in the South with sufficient capacity to really engage in the international debate about the pros and cons of corporate codes of conduct covering labour standards in global supply chains. AMRC has been very critical of Northern-based NGOs such as the US-based Council on Economic Priorities Accreditation Agency (CEPAA – now Social Accountability International), arguing that they are compromised in their corporate accountability work through their overly close financial association with the business community. They have expressed particular concern at the initiative's close relationship with commercial auditors and consultants who have subsequently sought accreditation against the resulting standard, SA8000.[11] SAI has responded publicly in full,[12] but this has done little to reduce concern that all-too-easily turns into suspicion and mistrust. The problems of NGO proximity to the business community have back, as well as front, door dimensions. One study of British NGO pension funds, for example, found that most of the major NGOs, including Christian Aid and Friends of the Earth Scotland, had some often significant funds invested in the very companies that they campaigned against, including the arms manufacturers GKN and British Aerospace Systems (BAe), developers of genetically modified crops including Novartis and AstroZeneca, and Nestlé. A spokesperson for these NGOs clarified that they were moving towards a fully 'ethical' investment portfolio, but added, perhaps sadly, that he 'saw it as the best deal on offer given the world that we live in'.[13]

This is not just a matter for traditional NGOs. The journalist John Pilger, for example, is renowned for his high-profile anti-corporate and anti-globalization position. In a recent article that was published at the same time as the article (quoted above) in *The Economist* on the events in Seattle, he wrote: 'The problem for the voluntary agencies is that they are already too close to government through funding and tax-exempt charitable status.'[14] Yet Pilger's main vehicle in the UK, the respected left-leaning weekly current affairs magazine, *New Statesman*, regularly carries advertisements from many of the companies he would criticize, including British American Tobacco (BAT). David Korten symbolizes for many the heartland of the intellectual opposition to the corporate community through his book *When Corporations Rule the World*. Yet he considered it reasonable to engage with the UK telecommunications giant, BT, in private, fee-paying discussion about sustainable development. Paul Hawken has been an increasingly vocal critique of the multinationals. Yet this has not prevented him from working as a consultant for many of those that he publicly challenges.

These cases are not offered up as examples of 'bad practice'. The author can equally recount comparable examples of his own practice.[15] Rather, these cases merely highlight the dilemmas of an interconnected existence where autonomy cannot be defined in terms of, and independence cannot be secured through, high degrees of institutionalized separateness.

There are examples, certainly, of both individuals and organizations structuring their approaches to secure a high degree of separation in strategically critical ways. Amnesty International does not, for example, accept public money given its historic role as challenger of state abuses of human rights. Oxfam (UK) has not accepted funding from corporations with which it has interacted, for example, through its involvement in the ETI, its examination of the practices of suppliers to Levi Strauss in the Dominican Republic, or its central part in the multi-NGO group that engaged in an exploration of the alleged human rights abuses associated with BP's Colombian operations. The Anti-Nike Campaign has adopted a public campaigning strategy that more or less excludes any serious engagement with Nike itself. The longest-running corporate accountability campaign, the International Baby Milk Campaign focused on the practices of Nestlé, has for 25 years adopted a strategy of not engaging directly with the company.

However, even in these cases, the dilemmas of what Geoff Mulgan terms 'connexity' cannot be avoided.[16] The fund-raising efforts of Amnesty International will almost certainly have been enhanced through their ability to actively participate in high-profile debate about corporate accountability issues. Some individual members of the Anti-Nike Campaign have certainly engaged directly with Nike. Indeed, some of its members have raised grants on the back of this multi-level approach, often from foundations that are funding activities involving the very corporations that are being campaigned against.

Interconnectivity and Accountability

Gone are the days, if indeed they ever existed, when social movements were homogeneous in terms of values and ideology. It is now more likely than ever that allies in one cause may be foes or at least bystanders in a struggle for some other end. Partnerships in this context become more transitory in their scope, form and duration. This in turn raises real issues about accountability. Consider for example the questions raised by a civil activist following the street battles that took place around the WTO meeting in Seattle.

> The question that came to my mind while seeing delegates from mainly developing countries excluded from the talks by protestors – and being sporadically assaulted and intimidated by them – while the US and EU negotiated inside – is when does one group's right to free speech outweigh another's right to free assembly? And when does obstruction of legitimate activity stop being 'non-violent'?

> Also what responsibility do the sub-group of NGOs who produce what are basically lies about the WTO take for winding-up naive – and very young – protestors so they go out and get tear-gassed? There was a lot of manipulation going on out there.[17]

The increased interconnectedness that has served the NGO community so well in bringing social and environmental issues into high profile has a sting in its tail. It makes it far more difficult to negotiate clear roles and responsibilities into relationships with those with whom one shares risks and opportunities.

This (or at least the danger of) disconnection and its causes effectively frames two key questions:

(1) What are the emerging patterns of accountability within the community of civil activists and NGOs?
(2) What are the implications of these developments for the role of NGOs in influencing business practices?

CIVIL WAVES

The rise and fall of NGOs can be understood partly – as for businesses – in terms of *generational waves*. If organizations fail to take account of emerging sensibilities, new organizations arise to take their place or at least work alongside them. For example:

- Human Rights Watch emerged as a major international human rights organization because Amnesty International was perceived to be too slow in taking up new issues, in part because of the very rules that had historically ensured their impeccable credentials.
- Plan International has grown to an extraordinary size because of its willingness to make use of hard-sell techniques in a market environment that has historically adopted a cautious, moralistic approach to marketing.
- A host of direct action groups have emerged in the 1990s, drawing on the experience and profile gained by Greenpeace, but attracting a younger generation with a taste for a more anarchic style of organization than Greenpeace's infamously autocratic organizational model.

NGO accountability is reflected in these civil waves. They can either signal substantive developments that need to be taken on, or constitute challenges to their institutional survival needs – or preferably both. As for businesses, however, the impact of these new waves can be affected by those organizations that are most influential at the time. Microsoft can and does seek either to marginalize or to replicate within its own products new potential developments in the markets in which it operates. So also do major NGOs seek to take-on the latest developments in thinking and practices that will enhance their institutional performance, as well as – hopefully – their development impact. Where this is not possible, it is hardly surprising that they seek to ensure that such developments remain subsidiary to the mainstream of its own operations and the attentions of its key stakeholders. Much is spoken about the increasing levels of intangible assets in the make-up of corporate balance sheets. Were it possible and worthwhile to measure the asset base of NGOs, the predominance of intangibles would for the most part far outstrip that of the business community.

Partnering Tomorrow's Waves

In early 1998, the Royal Institute of International Affairs (RIIA) hosted a one-day conference in London to explore the take-up of human rights issues by energy and resource companies. Three companies were profiled, BP, Rio Tinto and Shell International, each of which had incorporated elements of the UN Declaration of Human Rights into its core business principles with the help of, among others, the Amnesty Business Group.

It was a rather plush, high-profile affair, as these events seem to have become over the years. Outside, a demonstration was taking place, levelled squarely at BP over its human rights record in Colombia. It was raining, and the demonstrators were a rather bedraggled bunch surrounded by a cordon of only slightly less dejected-looking police. During the course of the buffet lunch, a small, impromptu, informal survey was carried out among the NGO representatives to determine their views on the demonstration that was taking place barely 10 metres away, clearly visible through the large picture windows of the Georgian building in which the RIIA is housed. The unaudited results of the survey were astonishing. The NGO representatives inside were completely uninterested in what was going on outside, which one NGO representative named without a trace of irony as '*an unbranded event*'.

With some prompting and considerable discomfort, the fact of the 'unbranded demonstration' and the perspectives revealed through the (very unscientific and possibly unethically implemented) survey were brought to the attention of the participants during the main afternoon session. Central in the ensuing debate (both during and after the event) was that the challenge for those in the conference was to remain relevant through, and at times despite, their growing levels of engagement with each other. Failing to do this would have one of two effects. One was that NGOs around the table would eventually be overtaken by emerging (and currently unbranded) NGOs and initiatives that would come forward and undermine the credibility of what some would see as today's increasingly unresponsive, mainstream NGOs. A second possibility was that today's leading NGOs would manage for long periods to maintain their grip on the mainstream debate and retain public support for their approach by effectively marginalizing emerging initiatives that challenged, quite rightly, their dominance.

In practice, these two possibilities are not exclusive but complementary pathways. There is little doubt that major NGOs *do* seek to retain a dominant hold over the discourse and associated resources in their main spheres of operation. However, there is equally little doubt that this is not a viable strategy for the long term, and that they will over time either adjust to new realities or find themselves making way for newcomers. These dynamics are clearly observable in the area of corporate accountability. Many within the main body of Amnesty International (AI), for example, have consistently resisted the strategy of engaging with companies that has in practice been pursued by its independent-minded infant prodigy, the Amnesty Business Group. It is only the tenacity of the leadership of the Amnesty Business Group and its ability to raise independent sources of revenue that has prevented the concerns within AI from halting the development of this increasingly effective part of the organization. On the other hand, a decision in the mid-1990s by Greenpeace to move away from its confrontational approach towards a more competency-based insider strategy was abandoned when it became clear that taking this approach would result in it losing its uniqueness, supporter appeal, and so its independent resource base, ultimately threatening the viability of the organization. The emergence over the same period of a host of new green direct action groups reinforced the institutional imperative to secure their role as the pre-eminent, high-profile, hard-hitting environmental group.

INFLUENCING RIPPLES

Such accountability dynamics have profound tactical and strategic implications for businesses seeking to understand and respond effectively to civil regulation. These perspectives suggest that companies will only gain a short-term advantage through co-opting NGOs in ways that will over time discredit these new-found partners in the eyes of their non-profit comrades. For Greenpeace to be a useful partner to Shell, for example, requires that the former remain credible so that it can not only encourage and facilitate, but also legitimize, the latter's (hopefully good) practice. The painful experience of the FLA in the US demonstrates the possible consequences of failing to achieve the required delicate balance. The FLA sought to strike a bargain between apparel and footwear companies, the labour movement, and the community of development and human rights NGOs, on how best to develop and implement codes of conduct covering labour standards in global supply chains. Towards the end of the process, however, the labour organizations involved – particularly UNITE, the main US textiles union – decided that there was no chance of achieving what they would have seen as an acceptable deal. As a result, they exited the negotiations with considerable, and very public, acrimony, doing serious damage to the credibility of the FLA in the process. Significant here is that the NGOs remaining in the FLA, especially the International Labor Rights Fund (ILRF), found themselves subjected to extreme public criticism for remaining in the partnership by those who were previously their allies, unions and other NGOs. Indeed, despite a sound and long history of labour activism, the ILRF found itself marginalized from significant parts of the labour movement in the USA – and hence also internationally – and so also ostracized by many NGOs working in the field.

It is not yet clear what are the full repercussions of the continued participation of the ILRF in the FLA. The ILRF has certainly been damaged by the experience. But it has also been nurtured and supported by those who see value in the FLA. In practice, the integrity of Pharis Harvey, the head of the ILRF, and his long-standing work as a civil rights and labour activist, has done much to protect the organization from being completely marginalized from its traditional community of individuals and organizations. If the FLA proves to be a demonstrably effective body in the field of labour standards, much of the reputational damage to the ILRF may well be recovered. However, it continues to be hard for the FLA to be effective without the support of the international trade union movement.

The FLA – and the ILRF's experience in particular – illustrates the accountability dynamics of the non-profit community, and points to some tactical implications for business and non-profit civil organizations. The ILRF and others were drawn into the negotiations preceding the establishment of the FLA in part for their expertise, certainly. But they were also drawn in so as to ensure that any deal struck would have a chance of being accepted by the wider community of people and organizations working in the field of labour rights. A balanced history of this negotiation has yet to be written (or at least published). However, what seems clear is that there was a misjudgement on the part of both the companies around the table and the NGOs over who needed to be – and stay – at the negotiations for credibility to be secured. It can be speculated that the tactical misjudgement had much to do with the strong wall of separation through secrecy built between those on the inside and those outside of the negotiation process. This secrecy generated an atmosphere among those outside the process of mistrust and a sense of impending betrayal. This in turn made it relatively straightforward for the unions to secure the high ground of moral and political credibility at the time of their exit from the process.

The strategic implications of the accountability dynamics within communities of non-profit organizations go well beyond the tactical responses illustrated above. Critical for business is that it does not misunderstand the nature of 'civil waves' that will eventually undermine any carefully constructed alliance that fails to address the issues that subsequent generations of activists see as important, and associated, attainable aims. These partners will almost inevitably be moved over time to one side by newcomers who have better caught the sense of the moment and have the energy, insight and commitment to effectively ride it.

The tactical issue for business in this context may well be to ensure that it does nothing to destabilize its existing partners and so inadvertently precipitate their demise. The strategic challenge, on the other hand, is to correctly identify and influence the next wave of NGOs and the agendas that they bring with them. As one business manager noted, resonating with John Jennings' statement quoted at the beginning of this chapter: 'When I engage with NGOs I see the future.'

The dramatic growth in the engagement of business with NGOs has impacted on its scope and depth of understanding of how society works and is likely to evolve in the future. This increased, and increasingly sophisticated, dialogue has enabled business to penetrate ever more deeply into the parts of society that have been historically largely free from corporate observation or intervention. Just a few years ago, for example, there were few businesses that would have even heard of the Malaysia-based Third World Network, a politically radical advocacy and campaigning organization. Today, its founder and Director, Martin Khor, writes regularly in the international media, and is known and courted by an increasing number of multinational corporations.

This increased visibility of the non-profit civil community carries with it both opportunities and risks. It creates windows of access to decision-making and resources for emerging social entrepreneurs. Simultaneously, it informs business of the futures they are most likely to encounter, and enables them to influence them in their formative states. In short, businesses can and are increasingly engaging down the 'food chain' of civil waves into the next generations of key actors. Two things can be expected to happen as corporations become increasingly adept at operating in these environments. First, is that corporations will increasingly have the opportunity to influence, and in some cases undermine, the institutional strength of new challenges and opportunities emerging with the development of new generations of NGOs. Second, is that this same deepening of corporate knowledge of civil society processes will enhance their ability to be able to respond positively to social and environmental challenges and to engage NGOs in a process of securing commensurate commercial rewards.

The key issue here is not whether corporations will use their deepening knowledge to respond positively to social and environmental challenges, or else seek to undermine the institutions that are driving these challenges. In practice both effects will certainly occur in differing measures depending on many factors. This analysis suggests, rather, that the continued ability of NGOs and other non-profit civil organizations to challenge corporate behaviour will not be secured through a sustained separation between corporations and their non-profit counterparts. Instead, what is likely is an acceleration in the pace at which the key parts of the challenge-based aspects of civil regulation are institutionalized in more intimate, binding relationships between business and the most powerful NGOs. That is the topic of the next chapter.

CHAPTER 8

The New Civil Governance

It is appropriate for companies to point out to governments the impact of their social and environmental policies on commerce. Just as it is appropriate for companies to point out the impact of fiscal policy on commerce... Sometimes publicly, sometimes quietly.

Peter Sutherland, former WTO Director-General, Chairman of Goldman Sachs and Co-chair of BP Amoco[1]

We believe in a global system that measures every multinational against a core set of universal standards using an independent process of social performance monitoring akin to financial auditing. This would bring greater clarity to the impact of globalization and the performance of any one company

Phil Knight, Chair and CEO, Nike Corporation.[2]

LET'S GET TOGETHER[3]

26 July 2000 may well go down in history as the day the roles of business in global governance were irrevocably changed. On that day, the UN Secretary General, Kofi Annan, flanked by the heads of key UN agencies, hosted the inauguration of the Global Compact. Together, the world's most senior international civil servants blessed a new partnership that aimed to further the penetration of the core UN conventions and declarations into global business and the markets within which they operate.

The name plaques announcing those in attendance highlighted the significance of the moment. Arrayed around the UN's semi-circular chamber in its New York headquarters were a powerful blend of business, NGOs and labour organizations, the architects of tomorrow's world. Present of course were the most well-known corporate giants such as BP, the Ford Motor Corporation, Rio Tinto, Shell and Unilever. Accompanying them were some of the newly emerging corporate titans, such as the Brazilian communications corporation, Globo, the Indian conglomerate, Tata, and the South African utilities, Eskom. Also arrayed around the table were business's traditional and new-found partners, including the mighty International Confederation of Free Trade Unions, Human Rights Watch and the World Wide Fund for Nature.

The UN's Global Compact is just one of a profusion of recently established private–public partnerships that are seeking to redefine the terms

on which companies go about their business, and how social and environmental goods can most effectively be delivered. These partnerships, while
diverse in scope and form, in the main share two core aims. They seek to
harness business in pursuit of such goods by mobilizing their capacities
and competencies. At the same time they seek to exert some level of control
on business's growing political and economic power. These two objectives
are clearly uncomfortable bedfellows. Yet they are the hallmark of today's
governance crisis – where increased expectations of what responsibilities
business can and should shoulder go hand in hand with a growing and
visible unease about the manifest inadequacy of existing governance
systems to accommodate these changing roles.

PARTNERSHIP BOOM

The current partnership boom is a predictable outcrop of the New
Economy. The world has become too complex and interdependent, and
resources too scarce, for any one institution or sector to effectively respond
to today's business or wider challenges and opportunities. Partnerships
are a means of getting things done that individual organizations would
be unable to achieve alone. Most directly, partnerships enable diverse and
complementary competencies and resources to be drawn together and
effectively applied. This is an aim underlying all partnerships, whether
it is the Star Alliance of airlines sharing codes to enable through-routing
and reduced overheads, or the European Rapid Response Force made up
of governments preparing to secure peace in our times.

There have always been partnerships. Companies come together to
drill for oil; NGOs join forces to campaign for new legislation to secure
environmental improvements; and governments join with each other
variously to fight wars and provide humanitarian aid. There have also
always been many forms of inter-sectoral collaboration between public
institutions, businesses, and NGOs. Governments have always contracted
commercial business and NGOs to deliver a multitude of public goods
and services; businesses have always donated money, goods and time
to community organizations and political parties. Strategic partnerships
between governments, labour and business have underpinned 50 years
of consensus-building and development since the Second World War in
several European countries, notably Germany, but also in less formal
terms, for example in Scandinavia and The Netherlands.

Yet partnership does seem to have been rediscovered.[4] Governments
and international development institutions talk about the importance of
partnership with business. The UK government's Department for International Development has a Partnership Unit to encourage such alliances.
The Danish government has established The Copenhagen Centre as a
semi-autonomous body focused exclusively on promoting partnerships.
The World Bank has a long-running programme, Business Partners in

Development, designed expressly to explore how best to make partnerships between governments, business and NGOs work.[5] Leading businesses advocate partnerships with governments, NGOs, competitors, and even those labour organizations that business did most to diminish in earlier decades. Many NGOs today are increasingly switched on to partnership. Indeed, an increasing number have been created with a partnership model in mind, particularly US-based giants like the International Youth Foundation and CIVICUS. Advocacy and politicized, representative, grass-roots NGOs are perhaps the most reluctant partners. More than others, they remain nervous to engage with governments that they have historically opposed, businesses that they have loved to hate, and labour organizations that they have often feared, partly perhaps because of their different and arguably more robust source of legitimacy in representing their membership.

These new forms of tri-sectoral partnerships, also called 'new social partnerships',[6] are being offered as a more effective way to address social and environmental problems where, for example:

- businesses and local government bodies join forces to re-integrate the long-term unemployed into work and society;
- businesses work with schools to build more effective bridges for students to the workplace;
- national governments encourage businesses to come together with NGOs and trade unions to improve labour standards in global supply chains; and
- volunteers from business work to build the strength of, and learn from, community organizations.

But such partnerships are more than a collection of inter-institutional competencies. They critically embody new governance structures and processes, often that evolve organically over time. Where these are intra-sectoral partnerships, these governance structures can in the main be handled through existing mechanisms, for example public regulatory bodies in the case of business-to-business partnerships, and supra-national public bodies when governments are creating issue or activity-specific alliances with each other. Inter-sector partnerships are, however, a different matter. The GRI, for example, is a multi-sectoral alliance created specifically to develop and promote guidelines for corporations to report publicly on progress in aligning performance with key parameters of sustainable development.[7] The many players around the table contribute their considerable expertise to the process, including corporations, labour organizations, UN agencies and human rights, development and environmental NGOs. Beyond this, however, as with the ETI and the Global Compact, these varied participants collectively create a sphere of legitimacy. This legitimacy – as well as the more traditional elements of competency-related benefits to partnerships – is in most instances core to the success of new social partnerships. This is particularly critical for the broader-based partnerships, also called Global Public Policy Networks. As Wolfgang Reinicke and Francis Deng clearly show in their study of these networks, legitimacy is not merely important, but is the critical ingredient that underpins the very possibility of creating synergies of, for example, operational competencies.

Box 8.1 *Reasons for Evolving Global Policy Networks*[8]

- Placing new issues on the global agenda

- Negotiating and setting of global standards

- Gathering and disseminating knowledge

- Making new and deepening markets

- Implementation mechanisms

TROUBLE WITH PARTNERSHIPS

The problem that many have with new social partnerships is not so much to do with what they make happen, but what they may make *not happen*. This argument is reflected in a letter sent to the UN Secretary General on 20 July 2000, just days before the launch of the Global Compact. The letter, sent by some of the world's best-known civil society leaders, provides an elegant summary of the potential trouble with partnerships.[9] The nub of its argument has three, linked levels:

(1) Companies build their reputations as good corporate citizens through associating with such partnerships while performing poorly away from the limelight.
(2) Business reduces the pressure for statutory legislation by being seen to be 'self-regulating' through such partnership processes.
(3) The current approach to globalization is further legitimized, thereby undermining the effectiveness of challenges to this development model.

The essence of the letter is clearly correct in arguing that some if not most companies actively oppose restrictive legislation. The two reasons most often given for this are that:

(1) Legislation can increase compliance-related costs and reduce the profitability of business opportunities.

Box 8.2 *Civil Society Challenges the UN Global Compact*

Mr Secretary-General

We are writing to express our concern and reservations about the Global Compact. . . we recognize the importance of bringing business behaviour in line with the universal values and standards represented by the nine principles of the Global Compact.

However, there are two aspects of the Global Compact that trouble us. . . Many sectors of society do not concur with the Global Compact's vision of advancing popular social values 'as part and parcel of the globalization process', to 'ensure that markets remain open'. Many do not agree. . . that globalization in its current form can be made sustainable and equitable, even if accompanied by the implementation of standards for human rights, labour and the environment. . . Our second concern is the purely voluntary nature of the Global Compact, and the lack of monitoring and enforcement provisions. We are well aware that many corporations would like nothing better than to wrap themselves in the flag of the UN in order to 'bluewash' their public image, while at the same time avoiding significant changes to their behaviour. The question is how to get them to abide by the principles in the Global Compact. . . we stress that markets cannot allocate fairly and efficiently without clear and impartially enforced rules, established through open, democratic processes. Asking corporations, many of which are repeat offenders of both the law and commonly accepted standards of responsibility, to endorse a vague statement of commitment to human rights, labour and environmental standards draws attention away from the need for more substantial action to hold corporations accountable for their behaviour. . . Although it may take years before we can hope to achieve a binding legal framework for the transnational behaviour of business in the human rights, environmental and labour realms, we believe it is necessary to start down that road, and to begin building the political support for that goal now. Therefore, the undersigned groups respectfully request you to re-assess the Global Compact, taking into account the concerns above.

Sincerely

Upendra Baxi (University of Warwick and former Vice Chancellor University of Delhi); Roberto Bissio (Third World Institute); Thilo Bode (Greenpeace International); Walden Bello (Director, Focus on the Global South); John Cavanagh (Institute for Policy Studies); Susan George (Transnational Institute); Olivier Hoedemen (Corporate Europe Observatory); Joshua Karliner (Transnational Resource & Action Center); Martin Khor (Third World Network); Miloon Kothari (International NGO Committee on Human Rights in Trade and Investment); Smitu Kothari (President, International Group for Grassroots Initiatives); Sara Larrain (Chile Sustentable); Jerry Mander (International Forum on Globalization); Ward Morehouse (Program on Corporations, Law and Democracy); Atila Roque (Brazilian Institute of Economic and Social Analysis); Elisabeth Sterken (INFACT Canada/IBFAN North America); Yash Tandon (International South Group Network); Vickey Tauli-Corpuz (Indigenous Peoples' International Centre for Policy Research and Education and Asia Indigenous Women's Network); Etienne Vernet (Ecoropa)

(2) Legislation too often proves to be a blunt and ineffective tool for achieving purported social and environmental goals.

There are many examples of active business lobbying against restrictive legislation formulated to address social and environmental goals. Environmental labelling is a case in point.[10] There has been active corporate opposition originating in the US against all eco-labelling. The US-based Coalition for Truth in Environmental Marketing Information Inc, representing corporations with US$900 billion of world-wide sales, opposes national and international eco-label schemes outright, with a number of individual companies lobbying against these and other schemes.[11] While not mandatory in the main, eco-labels have been discussed extensively by the Committee on Trade and Environment (CTE) of the WTO. The WTO's position is that trade-environment provisions that affect trade significantly must not discriminate between home-produced goods and imports, nor between imports from different trading partners.[12] At the time of finalizing this text, and following the European opposition to food goods containing genetically modified organisms, the US government, under pressure from US business, has signalled its intention to test through the WTO the right of the European Commission to insist on products containing GMOs to be labelled, arguing that this is effective discrimination against US-sourced food products that dominate this segment of the market.

The letter to Kofi Annan is also reasonable in arguing that 'voluntary initiatives' by business addressing social and environmental aspects of their business performance *can be* and *are* at times used to offset possible legislation. The International Confederation of Free Trades Unions has led the campaign for a workers' rights clause in trade regulations that would make trade dependent on demonstrable adherence to labour standards based on ILO conventions.[13] On the other hand, the vast majority of large businesses favour trade liberalization, and many see initiatives like the Global Compact as one way of offsetting challenges to the further extension of the liberalization process. Initiatives like the FLA in the US and the ETI in the UK are at least in part a route to avoid moves to establish labour standards at the heart of the WTO process, although the dominant fear is of reputationally damaging civil campaigning. Similarly, business support for initiatives such as the GRI have been seen in part as being about offsetting pressure for moves towards regulating for greater transparency of corporate social and environmental performance.

The UK Company Law Review provides a fascinating microcosm of the same line of debate about whether voluntary initiatives aim at, and succeed in, undermining attempts to legislate around social and environmental performance. During an extended collaborative process between government, business and 'interested parties', the core of the debate has concerned whether company directors should be made legally accountable for business performance to stakeholders other than shareholders, and whether there should be a legal obligation to report on social and environ-mental performance. The ball is still in play at the time of writing this book. However, the likely outcome will be 'no' on the first point, and 'yes' on the second, but only when directors think that the social and environmental dimensions of their performance might have significant impacts on the financials.

The relationship between the UK Company Law Review debate and 'voluntary initiatives' has been critical. Human rights, development and environmental NGOs have pointed to voluntary initiatives in the social and environmental fields, particularly major partnership processes like the GRI, as evidence that robust performance indicators are being used by leading companies. The fact that viability has thus been demonstrated, they argue, supports the view that they should be incorporated into law to ensure that all companies comply with what leading companies are already doing. Companies, on the other hand, have argued that the fact that there are effective voluntary initiatives involving 'all parties' demonstrates that legislation is not required in this field and that levels and types of social and environmental reporting should be left to the discretion of individual companies.

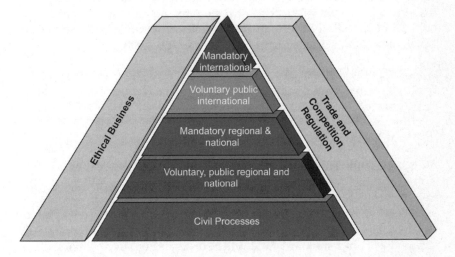

Figure 8.1 *Complementary or Competing Governance Hierarchies?*

But not all corporations are against statutory regulations. Corporations that lead in their handling of difficult social and environmental dimensions of their business impact can find it in their interests to advocate a regime that forces other companies to comply with the same standards to which they have adhered. Those leading companies will often have suffered the pain of being in the limelight for alleged misconduct. With often-considerable investment, these companies shift their practices over time and seek to rebuild their reputations. In some instances this strategy succeeds, as has been the case of Shell, and even perhaps of long-time 'class of one' symbols of the downsides of globalization like Nike. In the process, however, a number of other things happen. First, is that these companies incur substantial costs, some of which are ongoing. Nike, for example, has a team of close to 100 people working on the social dimensions of their business, particularly those dealing with labour standards issues in the company's supply chains. In addition, it finances regular social audits of all of their suppliers, and is a member of many initiatives involved in related issues and processes. Although these costs are certainly not sufficient to financially disable the company, they represent a significant additional cost that many of its competitors do not have to bear. For this reason alone, a company in this position might be expected to seek a stronger compliance regime applied to its competitors. In addition, a more effective international regulatory framework can lead to distinct cost-savings. For Nike, it is certainly now in the company's interests for the labour inspectorates in the countries where their suppliers are based to be strengthened. The company's own inspectorate – particularly the external auditing – is considerably more expensive for the company than would be its small share in the costs of building the capacities of government inspectors to do the job instead. It is perhaps not surprising that Nike's CEO and Chair, Phil Knight, made the following public statement at the UN Global Compact meeting in New York in July 2000.

> We believe in a global system that measures every multinational against a core set of universal standards using an independent process of social performance monitoring akin to financial auditing. This would bring greater clarity to the impact of globalization and the performance of any one company.[14]

A further reinforcement of the potential for positive relationships between 'voluntary' business practices and public regulation is created by the investment in the growth of new capacities within the company attuned to social and environmental issues. This certainly establishes a new pattern of internal lobbying, strengthened by the external pressures to continually ratchet up labour standards and other social and environmental aspects of performance. Beyond this, this capacity generates new thinking around how improved social and environmental performance might be more closely aligned to all aspects of business strategy. The wake-up call came to the Danish health care and enzymes group Novo A/S (previously Novo Nordisk) in the early 1980s when faced with technical quality shortfalls that placed it at risk in its major markets, particularly the US. The company's survival depended on a radical shift in all of its quality assurance processes. The company responded to this crisis with extraordinary vision, largely through the insight of its Chief Executive, Mads Øvlisen. Rather than simply solving the compliance problem, it adopted a radical strategy that placed sustainable development at its heart. What that meant, at least in the early years, was to make major advances in the ways in which it measured and managed its environmental and bioethics performance. More recently, this has extended to embrace a growing range of social issues.

The relationship between civil regulation, business responses, and the rule of law is rarely a straightforward one. US government pressure on other OECD governments to outlaw bribery for commercial gain was underpinned by US business seeking to offset any possible competitive disadvantage given the US statutes covering 'foreign corrupt practices' by US-domiciled corporations in their overseas operations. The fact that this legislation had rarely been used and had never led to any major fines or other penalties being imposed on any US corporation did not diminish the view of US business that the field had to be levelled in this respect, or indeed perhaps tilted in their favour. This was certainly the single most significant driver that led to the OECD *Convention on Combating Bribery of Foreign Public Officials in International Business Transactions* finally coming into force on 15 February 1999.[15]

At one level this is a fine example of public regulation emerging from a perceived need by the business community to level the competitive playing field, at least between the big players. As a corporate manager remarked during a meeting held in London shortly after the Convention was signed:

> We are in favour of the Convention. We do not see our competitive advantage as being in the area of bribery, quite apart from the moral issue. Our strength is in our investment muscle, our reputation for doing things well, and our political weight. If the field is levelled against bribery, we can only really gain.

There is, however, a sting to this particular tale, at least for the UK. In June 2000, the UK was heavily criticized by fellow members of the OECD for being the only country out of 20 member states that failed to ensure that the Convention was fully incorporated into domestic law. Over the same period, out of a total of 54 companies blacklisted by the World Bank for alleged corrupt practices in acquiring and implementing public sector contracts, 35 were British. According to one source, some OECD-based companies are establishing financial mechanisms in non-OECD countries for 'retaining the option to bribe'.[16] The issue here is not so much the recalcitrance of the UK government, although this is a cause for concern given its high-profile support for corporate citizenship as an integral part of its advocacy of increased trade liberalization. More fundamentally, the example illustrates the limitations of both voluntary agreements and mandatory regulations.

Certainly voluntary initiatives do not always lead companies to advocate related legislation, and the opposite is in practice often the case. Activists are right to be concerned at the possible downsides of high-profile partnerships that position major corporations in an ethical light. However, legislation can be and is at times enabled by voluntary partnerships. There is sufficient evidence to support the view, and logic to the argument, that companies that have effectively raised their social and environmental performance standards may in turn become advocates for a broader-based framework that applies similar standards to other parts of the business community. This is perhaps a pre-requisite for effective movement along some Mecca pathways. It would not seem unlikely that, in coming years, leading global corporations will increasingly support global regulations that establish a floor for environmental and social standards, and in the process consolidate their collective competitive positions against smaller, less powerful companies seeking to enter global markets.

Corporations Take the Reins

The underlying dilemma, however, is that such a seemingly 'progressive' outcome also points to a dramatic increase in the role of corporations in the formulation of the rules of the game. Corporations have of course always influenced public policy. What is new is that this influence is increasingly becoming formalized and legitimized through their involvement in partnerships with governments, international institutions and civil society organizations. This is as true at the national and local levels as it is for high-profile initiatives like the Global Compact.

The UK-based business membership organization, Business in the Community, gives annual awards for companies that have made notable contributions to the community. For the 2000 Awards, one of the winning partnerships involved News International and the potato crisp ('chip' for US readers) manufacturers, Walkers. Together with local education authorities across the country, they had operated a voucher system that enabled schools to acquire free textbooks by collecting coupons contained on Walkers crisp packets and newspapers produced by News International. Over the period in question this initiative resulted in the distribution of no fewer than 2,500,000 free books to schools. This was numerically comparable to the entire nation-wide, public sector provision for the same period.

While unquestionably a remarkable feat, this cause-related marketing initiative had two characteristics that highlight the underlying dilemma of the growing significance of these partnerships. First, was that the only eligible book provider through the initiative was HarperCollins, a company, like News International, that is within the Murdoch empire. HarperCollins is an extremely reputable publisher of education books, so that the quality of materials is not here in question. However, the partnership has clearly placed the company very well in gaining new contracts in the British education sector. As one person from News International privately commented during the awards event, 'There is no doubt that HarperCollins has benefited commercially from this initiative, and probably considerably so.' Second, and following from this, is that the continuation of the initiative depends on its on-going commercial value to the companies involved. News International and Walkers have gained in terms of reputation through the initiative, just as HarperCollins had gained directly in terms of book sales and share of the education market. But cause-related marketing often delivers only short-term reputational gains. Once consumers and other stakeholders have experienced the novelty value of the cause-link, they too often move on to other products that associate themselves with equally interesting images. Were the Books-for-Schools initiative to end, the fact would still remain that schools had acquired many free books and hopefully put them to good use. However, the dependence of schools on this initiative might well by then have been established, leaving the public school system at the mercy of other companies that might see the potential commercial gains in renewing the initiative in some other form. The greatest irony perhaps is, as Ed Mayo from the New Economics Foundation points out, that News International has led the press campaign for further reductions in tax levels, which in turn would further reduce the public sector's ability to supply (amongst many things) adequate levels of school books.[17]

THE NEW CIVIL GOVERNANCE

Partnerships are far more than 'at best more efficient and effective modes of delivery'. They embody an evolving set of organic governance structures and processes. This has particular significance for those partnerships that are between business, government and non-profit, civil society organizations in that:

● their basis of *legitimacy* is quite different, incorporating for example the trust afforded to civil society organizations and governments;
● the diverse *access to networks and relationships* afforded in particular through the involvement of NGOs increases the ability of the partnership to enter into areas of society that have historically been shielded from the business community; and
● the combining of organizational *cultures and competencies* enhances the ability and tendency of the partnership to initiate new formations of activities that more closely integrate into an almost seamless pattern of commercial and non-commercial interests and outcomes.

Civil partnerships are in practice an evolution in civil regulation. The previous chapter showed clearly how the cut-and-thrust form in which it is applied to particular aspects of corporate behaviour tends to evolve into more institutional rule-based frameworks. Although some of these frameworks may eventually find their way on to the statute books of national governments or international institutions, by far the majority will be developed and overseen by diverse configurations of civil partnerships. This is clearly true in the case of corporate codes of conduct, where companies increasingly seek to stabilize their commitments and risks by linking their codes to partnerships that involve human rights and development NGOs. Similarly in the area of disclosure, where companies once again seek to associate themselves with one or other reporting framework developed within a multi-constituency process. In some instances, elements of the rules will become law while others remain governed through partnerships.

Civil governance clearly does not carry the weight and possible implications of law, for example in terms of sanctions for non-compliance. At the same time, it has, or can have, a number of characteristics that take the position of the company beyond both 'self-regulation' and the early stages of civil regulation described in the last chapter. Civil governance:

- builds rules that the companies involved agree to abide to;
- rules are overseen by institutional structures and processes that involve non-commercial organizations, often NGOs, sometimes labour organizations and increasingly government and international bodies acting as facilitators, mediators and sometimes sources of financial support; and
- includes systems of penalties and rewards for non-compliance, although in most instances to date these remain weak and poorly defined.

Civil governance also has the critical effect of shifting the capacities and competencies of the organizations involved. The ETI brought together leading UK retailers, NGOs, labour organizations and the UK government in an exploration of how codes of conduct covering labour standards in global supply chains could be most effectively implemented. The initial 18 months of the initiative were taken up almost exclusively in the negotiation of a Base Code that member companies would sign up to. It was a difficult process; serious differences between the organizations involved surfaced, were worked through and solutions found. At various stages, organizations from all four constituencies were ready to leave the table over particular issues, notably over how best to handle the clauses covering child labour, freedom of association and collective bargaining, and basic income rights. In each case, there is little doubt that the negotiations would have failed if they had relied on the starting positions of the organizations involved. But at each stage, the representatives of key organizations evolved their understanding of the issues and the associated perspectives of others. Every organization changed during the process, although certainly some more than others. This learning process, and their ability to build this learning into the core of their respective organizations, enabled the initiative to move forward to what most would see as a successful resolution.

Civil governance lies at the heart of the New Economy of corporate citizenship. It is a key process through which rules are built that companies are willing to be accountable to. It institutionalizes the more chaotic and arguably transitory civil regulatory challenges that NGOs and other organizations are able to mobilize through popular and generally negative campaigning. Finally, it deepens the learning processes within companies, and also other constituencies, that act to shift their understanding of the issues and how best to be able to address them effectively within the competitive thrust of the global market place.

The potential benefits of civil governance should not be confused with an uncritical endorsement of all new social partnerships. So let me return finally to the example of the Global Compact with which the chapter began. The Global Compact marks a step up in the role of both business and non-profit organizations in global governance. Never before has a partnership been created between the highest levels of the UN, business, NGOs and labour representatives. Never before has such a partnership had the open-ended mandate of furthering the core UN conventions and declarations covering labour standards, human rights and the environment. For this first time in the history of the UN, the governments of sovereign states are not at the table, and can only exert influence indirectly, such as through their power elsewhere within the UN.

The stakes are high. The carrot offered by Kofi Annan in bringing business to the Global Compact has been to keep the trade liberalization process freer from the confrontational debate about its social and environmental impacts. For NGOs and trade unions, the Compact is a balancing act. It offers a new source of leverage over corporate practices, but it also carries the danger of diluting the impact of their calls for globally applicable legislation. The risk for business is that it projects them further into the limelight, potentially allowing them to be portrayed all the more as unaccountable usurpers of democratic institutions and processes. For NGOs and labour representatives sitting round the table, they may find their ethical future intertwined with some poor performing corporations, thereby earning the wrath of other NGOs.

But the potential gains are immense. It is a massive step forward for leading corporations to freely commit themselves to benchmark their performance against the closest we have to an international consensus on what constitutes civilized behaviour: core ILO conventions and key declarations such as the UN Declaration of Human Rights. Whatever the outcome of the Compact, its launch on 26 July 2000 will be looked back on as a red-letter day in the evolution of global governance.

Part 2

The Civil Corporation

CHAPTER 9

Foundations of Sustainability

TRIPLE BOTTOM LINE

Mads Øvlisen, until recently the Chief Executive of the Danish pharmaceutical and enzymes company, Novo Nordisk[1] offers his preferred definition of sustainable development at the outset of many of his public talks as being: 'A way of dealing with the planet as if it is on loan from our children rather than inherited from our parents.'[2] This striking and poetic metaphor invariably and rightly resonates well with his audience. Certainly, it provides a more accessible insight into the essence of sustainable development than most of the many hundreds of more technical definitions available.

Metaphor is well suited for establishing values and visions, but can be less useful for developing specific strategy, practice and learning. Practice alone can similarly fall short of providing a robust understanding of sustainable development. As a think-piece published by BT highlights, 'Although the Brundtland report incorporated the societal element into the original concepts of sustainable development, the most widely held perspective has been one of environmental protection and resource conservation.'[3] Indeed, how often have you heard the phrase, 'Oh yes, sustainable development is not just about the environment, one needs to add the social.' Very occasionally, a more enlightened phrase may drift by, of the form: 'Well of course we need to take account of economic effects as well when we think about sustainable development.' The underlying relationship between these elements remains, to those who are honest, unclear.

Increasingly we hear about the 'triple bottom line', a phrase coined by John Elkington in early 1994.[4] The triple bottom line seeks to encapsulate for the business community what are traditionally seen as the three spheres of sustainability, the economic, social and environmental. This useful metaphor correctly challenges the convention of taking 'sustainability' to be about the environment, thereby reinforcing an awareness that the three major dimensions are all relevant to an organization's performance, and tantalizingly suggests that each should and can be counted.[5]

The triple bottom line, like all metaphors that are effective through their simple message, has its limitations.

● The image of three columns of figures encourages the dimensions of sustainable development to be seen as separate, whereas John

Box 9.1 *Talking About Sustainability*

During the launch of the UN Global Compact, business leaders spoke of their companies' broader commitment to good corporate citizenship and sustainable development.[6]

The Chairman of the Brazilian mining and smelting company, **Aracruz Celulose S A**, gave testimony of the company's commitment to sustainable development:

'Aracruz consistently endorses the concept of sustainable development and conducts its business according to its main precepts.'

DuPont asserted its strategy as being 'sustainable growth', which it interpreted as involving:

'Creating shareholder and societal value while reducing our footprint throughout the value chain.'

The Swiss-based financial services group, **Union of Bank of Switzerland (UBS)**, confirmed that:

'UBS believes that sustainable development is an important aspect of responsible management.'

The South African state-owned utilities group, **Eskom**, was unequivocal in setting its own terms of responsibility within a sustainable development framework:

'When viewed from a sustainable development perspective, Eskom's electrification programme is closely aligned with the three pillars of sustainable development.'

The British water and energy utilities company, **United Utilities**, states in its annual social and environmental impact report:

'By combining our social and environmental impacts in a single report, we aim to provide a snapshot of our contribution to sustainable development and progress towards a better quality of life.'[7]

The **Ford Motor Company**, in its most recent Corporate Citizenship Report, sets out its ambition to:

'become a leader in corporate citizenship and a significant contributor to a sustainable world'.[8]

Elkington would of course be the first to stress the importance of their relationship.[9] Indeed, it offers no clue as to how to understand the relationship between social, environmental and economic performance and impact.

● By creating an image that parallels financial accounts, it unintentionally reinforces the view that what is important are those things that can be measured, or have a financial impact. While this imagery and its implications certainly catches the imagination of a corporate audience, it receives a less favoured response from, say, human rights activists who are not as wedded to the primary status afforded to those aspects of performance that can be readily measured.

Figure 9.1 *Triple Bottom Line: What Does It Mean?*

The metaphor of the triple bottom line has and will continue to serve a useful purpose in bringing elements of what is important into what are often conservative, risk-averse and not particularly well-informed people and institutions. But it is equally important to move forward in achieving a better understanding of both the conceptual dimensions and the practical applications if the challenge of sustainable development is to be effectively addressed.

A THEORETICAL DIGRESSION?

It is an oft-stated view, particularly in the Anglo-American world of business, that managers do not read (or at least do not read more than one page summaries), and are uninterested in either concepts or theory. From this it often follows that these debates concerning 'theory' do not really matter when it comes to the practical realities of running a business. Surely, many argue, the conceptual issues about sustainable development are better left to the academics.

This view of the archetypal business manager has always left me wondering whether it suggests that business only employs people with a characteristic lack of interest or ability in conceptual thought, or whether being part of the business community has the curious and apparently pervasive effect (presumably over time) of neutralizing any such interest or capacity. Of course neither of these explanations is correct. The real point is that people need to understand the relevance of things to what they do. Business, like politics, is quintessentially pragmatic. Products and services need to be designed, developed, produced and distributed in ways that enable the enterprise to see black rather than red ink at the end of the accounting period. Theory and concepts, from this perspective, are seen by some as time-consuming and distracting irrelevancies to the tough enough task of making business work.

But today's business activities bear little resemblance to their historical precursors. Design and development require ever-greater investment of money and people in ways that combine technical innovation with up-to-the-minute knowledge of rapidly shifting market conditions. Maintaining a clear 'licence to operate' with public regulators, employees, customers and non-profit advocacy groups is an ever-more complex task. Companies need to prove to prospective employees with valuable skills, for example, just how fulfilling as well as financially rewarding their work experience will be. Many businesses now collaborate with their competitors as much as they vie with them for market share.

Business is faced with an increasingly complex, dynamic operating environment. Dividing narrow skill-sets across traditional, functional hierarchies is no longer the way to organize a viable business. Flexibility, innovation, and working through dynamic networks of business relationships require the mobilization of knowledge that is either new or (desperately) under-applied within most business. As Chris Mellor, the CEO of the British utilities group, Anglian Water, commented, 'My greatest challenge is to identify and make use of the ideas and competencies of people working for us, and indeed those who are not.'[10]

Sustainable development reflects the ambition of securing an environmentally viable and socially just society, a modern-day utopia. Equally, however, it can provide the critical strategic and operational architecture of tomorrow's successful companies. Mark Moody-Stuart, Shell International's Chairman of the Committee of Managing Directors, sums up this proposition in the 1999 Shell Report: 'Our... commitment to contribute to a sustainable form of development... is inextricably linked to our long-term commercial success. Sustainable development builds the platform on which business thrives and society prospers.'[11]

Understanding what this means requires more than blind faith, crass cynicism, or simply a hit-and-miss approach to trial and error. Making sense of Moody-Stuart's statement needs an understanding of what sustainable development means in a business context. It may mean, for example, reducing a business's environmental footprint. But, again, at what cost? Certainly not at any cost, either from the perspective of the business or society at large. Improving labour standards in global supply chains is clearly desirable, as reflected in key conventions of the ILO. But at what cost and to whom? The confrontation around the WTO meeting in Seattle graphically highlighted the very different prevailing perspectives on the pros and cons to workers and nations alike of securing compliance to these internationally agreed conventions. As one person quoted in BT's *Changing Values* report puts it:

> You... *[those who are wealthier and safer]*... can afford to be concerned about the environment, the rain forests, the animals facing extinction – for us these issues are luxuries compared to the immediacy of social and economic survival.[12]

Trial and error is of course the life-blood of any evolving process or system. But to converge on an approach that meets the needs of sustainable development requires language and method that allow us both individually and collectively to analyse experience, learn from it, and so make better decisions in the future.

Theory is a practical necessity because we need commonly agreed conceptual frameworks that help us to understand what we and others are doing. We need robust ways of analysing what happens as a result of specific actions, and a common language that enables us to communicate this effectively to others. Most important, perhaps, is that we need ways and means of working out what are the trade-offs implied in different decisions and activities between varied and often conflicting interests and outcomes.

VISUALIZING SUSTAINABLE DEVELOPMENT

The conventional wisdom in working with sustainable development is to conceive of three interlocking spheres, the environmental, the social and the economic. Few would disagree with the UN statement following the 'Rio+5' event in 1997, that: 'Economic development, social development, and environmental protection are interdependent and mutually reinforcing components of sustainable development.' Intuitively this is an attractive place to start. We can think of the:

- *economic* as being about the creation of material wealth (including financial income and assets for the company);
- *social* as being about the quality of people's lives and so particularly about equity between people, communities and nations; and the
- *environmental* as being about protection and conservation of our natural environment.

This starting point is clarified further in the most recent version of the Global Reporting Initiative Sustainability Reporting Guidelines, as reproduced in Box 9.2.

Stressing the interdependent nature of these three spheres signals the need to understand the ways in which these dimensions affect each other. Greater material wealth can enhance the social, but does not necessarily do so; improvements in the quality of life for some can undermine or

Box 9.2 *GRI Perspectives on the Elements of Sustainable Development*

Environment
Organizations create environmental impacts at various scales, including local, national, regional and international. These occur in relation to air, water, land and biodiversity resources. Some are well understood, while others present substantial measurement challenges owing to their complexity, uncertainty, and synergies.

Social
The social dimension of sustainability captures the impact of an organization's activity on society, including on employees, customers, community, supply chain and business partners. Social performance is a key ingredient in assuring an organization's licence to operate, and supports the organization's ability to deliver high-quality environmental and economic performance. Many stakeholders believe that reporting and improving social performance enhances reputation, increases stakeholder trust, creates opportunities and lowers costs.

Economic
Organizations affect the economies in which they operate in many ways, including through their use of resources and creation of wealth. These impacts, however, are not fully captured and disclosed by conventional financial accounting and reporting. Thus, additional measures are required to capture the full range of an organization's economic impacts. Sustainability reporting has rarely embraced economic measures to date, although there is a lengthy history of measuring certain economic effects, for example, of company relocation, closure and investment.

Source: GRI Guidelines July 2000[13]

enhance that for others; and similarly the creation of material wealth can deplete the natural environment within which we live, and from which we draw resources both today and in the future.

Interdependence is therefore about the potential for mutually re-inforcing effects, but can equally be about trade-offs between and within each sphere. Understanding sustainable development therefore requires an appreciation of actual and potential causes and effects, the dynamic processes of change that yield impacts within one or more of these spheres.

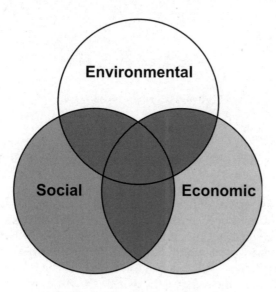

Figure 9.2 *Metaphoric Visualization*

Although attractive, this *metaphoric* visualization of the relationship between the three spheres of sustainable development suffers from fatal conceptual defects. It is difficult in practice to conceive of social phenomena that lie outside of the environmental sphere. Human society lies wholly within the natural environment, and every element of the social therefore has environmental roots and consequences. Similarly, the economic sphere comprises essentially social processes. The discipline of economics is, after all, the study of how people make decisions as to how best to allocate society's scarce competencies and available resources in the creation of products and services that are traded for consumption and investment.[14] Economics is therefore, of course, also about the manners in which limited resources drawn from the natural environment are exploited in pursuit of satisfying human needs.

It follows from this that a more appropriate visualization of the *literal* relationship between the three spheres of sustainable development is

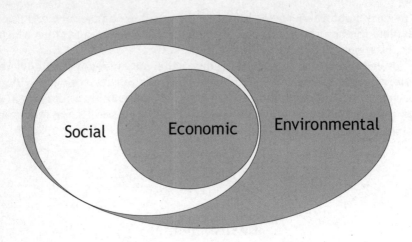

Figure 9.3 *Literal Visualization*

where the economic lies entirely within the social that in turn lies entirely within the environmental.

The literal is certainly more accurate than the metaphoric visualization, but equally has some significant disadvantages. Sustainable development is an entirely human, or socialized, conception. After all, it is about humans on planet Earth, and not the survival of the planet per se (which is not in doubt.) It offers a way of seeing things that, while certainly 'natural' (as are all things), arise through the peculiar manner in which humans perceive, interpret, and make their way in the world. The environmental element of

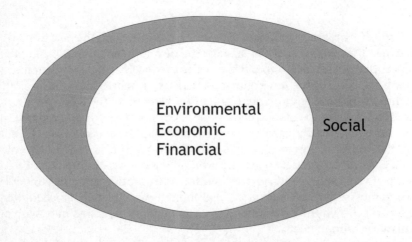

Figure 9.4 *Cognitive Visualization*

sustainable development is, similarly, an entirely socialized phenomenon. We judge what is good or bad for the environment, and even what is cause and effect, through an exclusively cognitive process. We see the environment, in short, through our ability to smell, touch, see and hear, with all the strengths and weaknesses that these capacities embody.

From this perspective, a *cognitive* visualization of sustainable development would place the social as the outer boundaries, and incorporate both the economic and the environmental entirely within it.

THE ECONOMICS IN SUSTAINABILITY[15]

Knowing that everything affects everything does not really help us to understand where to look and what to do. A different tack is to establish a hierarchy based on what we are interested in. The 'Rio+5' event in 1997 provides us with a clue in taking this approach: 'Sustained economic growth is essential to the economic and social development of all countries, in particular developing countries.'

Economics counts, but in what ways? The traditional view of the subject of economics is as being about how people use scarce 'resources' to satisfy society's many wants. Scarcity of resources means that we have to make choices between competing wants, individually and collectively. Economics is about why and how those choices are made, and to what effect.

The view of the subject of economics is useful in that it points to the need to understand and work with trade-offs, whereas the 'profits-with-principles' proposition has the danger of lulling us into a view that no such trade-offs need to be made. However, this view of economics is less helpful when we look to see what is not covered.

(1) *Economics in the environmental.* Economics is concerned with how human and natural resources are used in pursuit of human welfare,[16] both today and in the future. It is therefore not distinct from the environmental element of sustainable development.

(2) *Economics in the social.* Similarly, since economics is about how people allocate resources in pursuit of human welfare, it is clearly not separate from the 'social'. The economic is, rather, another way of looking at decisions and events that also have social outcomes. For example, an employee may see the social welfare gains from developing workplace skills, particularly if those skills increase her employability and her enjoyment of work. For an economist, this acquisition of skills was achieved at some resource cost, and yet (hopefully) adds to society's capacity to generate economic wealth.

(3) *Meeting human needs – or moulding them.* A crucial element of the interface between the economic and the social concerns the treatment of human needs. Mainstream economics generally takes needs as a 'given'

in its exploration of how scarce resources are allocated to meet them. In the real world, we need to distinguish what the Chilean economist Manfred Max-Neef calls 'satisfiers' from the underlying human needs that they may or may not fulfil.[17] For example, people have a basic need to relax and socialize with each other. Business of course does not offer relaxation and socialization, but products and services that give people an opportunity to satisfy their basic needs, for example:

- An airline will seek to associate in the minds of its potential customers leisure with travel, and travel with air travel, and air travel with that particular company.
- A telecommunications company, on the other hand, may seek to associate in the minds of its potential customers that the use of telephone and Internet is a core element of leisure, and that physical travel can often be avoided.

(4) There may well be some set of 'fundamental needs', but the means of their satisfaction are clearly subject to influence by, among other things, business.

The economics in sustainability, or indeed anywhere else, is therefore not a separate sphere of events or outcomes. The economic lies entirely within the social, since it is about what individuals and societies do in allocating and managing scarce resources to satisfy human wants. The economic therefore also lies within the environmental, since the social system is literally nested within, and is thus a subset of, the ecological system.[18]

In fact it is useful to go even further in concluding that economic is best thought of as being about means rather than ends. We are interested in generating economic wealth not for its own sake but for what it brings with it. The economic wealth generated through addictive and destructive drugs can enhance the prestige, lifestyle and power of those who produce and sell them. Economic wealth generated from the sale of armaments or by cutting costs through redundancies or skimping on health and safety supports the well-deserved lifestyles of those who have reached old-age and are fortunate enough to hold private pensions. But whether economic wealth produces what seem to be 'good' or 'bad' things, what is always the case is that its ends concern the production of social and environmental outcomes. From this perspective, economic activity is *no more or less than the process through which humans create social and environmental outcomes*.[19]

The implication of this way of looking at the economics element of sustainability is that we are only interested in it in so far as economic processes in turn generate social and environmental outcomes. Whether an economy, for example, has grown by 1 or 2 per cent should be irrelevant *in itself* in measuring progress towards sustainable development. What is relevant about that growth is what are its social and environmental implications both now and in the future.

This final visualization (Figure 9.5) therefore stresses a hierarchy of importance between the three spheres. The economic is a primary

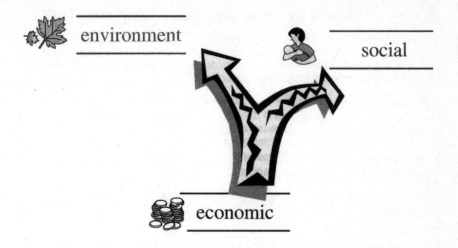

Figure 9.5 *Economics as Means Not Ends*

instrumental driver of social and environmental outcomes that are relevant to any benchmark of sustainable development. Both social and environmental outcomes can also be instrumental in that each can create outcomes in the other two spheres. But the social and the environmental, unlike the economic, also represent end goals.

BEYOND A CASH-FLOW WORLD

A company's cash-flow position tells us whether it has money in the bank. Its profit-and-loss statement tells us how it performed financially over the period in question. What neither tells us is whether the company is a going concern. In the context of financial accounting at least, we need the balance sheet to get to the matter of the underlying health of the company.

Similarly for the environment. Much time is spent measuring resource use and the levels of pollution created. Such measures are critically important in order to more effectively direct human affairs. However, we are ultimately interested in ensuring that the natural environment is a 'going concern'; that as a system it is viable in a form that ensures the well-being of those elements to which we attach value, notably but not necessarily exclusively humans. For this we need to know the state of the environment as well as the influences upon it. The Natural Step method, as summarized in Box 9.3, is a very helpful way of conceiving this way of looking at the world.

The social element follows from this. The perspective expressed in the core of sustainable development concerns our interest in both the current and future generations of people. We are interested from this perspective

Box 9.3 *The Natural Step's System Conditions*[20]

---

1 *In a sustainable society, nature is not subject to increasing concentrations of substances extracted from the earth's crust*

In a sustainable society, human activities such as the burning of fossil fuels, and the mining of metals and minerals will not occur at a rate that causes them to systematically increase in the ecosphere

2 *In a sustainable society, nature is not subject to increasing concentrations of substances produced by society*

In a sustainable society, humans will avoid generating systematic increases in persistent substances such as DDT, PCBs and freon

3 *In a sustainable society, nature is not subject to increasing degradation by physical means*

In a sustainable society, humans will avoid taking more from the biosphere than can be replenished by natural systems

4 *In a sustainable society, human needs are met worldwide*

Meeting the fourth system condition is a way to avoid violating the first three system conditions for sustainability. Considering the human enterprise as a whole, we need to be efficient with regard to resource use and waste generation in order to be sustainable. If 1 billion people lack adequate nutrition while another billion have more than they need, there is a lack of fairness with regard to meeting basic human needs. Achieving greater fairness is essential for social stability and the cooperation needed for making large-scale changes within the framework laid out by the first three conditions.

---

in securing the well-being of those to come, both the children of today and those not yet born. This can, as with the environment, be conceived of as a balance sheet over time. This can also be understood as meaning that the interests of the current generation extend beyond their own personal living futures.

Extending the financial accounting metaphor, sustainable development is therefore essentially about stocks as well as flows. We are interested in understanding and managing the effects of our actions on both today and tomorrow. But we cannot directly measure the 'facts' of what has not yet happened. Therefore, we need to find ways to model ourselves and our environment in terms of the balance sheet effects of what we do today on tomorrow's world. The model we need to do this must essentially capture the 'capital' as well as the 'cash-flow' or 'profit and loss' effects.

WHICH CAPITALS COUNT

We are interested in capital, but which ones? This is not a question about measurement, to which we will turn in due course. There is first the need to conceptualize how we want to ground our understanding of the building blocks of sustainable development. For example, the SIGMA (Sustainability Integrated Guidelines for Management) Initiative being implemented by the British Standards Institute, Forum for the Future, and the Institute of Social and Ethical AccountAbility (ISEA), has proposed five forms of capital as the conceptual basis for relevant tools: natural, human, social, manufacturing and financial.[21]

Box 9.4 *SIGMA's Five Capital Model*

Σ   *Natural capital* (also referred to as environmental or ecological capital) is any stock or flow of energy and matter that yields valuable goods and services. It falls into several categories: *resources*, some of which are renewable (timber, grain, fish and water), while others are not (fossil fuels); *sinks* which absorb, neutralize or recycle wastes; and *processes*, such as climate regulation. Natural capital is the basis not only of production but of life itself.

Σ   *Human capital* consists of health, knowledge, skills and motivation, all of which are required for productive work. Enhancing human capital (for instance, through investment in education and training) is central to a flourishing economy. Poverty is both morally indefensible, and socially inefficient in that it prevents millions of people from fulfilling their potential and becoming engaged in the creation of wealth.

Σ   *Social capital* is the value added to any activity or economic process by human relationships and cooperation. Social capital takes the form of structures or institutions which enable individuals to maintain and develop their human capital in partnership with others, and includes families, communities, businesses, trade unions, schools and voluntary organizations.

Σ   *Manufactured capital* comprises material goods – tools, machines, buildings and other forms of infrastructure – which contribute to the production process, but do not become embodied in its output.

Σ   *Financial capital* plays an important role in our economy, by reflecting the productive power of the other types of capital, and enabling them to be owned and traded. However, unlike the other types, it has no *intrinsic* value; whether in shares, bonds or banknotes, its value is purely representative of natural, human, social or manufactured capital.

Source: SIGMA

The approach advocated by SIGMA in many ways is 'best practice' thinking. However, a complementary but simpler approach is to retain the three-part taxonomy underlying the triple bottom line. From this perspective, we might say that:

- *Environmental capital* comprises the natural resources that are available to us to fashion into goods and services or to use as a 'sink' for our mounting waste. This is in some ways the easiest element to understand, and is equivalent to SIGMA's 'natural capital'.
- *Social capital* would be the skills and relationships that make up the capacities of societies to organize in order to meet selected perceived needs. This is the most difficult element of capital to conceive. Social capital has, following the seminal work of Robert Putnam and others, been understood to mean the:

  > quality of contacts people have and networks they plug into, and the norms of trust, reciprocity and good will, sense of shared life across the classes, and capacities to organize that these ties afford.[22]

Here, however, a wider sense of social capital is being defined that embraces the full set of human relationships and competencies that creates our fabric of social organization. Social capital would include, for example, the ILO conventions that define a set of social norms and expectations of behaviour, as it would include the organizing capacities of the ILO and others. In this sense, social capital here includes SIGMA's human capital, and also a range of key social dimensions not included in its five-piece formulation.

- *Economic capital* would be the material wealth that is produced by people by combining environmental and social capitals. This would then include both goods and services, and also financial capital.

There are, inevitably, limitations to this simple architecture. Phenomena do not always easily fit one or other type of capital. When exactly, for example, is a social relationship a service (and so is an element of economic capital), and when is it not (hence presumably becoming an element of social capital)? Normally one might argue that it falls into the economic category when it is traded, that is, there is an associated transaction involving money or some other means of exchange. The case of domestic labour, however, illustrates the difficulties that can arise; many argue that the non-traded value of the work of homebound spouses should be included in a nation's estimate of GDP.

A related dilemma is that the elements are not static or fixed members of one or other category. Clearly financial capital can be translated into goods and services, and yet will remain within the broad category of 'economic' capital. Similarly, domestic labour that changes from being unpaid to paid work could thereby move from social to economic capital without any real change in the activities involved. These types of problems, it must be re-stressed, are independent of the measurement problem that we will return to later in the book.

CAPITAL DYNAMICS

Of course the fact that activities 'move' between categories is part of the far broader issue of how to handle exchanges between capital accounts. Indeed, capital movements are a way of framing the core issues underlying this entire book and the whole field of corporate accountability. There are an enormous number of capital transactions when a company employs more people or uses more timber to generate goods and services that are sold for profit. At the first level, what is happening is that the company is using environmental and social capital to generate economic capital. Environmental capital may be bought using financial capital (a sub-set of economic capital). Similarly, elements of social capital may be rented using financial capital. But this is not the end of the story. The second level of effects of the company's activities may be the generation of new social capital; for example new skills, networks and organizations, and sometimes even laws. The activities may even lead to new environmental capital being created, such as new forests or existing forms of environmental capital becoming accessible for the production of economic and social wealth and outcomes, such as renewable energy resources.

Two distinct definitions of sustainability emerged during the 1980s and early 1990s. The first asserted that actions that were consistent with sustainable development neither reduced nor did damage to the world's stock of environmental capital. This 'strong' version of sustainability is perhaps most clearly articulated in the system conditions of the Natural Step. The second version, which became known as 'weak sustainability' stated that there could well be trade-offs between different elements of environmental stock, and indeed between environmental and other capitals, ie the social and economic. What was important was that the overall system remained both viable now and in the future, and satisfied human needs.

The distinction between the two views of sustainable development is profound. The first argues that any action that degrades the environment is *necessarily* a move away from sustainable development *irrespective* of its economic and social effects. The environment in its current form is sacred and forms the sole benchmark against which all decisions and actions are assessed. The second offers a permissive approach that argues for a multi-dimensional set of objectives, of which the protection of the environment is but one.

The approach implicit in the multi-capital model is what has historically been the 'weak sustainability' proposition.[23] This model is useful and

Box 9.5 *Weak and Strong Sustainability*[24]

The principle of *weak sustainability* suggests that what matters is the maintenance of the capital stock overall, not the amount of individual components of it. That means that there are no theoretical limits to substituting one form of capital for another (eg pristine forests being cut down to create jobs and new economic wealth) assuming most benefits can be demonstrated to outweigh the costs.

The principle of *strong sustainability*, on the other hand, holds that the substitution between different types of capital is imperfect at best, and that real sustainability depends on the individual components of different capital stocks, as well as on its overall level. There are clearly no substitutes for some of the 'services' (climate regulation, fertility building in the soil, etc) that the natural world provides.

---

relevant only if we are concerned with exploring the nature of the decisions being taken that lead to trade-offs between the various capital accounts, at least in the short to medium term. This can be justified on a number of grounds. Central is that there is no reason to assume, and many reasons to suspect the argument, that the protection of the environment today at the cost of social inequity yields a more sustainable development path. Put another way, there is every reason to argue that investments in social capital that secures livelihoods, builds human competencies and enhances harmonious relationships between peoples may offer essential foundations in securing a sustainable development path. It does follow from this that we cannot *automatically* assume that less profit today in order to protect the environment is a good thing. It may well be, but certainly not axiomatically.

This does not mean that every capital item is tradable within the constraints of limited knowledge and technology. The 'precautionary principle' is clearly relevant here. But it does mean that we are essentially concerned with the terms on which business translates one capital into others, *even where this is aimed at preserving certain types of capital.*

MODELLING SUSTAINABLE DEVELOPMENT

Any effective approach to modelling societal and environmental performance in the context of sustainable development needs to show how we impact on the various 'capital accounts' from which we draw, contribute to, and ultimately of which we are a part. This means moving beyond cash-flow accounting for our activities towards a balance sheet approach that allows us to understand a little about our longer-term impacts. It also means deciding which are the key forms of capital that count. This opens the door to addressing the question of how best to do such counting where the transactions or transfers between different capital accounts are complex and multi-layered.

A simple framework has been proposed here that retains the three basic forms of capital – social, environmental and economic – each of which can be sub-divided in various ways. However, within this, economic is seen as a sub-set of the social, and is relevant only in that it contributes to social and environmental outcomes.[25]

Critical in operationalizing the framework is an acceptance of the many possible routes through which organizations and societies can contribute to sustainable development. There are few if any fixed assumptions as to what kinds of transactions can or should not be seen in a positive light in this sense. We simply cannot get away from the challenge of valuation given diverse needs and interests. This standpoint takes us further in establishing that any meaningful accountability framework that takes sustainable development as its starting point will need to address centrally the question of *how* decisions are made, and by whom, or in other words, questions of governance. It is this domain to which we can therefore now turn in considering what we mean by the *civil corporation*.

CHAPTER 10

Sustainability as the Art of the Possible

> *Corporate Sustainability is a business approach to create long-term shareholder value by embracing opportunities and managing risks deriving from economic, environmental and social developments.*

Sustainability Asset Management[1]

DEBUNKING THE SUSTAINABLE BUSINESSES

There is a story of a person who, on offering help to someone she encounters one dark night looking for something under a streetlight, is told, 'Yes, I dropped it over there, on the other side of the road.' Puzzled, the would-be Samaritan enquires, 'Why then are we looking here under the streetlight?' to which the person responds without hesitation, 'Because it is light here, of course, and I have no hope of finding it over there in the dark.'

This age-old story mirrors how we deal with the relationship between business and sustainable development. We speak of 'sustainable business' because it seems to combine the laudable aim of addressing social and environmental challenges of our time with the accurate view that business has to 'do it' for us to have a chance of success. While understandable, this imaginative leap encourages approaches that in practice create more confusion than good. It is simply inaccurate and misleading to talk about a 'sustainable business'. The 'sustainable' in sustainable development is just not the same as the 'sustaining' of a particular business, *irrespective of its social and environmental performance*. The latter is a macro, system-level, condition. The former, on the other hand, is a micro condition to do with keeping an organization going, at best doing some good in the process and not too much harm.

We can and should conceptualize sustainable development as best we can, and make our concepts as useful as possible, as the previous chapter has sought to achieve. However, we do not know enough about the system to understand the total or perhaps even the critical dimensions of the relationship between the overall activities of one organization and the whole. We do not and cannot therefore really understand whether a company is 'more or less sustainable' in terms of its long-term impact on the overall system. This may seem strange or unhelpfully theoretical, particularly to those with a bias towards the environmental dimension of sustainable development. Surely, you would argue, we do know when a company is increasing or reducing its impact on the environment. This may indeed be the case for simple, short-term impacts, for example where a company reduces its level of pollution or achieves resource-use savings. But things become far less clear when long-term impacts are being considered, and where the social and economic dimensions of sustainable development come into play. At this point, the real dilemmas of trade-offs appear, as do the practicalities of what it is actually possible for the

Box 10.1 *Debunking the Sustainable Enterprise*[2]

The United Nations Environment Programme (UNEP) hosted a seminar on 'sustainable enterprise' in October 1998. Amongst its conclusions were the following:

Conceptual

Sustainable development is a concept that is dynamic, requiring a built-in flexibility in its application. Lessons from previous decades would indicate that we cannot be sure we have the right answers for future decades. As a 'meta-concept' similar in nature to 'justice' or 'democracy', the concept of 'sustainability' should be expected to change over time, becoming, in all likelihood, increasingly demanding.

Societal

A firm cannot be considered on its own to be 'sustainable' in isolation from its economic, social and environmental context. Sustainability is a holistic concept. Making the transition to sustainable development is a societal question that is answered at the level of policy.

Cultural/contextual

Environment is interpreted differently by different cultures and in different countries. It is over-ambitious to attempt to define what is a sustainable enterprise since the meaning of sustainable development is deeply rooted in culture.

Strategic

Sustainable development is defined in the aggregate. While it may be more possible to determine the sustainability of industries (firms in the aggregate), it is more difficult to determine the sustainability of individual companies, although the *direction* that is needed for a company to move towards sustainability can be determined.

Box 10.2 *Uncomfortable Trade-offs, Incomparable Valuations*

Advocates of the so-called Environmental Kuznets Curve like Grossman and Kruger have long argued that it is only by reaching certain levels of economic affluence that nations and communities will be willing to invest in environmental protection and conservation.[3] As Bhagwati argues:

'The fear is widespread among environmentalists that free trade increases economic growth and that growth harms the environment. That fear is misplaced. Growth enables governments to tax and to raise resources for a variety of objectives, including the abatement of pollution and the general protection of the environment. . . In short, environmentalists are in error.'[4]

This view is also shared by Frances Cairncross: 'As poor countries grow richer – and trade is a powerful source of wealth – their environmental standards will rise.'[5]

Empirical support for this proposition has long been put into question, most recently by Amory Lovins and others.[6] However, the fact that examples abound of cheap environmentally friendly production technologies and processes has not reduced the power of the political stance that was so vividly played out at the Seattle meeting of the WTO in November 1999 and summed up by Grossman:

'Attention to environmental issues is a luxury poor countries cannot afford. . . An open world trading system contributes to the prosperity of less developed countries and helps them get to the point of mandating and enforcing environmental standards similar to those in the developed world.'[7]

The problem is that it is not possible to predict (or at least agree on the relative merits of many different predictions) the impact of discrete actions today on the future shape of the system as a whole. This is not merely a technical issue of degrees of complexity that can be resolved through better data and more computing power. It is a problem of valuation, where we are *inherently unable* to determine how people as yet unborn will value the different options they face, and the starting points that we have created for them through our own choices today.

corporation to do at any point in time. These trade-offs at best can be observed at a macro level, such as those underlying the debate about environment and economic growth, summarized in Box 10.2.

REAL CHOICE OR NO CHOICE

Mark Moody-Stuart spells out Shell International's vision in the *Shell Report 1999: People, Planet and Profits*:

My colleagues and I are totally committed to a business strategy that
generates profits while contributing to the wellbeing of the planet and its
people. *We see no alternative.*[8]

In the same report, the Chair of SustainAbility Ltd, John Elkington,
reinforces this perspective in stating:

In February 1999, Shell reported its worst-ever financial results, in terms of
overall profitability. Chairman Mark Moody-Stuart warned that Shell faces
one of the toughest challenges in its history... Short-sighted shareholders
might argue that Shell must drop distractions like sustainable development
and concentrate on the real bottom line. But the real lesson is that business
success now requires economic, environmental, and social value added.[9]

On 15 December 1999, Royal Dutch Shell announced that it was to shed
about 18 per cent of its workforce, about 18,000 jobs, within 12 months.
The company also signalled its intention to buy-back up to US$10 billion-
worth of its own shares. The announcement, reported a *Financial Times*
article:

...pushed Shell Transport and Trading shares 5.4 per cent higher in London
to 499½... Mr Moody-Stuart said Shell... reaffirmed its commitment to meet
its target for Return on Capital Employed – a key indicator – of 14 per cent
by 2001.[10]

What is the relationship between these statements, decisions and actions,
and outcomes? Is this an example of a company cynically manipulating
the public imagination with pronouncements about its commitment to
sustainable development? Do Shell's actions indicate that the *real* story
is about short-term profitability achieved through externalizing social
and economic costs that are then borne by departing workers, taxpayers
through increased welfare payments, and society as a whole? Or is this
a case of a company doing what it can to balance competing demands?
In this case, the demands are between its long-term aspirations to build
business success based on its contribution to sustainable development, and
the short-term pressures of the financial markets to deliver shareholder
value in line with market expectations, benchmarked against companies
that make no such longer-term commitments. A further, more recent, FT
article entitled 'Oil's Giants Vow to Punch Their Weight' summed up this
dilemma in comparing Shell's two main sector rivals, ExxonMobil and
BP:

BP has staked out a 'progressive' public stance and image on controversial
issues such as global warming that contrasts sharply with the conservatism
of ExxonMobil... (but)... is there a danger that the focus on short-term
performance could undermine the long-term growth of the companies
involved?[11]

It is, furthermore, worth asking the question of how these cases differ (if at all) from those of the 1960s' icons of ethical business, such as Ben & Jerry's, The Body Shop and Levi Strauss. All three of these companies have implemented major redundancy programmes over recent years in efforts to enhance profitability. Indeed, how do these activities of publicly listed companies differ (if at all) from the decision by the small, British, Christian, fair trade company, Traidcraft, to shed one third of its staff in order, according to its then managing director, Phil Angiers, to bring the business to the necessary level of financial viability for survival?[12]

There are, of course, considerable differences between these cases. Equally, however, there are some important underlying similarities that need to be appreciated in seeking to understand the businesses involved and the roots of the decisions made. The real issue is what choices the businesses really had. This can be boiled down to three fundamental questions:

(1) What were its short- and long-term options given its external context?
(2) What would have been the implications, both for itself as a business and in terms of social and environmental outcomes, of the various options and in particular of not taking steps to secure short-term profitability?
(3) What was the businesses knowledge and understanding of its options at the time when decisions had to be made, and the state of its relevant competencies and overall ability to address the different available options?

These questions, of course, take us back to the three pathways discussed in an earlier chapter. The ability of a corporation to carve out a viable business that takes it along the Mecca pathway depends critically on how it handles the challenges and opportunities embodied in these three questions. The answers to these questions are critical since they define the benchmark against which these companies' performance should be judged.

Robert Fisher, at the time a board member of GAP Inc, was asked the following question following his plenary offering at the 1999 conference of BSR in San Francisco:

I have a lot of difficulty reconciling the fact that the GAP is worth billions and these people are living in poverty... One question that came to my mind is, given GAP's profitability, why not just start your own factories where you have control?[13]

Fisher responded without hesitation:

...regarding owning factories. You know, every company makes their own strategic decisions and has to decide what businesses they want to be in and what businesses they don't want to be in, and the manufacturing of merchandise in factories and running factories is not a business that we want to be in. We made that decision and that's the decision we're going to keep with and we're not gonna own factories.[14]

The reply brought an audible gasp from the 800 or so assembled part-icipants, most of whom it must be said were from the business community. Fisher's response clearly signalled that he viewed social performance as being at least one step (and probably considerably more) removed from business strategy. Strategy, his response clarified on behalf of GAP, was not up for debate through the spectacles of how best to secure acceptable labour standards.

Fisher might have answered very differently. He could have said that there was in his view a trade-off between financial returns and factory ownership. He might have continued that the company was under pressure from the financial markets to deliver financial returns that its management felt could not be achieved within a factory-owned business model. He could have emphasized that GAP was a very different business to those companies that had pursued the factory-owned approach, for example the world's largest toy manufacturer, Mattel Inc. He might even have explained that lower financial returns would endanger bonuses, share options, and ultimately risk a take-over bid if share prices fell too far. If Fisher had given these types of explanation in the short time he had on the podium, then it would have become clearer what trade-offs the company was really making, and where social performance fitted into these trade-offs.

Kevin Sweeny, then with the progressive textiles company Patagonia, invested a major part of his presentation at a meeting in Canada in 1998 hosted by the International Centre for Human Rights and Democratic Development in seeking to explain why it really was difficult to monitor labour standards down often long and complex supply chains. Neil Kearney, the Secretary General of the International Textiles and Garment Workers Union, offered the following harsh response:

> If a retailer can ensure that the stitching along the seam of every pair of trousers delivered to it are accurate to the millimetre, then it seems to me quite unbelievable that they cannot ensure that basic and internationally agreed standards in the workplace are adhered to.[15]

GAP and Patagonia are quite different companies. Yet both Fisher's and Sweeny's viewpoints can be seen as coming down to 'we do what the company has chosen to do', rather than 'what the company has to do given their situation'. For GAP, there may indeed be very sound reasons that make it impossible or at least undesirable for them to own their own production facilities. However, that was not what was said. Equally, Sweeny may well have been right in explaining just how difficult it is to monitor labour standards. But it was a viewpoint easily dismissed by Kearney because it bore the hallmark of 'we know what is right and what is possible'. Neither response was an acceptably fulsome account of the underlying business strategy and the alternatives. As a result, both speakers and their respective companies lost credibility in the eyes of their audiences.

FREEDOMS, CAPACITIES AND EFFECTS

Debate about corporate citizenship focuses as much on the question of choice than on the matter of impact. This is not because civil activists or indeed business people are not interested in outcomes. It is because people quite naturally focus on influencing the people or organizations that they believe are able to change the event or process in question. No one (so far) has put pressure on Reebok to seek to influence the International Monetary Fund (IMF), simply because the company is not seen to have any influence over that stately body. People, on the other hand, do pressure Reebok to increase wages in the factories of their suppliers *because they believe* that the company could do so within their current business model. BP, similarly, is lobbied by activists to pressure the Colombian or Angolan governments to make better use of oil royalties and find ways to reduce the incidence of human rights abuses precisely because it is assumed that BP might well be in a position to shift the behaviour of these governments.

Patagonia's Kevin Sweeny went to great lengths in his Canadian address to explain why increasing wages in supplier factories had major implications for overall costs. He argued that although factory labour costs made up only a small percentage of the total product cost, every cent of increased production cost had roughly a fourfold impact on the product price given the structure of the value-chain. Furthermore, he continued, there had to be comparable wage rates for workers producing for international and domestic markets, and for high-price branded, and low-cost unbranded, products. Paying higher wages to those producing one particular brand for export, he concluded, would create an impossibly chaotic and inequitable situation both within and between factories.

Sweeny was clearly right in highlighting some of the dilemmas of sharing the financial rewards of successful branding directly with the workers who produced the goods. It is unlikely, however, that his explanation would be acceptable to many as a justification for inaction. Surely, responded union and other labour activists, it must be possible for innovative companies like Patagonia, working with other corporations buying from the same suppliers, to overcome exactly these kinds of impediments to securing fair wages and conditions. Once again the issue was not only whether the final outcome would be acceptable, but also what the company should be expected to be *able* to do, and how this matched what it *actually did* in the circumstances.

Investment and Risk Hierarchies

A corporation's approach to addressing any challenge or opportunity, including those embodied in any vision of sustainable development, depends on how it deals with investments and risks. As Sustainability Asset Management (SAM) argues: 'Corporate Sustainability is a business approach to create long-term shareholder value by embracing opportunities and managing risks deriving from economic, environmental and social developments.'[16]

In applying this principle to BMW, for example, SAM sets a matrix of external risk and opportunities, and benchmarks the company against what it considers to be industry averages in handling both.

Box 10.3 *SAM's View of BMW's Strategic Opportunities and Risks*[17]

Strategic Opportunities

Manufacturing competitiveness is supported by the company's push towards build-to-order. The new Mini will contribute to implementing BMW's small car strategy

Major project under way to analyse the latest technologies and environmental costs of dismantling, recycling, and treating residue of scrap cars

Has pioneered an innovative process for final paint coating powder that produces no waste, needs no solvents, saves money, resources and protects the environment

Has implemented excellent programmes for further employee education, motivation and the possibility to take part in the company's financial success

Strategic Risks

Improved the fuel efficiency of cars by one-third since 1979

Was the first company in the world to introduce a car-recycling standard including guidelines to design

Components for improved recycling. In addition, BMW takes back used cars

All production plants are certified according to ISO14001 or EMAS

Uncertain whether BMW is as advanced in its fuel cell research as some other competitors.

SAM provides a similar overview of those companies that it considers to be leading their relevant sector in key aspects of 'corporate sustainability', such as the Japanese conglomerate, Teijin Ltd, as set out in Box 10.4.

There is a hierarchy in the *degrees of freedoms* facing any business that defines what they are able to do at a particular point in time. The degrees of freedom facing any particular company are defined by: (a) *general factors*, for example technological opportunities, competitor strategies and public

Box 10.4 *SAM's View of Teijin Ltd's Strategic Opportunities and Risks*[18]

Strategic Opportunities

Streamlined and amended the composition of the Board of Directors to ensure fair and transparent
Management and decision-making
Reorganizing head office personnel system to facilitate more effective strategic planning and ensure efficient use of human resources
Set ultimate environmental goals – Achievement of Zeros – attainment of zero emissions
Is a member of the Japan Responsible Care Council and has 4 of 6 factories certified under ISO14001

Strategic Risks

Introduced a ground-breaking recycling process for recovering useful substances from manufacturing
Process drainage, thereby reducing the volume of sludge significantly
Reforming its management system, to focus on increasing shareholder value, reinforcing consolidated
Group management, strict adherence to corporate ethics, and enhancing environmental, safety and health records
Established an independent Advisory Board, which monitors the performance of executives and advises on management issues

---

pressure; (b) *company-specific factors,* such as availability of finance, the quality of leadership and overall corporate competencies. Our views as to what a company should be expected to do therefore need to be grounded in an understanding of its real options given its external environment and internal technical and organizational competencies.

It is useful to identify a hierarchy of potential responses that any business might make. At the lowest level are those responses that involve *negligible investment and insignificant risk.* These are responses to opportunities where it is possible to reap social and/or environmental gains with neither increased net costs (and possibly net financial gains) nor notable uncertainty or risk. Paul Hawken and Amory and L Hunter Lovins provide a wealth of illustrations of these 'no brainers' in their publication, *Natural Capitalism.* For example, they argue that:

Chipmaking plants are consistently designed so poorly that most of their energy can be saved with 100-plus per cent typical after-tax returns on retrofit investments, better operations, and faster, cheaper construction of new plants.[19]

Similarly they argue,

> Managers can't afford *not* to retrofit buildings to save energy, because doing so can also make workers more productive. If labour productivity goes up just 1 per cent, that will produce the same bottom-line benefits as *eliminating* the entire energy bill.[20]

A failure to take advantage of these opportunities is almost always because of a lack of requisite internal competencies, which often revolve around management weaknesses that feed through into operational limitations, rather than technical shortfalls per se.

A second level of responsiveness involves *significant, but still relatively low risk, investment*. These are where some investment is required to secure social and environmental gains, but the net positive financial returns are significant and more or less assured. Many of the obvious examples here involve environmental investments, for example in energy-saving equipment, or systems and procedures for recycling. The British retail chain, B&Q, has made significant investments in training its employees to better serve disabled customers. The impact has in the event been a notable increase in sales and profitability, both through increased spend by disabled people and through the broader customer service quality effects of the training. BP and Shell's investment in internalizing carbon emissions trading would be a further case in point, where there is little risk, certainly not to the core business and its profitability, and yet the investment is significant.

Figure 10.1 *Hierarchy of Opportunities, Investment and Risks*

A third level of responsiveness involves both *significant investment and risk*. Here there may, for example, be an external reputational as well as financial face to the investment and the emergence of significant risk of negative financial returns. Codes of conduct covering labour standards in global supply chains would largely fit into this category. In this field there are under-specified direct financial costs that have to be borne somewhere in the value-chain. Furthermore, there are potential reputational risks as well as gains associated with having a more transparent supply chain in the face of having made often over-ambitious commitments. There has (at least to date) been an asymmetry in the structure of potential rewards. Codes of conduct can assist in the avoidance of significant reputational risk that could impact on the financial bottom line. At the same time, there is little evidence that good performance is consistently rewarded in the market for products and services by customers being willing to shift *towards* a particular company or brand as opposed to being willing to *shift away* where poor ethical performance is demonstrated. This level is clearly more complex than the straight win–wins. However, it generally involves short and medium rather than longer-term pay-offs that are relatively simple to both predict and quantify.

The final level of responsiveness involves major *strategic investment and associated risks*. Here the potential degrees of freedom may be great, but in practice they have to be created through market-making leadership. An example of this would be BP and Shell's significant investments in renewables, signalling their long-term strategies to reduce their dependence on carbon-based products. Another case would be moves within the automobile industry to push forward major investments in vehicles that use different fuels, such as the case of BMW highlighted above. A less-than-

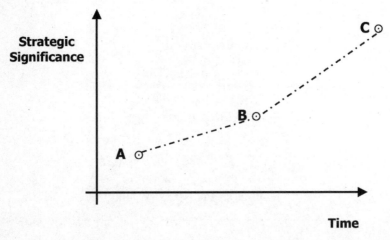

Figure 10.2 *Linking Tactics and Strategy*

successful case, at least to date, would be Monsanto's commitment to genetically modified agricultural products.

These differing levels of opportunity, risk and investment are rarely distinct choices for a company to make. Rather, companies seek to construct a cocktail of all of them that link short-term tactics to longer-term strategy, mitigating where possible the risks of the long-term strategy by enhancing the potential gains from short-term tactics. In this sense the hierarchy can be seen as existing on a time-continuum, both in planning and actual terms.

Hierarchies of Effect

Businesses do not only have differing degrees of freedom, but also different potential and actual levels of impacts depending on both their size and importance, and the level and type of investment in change being made. At the simplest level, companies will make investments that, even where successful, yield *in-market effects*. Most companies are able to make some adjustments that fall within their existing business model and process, and so that also fit within the existing norms of the market they operate within. For example, the decisions by Rio Tinto and other resource and energy companies to build elements of the UN Declaration of Human Rights into their core business principles do not in themselves shift the basic operations of the markets in which they exist, even though this may of course happen over time.[21]

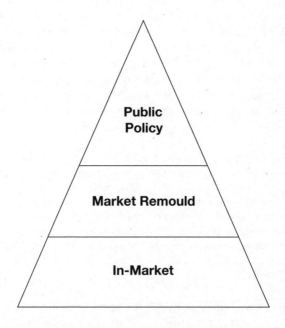

Figure 10.3 *Hierarchy of Influence*

At the next level, *market remould*, some companies make adjustments to the social and environmental dimensions of their business model that levers change at the level of the market. Where larger companies make shifts, they can often affect the wider markets within which they operate, and indeed other markets. The Body Shop, through a combination of a successful brand and product mix and a consistent powerful message against animal testing, has succeeded in shifting the mid-range body care market in which it had a powerful market niche. It is now difficult if not impossible, certainly in the UK and some other markets where The Body Shop has been most influential, to market body care products that do not explicitly state that they have not been tested on animals. Similarly, the move by Sainsbury's and other retailers in the UK to create the ETI, and by Liz Claiborne and other apparel and footwear companies in the US to create the FLA, created immense pressure on other companies to join, including those who traditionally have carved out their own pathway, such as Levi Strauss and M&S.

The third and final level, *public policy and frameworks*, is the highest level of influence, where companies affect the institutional architecture within which their markets exist and that dictate the legal and other frameworks that define how they are permitted to operate.[22] This might involve moving from good corporate citizenship practices into law, the possibility set out in the Mecca pathway. Suez, a French conglomerate with activities in energy, waste, water and communications employing 200,000 world-wide, built a national network of relationships in France with local public authorities to help young people suffering long-term unemployment back into work. The success of this approach has gained recognition from the government, elements of which have been incorporated into a recent regulation passed concerning social exclusion.[23] Alternatively, public policy influence may be more contentious, with many seeing it as having more to do with the Desert than the Mecca pathway. The Corporate Europe Observatory (COP), for example, concerned at the strength of the corporate lobby, records in its report on the COP-6 climate change negotiations at the Hague conference in late 2000:

> Over 1000 industry lobbyists attended the last climate summit of similar importance, COP-3 in Kyoto. The US, responsible for 25 per cent of the world's greenhouse gas emissions, is predictably home to some of the most aggressive corporate climate campaigns. Beyond the well-established major business groups like the Business Roundtable (BRT), the US Council for International Business (USCIB) and the American Petroleum Institute (API), corporate virulence towards climate change has also given birth to single-issue groups like the Global Climate Coalition (GCC) and the secretive Climate Council.[24]

For better or worse, public policy is for some – principally larger – corporations by far the most significant route through which it impacts on sustainable development.

Sustainability as the Art of the Possible

A corporation's degrees of freedom must therefore be understood in dynamic terms. It is not only a question of whether there are short-term, win–win opportunities, or potential gains that can be achieved at low risk and cost. The critical issue is more often the need for a company to satisfy the current market conditions while simultaneously investing in strategic change that may allow it to open up new opportunities that are consistent with sustainable development and competitive needs. The poor financial performance of, for example, many parts of the cooperative movement, does not make it any easier for them to be at the vanguard of social and environmental change. Similarly for the likes of Ben & Jerry's and The Body Shop. It is therefore hardly surprising that Shell, in exploring the shift from the 'carbon past' to the 'renewables future' describes the middle bit as the 'messy transition'.[25]

From this perspective, the statements, summarized earlier in this chapter, by Shell's Mark Moody-Stuart in support of sustainable development are not *necessarily* inconsistent with the decision to make 18,000 people redundant if, for example:

- the very viability of Shell was threatened by maintaining a cost structure that was higher than the industry norm; or
- Shell might have been taken over if its share price had fallen too far as a result of reduced profits and dividends, which again might have endangered the commitment to key aspects of sustainable development.

At the same time, there is clearly a trade-off involved in reducing costs through redundancies in order to secure the continued viability of the company by sustaining the level of short-term dividends. This trade-off is perpetuated as long as the corporation's profitability is not damaged by externalizing social and economic costs in this way. As the ex-President of the Jessie Smith Noyes Foundation, Stephen Viederman, argues: 'It will always be in the financial interests of companies to externalize costs until we establish laws that prevent this.'[26] This brings us straight back to the conclusion that Shell and indeed other companies will be forced over time to make these trade-offs (the 'Korten Effect' pushing us along the Desert pathway) unless they are able to build a competitiveness model that is rewarded for internalizing social and environmental costs (the 'Goyder Effect' helping us along the Mecca or at least the Oasis pathways).

Virtuous but uncompetitive companies will not be part of our future.[27] Our understanding of and practical approach to dealing with business's roles in forging sustainable development must lie in the art of the possible. The question then remains, how can we understand and best guide the 'possible' towards addressing the aspirational goals underlying sustainable development?

CHAPTER 11

Civil Learning

When I speak about civil society, I don't mean only non-governmental organizations, though they are a very important part of it. I also mean universities, foundations, labour unions and - yes - private corporations.

Kofi Annan, UN Secretary General[1]

CIVIL BENCHMARKS

Corporations need to be judged on the basis of how they perform relative to what they are able to do given their context and competencies.

It is unreasonable to deem companies to have failed if they *are* in fact doing all they can, and yet still cannot effect significant change or create noticeable social and environmental benefits. For example, it would be unreasonable to condemn Novo Nordisk, a major producer of insulin products, for the immediate lack of access to life-saving products for many millions of cash-poor diabetics. But it might be reasonable to enquire whether its research programme has sought to identify cheaper alternatives, or focused mainly on the life-style benefits of different and less intrusive forms of insulin delivery.[2] On the other hand, it would be reasonable to down-rate a company's performance that is doing good things but far less than it could do given its circumstances and competencies. For example, Philip Morris may indeed have fine philanthropic programmes, develop effective low-cost credit systems for small tobacco farmers in developing countries, or be a leader in social reporting. But this would simply not count for many concerned with the health effects of smoking.

Performance benchmarks are needed that calibrate what has been achieved in relation to what *could* have been achieved in the circumstances. Critical here is that such an approach bases its assessment on the will and ability to mobilize learning into relevant knowledge so that it can be and is effectively applied. In this way, the over-arching aspirational pathway and outcome of sustainable development can be meaningfully translated into a dynamic organizational form with real traction in terms of performance assessment, decision-making and accountability.

It is through this way of approaching the challenge of how best to direct the business community in pursuit of sustainable development that we arrive finally at the idea of the civil corporation. Civil has at least two possible connotations. First is the idea of 'being civil', a loose notion at best that suggests an adherence to the norms and expectations associated with reasonable behaviour. This is essentially normative in describing something that is deemed good. Second is an analytic perspective that describes 'civil society' as being the collective of associational relationships that form between individuals in pursuit of (varied) common interests. Axel Hadenius and Fredrik Uggla, for example, define 'civil society' as: 'a public space between the state and individual citizens where the latter can develop autonomous, organized and collective activities of the most varied nature'.[3] Larry Diamond confirms this but challenges the more limited institutional view of civil society, arguing instead that it is:

> ...the realm of organized social life that is voluntary, self-generating, (largely) self-supporting; autonomous from the state and bound by a legal order or set of shared rules... not some mere residual category synonymous with 'society' or with everything that is not the state or the formal political system.[4]

These two views of 'civil' are of course linked. David Korten reminds us of the Aristotelian roots of contemporary notions of 'civil society':

> ...civil society is an ethical-political community of free and equal citizens who by mutual consent agree to live under a system of law that expresses the norms and values they share.[5]

Such engagement, from this perspective, is not for personal gain, but rooted in a sense of civic duty, or even a desire to contribute to the well-being of society at large. 'Civic participation is not driven by the quest to increase mutual advantage but rather by a desire to be a responsible contributor to the life of the community.'[6]

Gavin Andersson extends and in a sense concretizes this normative view of civil society in describing it as:

> organizations that do not organize for political power or the pursuit of profit. They have been described as 'the connective tissue of a democratic political culture'; private organizations which work for the social good and which can serve as the means to counter excesses of the state as also the whim of the market and the power of private shareholders.[7]

Korten reinforces this view in stressing that 'civil society' is not a particular part of society, but a way in which a society might work.

> The term civil society refers to a type of society... in contrast to its contemporary usage, which refers merely to the sector that is neither government nor business and led by not-for-profit organizations.[8]

'Civil society' from these perspectives therefore embodies at least two key propositions:

(1) *Values and purpose* that concern the pursuit of individual and collective perceptions of the 'common good', although certainly not necessarily what all might consider as such.
(2) A way of *organizing*, as reflected in the notion of freely chosen, associational relationships underpinned by common values and driven, at least in part, by common purpose.

It is the relationship between this, very distilled, view of civil society and the learning-based approach to understanding and guiding the relationship between business and sustainable development that sets the scene for the *civil corporation*.

THE MATTER OF PURPOSE

It is a given to most social activists and writers on civil society that the business community is not part of civil society. The main reason given for this is the view that the primary purpose of business is the pursuit of profits rather than a 'collective social interest'. This critical distinction underpinned, for example, comments by Nicola Bullard, the Deputy Director of Focus on the Global South, on Kofi Annan's moves to build closer ties between the UN and the business community.

> In his opening speech to the Geneva 2000 Forum on the eve of the Social Summit, Mr Annan told the predominantly NGO audience that 'people are poor not because of too much globalization but too little'. And, just to drive home the point, he added that private corporations are no less a part of civil society than NGOs![9]

It is understandable that most see it as a simple truism that business is driven by financial interests. Financial returns to capital clearly underpin the core measures of success applied to many businesses, notably publicly listed corporations. Short-termism within the financial markets, already discussed in earlier chapters, consolidates the importance of these measures and their implications for corporate decision-making, behaviour and outcomes.

What is perhaps somewhat stranger is the equally pervasive view that business should be understood as *necessarily* having financial interests as the primary and dominant purpose. Civil society leaders are particularly adamant about this. Indeed, one such leader concluded in a closed workshop on the topic that this was not just the way things were, but the way things *should* be:

> We all have different roles in society. Business exists to make money, and ours is to ensure that they do this according to acceptable rules of the game. It just confuses the picture when some argue that business can have a social purpose beyond making money.[10]

This view, although understandable, is both historically and aspirationally suspect. It is one thing to argue that companies have to make money to survive, but quite another to argue the far stronger position that companies exist exclusively to make profits for shareholders. This is of course not news for those who have long argued that the growth of managerial power has usurped the critical basis for business's accountability to its shareholders. However, there are several more fundamental senses in which financial returns to capital are not the sole or even necessarily the central aim of many businesses.

(1) The large number of 'business vehicles' designed specifically to deliver social and environmental 'goods'. Co-operatives, for example, do business on behalf of over 150 million members worldwide. Many of these were initiated to provide affordable and high quality goods and services and livelihoods to their, largely lower income, members.[11]
(2) The burgeoning non-profit sector comprises an extraordinary assortment of organizations designed to deliver social and environmental benefits. Increasingly this sector includes many enterprises providing goods and services. The measured financial income flows through this sector in most developed countries amount to anything up to 3–5 per cent of GDP. The non-profit sector is currently one of the most rapidly growing parts of many economies.
(3) The millions of small businesses that are vehicles for securing the independent livelihood of the families that initiate, own and run them. Financial rewards are of course important to these families, but this is in order to secure the future of the family, first and foremost a social aim.

What these non-trivial examples highlight is that not all businesses have the primary purpose of making money, even though they all have to make money one way or another to survive. The typical response to this line of argument is that this may indeed be true for these particular categories of business, but that this is not a useful way of looking at the main rump of the corporate community. The argument that corporations are solely interested in financial returns is situated in a view of them as institutions that have unitary purpose, or at least a clear hierarchy of purposes. So, the argument runs, it is all very well to say that 'corporations are full of people, and people have diverse visions and interests', but this denies the fact that they are working for an institution that is structurally driven by its location within a capitalist system. From this view, while individuals may struggle and at times succeed to get companies to do good things, this will only be possible so long as their vision and actions do not significantly challenge the corporation's primary purpose (or, put positively, can advance the achievement of the corporation's primary purpose).

There are two interrelated problems with this view. First, if one follows the line set out above that the interests of the owners of capital will always ultimately win out, then completeness requires that one turns to examine the behaviour of the real owners of capital, individuals for example who own insurance policies and pensions. The dramatic growth of socially responsible investment is testament to the fact that social and environmental criteria can enter into investment decisions in a manner entirely consistent with perceptions of the wider 'public good'. If consumers are willing to buy ethically, employee motivation is fired by socially responsible behaviour, and communities make hell for companies that behave badly, then it increasingly follows that it is in the investors' interests to take these factors into account. Just as Bob Monks and Jeff Gates argue for the need to erode the 'market failure' of over-played managerial power, so then it must follow that the failure of the interests of the ultimate owners to shine through the institutional mask of fund managers is a market failure that needs to be overcome. More generally, to argue that this all simply means that profit-making corporations are just being smarter is arithmetically correct, but adds little insight to the fact that corporations *in practice* act essentially as mediators of their stakeholder interests with certain conditions that underpin their continued operation, one of which is financial viability.

The second level to the argument supports the view that corporations can, and do, embody significant non-financial interests. In challenging the view of corporations as unitary entities, this goes beyond the previous argument that corporations can be concerned for social and environmental issues for the instrumental reasons of enhancing financial performance. Again, this is far from a new view. John Kenneth Galbraith, writing in the 1960s, argued that strategic decision-making in large technocracies is deeply influenced by the 'distortions' introduced by the vested interests of technocrats as information flowed up the organization towards the most senior ranks.[12] CEOs make rational decisions on the basis of what emerges from this distorted process. The corporate world today is very different from the experience of the world that informed Galbraith's early thinking. Critical is the shift away from deep hierarchies towards flatter organizations, and the impact of information and communication technologies on the pattern of internal and external communications. But Galbraith's essential argument still holds, where the geographic, legal, cultural and linguistic extension and dispersion of the corporation all add layers of diverse meaning to the information on which basic decisions are based. Corporations are in effect made up of hundreds of communities of interest, and many thousands more if external as well as internal stakeholders are included.

To argue that corporations *necessarily* have the primary purpose of making money is a sociologically weak proposition that glosses over their complex structures and organizational dynamics. It resembles the equally flawed psychology embodied in the view of conventional economics that depicts us as all as 'economic beings' who rationally maximize our personal utilities. At best it is a weak approximation; at worst it is an ideological fixture that constrains innovation and progressive change.

PAVLOV'S CURSE

In early 1999, Joseph Ha, a Vice President of Nike and Special Adviser to the company's CEO, wrote a letter to the President of the Vietnam General Confederation of Labour in which he wrote:

> A few US human rights groups, as well as a Vietnamese refugee who is engaging in human rights activities, are not friends of Vietnam... They target Nike because Nike is a high profile company and a major creator of jobs in Vietnam. Nevertheless, this is the first step for their political goal, which is to create a so-called 'democratic' society, modelled after the US.[13]

The Vietnamese and international human rights movements were outraged. Thuyen Nguyen, the head of Vietnam Labour Watch, set out the implications of Nike's public stance:

> With this accusation, Nike has taken the (labour standards) protest into the political arena... by equating monitoring Nike factories with being political extremists, Nike has made it dangerous for these people.[14]

Nike responded by sending a letter to various Vietnamese organizations, the key element of which read:

> Nike's position on this letter is perfectly clear – the views expressed in the letter were Dr Ha's and Dr Ha's alone; they do not represent the position of Nike and are inconsistent with what we have been saying and doing as a company... We do not believe that one remark by one executive in a private exchange should be the basis on which our key relationships with the NGO community are predicated.[15]

Researcher and writer Christopher Amery, examining the publicly available facts about the incident, concluded in a moderate tone:

> It is difficult to understand how a man so senior in the company could have been so out of touch with the company's high profile, highly publicized approach to human rights. Whether or not Joseph Ha's letter reflected Nike's thinking, the incident is a reminder that when a company commits itself to a human rights policy, the commitment needs to be internalized into its corporate culture. Announcing a new policy is not enough.[16]

Cut-and-thrust dialogue between business and NGOs tends to be of course more renowned than the often less flamboyant instances of more relaxed interactions. Dialogue that finds its way into the mass media is usually by definition simple, and generally carries confrontational views about people and institutions. Most often, it focuses on alleged misdemeanours of specific institutions and individuals.

There are, unfortunately, ample opportunities for such aggressive interactions to highlight what for most would be deemed totally unacceptable corporate behaviour. The alleged bribery associated with sales of arms to the Indian government by the Swedish manufacturer, Bofors, is certainly a case in point.[17] The US company, Union Carbide, would for many activists be more than eligible for inclusion in the list of those companies that deserve public pillorying for its alleged attempt to avoid legal liability in the US courts for the human tragedy in Bhopal. Monsanto became the activists' bête noire in the late 1990s for its aggressive marketing of genetically modified agricultural and food products; and a host of German companies, and a few US companies with German subsidiaries, have been dragged into the public limelight for their active participation in the use of slave and forced labour under the Nazi regime in Germany during the Second World War.

This type of confrontational conversation encourages us to think about corporations a little like the behavioural psychologist Pavlov thought about dogs. Pavlov, you will recall, argued that a way to train his dog to do what he wanted was by linking rewards and penalties to behaviour in a systematic, repeated manner until it took the hint about what constituted acceptable behaviour. This learning model, while painfully crude, may at times be effective in shifting behaviour in instances where a response requires a clear prospect of punishment. That is, after all, why we have laws against what we deem unacceptable behaviour, such as corruption, theft, rape and murder. Equally we do find ways to reward good behaviour, for example through public recognition of contributions to knowledge or to the arts and music.

Such a short-term behavioural model, however, presents a disturbing and inaccurate vision of how we learn both individually and collectively. Must we assume that only the stick and carrot will mould a company's practice away from bad, and towards good, behaviour? Businesses should not be expected to do things that are directly against their interests, that much is clear. But as we have seen, their interests are far from being confined solely to the over-arching institutional imperative of profit maximization.

CIVIL LEARNING CYCLES[18]

Behavioural changes require learning, which in turn has to be under-pinned by the appropriate process of knowledge acquisition. This is true irrespective of what are the behavioural norms that undergo change, and it is equally true in the light of the myriad ways to learn, some more painful than others. There is an enormous literature on organizational learning, from Peter Senge's ground-breaking work[19] through to the more recent outpouring of material on learning and knowledge management.[20] It is important in this context to clearly distinguish data from knowledge; it is the latter which is the basis for durable, organizational as well as individual learning. That is the problem, Probst argues, with most so-called 'knowledge management systems', that actually relate to the informational rather than knowledge base of the organization. He stresses, furthermore, that knowledge is in this sense relational in that it is rooted in people and the quality of their interactions over time:

> ...*knowledge*, however, is the whole body of learning and skills that *individuals* (not machines) use for solving problems. Knowledge is always tied to people, and is not reproducible in information systems. Companies that content themselves with adjusting the structure of their Intranets and databanks do not deal adequately with most of the knowledge problems that arise in organizations.[21]

Data .... Information .... Knowledge
Unstructured .... Structured
Isolated .... Embedded
Context-independent................................ Context-dependent
Low behavioural control .... High behavioural control
Symbols...................................... Cognitive patterns for action
Distinction... Mastery/capability

Figure 11.1 *The Data–Knowledge Continuum*[22]

Knowledge serves many purposes. At the minimum level of effective exploitation, it enables more efficient processes while leaving aims and approaches broadly intact. At higher levels of learning, the acquisition of knowledge enables qualitative shifts in approach and also critically in purpose, as Tissen and others describe in Box 11.1.

In moving from the possible uses of knowledge to its acquisition and management, Huber identifies four key 'constructs and processes' as critical for organizational learning:

(1) *Knowledge acquisition*: the process by which knowledge is obtained.
(2) *Information distribution*: sharing information to broaden the new understanding.

Box 11.1 *The Knowledge Dividend* [23]

Knowledge efficiency	*Knowledge connectivity*	*Knowledge innovation*
Knowledge at work	Benefits the whole	Provides future value
Who knows what, and	Cross-unit knowledge	The why, what and
where to find it	Knowledge = sharing	when of knowledge
Easy to access and use	power	Inspires and connects
Prevents reinventing the	Develops 'one-firm'	people
wheel	potential	Develops new
Exploits available	Adds value through	combinations
knowledge	identifying company	Reinvents existing
	best practices	knowledge
'Clickable knowledge'	*'Collaborative*	*'Combinable*
knowledge'	*knowledge'*	

(3) *Information interpretation*: distributing information to give it one or more commonly shared understandings.
(4) *Organizational memory*: storing knowledge for future use.[24]

Learning at an organizational level requires all of these to be present. These can be considered in terms of a learning cycle that can be characterized as follows:

➜ Engaging with *people and organizations* that see, experience and respond to the world in different ways... leading to...
➜ changes in the *information* acquired by the organization (and its stakeholders)... resulting in...
➜ development of new *knowledge* for use by stakeholders and the organization for mutual benefit... opening the way to...
➜ a recognition by an organization's leadership of *new patterns of opportunities and risks*... allowing for...
➜ *commercially successful innovation* that is aligned with stakeholders' vision, values and behaviour... creating the need for...
➜ *re-codification of organizational behaviour* to enable effective management in relation to newly aligned business activities, including in particular the basis for personal rewards and overall measures of success... reinforcing...
➜ *shifts in approaches to communication and engagement* with stakeholders critical in securing the success of the underlying business proposition... which...
➜ once again changes the *information* flowing into the organization... revealing...
➜ *new patterns of opportunities and risks*... and so on.

Needless to say, the order of events described in this cycle of civil learning might vary, and certainly would have many sub-systems that complicate the real process. However, this *civil learning cycle* contains the basic ingredients to deliver usable forms of new knowledge to the organization in ways that create new and viable processes and outcomes that reinforce the patterns of learning and change through rewards that in turn strengthen the organization. This is summarized in Figure 11.2.

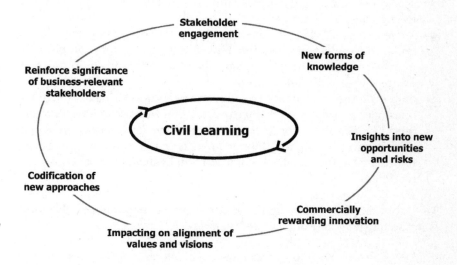

Figure 11.2 *Civil Learning Cycle*

BROKEN VIRTUES

There are, unfortunately, a host of reasons why this process can be and in practice often is, broken, undermining its potential as a virtuous cycle for aligning purpose, strategy, operations, and results to the broader imperatives of sustainable development. Learning can break down in many different ways. Reflecting on specific elements in the engagement–knowledge–action cycle, a number of clear candidates arise:

● *Leadership fails to recognize the opportunities or risks* associated with the organization's social and environmental performance, and does not initiate new patterns of learning, organizational and behavioural change. Alternatively, leadership changes reverse and undermine historic and progressive learning patterns.
● *Usable knowledge is not created* from the new information within the organization. It is deemed unhelpful, irrelevant and unintelligible;

it is seen as inaccurate because it has emanated from non-business sources or because it is qualitative rather than quantitative, or not seen as relating to financial performance priorities.

- *Competency gaps* result in the organization not being able to access information or make good use of it even where it realizes that it is relevant. This may be a matter of individual or embedded organizational values and attitudes that block learning or, for example, an inability to innovate in the design and delivery of new products and services even where the organization understands the implications of its changing environment.
- *Rewards are not forthcoming* because the market does not recognize the underlying values of new directions. For investors, for example, this may mean a failure to believe that enhanced social and environmental performance will yield improved financial performance. For customers, on the other hand, this may mean an unwillingness to confer financial rewards through their purchasing decision, either because they are themselves not willing to trade-off social and environmental gains against additional time or financial costs, or because they do not believe in the social and environmental value of the new business offerings.

This is not simply a matter of 'not learning'. As Huber points out, the issue is not so much *whether* but *how* and so *what* one learns.

> (A)n entity learns if, through its processing of information, the range of its *potential* behaviours is changed... (but learning)... does not always increase the learner's effectiveness... (Entities) can incorrectly learn, and they can correctly learn what is incorrect.[25]

Only when these matters are clear is it possible to understand why certain things are not being learnt. In the case of Nike outlined above, what would need to be explored is whether Joseph Ha's expressed views did or did not reflect Nike's institutionalized knowledge. This is not a matter of whether Nike employees, even Mr Ha himself, do or do not want the weight of Nike to support the furtherance of human rights. It is a question of what are the signals they receive *familiarly* in their role as Nike employees about what constitutes behaviour aligned to the organization's interests, and what does not.

The role of the CEO is clearly crucial in providing a basic framework within which some of the internal signals evolve, are reinforced, or in some cases marginalized. This is why, as Sir Geoffrey Chandler, until recently Chair of the Amnesty Business Group (UK), has consistently argued, publicly stated commitments by senior corporate managers are by no means irrelevant even if they often seem little more than public relations management. Despite the importance of the role of the CEO, however there are certainly limits to what she or he can do. The CEO can clearly set out the values on which the company is to be run, and plot the basic course. But the CEO neither steers the boat nor often, if ever, visits the engine room or checks out the basement toilets, particularly in large corporations. It is a sad truth that it often only takes a few brief encounters with site-level business managers and suppliers, never mind people from outside the business community, to discover the often-murky underbellies of what otherwise seem in the main progressive companies.

But the case of Joseph Ha and Nike does not simply tell a story of institutionalized misinformation. Mr Ha was a Special Advisor to Phil Knight. Presumably he had some access to him and so a direct sense of his values, visions and views. This cannot therefore have been a simple case of errors created by extended lines of communication. Something else must have gone wrong that led Mr Ha to publicly reflect either what were Phil Knight's confidential views, or else to misrepresent him based on Mr Ha's misreading of what the company was or should have been about. Either way, what is certain is that Mr Ha was not working in a vacuum, or at least if he was it will have been one that reveals dilemmas about Nike's underlying organizational culture.

This issue is of course one not only for Nike. It is not odd or unusual when organizations demonstrate a lack of internal coherence and consistency, or an inability to effectively or at least adequately manage their own learning processes. Relatively high levels of incoherence, inconsistency and disabled learning are the norm, not the exception. This is hardly surprising in a world characterized by increased, and ever faster moving forms of interrelated (or perhaps it is more honest just to call it more 'tangled-up') change. Dysfunctional repercussions of these dynamics can be seen in many companies, from high-profile cases such as Monsanto, Nestlé or Shell, through to The Body Shop, Levi Strauss, and Coca-Cola. How was it possible that Monsanto thought it could effectively penetrate the European market with its high-pressure tactics when not only NGOs, but also high-level advisers and other senior people from the business community were telling the company that such an approach would not succeed? What made a company like M&S continue to believe for so long that it could ignore the wave of public opinion in favour of it taking fuller responsibility for labour standards in its global supply chains?

In the emerging New Economy, our competencies are often redundant before they have had a chance to mature, both at individual and institutional levels. Organizational change processes on their first outing are already knocking elbows with the next generation of change agents who have arrived complete with new language and models, and a fresh set of threatening stories and alluring 'empowering pathways' with which to engage the anxious, distracted and over-worked manager's attention. What is amazing is that Mr Ha, or his equivalent in a hundred thousand other organizations, did not say or do something even more absurd. Actually, they probably did, but we were ourselves too frantic and distracted to even notice.

The issue at hand is not, to re-emphasize the point, *whether* one learns, but *what* one learns. Learning is an organizational phenomenon, whether at an individual or an institutional level. The type of learning that takes place depends on how people relate to each other, what information is shared and what forms of communication are relevant to the quality of their interactions. Learning is about what counts in what ways. That is why creating the civil corporation requires above all else a shift in the types of information flowing through and around it, the ways in which this information is received and turned into usable knowledge, and the corporation's ability and will to act on its different components. This is the topic of the final section of this book.

BUSINESS IN CIVIL ORGANIZATION

Civil society cannot be defined in terms of particular categories of *institution*, but in terms of ways of, and reasons for *organization*. The implication of this for how we think about corporate behaviour is profound. It makes little sense to look at a corporation as a single system. What is needed is to explore which bits function in line with an understanding of civil society that focuses on voluntary and associational organizing in order to realize aims that are perceived as being for the common good. Within this framework it then becomes possible to address questions about the extent to which a particular corporation displays these characteristics. It is perfectly possible for The Body Shop to work with community producers in developing ways to trade that both sides deem 'fair and reasonable' while at the same time having an approach to inventory control that creates real dislocations for the same set of suppliers. Similarly it is more than possible for Oxfam to have a trading company that is progressive in promoting fair trade while not having an effective mechanism for managing its own procurement according to ethical as well as financial criteria. Grant-giving organizations like the Ford Foundation may well give money to organizations promoting socially responsible investment while applying no social and environmental criteria whatsoever to their own, often massive, investment portfolios.

Civil organization is about being able and willing to internalize learning from broader society, including through engagement with civil society actors concerned with addressing social and environmental challenges and aims. Thinking about civil learning in this way does not make life easier, but it does open up quite different ways of looking at organizational behaviour, including businesses. It leads one to a more realistic analysis of domains of organization rather than taking the formal institutional framework – the 'corporation' – as the starting (and often end) point. It understands 'civil society' as a phenomenon that exists and evolves within and around institutions across the spectrum, from state bodies, to non-profits to the largest corporate entity. Most of all, by understanding the civil corporation as a dynamic process of learning and change, it allows the focus to shift from a static 'sustainable development' framework to one that is more sensitive to the underlying drivers and enablers of change.

Part 2

Building the Civil Corporation

CHAPTER 12

Building Civil Corporations

BENEATH THE MAGIC BULLET

A civil corporation is one that takes full advantage of opportunities for learning and action in building social and environmental objectives into its core business model by effectively developing its internal values and competencies. This must be the basis for our expectations and judgements of business in addressing the aspirations and challenges underlying sustainable development. But the question remains both how to build and judge corporate behaviour against such a benchmark.

There are no magic bullets that will create civil corporations. There are no standard systems that substitute for real-life, messy solutions made up of cocktails of unusual leadership, coincidence and luck, and really hard work. But the effective systematization of such cocktails is, nevertheless, a critical ingredient of success. The last ten years have seen the emergence of many systems aimed at aligning core business strategies and processes with elements of social and environmental aims and outcomes. Equally prolific has been the outpouring of books and reports either advocating their development and use, or admonishing their inventors for their ignorance or deception. For most, and most of all for business, it is all rather confusing, and also increasingly irritating. In fairness it must be said that 'it is early days', which both explains and in a sense justifies the rich chaos. After all, it is barely 15 years since environmental management systems have been taken seriously by the mainstream business community. Human rights, save for leadership icons like The Body Shop and Ben & Jerry's, began to enter the mainstream world of corporate management barely 15 months ago. It is only five years ago, during a boardroom presentation to a major insurance company about the practice of social auditing that I was accused, only half in jest, of being either a communist or a Christian evangelist.

It is too early to say which standards, guidelines, systems, procedures and practices will turn out to make most sense for any one company, let alone for the wider business community. It is unclear, for example, whether the more daunting Natural Step will prevail over the pragmatic ISO14000 series, or whether the labour code and monitoring standard, SA8000, will do the job. How will this fit into the Balanced Scorecard or Total Quality Management, always supposing that these tools will survive the coming years? Furthermore, it is a complete mystery to most people how such approaches – all designed for relatively stable manufacturing systems –

will fare in a New Economy where the social and environmental footprints of dominant corporations are less clearly defined. The Chairman of Cisco Systems, when asked at one prestigious meeting in the chambers of the UK Chancellor of the Exchequer, Gordon Brown, why his company did not report on its environmental and human rights performance, replied unequivocally, 'We do not really have any significant environmental or human rights impacts.' There is a long way to go in establishing and legitimizing approaches for addressing the pervasive but indirect social and environmental footprints of such companies.

The trick, then, is not to place one's bets on particular systems, but to look for the underlying principles that will need to guide the evolution of appropriate approaches in the future. This is the aim of this final section. It identifies and explores the fundamental principles underlying not only today's but tomorrow's quality systems and tools that will deliver what corporations will need to adopt in becoming demonstrably more civil in their approaches to business.

THE YOGI AND THE COMMISSAR

Businesses, like all organizations, need to be managed. Even the most loosely knit associations of people who come together with some common aim need to have agreed rules of engagement and operations. Indeed, the more complex the environment and the more daunting and multilevelled these aims, the more attention needs to be paid to how best to manage the process of organization towards, hopefully, successful ends.

What makes effective management is probably the most written about subject of the modern age. Books, papers, videos and web-conferences have swarmed to capture the imagination, and buying power, of a somewhat self-absorbed cadre of business managers facing an increasingly difficult, stressful life. This massive and often hyped output is perhaps a rather sad reflection of our modern times. But it is nevertheless completely understandable. Managers have never had such a difficult job. They have to steer their organizations through waters that have more unexpected low-lying rocks, unexploded mines and frenzied sharks than ever before. Businesses are challenged by newcomers from entirely different sectors, using innovative selling routes or production and distribution channels, breaking-down traditional barriers to entry and capturing the imagination of those in both the markets for goods and services and for critically needed expertise.

Managers have responded to this in two distinct ways:

- where possible, to develop approaches that simplify management through codification, and;
- where this is not possible, build new competencies that secure high levels of strategic and operational flexibility.

To aid simplification through codification, there has been a burgeoning of 'toolboxes' for almost every field of management endeavour from doing a job review and bonding with colleagues through to memorizing the ten things one should, or perhaps shouldn't say to a potential customer. These checklist approaches support much-needed simplification and have generated larger scale quality assurance systems like the Business Excellence Model developed by the European Foundation for Quality Management; the International Organization for Standardization's ISO9000 approach for building organizational systems and procedures; the European Commission-sponsored EMAS model for environmental quality assurance; and the Investors in People method for building an organizational process attractive to your employees, to name just a few. There are today hundreds if not thousands of codified methods that have been designed to operate in different parts of the business, or that sometimes approach the same parts or processes in different ways. The common feature is that such tools provide the basis for reducing complex processes to simple repetitive tasks.

At the other end of the spectrum are the developmental methods used in efforts to mobilize people's ability to empathize, to think laterally, and to move beyond information management to creating and applying relevant knowledge to the business. Once again, the gurus and large-scale service providers have busied themselves in creating well-bounded processes that intend to provide, or at least offer the promise of delivering, well-rounded people working in innovative communities on behalf of the business. Alistair Mant, for example, talks of Intelligent Leadership;[1] Peter Block reveals the Empowered Manager,[2] Donar Zohar talks of quantum-transformation,[3] and Charles Handy describes through poetically simple stories the New Alchemists who have retuned their minds to the complexity of modern-day business.[4]

Codification and innovation are uneasy bedfellows, and indeed are often presented as being in opposition to each other. At a seminar in Denmark in 1997 co-hosted by the Copenhagen Business School and the Aarhus Business School, much was made of this supposed opposition. Those from Aarhus presented the argument that rule-based systems undermined deeper learning and change, while others argued that rule-based systems are an essential element of organizational and personal change. Codification and innovation are of course complementary in securing organizational effectiveness. For example, criticism has been levelled at the 'check-list' approach that SA8000 and other highly codified approaches use in monitoring labour standards compliance in global supply chains. Surely, argue labour activists, such codes are misconceived in applying approaches more suited to checking product production quality to the entirely different and infinitely more complex sphere of working conditions. Those with a classical auditing background, on the other hand, argue that the more tactile, dialogue-based approaches to monitoring labour standards preferred by the NGOs generates anecdotal information that is often unverifiable, has no clear relationship to the experience of the whole population of workers in a particular factory, and cannot be benchmarked across a company's supply chain as a basis for making management decisions, often in relation to thousands of suppliers.

At the other end of the spectrum, there have been concerns expressed about what some see as the 'over-flexibility' within AA1000, the foundation accountability standard developed by ISEA. Here the concern is that there is an inadequate level of detailed codification that would bind companies claiming to have achieved specific performance standards. Others, on the other hand, including many people equally concerned with issues of social and environmental accountability, have welcomed this feature of AA1000. For them, there is a need for companies to experiment and innovate, rather than binding themselves into straitjackets that would, they argue, do little to advance the evolution of socially and environmentally responsible companies.

Effective organizational learning needs a balance between codification and innovation. An over-emphasis on either codification or values and culture can be and in most instances will be counter-productive, as caricatured in Arthur Koestler's *The Yogi and the Commissar*.[5] A balance

Box 12.1 *Getting the Balance Between the Yogi and the Commissar*

Over-Emphasis on Codification	*Over-Emphasis on Values, Culture and Leadership*
● Restricts the possibility of shifts in the underlying culture and values of the organization.	● Introduces a fragility to the change process through a focus on the transformative capacity of those people in place today.
● Does little to strengthen the quality of relationships with stakeholders who are looking for shared purpose as well as behavioural changes.	● Is likely to restrict the degree to which the change permeates the entire organization.
● Does not build a culture of trust and so maintains the high costs of having to continuously demonstrate each element of behavioural change.	● Can lead to a failure to establish a commonly agreed language that reveals the relationship between values and behaviour.
● Restricts the likely rewards to the organization and so acts to break the virtuous circle that is needed confirm the positive effect of the shifts in behaviour on institutional viability.	● Allows distrust of the organization to be sustained despite a growth in stakeholder trust in a few people leading the change process.

is needed between codification on the one hand, and the deeper process of shifting the values of individuals and of the organization as a whole. Critical, indeed, is the relationship between the two dimensions of learning and change.

THE KEY QUESTIONS

Identifying and developing fundamental principles that can underpin answers to the 'how' requires being very clear about the practical questions being addressed in meeting the business challenges and opportunities associated with sustainable development. Given how this question has been framed by the idea of the civil corporation, some of the key questions that can govern our selection and development of method must include:

- How do we assess and build an organization's *degree of freedom* in making operational and strategic decisions that align a viable institutional process with social and environmental goals?
- How do we assess and build an organization's *willingness and ability to engage, and practice in engaging, with stakeholders* in ways that allow decisions to be reached, and to explore how to enlarge the opportunities for acting that are consistent with organizational viability and sustainable development?
- How do we assess an organization's *social and environmental performance*, the trade-offs being made between these different spheres and outcomes, and their causal relationship to key aspects of the business process and to critical operational and strategic decisions made by management?
- How do we more effectively *bring relevant information and knowledge* to decision-making processes, both within the organization and where external stakeholders are making decisions in relation to the organization?
- How do we create a framework of *incentives and penalties* that will encourage the organization to align its processes to social, economic and environmental goals?
- How do we understand and work with an organization's *purpose and values* in deepening and more permanently embedding a pervasive sensibility about sustainable development?

The remaining chapters in this section seek to elicit the principles that are needed to underpin suitable answers to these questions.

CHAPTER 13

How Much Is Enough?

As a water utility we are a major landowner. We have been approached by representatives from the anti-hunting league and asked to stop renting out a parcel of land for use by sports-hunters. To be honest, we don't have a corporate view on hunting, and do not particularly want to have one. Where does this all end? If there is a church but no mosque on our land, will we eventually have to have a view on God?[1]

How is it possible that oil companies that state their commitment to sustainable development remain unwilling to take any responsibility for their single most significant impact on people, the planet and indeed profits – the use of their products?[2]

TROUBLE WITH BOUNDARIES[3]

The post-privatization experience of the British utilities companies has in the main been a fraught affair. The initial period of relative calm supported by booming share prices and near-monopoly conditions was soon followed by a series of high-profile problems. These ranged from an exploding number of people unable to pay their rising bills being disconnected from basic water and energy services, through to accusations of 'fat cat' pay for directors who had often acquired their position through easy routes from long-term civil service to boardroom supremacy. It is perhaps not surprising that these utilities have been some of the early adopters of environmental and then also social programmes, and associated stakeholder dialogue and reporting. United Utilities, which is responsible for the provision of water and electricity supplies throughout the North-west of England, produced its first social report in 1999. Not surprisingly it highlighted its philanthropic activities. However, in line with the times, it embraced the view that social responsibility is critically about the 'business basics'.[4] For example, the company reported that water disconnections had fallen from a high of about 2000 per annum in 1992/1993 to a low of less than 100 in 1998/1999; that water leakage had fallen by 45 per cent since 1992/1993; and that all of their systems were Y2K compliant by the end of 1998.[5] So far so good.

At about the same time that United Utilities was preparing its report, a manager from another British utility met with me and posed the following question:

As a water utility we are a major landowner. We have been approached by representatives from the anti-hunting league and asked to stop renting out a parcel of land for use by sports-hunters. To be honest, we don't have a corporate view on hunting, and do not particularly want to have one. Where does this all end? If there is a church but no mosque on our land, will we eventually have to have a view on God?[6]

Extreme perhaps, certainly ironic, but absolutely relevant. Businesses that publicly seek to demonstrate their responsiveness to society's social and environmental challenges find themselves vulnerable to ethical challenges from almost any quarter on any topic.

Box 13.1 *Conversations about Boundaries*

Author: Can you explain why you are not applying any social or environmental criteria to your investments where you have publicly embraced the whole corporate social responsibility agenda?

Insurance Company: Because we have a legal and moral responsibility to our policyholders to ensure that financial returns are maximized.

Author: But the weight of evidence is overwhelming that the application of social and environmental criteria need not cost you anything, and may even lead to better long-term financial performance of your portfolio.

Insurance Company: Be that as it may, it would be impossible to apply formal criteria. There are none that would always hold true.

Author: Really! Surely there are no circumstances, for example, where you would invest in companies knowing that they used bonded or slave labour.

Insurance Company: Of course not, and in fact we do check up on all sorts of things like that. We are very ethical in our approach. But we can't formalize it. The moment we said publicly that we were screening one thing out, people would ask why we were not screening out other things. It would never stop.

There is a real boundaries problem. Sometimes boundaries are reasonably clear, such as the time it takes for a company to settle suppliers' invoices. Indeed, boundaries of responsibility are often framed by law, such as a company's responsibility for safety in the workplace. But tradition and law are increasingly inadequate bases for defining such boundaries. There is no clear legal framework or tried-and-tested convention for the responsibility that GAP takes for the millions of people working in its legally separate suppliers. It is not at all clear what are the implications for energy and resource companies like BP or Rio Tinto if governments use part or all of the royalties these companies pay under licence agreements for their own aggrandizement, whether legally or otherwise. There is no obvious route for the Danish provider of insulin products for diabetics, Novo Nordisk, to take in dealing with the fact that many public health services around the world are unable to afford the volume of insulin needed to prevent the otherwise avoidable death of diabetics.[7] It is all very well telling companies to be accountable for more, but how much more?

THE CIVIL ACCOUNTING ENTITY

Defining boundaries of responsibility is the single biggest dilemma for companies wishing, or having been pressured, to take fuller account of their responsibilities. Indeed, boundary setting can be seen as *the* heart of the field of corporate citizenship and its relevance to sustainable development.

It is useful to start with several *de facto* boundaries of what companies take into account in describing themselves and the world around them, that is, what companies in practice have done, and how the boundaries are set. In the first instance, a business's boundaries have traditionally been defined in three broad ways. First are their *legal characteristics*. This is essentially concerned with:

- *Ownership*, and associated rights and responsibilities.
- *Spheres of control, risks and responsibilities* that carry with them legal implications.

Beyond this legal foundation, business has focused almost exclusively on the *financial characteristics* of their operations. From this perspective, businesses have defined their boundaries according to two main criteria:

- *Stakeholders* considered relevant are those that impact on their financial position, for example shareholders as owners and earners of dividend, or staff as receivers of income.
- These relationships have been defined primarily in terms of *financial flows*, and financially denominated assets and liabilities, often both historic and predictive data.

The third conventional means of defining an organization's boundaries has been by setting out its *operational characteristics*. This involves the use of non-financial measures covering, for example:

- *Technical features*: what they make and how they make it.
- *Market and marketing*: who are the actual and potential customers, how are they reached, and what are their responses and why?
- *Competencies and their management*: what staff do and how their skills are developed.

Box 13.2 *Characterizing Organization*

The Old	*The New*
	● Strategy
● Legal	● Risk
● Financial	● Value Chains
● Operational	● Information and Knowledge
	● Values

More recently, there have been major shifts in the ways in which businesses describe themselves. This shift has in no way excluded any of the above, but has included it with other elements in ways that signal a quantum change in how business is characterized. The first piece of this *new organizational characterization* is the attention paid to *strategy*. Strategy has always been a core element of business planning, particularly for larger business organizations. What has shifted is the level of complexity and therefore challenge in conceiving of tomorrow's operating environment, a particular business's role in it, and how best to get there. Far more is invested today than ever before in working out the future characteristics of a business, and often the quality of this work is the key difference between success and failure. This focus shifts the basis on which organizational boundaries are conceived. Electricity utilities, for example, have increasingly realized the potential value of their primary tangible asset – electricity cabling – in meeting the emerging demand for increased bandwidth for delivering telecommunication services. An implication of this is that these companies acquire a whole new set of stakeholders that they need to take into account, including the potential customers of such services, people with skills that they will need to employ, and telecommunications regulators.

The second piece of the new organizational characterization is that businesses increasingly define themselves – and are defined for example through stock markets – in terms of their *risk* (and opportunities) profile. It is no coincidence, for example, that the newly created Sustainability Advisory Service of the accounting and consultancy giant, KPMG, is located within the company's division that handles risk assessment and management services. Similarly in the case of its competitors, PricewaterhouseCoopers, which has located its key teams of 'ethics advisers and auditors' under 'global risk'. Key here again is that the boundary conditions both extend beyond the conventional approach *and* are lateral or crosscutting rather than departmental or even divisional. Risk in this context would therefore cover:

- *financially definable and measurable risk,* including in some instances environmental and other liabilities that would appear on the balance sheet; and
- *qualitative risk and opportunities* that might involve the potential for reputation damage and so ultimately financial losses, even where they are not quantified in financial (or indeed often in any other) form.

The third piece concerns the new focus on *value-chains*. These are characterized in terms of the financial and operational features of the entire chain of business from which the company draws and to which it contributes, and so from and through which financial value is either gained or lost. The critical shift here is that this reaches beyond the legal boundaries of the business through its customer and in particular its supply chain relationships.

A fourth piece of the new organizational characterization concerns the increasing importance of *information and knowledge* in creating and underpinning successful businesses, as discussed in an earlier chapter. This is partly a matter of new market opportunities. One estimate puts the current annual value of the global markets for the supply, organization, and retrieval of information at US$1.5 trillion, or about 5 per cent of annual global income.[8] But an increasingly critical element of this characterization concerns the need for businesses to be able to mobilize and focus ever-more complex arrays of knowledge, part of which is disembodied from any particular person or group, and other parts of which require interactions with specific people who are capable of adding value through the application of the knowledge set that they embody. The explosion of systems and processes for handling information and converting it into useful knowledge is testimony to the central importance of this development. The implication here is that information and knowledge, and a business's ability to control and manage both and the alchemy between them, has in itself become a defining element of the organization.

The fifth and final piece of the new organizational characterization concerns the matter of *values*. Although this piece is often assumed to be the same as some expression of 'social responsibility', this is far from the case. Values are the glue that hold together businesses that are becoming diversified in terms of geographical spread and products and markets, and in terms of the varied and dispersed competencies that have to be mobilized across time, space, language and culture, and institutions. They offer a means to reduce transaction costs and improve quality at all levels by deepening relationships and enhancing trust. This is not, therefore, necessarily about 'good or bad' values, as Porras and Collins point out in their groundbreaking work linking company values and long-term stock market performance.[9]

The *new organizational characterization* re-positions, rather than downgrades, the importance of legal, financial and operational information. These traditional features are integrated into ways of describing the business that are more dynamic and that lose many of the conventions of distinguishing what is in and what is out. This is the basis for a redefinition of what we understand as the accounting entity into what we might call the *civil accounting entity*.

CREATING BOUNDARIES

Contingent Boundaries

Business boundaries are contingent. This is a horrible truth for managers trying to manage in relation to operational and financial – let alone social and environmental – goals. This fact poses particular dilemmas for those who are mandated to build robust, codified accounting and disclosure mechanisms in their organizations that can underpin better overall business performance.

Contingent boundaries make life hard for people trying to manage organizations, but they are a fact of today's world. The manager from the water utility recognized this in his exasperated enquiry about whether he would eventually need to have a view on God. Automobile companies note this with some fear as they see the emergence of ever-costlier 'take-back' legislation that extends their responsibilities for reusing or recycling the products they produce deep into the future, and indeed possibly into the past. Companies from Disneyland to Reebok recognize this as their social and environmental responsibilities extend further and further into their global supply chains, and now out into the families and communities of the workers in their supplying companies.[10]

Acknowledging the contingent nature of an organization's boundaries is one thing; but contingent on what? A business generally identifies its organizational boundaries at any particular point in time through the use of two core reference points:

● *Vision, mission, strategy and goals* are clearly core in identifying key stakeholders and other parameters of the organization's boundaries.
● *Risk assessments* are critical in defining what issues and associated people, institutions and processes are likely to be relevant in the short and longer term.

These reference points may help, but may equally be part of the problem. A meeting of European and US corporations took place in early 1999 in New York under the auspices of the Conference Board to discuss developments in 'corporate global citizenship'. A senior manager from Monsanto made a presentation that highlighted the complementarity between global concerns and solutions, and their controversial promotion of genetically modified agricultural products. At the end of the presentation, a representative from a major European oil company made the following comment to the presenter and the gathered assembly:

I am surprised that you do not seem to have learnt the lessons of the Shell experience and since then many others. You can argue until you are blue in the face that your business vision and that of feeding the world's poor are one and the same. But I have to tell you that you are not believed in Europe, and repeating it endlessly will simply deepen the distrust.

This proved to be a prescient statement. Monsanto was following its vision and had undoubtedly undertaken its own risk assessment. Both were fatally flawed.

Negotiated Boundaries

Businesses, including some of the world's largest that are well able to finance virtually any level of investigation, have repeatedly found themselves wrong-footed by poor advice and overly arrogant views over where effective vision and policy are made. It is clearly the business of managers to manage, and the task of senior directors to clarify and order the organization's vision, mission and strategic policies. But it is not up to them whether these orientations, once set, are the foundations of success or failure. The right to decide falls to the stakeholders that are able to make or break the business by refusing for example to buy, to invest or to work productively. These stakeholders are in general not revolutionaries; few of them graced the battles on the streets of Seattle or, despite the hype, have a clue of what the WTO is about. But these stakeholders *are* influenced by the moral moods that wax and wane through their communities, the debates in their local shops and pubs, and perhaps most of all the views of their children. They are willing to respond to the moral call-outs by environmental and human rights organizations. This is not because they are sure about what is going on or how to fix it. It is because they sense that something is very wrong, and that the most powerful institutions around them – corporations and governments – are either ignoring the problems, unable to come to grips with them, or are themselves part of the problem.

The real boundaries of responsibility of any organization are therefore essentially set through negotiation with those stakeholders who can penalize a business for 'getting it wrong' and equally those that can reward it for getting it right. This may not be objective enough for some; it is certainly not a stable cocktail of collective subjectivity. There is no doubt that everything seems to become more and more muddled the more diverse and dynamic are the array of views that can, if acted upon, affect a business's fortunes. This is all true, and may (and often does) lead the exasperated business manager to declare the 'end of rational debate'. As one manager muttered following a particularly humiliating media debate about the company he worked for, 'We are clearly going to have to take greater account of the public's concerns, even if they are totally wrong.' This *is* the environment facing an increasing number of companies today, and there is no reason to suspect that it will get any less complex and dynamic in tomorrow's world. Globalization has many – and many-layered – forms and effects. For companies, however, there is a recognition that it brings with it the need to handle socialized markets that are quickly influenced by the cut-and-thrust of global events and debate.

Many a mistake is made by a corporate team arguing that, 'these stakeholders are in, but *those* we want nothing to do with'. It is simply not really the company's choice who is and who is not a stakeholder, at least not in the short term. The Body Shop could not decide during the media onslaught against it in the mid-1990s that the journalist, Jon Entine, who led the pack in baying for blood 'did not count'. What a business can do, however, is to *ask* 'who and what counts?' Furthermore, it can ask the more difficult question, 'What and who will count tomorrow and the day after?' With these questions in play, a business can then also ask a question that lies at the heart of its own future, namely, 'Who and what do we actively want to count rather than merely respond to as a matter of tactical convenience?'

It is at that point that the matter of values and vision comes back into the picture. But in this form and context it has a powerful new place in the discussion. Rather than it emerging as the 'view from the top', it evolves from a more subtle and engaging dialogue about the world within which the company finds itself, and the manners in which it would wish to respond.

Evolving Boundaries

Boundaries evolve over time in several quite distinct ways. First, is that our understanding of what is most important in pursuing sustainable development changes over time. As UNEP points out:

> Sustainable development is a concept that is dynamic, requiring a built-in flexibility in its application. Lessons from previous decades would indicate that we cannot be sure we have the right answers for future decades. As a 'meta-concept' similar in nature to 'justice' or 'democracy', the concept of 'sustainability' should be expected to change over time, becoming, in all likelihood, increasingly demanding.[11]

Second is that what is salient changes over time. As the world's cities are increasingly clogged by cars and the associated pollutants, there is an increasing interest in how best to design both cities and cars in ways that can rid us of this combined health hazard and dis-amenity. With increased evidence of the effects of human activity on climate change, and the acceptance of that evidence, there are new efforts at both governmental and business levels to reduce the extent of this negative externality through a combination of technological developments and regulatory adjustments. With the rapid growth in the adoption by businesses of codes of conduct covering labour standards in global supply chains, there is an evolution of the debate towards the matter of a 'living wage' that is contained aspirationally within many of these codes and within key international conventions including the UN Declaration of Human Rights.

Third in the chain is that there are developments in our ability to address key dimensions of sustainable development. Paul Hawken and Amory and L Hunter Lovins, for example, set out in *Natural Capitalism* a veritable treasure-chest of ways in which the adoption of existing technologies could improve both environmental security and open new opportunities for employment. The author and Susan Scott-Parker highlighted in a recent report, *Unlocking Potential*, how new employment opportunities for disabled people are emerging as a result of the forms of business organization, and in particular the role of telecommunications in affording greater access.[12]

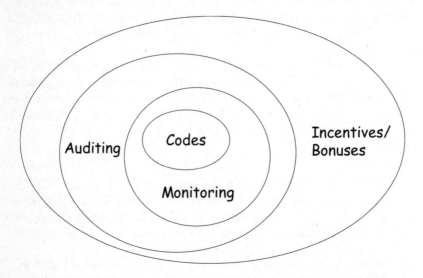

Figure 13.1 *Evolving Boundaries: the Case of Labour Standards*

Evolving boundaries are not so much a sign of confusion or chaos as a signal that learning is taking place. New insights into sustainable development emerge principally through practice, and in particular leadership in forging new best practice. The increased salience of aspects of sustainable development emerge through new knowledge, innovative ways of communicating that knowledge, and a belief rooted in some practical basis that the issue could be effectively addressed.

Standard Boundaries

Negotiations move boundaries in fits and starts that are often marked out over time by new standards. It is important here to understand their role in the development, contestation and acceptance of boundary conditions at any point in time.

The short history of the GRI illustrates how standards both influence and are driven by the shifting terms of the debate. The GRI itself was initiated by the CERES. CERES is a coalition of US-based NGOs that came together following the Exxon Valdez oil spill and created a voluntary corporate environmental reporting standard based on what eventually became known as the *CERES Principles*. In 1997, CERES decided to expand the CERES Reporting Standard to enable and so encourage multinationals to use it across their global operations, as well as drawing in non-US companies to adopt the reporting standard.

The GRI is currently the only corporate reporting standard aspiring to span the entire territory of sustainable development. The initial 'exposure draft' was launched in March 1999 following a two-year, extensive consultation process that engaged experts in the key areas: key institutions from the UN family, for example, UNEP; from the business community, in particular the WBCSD; from the accountancy profession, such as the Association of Chartered Certified Accountants (ACCA); and from the NGO community, such as the NEF.

At the outset the vision was for a global *environmental* reporting standard. Half-way through the process that took them to the 1999 spring launch, however, CERES and its mainly environmentally focused networks and collaborators found themselves pressured to extend the vision to embrace the wider sense of sustainable development. New people and institutions were recruited into the consultation process, and focus was placed on the development of social indicators and a framework for handling the crosscutting dimensions of sustainable development within a business context.

A number of critical new factors have come into play since the launch of the exposure draft. First, about 20 companies agreed to pilot the reporting

Box 13.3 *Evolution of GRI Standard*

Fall 1997: First organizational meetings of the GRI

February 1998–March 1999: Quarterly public meetings for developing the draft *Guidelines*

March 1999: Public release of the exposure draft *Sustainability Reporting Guidelines*

April 1999–spring 2000: Pilot testing and comment period

June 2000: Release of revised *Guidelines*

November 2000: GRI Symposium, Washington, DC

By 2002: Establishment of independent GRI institution

2000–2002: Ongoing application of and feedback on the *Guidelines*

standard on the basis that this experience would inform the next set of guidelines (subsequently released in July 2000). Second, the GRI has become more closely associated with the UN Global Compact. Third, attention has shifted to the institutionalization of the GRI, and in particular the role that non-profit civil organizations and businesses in developing countries are likely to play in the next round of its development. Fourth, there has been an increasing interest in the 'economic' element of the standard, which was almost entirely unspecified in the initial draft.

The GRI has successfully captured the imagination of a growing number of people in key institutions who realize the need to develop a clearer framework for corporate reporting against the key dimensions of sustainable development. Participants have quite varied reasons for advancing this agenda through the GRI. For some, it is a way of moving previously marginalized issues on to the mainstream corporate agenda. For others it is a way of seeking to regularize and for some to moderate the emerging challenge of sustainable development as it impacts on the business community. Whether for these or other reasons, the GRI has at least for now provided a focus point for the negotiation of boundaries.

For the GRI to continue to play this role, it will need to 'move with the times' as well, of course, as influencing them. It will need to ensure that the understanding of sustainable development reflected in the guidelines, and in particular the manner in which they convert complex issues and dynamics in manageable operational characteristics, are reasonably acceptable to those who count. In this sense, the GRI as a standards initiative finds itself not only part of the negotiation of boundaries, but also subject to many of the same challenges as the businesses that it seeks to influence.

Committed Boundaries

It is necessary to have an *appreciation* of the contingent, negotiated, and evolving nature of organizational boundaries in order to understand the *civil accounting entity*. But an appreciation is not sufficient alone for businesses to be able to establish appropriate organizational and so accountability boundaries. The practical question still has to be answered; namely, what does a business take into account now and tomorrow (and what does it not)? Where, in short, does one start? Best practice today offers the key lessons to enable one to answer this question:

● *Acknowledge the broadest possible 'boundaries-in-principle'*. There is nothing to be gained by denying the legitimacy of key stakeholders or issues, and so in this way trying to maintain them outside the boundaries of business accountability. Legality clearly counts, but arguably for less then ever before as stakeholders find other ways to impact on the business. It may appear scary to GAP or Mattel to acknowledge that it needs to engage in debate about a 'living wage' for workers in its supply chains even if it seems on the surface to be a completely unmanageable dimension in seeking to run a viable business. Similarly, it may appear suicidal for major oil companies like ExxonMobil to acknowledge that climate change not only exists, but that they as energy companies need to play a role in finding ways of heading off the predicted calamity. Acknowledgement that aspects of the business create social or environmental effects that need to be understood and reduced (or indeed enhanced) is an absolute pre-condition to any engagement in the challenge of sustainable development.

- *Commit to engagement and transparency.* A commitment to explore what are the implications of the acknowledgement is clearly the next step. Shell published their first report in 1998 amid what was arguably one of the bleakest periods in its long history following the episode with the Brent Spar oil platform and the execution of Ken Saro-Wiwa in Nigeria. The most talked about and in the main celebrated single element of the report started only at page 49 of the 56-page document. It was entitled 'Road Map' and set out in very general terms a commitment by the company to measure, disclose publicly in externally verified reports, and develop systems to more effectively manage all elements of the business that impacted on the goal of sustainable development.[13]
- *Start, Start Small, But Focus on What is Significant.* Some of the earlier examples of social and environmental reporting sought to achieve a very high coverage of stakeholders and issues from the outset. The Body Shop's *Values Report* (1996) was a four-volume boxed set that ran to several hundred pages covering the environment, health and safety, social issues and animal rights.[14] The Social Statement alone covered 10 stakeholder groups across 135 tightly packed pages. Such an extensive level of public reporting was exactly what was needed at that time to demonstrate what was possible; to point the way in particular beyond the public relations 'sound bite' to a self-consciously over-detailed disclosure of the company's performance from stakeholder perspectives. More recently, there has been a shift in the interpretation of completeness towards providing strategic clarity rather than operational detail. The first Shell report led the way in forging this trend, which was made possible precisely because the company had set out their 'Road Map' and associated commitments.

These are some of the fundamentals that any business must undertake in addressing the challenge of sustainable development. It does not, it must be stressed, mean that an organization that has taken this first step is acting consistently with the sustainable development challenge; this takes considerably more, much of which will be discussed in the following chapters. What moving in this direction does mean is that the business is taking on the very basic conditions for being, and being seen to be, a civil corporation.

CHAPTER 14

Useful Measures

Citizenship needs to move from the realm of social philosophy to the realm of management science and the measurement agenda is central to this transition.

David Logan, Corporate Citizenship Company[1]

Normal professionals face the core
And turn their backs upon the poor
New ones by standing on their head
Face the periphery instead.

Herbert Butterfield [2]

THE MEASUREMENT INDUSTRY

The single largest area of endeavour in the field of corporate citizenship in the last decade has been in the development of new measures of progress. A seemingly endless procession of consultations, research and reports has flowed from the view that non-financial aims and outcomes will only count when they are effectively measured. At its most basic level, it embraces the argument that 'if you can't show how it impacts on the (financial) bottom line, it just doesn't count'.

Millions of person hours, and tens if not hundreds of millions of dollars have been invested in this quest, particularly when one adds on the systems and procedures, equipment, training and of course auditing that follow the measurement bandwagon. Company, multi-company, and multi-sectoral initiatives have proliferated, all seeking to identify and develop SMART (simple, measurable, accurate, relevant and timely) indicators that effectively measure corporate social and environmental performance.

Measurement work has covered quite different aspects of corporate social and environmental performance. The ETI, for example, requires its corporate members to report publicly on their progress in managing and enhancing labour standards in their global supply chains.[3] Work by the IBLF has focused on measuring the impact of partnerships.[4] The Corporate Citizenship Company has developed indicators to measure the impact of companies on the communities in which they are based.[5] Initiatives on measurement have not only covered different aspects of corporate performance, but also different institutional forms of indicators. Beyond individual indicators for specific companies, much work has been invested in the development of standardized indicators. The Social Venture Network, for example, has produced a set of proposed standards for corporate social responsibility,[6] as has Instituto Ethos in Brazil.[7] Others have been more ambitious in their scope, notably the GRI's ambitious agenda for covering a corporation's total performance.[8] Beyond the indicators themselves are the standards against which performance is to be measured. This goes further than indicators in setting out a normative framework of what constitutes good performance. Most of these have been specialized in their approach, such as the work of the CEPAA (now renamed SAI) in defining performance measures covering labour standards in global supply chains; the UK-based 'Investors in People' with its focus on treatment of employees; and 'Transparency International' with its ongoing work in developing an 'integrity' standard for assessing levels of corruption and bribery.[9]

THE MEASUREMENT EFFECT

Measurement is clearly an important element of any attempt to make issues more visible, effectively managed and integral to performance assessment. But this does not help very much in deciding what kind of measurement makes a difference in what situations, and to what degree. Famously, John F Kennedy is alleged to have said:

> GNP measures neither our wit nor our courage, neither our wisdom nor our learning, neither our compassion nor our devotion to country. It measures everything, in short, except that which makes life worthwhile.[10]

Wise words certainly, but they have done little to erode the pivotal role that measures of gross national product (GNP) have played over the last half a century in reflecting and reinforcing the overwhelming importance of financial wealth and economic growth as *the* key national success indicator of modern times. Mark Goyder of the Centre for Tomorrow's Company, and many others, have similarly argued that tomorrow's successful companies will have embraced 'inclusivity' as the pivotal foundation of their strategic positioning and thrust.[11] This has not, however, significantly eroded the dominant role of measures of short-term financial performance as the basis for most investors to make decisions to buy or sell. Public opinion surveys repeatedly conclude that an overwhelming proportion of the consuming public are willing to reward or penalize companies through their purchasing decisions on the basis of their social and environmental performance.[12] Yet, as earlier chapters here revealed, data about actual market transactions tell us that a far smaller proportion of the consuming public act out this viewpoint in practice, even when there is no obvious financial penalty to including ethical criteria in buying decisions.

We should not confuse measures that seem vitally important to some of us, with those measures that *really* count. Furthermore, we should not assume that the very fact of measuring something that seems important makes it so in the eyes of those who make decisions that really do count.

The *Financial Times Annual Survey 2000* found that General Electric was deemed by the 750 or so business leaders consulted to be the 'world's most respected company' for the third year running.[13] One fund manager quoted following last year's survey offered the 'no brainer' reasoning:

> It is not hard to see why General Electric is so widely respected... few companies have ever created so much wealth for their shareholders in so short a period... The company had a market capitalization of less than US$20 billion when Jack Welch took over as chairman in 1981: last month, as share prices recovered from their early autumn swoon, it topped US$300 billion.[14]

This, despite Allan Kennedy's persuasive argument in *The End of Shareholder Value* that GE's CEO, Jack Welch, has failed to establish the basis at General Electric for excellence in long-term financial performance (let alone social and environmental performance). Whether or not Kennedy is correct in his prediction about GE's long-term prospects, the survey confirms that the stock market does indeed focus on short-term returns. This is perhaps not surprising given that the average time that an investor holds on to GE stocks is only about 33 months, short but relatively loyal compared with the equivalent figures for IBM, Delta Airlines and Amazon. com of 14 months, 4 months and just 7 days respectively.[15]

The *Survey* for 2000 for the first time included a whole section on perceptions of 'corporate social responsibility'. Interestingly, over 50 per cent of those fund managers surveyed took the view that social responsibility was really important. But this stated view did little, it seems, to influence how they vote in their day-to-day buying and selling. The simple lesson here is that the most important of the SMART characteristics of indicators is 'relevance', and that relevance has to be to decision-makers for the indicator to influence behaviour. Without this 'fit' to decision-makers' perceptions of what is important, an indicator may be elegant and appropriate to the agenda of many stakeholders without it having the slightest effect on corporate performance and outcomes. The question is, then, what makes an indicator relevant?

Financial Twinning

The most obvious reason why companies choose to adopt and be responsive to particular indicators is that there is a demonstrable linkage to financial performance. Some of the key arguments and empirical studies in this area were reviewed in Chapter 5. Relevant here is that the underlying measurement approach is to *twin* non-financial with financial indicators. Some twinning allows for a direct demonstration of cause-and-effect.

For example, Amory Lovins at the Rocky Mountain Institute is the quint-essential expert in this when it comes to environmental performance. His recent book with Paul Hawken and L Hunter Lovins is replete with comforting statistics that demonstrate to great effect that environmental savings are a fast and virtually risk-free way to increase profitability.[16] The medical products company, Baxter International, has taken the quantification of financial benefits arising from environmental initiatives further than most. For example, in its *Environmental, Health and Safety Performance Report* 1998, the company concludes:

> Cost avoidance in 1997 from efforts initiated in prior years back in 1990 was US$86 million. This means that Baxter would have spent US$100 million more in 1997 for raw materials, production processes, disposal costs and packaging if no environmentally beneficial actions had been implemented since 1990.[17]

Other twinning exercises imply cause-and-effect but can in reality do little more than suggest that the financial and non-financial performance measures tend to track each other. A good example of this is the argument that companies that pursue strategies consistent with sustainable develop-ment will perform better financially. A number of indexes have been constructed to demonstrate this proposition. The Dow Jones Sustainability Index (DJSI), for example, has been compared with the other indexes of share portfolio performance without any social or environmental screens. The data suggest that the DJSI performs at least as well as the equivalent Dow Jones (unscreened) portfolio indexes.[18] The earlier quote by the President of SAM, reproduced below, is evidently a 'twinning' argument that this proves that 'being sustainable is better for business':

> Companies which are better managed environmentally indicate more sophisticated management throughout the company... And good manage-ment is the single most important factor in corporate profitability, growth and future earnings.[19]

Twinning non-financial with financial measures is not confined to initiat-ives that promote better corporate social and environmental performance. A study by Ernst and Young's Centre for Business Innovation suggested that only 70 per cent of a stock analyst's recommendation decision derives from financial data, the remainder being based on non-financial proxies for the underlying strengths of the business.[20]

There are of course instances where quantified metrics are put to use in analysing possible actions. These metrics are particularly important for portfolio investments and where large-scale, lumpy, non-reversible investments are being contemplated. There is surprisingly little consensus even in this sphere on which are the most effective indicators of financial performance. In the 1970s, earnings per share and price-equity multiples

Box 14.1 *Which Non-financial Measures do Investors Value Most?*

Execution of corporate strategy
Management credibility
Quality of corporate strategy
Innovativeness
Ability to attract and retain talented people
Market share
Management experience
Alignment of compensation with shareholder interests
Research leadership
Quality of major business processes

emerged as lead indicators of financial performance, whereas the 1990s saw the emergence of economic value added (EVA) as a favoured formula.[21] It must be said that the emerging evidence regarding the use of hard-core financial measures such as EVA suggests patchy effectiveness. Although EVA can in theory be cascaded down the organization, it is in practice poorly understood and applied at the level of the business unit. Furthermore, EVA is an outcome measure and therefore cannot usefully drive organization behaviour. As Marcos Ampuero and his colleagues conclude: 'EVA must exist within a larger universe – a universe that often includes non-financial measures.'[22]

Indicators that aspire to measure and predict the financial implications of social and environmental performance are therefore of very differing levels of meaningfulness, credibility, and so relevance to decision-makers. Often the determining factor is the type of investment being considered. At the simplest level, the larger and lumpier the investment, the more pressure there is to produce data in support of its likely financial benefits. The smaller and less risky the investment to the business as a whole, the less precise will be the associated financial predictions. But precision has little to do with accuracy. Research into the financial consequences of major mergers and acquisitions shows that the predicted financial results rarely materialize.[23] Indeed, one need look no further than the recent performance of investments in Internet companies to realize that projections of likely financial returns are based as much on the alchemy of intuition, judgement, perhaps prejudice and habit, or just plain old copying, as they are on the scientific calculus of cost-benefit analysis.

Divergent Relevance

Companies within the same sector – particularly those operating globally – might be expected to respond in broadly similar ways to comparable social and environmental indicators. However, this is far from the truth. BP and Shell, the world's second and third largest energy companies, have gone to considerable lengths to demonstrate their positive social and environmental credentials.[24] Both companies found themselves at the heart of the European and particularly the British surge of NGO activity in the second half of the 1990s. On the other hand, the world's largest oil company, ExxonMobil, has chosen not to respond to civil pressures to demonstrate greater awareness of social and environmental issues. Clearly its judgement of the relevance of civil pressures is quite different from that of its two European industry cousins. Similarly for the case of food retailing. British food retailers like Sainsbury's and Waitrose have engaged with NGOs and labour unions in addressing the complex issue of labour standards in their global supply chains. The world's largest retailer, Wal-Mart, on the other hand, has consistently refused to disclose information about its supply chains, and has equally refused to engage constructively with NGOs and labour organizations in the design or implementation of codes of conduct.

There is no one simple reason for these differences between companies within the same sector. Often quoted are the very different ways in which US-based companies respond compared with European companies. This may well be a factor, but there is ample evidence that undermines this as generally applicable. The world's two largest automobile production companies, General Motors and more recently the Ford Motor Company, have sought to secure their reputation for engaging in the social and environmental challenges of the time, both focusing particularly on the environmental dimensions of their production processes and product use. General Motors has been a lead company in the GRI,[25] and Ford has taken a lead in producing a European-style public report outlining its commitments to social and environmental accountability.[26] The major European producers, Volkswagen, DaimlerChrysler, BMW and Fiat, on the other hand, have made almost no moves to demonstrate this type of public accountability. Similarly in the apparel and footwear sector, where the world's largest operator, San Francisco-based Levi Strauss, led the way in the 1980s in the development of codes of conduct covering environmental and social dimensions of supply chain performance. This compared extraordinarily well with Europe considering the almost complete dearth of comparable work by European companies until well into the 1990s.[27]

The relevance of particular indicators is underpinned by factors that extend beyond the traditional sector distinctions and, equally, is not obviously equated to brand value or company nationality. Crisis can be an influential driver, but there are ample cases that demonstrate both that some companies continue their traditional practices despite crisis, and that other companies seem to be able to develop a culture of handling social and environmental information, indicators and goals well beyond any obvious source of external, threat-based pressure.

Windows and Mirrors

The single most common view of indicators is that they work by simply communicating complex information about a situation or event on which the audience wishes to be informed in order to make decisions. Product labelling is a case in point.[28] There has been a proliferation of labels intended to inform the consuming citizen about the social and environmental characteristics of particular products. Most common are those that are anti-sweat, no child labour, and green. However, there are many other labels that seek to link the product or the company to aspects of non-negative or positive social and environmental performance.[29] Labelling schemes strengthen the ability of more powerful stakeholders to support those who are less powerful, or what has been referred to in work by the NEF for the UN Human Development Report Office as 'lent power'.[30] Children in Bangladesh, for example, have little power alone to influence their employers, but gain leverage through the influence of NGOs like Oxfam and Save the Children Fund.

Shoppers are often dismissed as irrational; they fail to consider the information on offer or to search out other sources of information. However by adding the 'time cost' into the equation we can see that in shopping decisions which involve little risk, the time which would be needed to make a 'rational' decision on the basis of all available information would

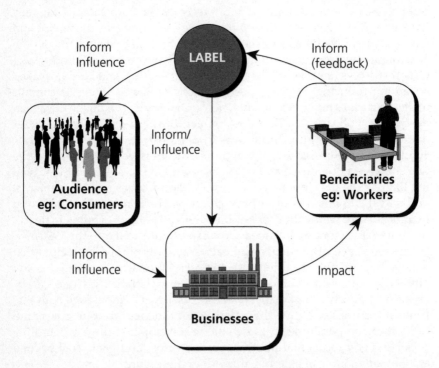

Figure 14.1 *How Labels Work*

outweigh any benefit to the consumer. Therefore purchasing decisions are largely dictated by habit and consumers rely on brand names as a guarantee of quality.

Social labels reduce the costs to consumers primarily by reducing the time it takes for them to find an 'ethical product'. In this way they act in a similar way to brands, offering consumers an easy (low time cost) means of quickly singling out a product as the one to choose from the array of alternatives.

However if social labels are associated with other 'costs' such as quality, or price differentials this will tend to reduce their uptake. For example, in the 1980s Nicaraguan Solidarity coffee was costly: it was expensive, hard to find and hard to drink and all but the most dedicated activists gave up drinking it. On the other hand, the main UK brand of fair trade coffee, Cafédirect, can compete on price and quality with the brand leaders, and is available in mainstream outlets. Directly as a result, it has achieved much greater market penetration. Retailers who have experimented with social labels attest to the importance of eliminating these costs. Peter Rogan of the UK retail chain the Co-operative Wholesale Society, states that 'social labels are only a competitive factor if everything else is equal'.[31] Others feel that social labels – like lead free petrol – only gain significant market penetration if they are associated with cheaper or equivalent prices to the traditional alternatives.

Ethical consumerism is sometimes presented as a purely altruistic act; as the National Consumers' League puts it:

> Consumers who are educated about exploitative working conditions and feel a sense of responsibility to act upon this knowledge find frustration in the marketplace. As a reaction to a lack of information and labels to help the conscientious consumer identify products made under decent conditions, many consumers are taking personal action – to include even personal boycotts of certain products, companies and countries.[32]

Social labels and associated publicity and educational activities provide this necessary information – both about issues and about products – to allow concern to be turned into positive action. But ethical consumerism, like other forms of social behaviour, is also a means of establishing and reinforcing identity. The idea of using purchasing (or non-purchasing) as an act of belonging, and therefore a positive attribute or benefit, goes some way to explaining how different social and environmental issues have come into 'fashion' at different times; for example, CFC-free aerosols in the late 1980s, animal testing[33] in the early 1990s and child labour currently. Writing about union-led boycotts at the turn of the century, Wollman recognized the consumer choice as a collective action and the importance of a supportive culture: 'Where the labouring community is a closely knit, intimate assembly, the boycott is waged by collective efforts impelled by a collective conscience.'[34]

More recently the National Consumer Council remarked in their research on consumer attitudes to environmental claims:

> People talked at length about detergents, the brands they used, and the environmental issues they perceived to be connected to them. For people [in the focus group], use of 'green' detergents and cleaning products was almost a credential for judging environmental awareness.[35]

This begins to suggest that labels do not function primarily through an *informing* process but that their *influence* is also about building a sense of identification.

This notion, as well as that of costs and benefits associated with labels, is captured in the idea of 'windows and mirrors'. From the consumer point of view, social labels can be thought of as acting as both 'windows' and 'mirrors'. In its function as a 'window', a label needs to provide information that is accessible and trusted and which provides consumers with a useful basis on which to make decisions. They need to know that a label exists and what it means. In its function as a 'mirror', the label's effectiveness as a marketing tool is secured by being associated with the triple benefits of self-expression, 'feel-good factor' and positive social identity.

Box 14.2 *Criteria for Effective Social Labels*[36]

Relevance	Is the issue important to the *consumers* and intended *beneficiaries*?
Clarity	Do *consumers* understand the label?
Trust	Do *consumers*, *businesses* and *beneficiaries* believe in the legitimacy of the label and the way it operates?
Accessibility	Can *consumers* buy labelled products? Can willing *businesses* participate in the initiative?
Accuracy	Can *businesses* participating in the initiative be assured that the label's claims are verified?
Financial viability	Is the label consistent with the financial goals of participating *businesses*? Does it add additional assurance to that contained in the brand? Are *consumers* able to afford labelled products?
Legal viability	Will participating *businesses* be acting within national and international regulations?
Impact	Does the labelling initiative have 'positive' effects on *beneficiaries*? Do these outweigh negative side-effects?

Clearly, these intangible benefits are not only provided by the label itself since often the only information provided at the moment of decision-making (eg at the point of sale) is the name of an organization or a logo. We can think of a label as being the tip of an information iceberg. Information comes both directly from the labelling initiative, the retailer or manufacturer and from other sources such as schools, the media and campaigning groups.

The effectiveness of a label itself needs to be understood in a wider context of awareness raising and education on the issue concerned. This point is crucial as it implies that the main mechanism for labels to work is not to change or make up the mind of a consumer in a shop, but to confirm an earlier decision made outside the market place influenced by marketing, the media and, crucially, civil processes. Many labels such as the Forest Stewardship Council labels and the Rugmark have emerged out of consistent NGO campaigning and media attention that effectively raised the heat on an issue.

This way of understanding product labels can be applied equally to other indicators. Accurate and meaningful indicators will not necessarily capture the interest of key decision-makers unless they believe that such responsiveness would be in line with the expectations of their peers. This perspective goes some way to explaining why some communities of businesses adopt and use social and environmental performance indicators while others do not. The hot-housing effect, for example, of the concentration of major multinationals in and around London has in itself created pressure for those companies to use indicators adopted by their peer companies. Business groups like the London Benchmarking Group, ISEA, and Business in the Community tend to reflect and reinforce this group effect. This is still further reinforced by the relatively small group of opinion leaders, often acting as consultants, driving the adoption of particular approaches.

Completely erroneous, or at least decidedly unhelpful, indicators will of course eventually be discredited and discarded. However, this can take some considerable time, as is clearly the case for financial accounting, where much of what is measured today is not effective in informing the investor of past, let alone, future likely performance.

There is a link between indicators that work through 'financial twinning' and those that work mainly through peer group mimicry. Clear predictive links between actions and bottom line financial impact are becoming increasingly rare as business pathways and performance become more dynamic and volatile. The effect of this is to increase both experiment-ation and mimicry. Many of today's innovative measures of corporate performance – including those that focus on social and environmental performance – are early steps in the development of entirely new ways of looking at business performance.

Conversational Performance

The supposed differences between US and European approaches to business are also highlighted in the area of performance measurement. This became apparent in an exchange between myself and a US-based staff member of the consulting firm, KPMG, summarized below.

KPMG: The indicators work going on in Europe, and in particular in the UK, is clearly innovative and we can learn from it in the US.

Author: Well, what is clear is that in the US you have a far greater orientation towards compliance than in Europe.

KPMG: What remains unclear to me, however, is how these indicators fit into policies and procedures. It almost seems that you have jumped the step where we have done most work with the result that the indicators are not tied in to robust and auditable procedures that allow compliance to be really assessed and reported on.

Author: I am sure that this is partly right, but I also think that there is an underlying difference in the way indicators are being used in the US compared with Europe. In the US, indicators really are intended as 'performance indicators' and so policies and systems need to be in place to allow systematic, consistent and auditable measurement processes. In Europe this is sometimes the case, but more often indicators are used as part of a conversation about the role of companies in society. This sounds esoteric, but it is immensely practical. Leading companies are offering up measures and thereby asking 'is this the basis on which you want us to measure our performance – is this a reasonable basis for a renewed social contract?'

Indicators aim to aid communication. Most contemporary social and environmental indicators published in corporate reports appear to be performance indicators. They are in the sense that they describe a way of looking at performance. But they are not fully developed performance indicators in that they are often not embedded in the organization. This is assumed to be 'bad', but in practice it may not always be. Unembedded indicators can be those that companies are willing to 'trial' as part of their conversation with stakeholders. If they bear the test of time, then they are likely to be linked more closely to policies and robust accounting systems, particularly management accounts.

CIVILIZING THE PROFESSIONALS

Disabled people make up a large and increasing proportion of the population in most industrialized countries. Their roles as employees, consumers, investors and voters are therefore a topic of growing interest and concern. A recent study for the UK-based Employers' Forum on Disability highlighted some of the demonstrable facts about disabled people in the workplace.[37] They:

- are as productive and reliable as any other employees;
- have better attendance records, stay with employers longer and have fewer accidents at work;
- develop transferable problem-solving skills invaluable to the workplace;
- rarely require significant 'adjustments', and often when they do these are covered through government assistance programmes;
- enhance staff morale when their employers are seen to be responsive to the needs of the disabled; and
- are well placed to show their employer how best to serve the disabled market, which in the UK is estimated at US$70–90 billion per year.

This is the financial twinning strategy at its best, with strong evidence of links between financial and social performance. Unfortunately, even the most sophisticated twinning strategy of this kind does not always do the job of encouraging behavioural shifts where people and organizations reject change because of, to be blunt, prejudice. As a survey undertaken for the US-based National Organization on Disability concluded:

> One survey of the attitudes of non-disabled towards disabled people found that 58 per cent felt awkward and embarrassed in encountering disabled people, 47 per cent felt fear during such encounters because they saw what might happen to them, and a further 25 per cent felt resentment or anger during such encounters.[38]

This problem is not confined to disabled people, but marks a broader pattern of discrimination. As a study published by the UK Equal Opportunities Commission concluded:

> Institutionalized and internalized discrimination is not uncommon whether in relation to disabled people, people of colour, older people, gender, and others. Our knowledge of the deeply irrational prejudices and stereotypes which underpin discrimination should inform us all that genuine attitudinal change requires more than the 'cold logic' of statistical evidence.[39]

Far more is needed in these circumstances than 'the facts of the matter' or the 'hard-nosed proof' of the relationship between financial and socially responsible performance. That is not to say that measures become unimportant. It is to say, however, that very different measures are needed, often ones that bring out the underlying prejudice in a controlled and manageable manner. In the case of disabled people, it is often by non-disabled people having *direct* workplace experience with disabled people that they are able to overcome their fears and ignorance and accept the productive role that disabled people can play in the business. Along the same vein, it can be more effective in such situations for managers to hear directly from other non-disabled managers about their positive experiences rather than having such experience filtered through statistical screens. In the broader field of corporate citizenship, it is not surprising in this light that Business in the Community in the UK sees its 'Seeing is Believing' programme, which takes business managers out into the wide world, to be one of, if not *the* most effective that it runs. These are 'measures' that focus on the 'see it, hear it' mode of informing and influencing as a means of eroding, or at least circumnavigating, the constraining mindsets. Without such underlying attitudinal shifts, indicators are not only unproductive, but their inevitable weaknesses are often used to legitimize inaction on the part of those resisting because of fear and prejudice.

The application of this to discriminatory practices against the disabled and other of society's distinguishable groups is perhaps more obvious today than in the past. The same issue of prejudice is, however, true of other aspects of corporate behaviour. The single common thread that links the experiences of Monsanto in relation to genetically modified foods; Nike in relation to labour standards in global supply chains; Nestlé over baby milk; and Shell over the Brent Spar oil platform and the situation in Nigeria was the initial absolute confidence by the companies that they understood the situation, and were responding in a manner that was appropriate given their information and who and what they were. Even when this – misplaced (as in each case it turned out) – sense of security was effectively rattled, corporate prejudice too often remained unshaken. As one senior corporate executive concluded in a business-only seminar on non-financial performance measures:

> We understand now that stakeholders need to feel appreciated, to be listened to. We need to be seen to be listening to them – even when they are ignorant or deeply misguided.[40]

Such prejudice is not of course unique to the business community. It is a feature of 'the professions' in whatever institutional guise they find themselves. Those in the professions have been trained in the main to see themselves as the holders of the 'expert view'. Equally, those who consult them have been trained as believers in this view. One of the leading advocates of participatory development, Robert Chambers, based at the Institute of Development Studies (IDS) in the UK, sums this up:

> Normal professionalism refers to the thinking, values, methods and behaviour dominant in a profession or discipline... (it) maintains itself through a repertoire of defences against discordance and threat. It seeks security through specialization, simplification, rejection, and assimilation... Power, wealth, knowledge and professionalism are intimately linked.[41]

The unchallenged position of the professions has in recent years come increasingly under threat. Doctors have found themselves having to justify their diagnosis and their bills like never before; educationalists have been challenged over their failure to fulfil the modernist dream of an educated, knowledgeable and trained citizenship; and politicians have been called to account for their personal and often would-be private behaviour. As Herbert Butterfield quips:

> Normal professionals face the core
> And turn their backs upon the poor
> New ones by standing on their head
> Face the periphery instead.[42]

Such a message may seem a long way from the issue of corporate social and environmental accountability; and even further from the practical concerns and constraints facing business managers. Far from it. Professor Michael Power, writing about the future role of that most sober of the professions, the financial auditors, concludes:

> We need to reposition audit as a local and facilitative practice, rather than one that is remote and disciplinary, so as to enable rather than inhibit public dialogue... In this way we may eventually be in a position to devote more resources to creating quality rather than just policing it.[43]

These attitudes are *not* 'unbusiness-like', but increasingly reflect the sorts of values that underpin best practice management. As the UK-based Industrial Society concludes in a pamphlet that describes the new generation of business leaders:

> [they base their leadership] on mutual trust, shared beliefs, and strong relationships... [they] recognize the leadership potential in everyone... they have the values, the integrity, the enthusiasm, and the ability to gain trust.[44]

We have entered a period where the tradition of acceptance of the 'superior insights' of others in determining the lives of individuals and communities has collapsed, or is in the process of doing so. This is the wider context in which the growing – and increasingly vocal – questioning of corporate behaviour needs to be understood. This period is marked by a renewed, and in the main welcome, assault on the traditional role of class, of age and of gender in determining society's political and ethical benchmarks. These assaults are not welcome because they are comfortable or easy, but because they challenge deeply rooted elitism that has systematically favoured one over other groups, and has thereby entrenched decisions and actions that have had corrosive effects on cultures, communities and their social, political and economic institutions.

The 'old professionalism' too often perpetuates the habits that prevent us from innovating in addressing the broader challenge of sustainable development. Equally to the point, it is simply not good for business.

WHOSE INDICATORS COUNT?

The fair trade company, Traidcraft, built an extensive dialogue with its employees into its first social accounting cycle in 1993.[45] During the course of this dialogue, it became clear that a majority of non-management employees felt strongly that the bottom tier of wages paid were unacceptably low. The company's senior management was, however, of a different mind. To support their view, they provided clear proof that the lower levels of wages paid were certainly no less than those prevailing for comparable jobs within the local area.

As part of the company's social accounting, the views of employees were again solicited with this information in mind. The overwhelming response was summed up by one staff member during a group discussion:

> Benchmarking wage levels with other firms in the area is wrong. This company says it trades 'fairly'. This cannot mean that it pays badly just like everyone else. Many of the lowest paid staff here are eligible for government income support. That means that by national standards they are below the poverty line. That cannot be fair.[46]

Management appreciated but was not impressed by this argument on three counts. First, they argued, the company was in a competitive market and could not pay more than the going wage. Second, the company was in business first and foremost to help community producers in developing countries. Any 'affordable excess' should go to them. Third, senior management were all paid significantly below the market rate. Surely, they argued, this demonstrated the fairness with which the company's underlying ethos was being played out in practice.

Box 14.3 *Traidcraft on 'Fairness'*

For Management	For Employees
External benchmarks with jobs involving similar tasks in other companies	Lowest paid being eligible for income support
Their own salaries being significantly below market rates	Company's commitment to fairness as its core business principle
Community suppliers in developing countries having the first bite of the financial cherry wherever possible	Degree of staff involvement in deciding how best to share out what was available

The conversation continued, suitably framed within the social accounting process. Employees were divided. All agreed that the company should aim to help community producers by offering them better market conditions for their products, including a higher and more stable price. Different views emerged, however, as to how much, and at whose cost. While it was true, some argued, that management were paid below the market rate, their salaries might nevertheless be anything up to just under three times that of the lowest paid.[47] The underlying problem, others argued, was in the process, not the outcome. Wage negotiations were always over the residual monies available once community suppliers and everyone else's deal had been settled. Surely, this group argued, there was a case for having a process that allowed for a debate over how the overall cake was divided.

This debate was of course not created by the social audit process, but rather surfaced through it. At the heart of the debate were varied interpretations of the company's underlying value, 'fairness', and so what constituted suitable measures to calibrate performance.

Mediating Indicators

In these, somewhat simple, distinctions between perspectives are clear underlying variations in what were considered reasonable performance measures in this aspect of the company's activities. Some saw external benchmarks of wages as the key indicator, a view that would certainly

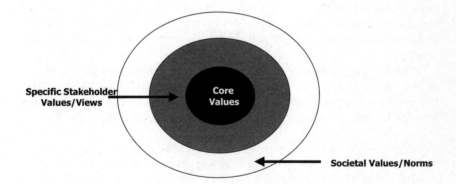

- The company's **own values and stated mission**. This may imply or explicitly set out social and environmental goals.
- The values and interests that reflect **views and aspirations of key stakeholders**.
- Values **institutionalized in law, conventions, or rooted social norms**, including for example key international agreements and conventions.

Figure 14.2 *Mediating Indicators*

have credence within many parts of the business community. Others saw external benchmarks taking into account 'need' as the key, such as the proportion of staff eligible for government income support. Still another group took the viewpoint that it was a measure of the level of participation in decision-making that best revealed the company's degree of fairness.

Equally clear is that neither one nor the other side of the debate was 'right'. There was nothing really to prove or disprove. This was not a debate about facts where verification provided the basis for a decision-by-accuracy. This was more a question of how to interpret what were in the main shared values, and how to judge performance within what was actually a reasonably common view of the company's core vision.

Indicators that pinpoint people's understanding of what values, visions, policies and aims should or do mean in practice are essentially communication tools. They are of course a way of measuring performance, the conventional understanding of their use. But more importantly, or at least as a pre-condition to playing that traditional role, indicators need to provide a foundation of common language and shared understanding of what are the critical benchmarks against which performance is judged, and how that judgement is to be made.

Indicators are in this sense inter-subjective; they are ways for one group of people to say to another 'this is how we see the world'. That does not mean that everyone's view is equivalent, or that we have no basis to rank importance or calibrate against a sense of accuracy or inaccuracy. Traidcraft's employees were not saying that external wage comparison was fictitious or even irrelevant. Equally, they were not saying that community suppliers were being paid too much. What they were saying, however, was that management was over-assertive in their view as to what counted, and therefore no longer heard what staff felt were their valid and relevant concerns.

Mark Lee, now Director of Member Services at BSR, reflected at ISEA's annual conference at Nijenrode Business School in The Netherlands on the use of indicators for engaging with stakeholders by his then-employer, VanCity Savings Credit Union during their first social audit cycle:[48]

> I would expect the indicators we use next year to be at least in part different from those we have used this year. They will change as we learn more about what is important for stakeholders and how best to measure this. Change will, or should, reflect learning. Since it would be most unlikely that we have got it right the first time around, I would be worried if they did not change over time.[49]

That also does not mean that people have to agree with each other. But it does mean that there must be language that at the very minimum offers insights for each side to base an understanding of the nature of their disagreement. Indicators are therefore a prerequisite (although not necessarily sufficient) for rational – or civil – conversation. Without shared language about what's what, there is little chance of moving on to the debate about what can or should be.

STANDARD MEASURES

The downside of using measures in this way is that they are often unique to the situation and also change over time. As a result, the exclusive use of indicators developed through dialogue between the company and its stakeholders makes it difficult to track performance over time, or to benchmark performance with other organizations or industry or societal norms.

The need to compare in these ways is a key driver behind the call for standardized performance indicators in the environmental, social and economic spheres. Standardization as a means of comparing helps in a range of decision-making spheres, including 'ethical screening' of investments, in choosing a potential employee, and where consumers seek to distinguish between different product and service offerings according to their social and environmental characteristics. Standardization can also be a boon for companies that want, for example, to minimize the cost of collecting data, of communicating performance, and for easily benchmarking their performance against others.

Measuring Basic Livelihoods

The question of course is, which measurement standards? Take the critical and complex case of human rights. A consortium of organizations has recently analysed some of the main conventions and codes that can or are being used as standards by the international business community on issues of human rights.[50] There are a lot of them, as the selected discussion of them below clearly demonstrates. What makes things particularly complex is the basis of the difference between them. These differences are not only a matter of scope, but also depth, interpretation and the institutional constellation through which the standard was evolved.

Consider one element of human rights, that of earning through one's labour enough for the basics of life for oneself and one's dependants. The principle of a 'basic livelihood', for example, is enshrined within a number of the conventions and codes. The UN Declaration of Human Rights (UNDHR) states as its purpose to assert a: 'common standard of achievement for all peoples and all nations', recognizing the 'inherent dignity and... the equal and inalienable rights of all members of the human family'. In pursuing this purpose, it highlights 'basic livelihoods' as a human right, arguing that it should comprise a: 'standard of living adequate for the health and well-being of all and the right to security in the event of uncontrollable lack of livelihood'.

The SA8000 code of conduct covers labour standards in global supply chains and has the following stated purpose:

> This standard specifies requirements for social accountability to enable a company to:
>
> - develop, maintain and enforce policies and procedures in order to manage those issues which it can control or influence;
> - demonstrate to interested parties that policies, procedures and practices are in conformity with the requirements of this standard.[51]

Based on the core ILO Conventions, the code contained within the SA8000 Social Accountability Framework sets out its understanding of 'basic livelihood' as it applies to the workplace:

> Wages paid for a standard working week shall meet at least legal or industry minimum standards and shall always be sufficient to meet basic needs of personnel and to provide some discretionary income.[52]

The third example of a standardization approach is the GRI, already discussed at some length elsewhere in the book, which aims to:

> Design, disseminate, and promote standardized reporting, core measurements applicable to all enterprises, and customized, sector-specific measurements, all reflecting the environmental, economic and social dimensions of sustainability.[53]

Box 14.4 *GRI Spheres of Reporting*

1   CEO Statement

2   Key Indicators

3   Profile and Financial Performance

4   Policies, Organization and Management System

5   Stakeholder Relations

6   Management Performance

7   Operational Performance

8   Product Performance

9   Sustainability Statement

The GRI, while seeking to be comprehensive, currently covers the matter of human rights in little more than the following statement:

> (the GRI)... recognizes that established indicators/metrics may not exist for many of the aspects listed... GRI seeks input on defining and developing indicators for the various aspects... (including) Human Rights.[54]

Box 14.5 *Measuring the Living Wage*[55]

Take home wage (1) = (average family size (2)/average of adult wage earners) x (Cost of nutrition + clothing + health care + education + potable water + child care + transportation (3)) + (housing + Energy (4)/ average of adult wage earners) + Savings (10 per cent of income)(5)

The take home wage is based on the number of hours worked in a legal working week (not exceeding 48 hours in one week). The take home wage is the worker's weekly net wage (subtracting out union dues, taxes, etc).

The average family size is divided by the average number of adult wage earners in a family. As noted in the text, it has not yet been determined what data would be used to quantify this analysis.

This list of 'basic needs' was derived from a larger list that also included: entertainment, vacation, paid family leave, retirement, life insurance and personal liability insurance. This list is not definitive and may vary depending on regional factors.

The cost of housing and energy is divided by the average number of adult wage earners. Housing and energy needs are considered to expand in proportion to the number of wage earners in the household.

A random factor of 10 per cent has been included for savings in order to permit workers to have some discretionary income and to allow workers to send money home to their families.

These three versions clearly differ, but in painfully awkward ways. First are the substantive differences in content. The UNDHR refers to health and well-being, essentially *outcome* indicators. The SA8000 Code, on the other hand, refers to *output* measures in benchmarking legal minimums, and also to a measure of *outcome* in the idea of 'sufficiency'. This in turn almost certainly implies something less than what is set out within the UNDHR, assuming that well-being involves something more than the satisfaction of basic needs (and a bit of discretionary income). The GRI, on the other hand, is wholly under-specified, to date largely because the initiative has focused more on environmental indicators.

A second difference between the three concerns the standard's level of detail. Clearly the GRI has very little detail on human rights. The UNDHR statement is, however, differently but in some ways equally under-defined, since it offers no tangible indicators with which to establish its meaning 'on-the-ground'. The SA8000 and ETI codes go considerably further in this regard, providing at least the legal or industry norm as benchmark, and also possibly implying a cost-of-living approach to establishing what would be appropriate in relation to 'basic needs'.

A third major difference between the three approaches to creating a basic livelihood standard concerns the very different institutional constellations through which they were created. The SA8000 standard was developed over a period of two years and involved extensive consultation with the business community, NGOs and trade unions, and inter-governmental bodies, including key UN agencies. SA8000 has been endorsed by the international trade union movement, particularly through Neil Kearney of the International Textiles and Garments Workers Union (ITGWU), and has been embraced by a number of leading multinationals. UN agencies do not endorse private standards, but the ILO and other bodies have responded positively to the fact that SA8000 is rooted in the core ILO conventions. The standard has, however, been severely criticized for not reflecting the views of NGOs in developing countries, and directly for the lack of real consultation and representation from developing country organizations. The AMRC based in Hong Kong has been particularly vocal in this criticism:

> There are altogether 26 members in CEPAA's advisory board. The criteria for appointment are unknown. The majority come from the business sector, including Reebok, Toys R Us, Avon Products, etc. Only one member comes from a union background and a few are from non-governmental organizations. The imbalance of interests on the board is obvious, bringing its impartiality into question, and suggests that any pro-labour proposals would be automatically vetoed because of the in-built business bias of the board.[56]

The GRI has similarly evolved through a lengthy informal consultation process. There have been some distinct differences in the pattern of participation compared with the SA8000 process. First is that the GRI has been initiated and led by an alliance of US-based environmental NGOs, CERES. Second has been the absence of any trade union involvement until very late in the process, explainable although not really justifiable by the broader sustainability, rather than labour standards, focus. Also different has been the direct UN involvement, principally through UNEP, and following the launch of the guidelines in 1999 through financial support from the UN Foundation and the visible encouragement of the initiative through its association with the UN Global Compact. Finally, the business community has been represented not only through individual companies, but also through the active involvement of the WBCSD.

The UNDHR was created through negotiations between the governments of sovereign states. Like most UN conventions, it was confirmed through the UN's General Assembly. While in this sense having arguably the most broad-based and well-rooted legitimacy possible in this messy age, NEF and others remind us that:

> The UNDHR has no legal effect in itself – rather the legal force of the Declaration springs from its related Covenants and Conventions. There are some 49 UN members who have not ratified the Covenant on Civil and Political Rights and some 140 who have. These include states such as Turkey and Myanmar. Similar numbers have not ratified the Covenant on Economic Social and Cultural Rights, including the United States for example.[57]

The legitimacy of the UNDHR and other UN conventions in the eyes of the business community is even weaker. Christopher Amery in a study of business and human rights confirmed that few business leaders see any meaningful relationship between non-mandatory decisions made by governments through the UN and their own policies and behaviour.[58]

Standard measures are therefore not merely about *what* measures but *who* created them and *for what* purpose. What makes a 'good' standardized indicator is not only its accuracy in measuring something considered important, although that is certainly a necessary condition. Also needed is a broader legitimacy rooted in the indicator's ability to mediate across critical frontlines of difference in perception and interests, and for it to be institutionalized as a living element of that mediated process. In this sense, *standard* indicators can be understood as institutionalized mediations, and effective standard indicators are those that have succeeded in mediating and remain alive and responsive to the evolving dialogue between key stakeholders.

USEFUL MEASURES

It is hopefully now clearer what the principles should be underlying the selection, development and application of indicators. For them to be useful requires that they provide a frame of reference for 'measuring what needs to be measured' that is agreed between those who count. This is of course complementary to the discussion about setting boundaries in the previous chapter. A remaining unanswered question is therefore how to ensure that indicators make sense to stakeholders as well as the organization.

Children, family therapists argue, are often the best informants about what is going on within a family. But because they are children, they are rarely asked. This is equally true for many of an organization's stakeholders who are assumed not to know what is going on; or have views that need to be discounted because of their 'partiality' or bias; or else are unable due to a lack of professional training to offer up indicators that effectively capture the essence of what they think should be measured.

This is not the place to have a romantic or sentimental view of stakeholders, either in general or very specific terms. A child will often be inarticulate when asked for the first time to clearly express how they see what has until now been deemed an 'adult affair'. So too are many stake-holders (adult or otherwise) when asked for the first time to define in words of one syllable (or even worse, in numbers) what they sense to be the case. This is often precisely because of their own history of being subject to 'professional dictate' where performance is defined on their behalf by those with the firmest grip on language and power.

It is therefore often not straightforward to work with stakeholders in developing indicators that both mean something to them *and* effectively and cost-efficiently communicate the essence of that meaning to others. Indeed, stakeholders are generally 'at the table' not because they want to define indicators, but because they want the organization to do something different in the future. Furthermore, many stakeholders are, or feel themselves to be, vulnerable in engaging with an organization that may hold the key to their continued source of livelihood, or even at times their physical security.

Useful measures therefore have to be developed with the stakeholders whose lives and experience they describe and thereby also influence. This is a pre-condition for securing high quality measures that effectively serve the role of communicating accurate, intelligible and useful information. Useful measures therefore emerge from meaningful engagement with stakeholders, the subject of the next chapter.

CHAPTER 15

Conversational Corporations

Normal professionalism refers to the thinking, values, methods and behaviour dominant in a profession or discipline... (it) maintains itself through a repertoire of defences against discordance and threat. It seeks security through specialization, simplification, rejection, and assimilation... Power, wealth, knowledge and professionalism are intimately linked.

Robert Chambers, IDS[1]

SET PIECE CONVERSATIONS

The Body Shop published the results of its first 'social audit' in 1996. This followed its public commitment in 1994 to measure and report on its social performance as a way of holding itself to account and encouraging others to do the same.[2] The published report, *The Body Shop Social Statement 95*, was part of a four-volume set running to over 300 pages that made up the company's overall 'Ethical Audit' for the period, including environmental and animal audit reports and a document describing the method adopted.[3] The underlying approach taken by The Body Shop in its social audit was to focus on the interests and perspectives of stakeholders and so measure the company's performance from that vantage point, at least in part. Stakeholder dialogue was clearly a core element of this approach, without which the relevant data could neither be acquired nor validated. The Body Shop, very keen to adopt the most professional approach possible to avoid accusations of bias or incompetence, invested heavily in creating a highly transparent, systematic method for stakeholder dialogue that included the following:

> We have been careful to avoid direct interpretation of results other than drawing attention to or summarizing responses which exceeded a rule-of-thumb threshold of positive or negative perceptions... Where appropriate we have provided context and interpretation to avoid misconceptions... Results of surveys are set out in bar form for ease of interpretation... Throughout the text we have inserted comments and quotes from stakeholders. The quotes were selected by NEF (the external verifiers) from comprehensive digests of comments... from the confidential questionnaires... We will be convening meetings with our staff and other stakeholders... The results of these discussions will feed into future decision-making and priority setting.[4]

Box 15.1 *The Body Shop's Formal Stakeholder Dialogue*[5]

Stakeholder Group	Population	Sample
Staff (UK)	2199	2199
Staff (US)	866	0
Suppliers	1309	285
Shareholders	6809	1473
Customers (UK)	34 million	1000
NGOs (UK)	352	137
International Franchisees	40	40

The bulk of the *Social Statement 95*'s 134 pages of dense grey text was made up of detailed survey responses, linked to policy statements, indicators, stakeholder quotes, and lastly company responses to the data in the form of commitments signed off by the responsible senior managers. There have been many social reports published since then, both by other companies and by The Body Shop. However, the stakeholder dialogue underlying The Body Shop's 1996 report remains one of the technically most sophisticated in recent times in terms of its structure and handling of data, and one of the most sensitive in feeding stakeholder concerns into the design of the survey and other dialogue tools.[6]

ORGANIC DIALOGUE

Effective engagement with stakeholders lies at the heart of the civil corporation. It is through this route that knowledge can be generated and exchanged, mutual understanding and trust developed, and loyalty established and sustained. These are the features of stakeholder relationships that can underpin productive and mutually beneficial decisions and actions. Structured dialogue with key stakeholders of the kind described above is increasingly a feature of corporate-led social accountability initiatives. But such dialogue often sits in the context of an ongoing, more cut-and-thrust conversation. The Body Shop's first social report followed hard on the heels of the reputational assault led by the US journalist, Jon Entine. Entine was excluded from the structured process, although his public critique of the company clearly influenced both the design of its first social audit cycle and the views of some of those stakeholders included in the more formal conversation.

There is an enormous amount of complex, organic, institutionalized 'stakeholder dialogue' that at times sits uneasily with the more set-piece, almost scientific approaches. In 1991, Placer Dome De Venezuela (a subsidiary of Placer Dome) entered into a joint venture agreement with the Corporación Venezolana de Guayana (CVG), a public organization with responsibility for regional mining development. The joint venture's goal was to secure the systematic exploration and, if feasible, the large-scale commercial development of the Las Cristinas gold deposits. There are many layers of regulatory oversight at Las Cristinas. In addition to CVG's role, other governmental agencies with jurisdiction over the Las Cristinas site include three national government agencies, the national Supreme Court, a regional government agency, and the local mayor. In addition to formal governmental actors, the local community members themselves were extremely interested in involving any parties that they believe may provide assistance to them in increasing their social services (health, education, water supply) and promoting economic development.

The political and social situation around the potential mine is turbulent, as can be seen in the following example.[7] When mining activities were suspended temporarily due to a drop in gold prices in 1999, a delegation of miners and community leaders appeared at the joint venture's camp gate, demanding that the joint venture open up the property to small-scale miners who had been displaced when the joint venture started exploration. They threatened disruptive actions, negative press coverage and application of community pressure in order to force the company to respond to community livelihood needs in the aftermath of the suspension of activities. The joint venture was able to work with the community through two newly formed miners' associations, and came to an agreement on a legal framework permitting small-scale mining under company supervision. As part of this process, Placer Dome also sought to identify ways in which they would be seen to be responding to the expressed needs of the community. The company, acting through the joint venture, developed two partnerships involving business, the community, NGOs and governmental agencies. The first partnership aims at developing a health clinic for the Las Cristinas area. The second partnership aims to increase the capacity of small-scale miners to earn a living without degrading the environment, and without needing access to the joint venture's land and financial support.

On-the-ground stakeholder dialogue around corporate social performance is not always precipitated by a crisis such as the one Placer Dome found itself facing. Programmes to tackle social exclusion in The Netherlands have shifted in recent years to the large housing estates on the outer urban rims. Most government initiatives have been focused on housing, education and health. Few have effectively addressed the systemic, deeply rooted economic malaise apparent in these areas. Ahold is The Netherlands' largest retailer, principally focused on food. It employs 230,000 people world-wide, about 60,000 in The Netherlands. Ahold's increasing client-focus has driven it towards a greater appreciation of the need to be sensitive to the varied needs of different communities. For example, whereas in earlier periods Ahold in the main built larger supermarkets, it is now increasingly developing different size units and also developing new services, such as financial services, for its customers.

Ahold saw that operating effectively in deprived urban areas would require working with government and other companies in developing an integrated approach to urban planning. This approach, in their view, would enable government to work effectively on the 'economic' piece of the puzzle. 'Overleg Platform Stedelijk Vernieuwing' (OPS) therefore came into being. Comprising ten non-competitive retailers including Ahold, Rabobank and McDonald's, its aim was to work with government in creating a sound 'investment climate' in outer rim urban areas.[8] The design approach was for OPS to work with local authorities in creating urban development plans that would subsequently enable OPS members to make investments in the areas.

The first project was in the Dutch town of Enschede. In a high profile process, OPS worked with the local authorities for six months up to the end of 1998 in developing a plan for the area. 'It was a very tricky process,' reflects one of the business participants. 'There were repeated misunderstandings about roles. We had to keep reminding them that we were not here to sponsor... but to create an investment climate that would get people back to work.' There were also real differences between the companies involved. Those involved in property development, for example, tended to have a longer time frame than other retailers that were forced to focus almost entirely on 'next week's turnover and profits'. Also some business members of OPS such as Rabobank were more experienced than others in community initiative. Indeed, such differences led to OPS creating two sub-groups, one comprising companies more able to commit time, energy and money to these experimental processes.

ENGAGING TRUTHS

How can one best understand and engage in stakeholder dialogue? Structured and organic dialogues are neither mutually exclusive nor straightforward substitutes for each other. The former, however, is often initiated in an attempt to better understand issues and perspectives that have arisen in organic dialogue, to demonstrate a willingness and ability to listen, and to define concrete actions that are seen by all sides as reasonable, legitimate and feasible. The UK-based Environment Council, for example, explains its understanding and practice of building dialogue as opposed to consultations in arguing that dialogue uniquely involves:

- a search for win–wins;
- an exploration of shared and different interests, values, needs and fears;

- a focus on process rather than issues; and
- strengthening and building relationships.[9]

There are now several decades of experience in evolving and implementing 'participatory' approaches to development practice and research. This has been particularly focused on how best to bring in people who have traditionally been marginalized from decision-making in institutions that deeply affect their lives; for example peasant farmers in relation to the activities of agricultural ministries and research institutes. The objective of such approaches has been to push the activity in question up the 'ladder of participation', moving it beyond functional or consultative participation towards a degree of involvement by multiple stakeholder groups that allows effective change to occur beyond a rhetorical engagement.

Box 15.2 *What is Stakeholder Dialogue?*[10]

'A genuine process of sharing each other's perspectives with a view to tackling a joint issue. It assumes you are willing to change your views. It is the spirit of seeking out and valuing the views of others'

'A two way process between a company and everyone who has a legitimate interest in the company'

'The common-sense approach to understanding the needs of key audiences'

'Positively engage with stakeholders in a collective, solutions-based process'

'Different kinds of interaction that define different types of learning, responsibility, accountability between the different actors – individuals, collections of individuals, institutions'

'A genuine process of sharing each other's perspectives with a view to tackling a joint issue. It assumes you are willing to change your views. It is the spirit of seeking out and valuing the views of others'

'It now means having a formal programme of consultation with key stakeholder groups'

The NEF publication, *Participation Works!*, drawing on the work of others, reproduces a well-used approach that identifies eight levels of participation, from 'manipulation' at the bottom through to 'delegated power' and 'citizen control' at the upper end.[11] Another version has been produced by the International Institute for Environment and Development, as set out in Figure 15.1.

There have been many attempts to operationalize these ladders. Initiatives for community-based policy monitoring in the US, for instance, have

| Self-Mobilization Passive |
| Information Gathering |
| Consultation |
| Material Incentives |
| Functional |
| Interactive |

Figure 15.1 *Participation Ladder*[12]

evolved indicators for the socio-economic and political impact and citizens' involvement of 'empowerment zone' policies by national government.[13] Development project indicators on different forms of engagement, or types and quality of participation, by different stakeholders are being sought through different approaches.[14]

Participatory learning approaches address issues of standards through a number of methods such as matrix ranking and prioritization. Well-being or Wealth Ranking has been further developed by using it for institutional power and impact ranking. The Inter-American Foundation (IAF), for example, has developed an assessment framework, the 'Cone', in seeking to have a comparative tool for understanding quality of impact and process, including participation across a number of projects.[15] Evolving techniques for participatory monitoring and evaluation of participation seek to contribute to the strengthening of the quality of participation being practised in any given project.[16]

DIALOGUE SHIFTS

Dialogue can usefully be understood as being made up of a series of evolutionary stages. At the lower levels lies the static process of identifying what common ground exists. This is essentially the search for 'low hanging fruit', or what we referred to in a previous chapter as being the zero-cost, low-risk degrees of freedom. Companies do and should seek out and build on these areas where they exist. Higher up the evolutionary ladder lies dialogue that involves the exploration, appreciation and in some instances acceptance of the interests of others. In these situations, change is required in the way you understand what your environment is like, how people see you, and what are your immediate or medium-term opportunities and risks given your more or less given interests. This then is an exploration of what we have referred to earlier as the medium cost and medium risk areas of investment for change.

At the very peak of effective dialogue one finds an evolution of purpose itself. At this level, there is a shift beyond the 'give-and-take' that is rooted in each participant working out what they need to do for the other that will deliver outcomes in their own best interest. The shift is in understanding one's own interests. The dialogue that was initiated with one's own personal or institutional aims in mind has in these instances had the effect of altering these aims. Donar Zohah, the doyenne of accessible quantum mechanics, highlights this higher level in *Rewiring the Corporate Brain*. In distinguishing 'debate' and 'dialogue', she argues that dialogue is: 'a powerful means by which we can grow new neural connections'.[17]

The key point here is that this 'dialogue shift' is far more mundane than the mystical experience that some explanations would have us believe. It signals merely that we have come to *understand* something differently, and therefore seek to realize a different aim rather than only finding better ways to achieve the same aim.

Learning takes place at all levels of dialogue. But only the lowest level is adequately captured by the supposed experience of Pavlov's dog discussed in an earlier chapter. This is the essence of the cut-and-thrust tactics that typify most public debate about corporate social, economic and environmental performance. Most consultation lies equally on the lower rungs of the ladder. Usually it involves the confirmation and external and internal communication of what the company concerned already knew to be possible within its current, underlying frame of reference. The higher levels of dialogue are scarce, it must be said, but do exist. However, they are rarely defined as are the others in specific time and space. This form of learning is of a more lateral nature, usually involving:

- A series of *iterative organizational shifts* in perception and practice that resonates between the higher and lower levels of the organization for confirmation and testing at operational and strategic levels.
- *Discontinuities in organizational experience*, usually a crisis of some kind.
- *Personal messengers* committed to the task within the organizations, often working over years to bring change. Those within the organization are what I have called elsewhere the *ethical intrapreneurs*.[18] Usually there are also key outsiders who act as what Ros Tennyson from the IBLF calls *brokers*, placed between the outside and inside realms of the organization.
- *New language* that can effectively play the bridging role between the organization's 'now' and its possible 'then'.

Some forms of participation are better than others. But crucially, they are all interdependent. It is unlikely that higher level dialogue and associated learning can happen without the organization having first experienced a cruder variant of conversation; the symbolic discontinuity that historically marks the shift and its incontestable rationale. This experience need not be direct, of course, but may be of the vicarious kind. Energy and natural resource companies around the world have learnt from Shell's experience, as have life-science companies resonated with the crashing fall from grace of Monsanto. These cruder experiences, however, are rarely sufficient in themselves to set any organization on a radically different course. Fear can precipitate action, but it also dims as a driver over time. Imperatives arising from 'that terrible event' soon pale as institutional story-telling and inertia combine to tell of that event that 'can never happen again' because we are 'all prepared'. A deeper level of learning has to take place for cruder signals to translate into sustainable change.

MEASURING QUALITY DIALOGUE

Fine words, but how does one do it; and how can one tell the difference between good and poor dialogue? There are four broad dimensions of dialogue that should be taken into account in any quality assessment, as set out below.

(1) *Inclusiveness*, or who is included in the dialogue.
(2) *Procedural*, referring to the basis on which the dialogue is designed and implemented.
(3) *Responsiveness*, referring to the degree to which the various parties respond to the dialogue, particularly but not exclusively the organizational subject.
(4) *Outcome*, which is the question of what actually happens and who reaps the associated costs and benefits.

These four quality domains are in practice interrelated, often in seemingly quite contradictory ways. Consider for example some possible dynamic results that can arise from a greater level of inclusion and higher procedural quality of dialogue:

● The greater the level of *inclusion*, the more complex and difficult it becomes to deal with the *procedural* side, the more unlikely it is that the degree of *responsiveness* will meet the needs of those around the table, and the greater the likely level of *outcomes* in relation to the issues debated.
● The higher the quality of the *process of dialogue* in terms of giving voice to those around the table, the greater is likely to be the level of *responsiveness*, and the less powerful will be the *outcomes* in relation to the issues raised and debated.

Procedural Quality

Consider first *procedural* quality. The process accountability standard, *AA1000*, produced by ISEA, advocates the centrality of 'stakeholder inclusivity', by which it means:

> Organizational accountability is directly addressed by the *inclusivity* of the social and ethical accounting, auditing and reporting (SEAAR) process. Inclusivity concerns the reflection at all stages of the SEAAR process over time of the views and needs of all stakeholder groups. Stakeholder views are obtained through an engagement process that allows them to be expressed without fear or restriction. Inclusivity requires the consideration of 'voiceless' stakeholders including future generations and the environment.[19]

The standard continues by setting out the basis of good dialogue.

> But what does it mean to have meaningful engagement? At a high level, it requires that the organization is accountable (transparent, responsive and compliant), and that its leadership make decisions based on an accurate and full understanding of stakeholder aspirations and needs. To achieve this, engagement needs to:

- Allow stakeholders to assist in the identification of other stakeholders.
- Ensure that stakeholders trust the social and ethical accountant (internal or external) that is collecting and processing the findings of the engagement.
- Be a dialogue, not a one-way information feed.
- Be between parties with sufficient preparation and briefing to have well-informed opinions and decisions.
- Involve stakeholders in defining the terms of the engagement. The terms will include, but are not limited to, the issues covered, the methods and techniques of engagement used, the questions asked, the means of analysing responses to questions and the stakeholder feedback process.
- Allow stakeholders to voice their views without restriction and without fear of penalty or discipline. However, stakeholders must be aware that if their opinions are taken seriously and acted upon, this will have consequences upon them and other stakeholder groups.
- Include a public disclosure and feedback process that offers other stakeholders information that is valuable in assessing the engagement and allows them to comment upon it.[20]

The AA1000 standard goes some way in setting out the underlying principles of quality as they should apply to the process of dialogue. Many of them do not so much concern the techniques that are used as the rights and responsibilities of those involved in the dialogue. This view is confirmed by the Environment Council which, while setting out a similar process model in its own guidelines, argues ultimately that it is *how* more than *whether* a particular technique is used:

There is nothing very mysterious about the actual techniques of stakeholder dialogue. The complexities and subtleties come in *how* to use which technique at what moment with which group of people.[21]

This focus on process rather than technique stresses the significance of the terms on which the dialogue takes place. So, for example, it stresses the importance of all participants being resourced with equivalent and relevant information, and furthermore establishes the legitimacy of the organization's stakeholders having a right to define for themselves the routes and pathways along which dialogue will take place. There has been much criticism, for example, of dialogue with vulnerable workers that has taken place within the factories, and at times using translators hired by management. As the Maquila Solidarity Network Canada point out:

> Even with proper training, we question whether Northern private sector auditors, who will inevitably be seen as company representatives, will have sufficient trust of Southern workers to receive their full story.[22]

In other instances it has become clear that, for example, suppliers dependent on continued orders for their livelihoods will only share their views through one-to-one interviews, not even trusting each other to maintain much-needed confidentiality. Indeed, in the first cycle of the social audit of The Body Shop, its head franchisees as a group refused to complete the survey unless there were guarantees that any negative views voiced about the company that might damage its – and therefore their own – business prospects, would be held in confidence between them and the company. They wanted the company to hear their views, but not their own customers![23]

AA1000 is therefore useful in bringing the issues of rights and responsibilities to the fore. However, it does not by itself offer sufficient detail and precision to provide more than a broad basis for calibrating the quality of dialogue. Some further elements are needed to be able to determine whether a particular dialogue process has been of a higher order quality or has been little more than a confirming, communication or – at the lowest end – a manipulative process.

Outcome Quality

Turn now to the *outcome* basis for assessing the quality of dialogue. Can we say, for example, that it worked well when people emerge smiling, and poorly when they emerge dissatisfied, upset or possibly angry? The fact that a peace accord has broadly held fast in Northern Ireland is surely a reasonable indicator of the quality of the preceding dialogue. Similarly, a failure in some other situation for hostages to be safely released must be at least one basis on which to assess the quality of the negotiations. Yes and no. At times there are simply very real conflicts of interest for which a mutually acceptable solution cannot be found at that point in time. A failure to date to deliver a deal between Syria and Israel over the Golan Heights or between Israel and the Palestinian Authority over the future contours of a Palestinian state, for example, are not necessarily indications that the process has been badly handled.

Furthermore, a deal may be done that only resolves the matter because one side had far more power than the other. There is little to compare the situation of Bhopal's citizens whose family members had been maimed or killed by the chemical disaster at the Union Carbide plant with the position of people who had been used by business as slave and forced labour in Nazi Germany. For the former, there proved to be no possibility of getting redress through the US courts, with the result that a far lower settlement was reached through the Indian courts.[24] The latter group, on the other hand, have been able to effectively mobilize the US government in realizing a claim of several billion dollars for actions undertaken some 50 years previously. No court action was needed in this case since Swiss and German companies felt obliged to respond in view of the political weight and therefore ultimately the potential economic sanctions that lay behind the campaign.

A further case in point may be where the decision is made through an interpretation of the law, but this does not necessarily mean that it is the preferred outcome for many of the participants. The decision in favour of the US in the WTO arbitration over access of Latin American bananas to the European Community was perhaps a reasonable interpretation of international trade law. But the dire consequences for the fragile economies of the Eastern Caribbean islands raises considerable doubt over whether it was a preferred outcome to any but the US corporations seeking to enhance access for their relatively low-cost Latin American bananas. Finally, outcomes are often temporary pauses in ongoing conversations. Achieving an outcome in the short term might well prevent longer-term and possibly more significant outcomes being realized.

In summary, outcomes are obviously an important indication of the quality of dialogue. However, there are numerous reasons for caution in their use given the many possible disjunctures between the fact of an accepted, observable result and any other measure of quality of process or outcome.

Responsiveness Quality

Finally turn to the *responsiveness* criterion for assessing the quality of dialogue. When John Elkington withdrew his company, SustainAbility, from its retainer-based relationship with Monsanto, he cited Monsanto's unwillingness to enter into real dialogue with concerned consumers, farmers and their representatives. This was not a matter of inclusiveness, since Monsanto had ensured that all parties had at some stage or other been included in the dialogue. Neither was it an issue of procedures, since concerned external stakeholders had certainly found clear ways to express themselves. Equally, this was not a matter of outcomes, since John Elkington's withdrawal was not based on a view he had taken concerning the substantive issue of genetically modified organisms. At the heart of the issue was the perception that the company was unwilling to *respond* to stakeholder concerns. The company included stakeholders, discussed and listened – and then proceeded as previously planned.

Whether or not a corporation is being responsive to stakeholders' interests lies at the heart of most of the confrontations about corporate behaviour. The call by labour rights campaigners for a 'living wage' for all, for example, is ultimately about outcomes, in this case the economic welfare of workers in global supply chains. However, the critical battle line in the debate is really about what the companies can afford to pay, and so by implication the degree to which they are being responsive to the degree possible within the framework of a competitive business environment. From this perspective, responsiveness is actually the same dimension that we have built into the core proposition of the civil corporation. It concerns the degree to which a company engages, learns and responds to the degree of its ability in enhancing its own social and environmental performance.

DIALOGUE WORKS

Stakeholder engagement is arguably the most critical ingredient in the development of the civil corporation. Done well, it can underpin a powerful change process that benefits all. Handled badly or implemented in bad faith, however, it can equally be an expensive, time-wasting and counter-productive activity that neither builds understanding and trust, nor establishes and enhances long-term mutual commitment and productive collaboration. There is no one way or formula that ensures that one 'does it right' in terms of levels of participation, techniques or even outcomes. However, there are some simple guiding principles that are likely to be useful in most instances.

- *Included stakeholders should grow over time.* This is a healthy sign that the company is seeking ways to extend its boundaries of responsibility in line with its understanding of the issues and its investment in identifying how best to handle them. This is consistent with the earlier discussion of extending accounting boundaries over time.
- *Framing the dialogue.* The productiveness of any dialogue is rarely a function of the techniques adopted, but of the quality of, and intentions behind, their implementation.
- *Stakeholder dialogue underpins indicator development and use.* Performance indicators need to reflect stakeholder interests as well as stated corporate policies and commitments. Indeed, the development of indicators through the dialogue process both grounds the process, and generates legitimate measures that can form the basis for building

'shared facts' and so trust and commitment. Again, this reflects the discussion in the previous chapter.

- *Process is not a long-term substitute for substance.* There does ultimately have to be something on the table that is of significant relevance to stakeholders and can form the basis for corporate commitments and targets for change.

CHAPTER 16

Professionalizing Credibility

THE VERIFICATION CONUNDRUM

Trust is deeply rooted in people's values, visions and personal experiences. At the same time it is fluid, moulded both deliberately and organically by the complex interactions of people's internal and external worlds. At one level it can provide a stable basis on which to build long-term relationships, shared values, and pursue common aims for mutual benefit. At another level, trust can be an unstable cocktail of fact and fiction, of utopian desire and pathological hopelessness.

Trust is, perhaps most of all, not to be trusted.

NGOs and others have taken this view in demanding that corporate social and environmental performance be subjected to the rigour of external verification as well as the cut-and-thrust of public view. Without disclosure and formal external verification, they argue, credibility is far from assured. However, the use of external verifiers has by no means become standard for social or even more traditional environmental, health and safety reports. A recent study of social and environmental reporting by companies by BSR, for example, found that only seven reports by Fortune 100 companies included independent verification of social and environmental performance.[1] NEF, similarly, in a recent study of social reporting practice, found that only 15 out of 100 reports considered had any level of external verification.[2] However, there is an increasing incidence of external verification, notably for high-profile, consumer-oriented corporations, and notably in the UK. As Shell reflects in one of its reports:

> We have begun the process of getting independent verification of the social information we publish, as we do already with our financial, health and safety and environmental (HSE) data... We are working with our verifiers to ensure steady progress because we need it and know that the public demands open, candid and honest reporting.[3]

The question, however, remains how best to secure a robust and credible process of external verification. Patrice van Riemsdijk, a founder member of ISEA, sums up the challenge:

> ...(external verification) is becoming very important – because corporations need increased legitimacy, assurance and transparency. But it will only be

useful if the verification process is different from the environmental and financial models.[4]

The Danish enzymes and health care group, Novo Nordisk (now the Novo Group), similarly argued in its first Social Report:

> Building credibility requires transparency in the data and information we put forward... We also realize, however, given the nature of the inform- ation... (that)... traditional methods of auditing may not be the most suitable way.[5]

An underlying consensus has evolved that the traditional approaches to auditing are unlikely to be adequate to attest to meaningful accuracy and completeness in public disclosure. As the *Guardian* journalist, Melissa Jones, argues:

> So far, most multinationals are happy to leave [social auditing] to friendly corporate accountancy firms instead of bodies with no commercial conflict of interest. Even Rio Tinto, however, accepts that social auditing can sometimes amount to no more than a 'box-ticking' exercise.[6]

This challenge has by no means been dismissed by the accountants themselves. As James Schiro, CEO of the world's largest accountancy firm PricewaterhouseCoopers, argues:

> New rules must reaffirm the independence of the auditor as trusted third party... We support limitations on the services accounting firms can provide to their audit clients... disclosure by public companies of the aggregate audit fees and aggregate non-audit fees... (and)... efforts to strengthen the roles of audit committees... New rules are needed now.[7]

Concerns about auditor independence and aspirations for the future have not, perhaps unsurprisingly, prevented the leading accountancy and management consultancy companies from developing and offering services in the field. Rio Tinto's *1998 Social and Environmental Report*, for example, has neither pictures nor words from any celebrities.[8] Instead it offers at the end of the 42-page document an 'Independent Report' by the firm Arthur D Little that seeks to confirm the relevance of the data included in the report, and the robustness of the systems and procedures for collecting these data. UDV Polska, a Polish subsidiary of the food and drinks conglomerate Diageo, produced its first report in 1999 covering its 'economic, social and environmental' performance.[9] The report carries with it a statement by the firm KPMG. Like the A D Little report for Rio Tinto, the KPMG statement falls short of offering a formal audit to verify accuracy or completeness. Instead, it concludes that: 'Nothing came to our attention during our review that is in conflict with the information contained in the report.'[10]

Novo Nordisk's Social Report similarly contains a verification statement from KPMG. In it they state:

> The verification work performed by us does not constitute an audit in the
> sense of a financial audit and therefore we do not express an opinion... (so
> in conclusion)... In our view, the data included in the Social Report 1998 is
> consistent with the documentation presented to us.[11]

The commercial service providers have by no means, however, had the
field to themselves. The second Social Report by the progressive Canadian
financial services institution, VanCity Savings and Credit, has made use
of Susan Todd of Soltice Consulting for their external verification, who
concludes in a far more confident fashion than statements by the conservative, and perhaps more litigation conscious, mainstream accountancy
firms: 'I am satisfied that VanCity's 1998/99 Social Report is reliable,
balanced, and a reasonable representation of the organization's social and
environmental performance for the period.'[12]

Similarly, a recent report by the UK-based utilities group, United
Utilities, carried within it an 'independent view' from Andrew Wilson,
the Director of the Ashridge Centre for Business and Society, and
Adrian Henriques, then Head of Corporate Accountability at the NEF.
The statement lays far greater emphasis on the process underlying the
preparation and publication of the accounts, and also highlights the role
that both external organizations have played in advising the company
of its social accounting method. In summarizing, the statement gives a
broad endorsement, while highlighting the areas in which it could and
should do more.[13] Andrew Wilson also acted as adviser in the preparation,
and external verifier, of BT's first Social Report. In his verification report,
he makes what is probably the most bullish statement of all the current
attempts to provide external attestation:

> On the basis of our involvement, Ashridge is satisfied that the information
> presented in this report... presents a far-reaching picture of the way in
> which BT activities impact upon UK society.[14]

Contemporary approaches to external verification have been subjected to
serious criticism. For example, Professor Rob Gray, founder and Director
of the Centre for Environmental and Social Accountancy Research at the
University of Glasgow, argues that there is little value being added by
way of quality assurance by the current verification statements, and that
this is leading to serious misrepresentations of the facts of the matter. 'The
combination of partial (cherry picking) reporting, mis-labelled reports
and potentially misleading attestations give the impression of a far more
substantial progress than is actually the case.'[15]

Gray and Owen are not lone voices with this view. Shell and other
companies that have seen the need to bring in verifiers have privately

complained bitterly at the perceived lack of a clear basis on which verification can be carried out, and the very varied competencies that both commercial and non-profit service providers have brought to bear.

HYBRID VERIFICATION

There has been a growing recognition of the need to essentially reinvent external verification as it applies to organizations' performance benchmarked against sustainable development.[16] Three dilemmas underpin this need, both of which emerge from the experience of the 1990s summarized above.

(1) *Beyond Technique.* What needs to be taken into account is, as we have discussed in a previous chapter, not a purely technical matter, but emerges from stakeholder dialogue and the broader evolution of thinking and practice about corporate responses to sustainable development. Traditional approaches to verification cannot define its own boundaries, and so can do little more than to look where the company tells it to look, which might in a very public manner miss the point altogether.

(2) *Competency Gaps.* The range of competencies required for effectively finding out and making sense of what is going on span from the traditional accounting arena of handling quantitative data and testing systems and procedures through to the ability to gain the trust of vulnerable stakeholders in order to obtain their personal testimonies.

(3) *Independence Dilemmas.* Close-up involvement in the process of accounting is essential if the quality of dialogue is to be assessed, and yet this compromises the independence of the verifiers as they fall foul of the dictum that one can never check results that one has been involved in creating.

There have been a number of attempts to address these methodological challenges by extending the breadth of institutional involvement and by adding new levels of oversight to the overall process. Several companies have sought to overcome the need to have a broad range of competencies that are not available in any one institution by drawing several institutions into the verification process. The *Partnership Report 1999* of the Co-operative Bank in the UK, for example, went for breadth in engaging David Cook, the Chief Executive of the Natural Step in the UK; Mark Goyder, the Director of the Centre for Tomorrow's Company; and Richard Evans of the consultancy Ethics Etc., to assess its reported performance in the ecological, commercial and social areas respectively.[17] Novo Nordisk, on the other hand, sought to address the issue of boundaries through a two-level approach to the external oversight of its first Social Report, using KPMG to check quantitative data and related systems and procedures, and using the author of this book in providing an overview of the appropriateness of the method employed and the boundaries set.[18]

A further innovation has been the use of expert panels with the duty of overseeing the verification process. This was first tried out by the author working through NEF in its work with Richard Evans and Traidcraft in developing and applying a 'social audit' process to the company.[19] The principle aim was to overcome the double-bind arising because the external auditor was structurally compromised through his or her engagement in the process itself as a means of improving and monitoring its quality, particularly with respect to stakeholder engagement. The panel's role in this situation was to challenge the auditor more than the company. The panel was not asked to sign-off the accounts, this being the role of the external auditor. However, the panel did have considerable power over the process by virtue of their right to add their names to, or withhold their names from, the bottom of the published verification statement. Given that panel members were chosen for their considerable reputation in key fields, this represented a significant endorsement where it was forthcoming. As a third option, individual panel members could add their names to the statement as being 'unsatisfied' with the conduct of the audit.

Box 16.1 *Panel Members Make Their Choices*[20]

The panel members will be asked following the final meeting to consider whether and in what ways they would wish their contribution to be noted in the published reports. The options will be as previously:

- Noted as having contributed to the process as a member of the panel.
- Noted as having contributed to the process as a member of the panel, but on balance not being satisfied by the overall process.
- Not being noted in any published report.

This innovation has stood the test of time in various guises. This is largely because it has effectively served several needs: a real source of quality control at a critical juncture in the process; an opportunity to solicit implicit endorsements by known people in the field; and a route through which the particular process and its outcomes can be communicated to and through key opinion leaders.

As a method for securing quality, the approach has real advantages so long as the company is willing to bring in people who are likely to offer real challenges, and depending on the willingness of panel members to step out from the group and introduce a negative view publicly about the verification. In practice, these have both proved limiting factors, although certainly not damning ones. There are in fact *no* instances to the author's knowledge of a member of such a panel availing themselves of the option of registering a negative view in the company's published report. This is unlikely to have been because people have been silenced; the people involved have too high a reputation and too much integrity for this to be possible. More likely is that people have been chosen for their willingness to fundamentally embrace the company's basic approach to its business and to the accounting and verification process. This brings us back to the boundaries problem discussed in an early chapter, only this time the boundaries are being set indirectly by the company through their choice of panel members and also, of course, of external verifiers.

STANDARDIZED CREDIBILITY

The final stage in the institutionalization of trust is through the development of more formal standards in the areas of method and the evolution of a profession. This requires four conditions to be satisfied:

(1) *Boundaries*. Agreement of what is being looked at and how; for example how the entity is defined, the boundaries set, and so on.
(2) *Reporting Elements*. Agreement on how what is being publicly disclosed or otherwise reported to provide an indication of agreed measures of quality or performance.
(3) *Verification*. Agreement on how the accuracy, completeness and meaning of the reported items are to be assessed, or 'verified'.
(4) *Professionalization*. Agreement on what are the competencies required to carry out such verification, and how the quality of these competencies can be developed, attested to through some form of professional accreditation, and overseen through relevant institutions.

This approach to standardization follows to some extent the financial accounting and auditing model, but equally is comparable to the evolution of many different professions across for example health, law and education. Environmental accounting and auditing has also progressed far in this direction, with several standards for accounting and auditing, and a host of different routes through which professional skills are developed and overseen. The most well-known and used is the ISO14000 environment standard and the European equivalent, EMAS. There have historically been many standards covering elements of the social dimension of sustainable development, ranging from human resource development through to philanthropic activities. In the UK, for example, Investors is People is now a widely used procedural standard in the employees area, and the London Benchmarking Group has evolved a sophisticated tool for measuring and benchmarking corporate activities in the community. SA8000 seeks to offer a standardized approach to monitoring and ultimately improving labour standards in global supply chains by offering: (1) a code that defines what is covered; (2) an approach to accounting and non-public reporting; and (3) a training and accreditation route for auditors, complete with a professional oversight body, SAI.

Several more integrated standards emerged towards the end of the 1990s that sought to bring together the overall social area, and indeed began to pull together the social with the environmental and the economic. The GRI Sustainability Reporting Guidelines, for example, aim to offer a standardized public reporting format for social, environmental and economic elements of sustainable development, and indeed their relationship (thereby seeking to fulfil conditions (1) and (2)). In some ways this reporting standard supersedes what for a number of years has been a key 'environmental plus' reporting standard developed by the consultancy SustainAbility Ltd in association with UNEP. AA1000 is a further attempt at an integrating standard, only this time focused on the stakeholder engagement, accounting and auditing elements of the cycle. AA1000 has been designed, like SA8000, to be linked to a professional training and accreditation process.

There are significant qualitative differences between these emerging standards that reflect their different intended uses and link back to the earlier discussion about the need to balance codification against flexibility for innovation. The GRI, for example, is intended to evolve to a highly codified level with specific indicator reporting requirements in all of the key areas. This reflects the emphasis on public accountability, and in many ways the US-focus on measurement and comparability. Only in the 'sustainability' area of the reporting guidelines is there designed flexibility, where the reporting entity is invited to reflect on its overall perspective and approach to sustainability. AA1000, on the other hand, is far more flexible, to such a degree in fact that some see it as a quality assurance framework rather than a standard. There are no specific metrics within the standard, and in its initial form there is also an open approach to validating differing approaches to verification. What it does offer, however, is the broad architecture of the process, and emphasizes its core underlying principles.

It would be misleading to suggest that there is currently a preferred approach to standardization at any of the four levels set out above. Each has its advantages and potential dilemmas to overcome. The most significant dilemmas all arise from issues raised in the preceding elements of the chapters in this section, and include the following:

● *Boundaries* evolve over time and reflect ongoing, negotiated patterns of responsibilities. This makes the codification requirements associated with defining the 'entity' quite unlike, for example, those historically used for financial and environmental accounting and auditing. Codification will critically require a *process* element that reflects on the quality of dialogue that goes into defining the boundaries at any point in time.

- *Reporting Elements* will, similarly, change over time as the learning of the organization evolves through, for example, dialogue and reflection. These changes will partly reflect boundary shifts, but also the evolving understanding of how best to measure performance of identified elements of behaviour, activities and outcomes.
- *Verification* to gain credibility for what has been reported will almost certainly evolve into a multi-layered process involving different institutions with varied competencies and reputations. Quantitative accuracy and procedural robustness will be subjected to increasingly professionalized inspection by in the main traditional service providers, the accountants and management consultants. Definition of boundaries and reporting elements, on other hand, are more likely to be handled by organizations with skills in facilitating and overseeing dialogue and with reputations for integrity in their social and environmental purpose as well as their competencies. In this last sense, the emphasis of independence through 'studied neutrality' will shift more towards providing credibility from those with a strong values-alignment with the issues and people concerned.
- *Professionalization* should involve the evolution of appropriate training and accreditation by suitable institutions. In practice, this traditional professionalization process will be challenged on many counts, and so to a degree is likely to be re-moulded, by civil activists. At the heart of this already lively debate will be the matter of how competencies relate to trust and integrity.

Purpose is difficult to institutionalize. Indeed, in many ways the codification that underpins effective professionalization is precisely to overcome the diversity of purposes of those who may engage in a field of endeavour. But even from this perspective, professionalization does not overcome the matter of purpose: it simply raises it from the level of the individual to that of the institutional framework within which the professional evolves. That is why a critique of the GRI, AA1000 or SA8000 is as likely to focus on the question of governance of the overseeing institutions as it is to light on one or other specific elements of method. Governance of standard-setting bodies lies at the heart of the discussion of the New Civil Governance in an earlier chapter.

BEYOND VERIFICATION

The use of expert panels and other hybrid approaches to external verification is a positive and productive development during this period of experimentation. They seek in different ways to bring together the requisite combinations of competencies and credibilities needed to deliver a reasonable degree of trust in the finished product. Emerging approaches to standardization of external verification also helps, certainly. It regularizes what can be expected of external auditors and verifying processes, the competencies that they need, and therefore what their involvement does, and does not, signify. It is certainly crucial that the process of standardization continues, although it carries with it the dangers of over-simplification, at best, and at worst a re-marginalization of the underlying performance issues under the guise of pragmatic professionalism.

But these approaches (including some of those that the author has helped in designing) are unlikely to form the basis for more stable, robust and credible approaches for the longer term. This is because they are seeking – and largely failing – to deal with issues that should properly be dealt with elsewhere in the overall process of corporate and societal governance. Financial auditing seeks to hold the executives of a company to account, especially its directors, particularly on behalf of its shareholders. The external verification process built into (most) financial auditing is part of a far broader set of rules and regulations that make up the overall framework within which companies are governed. This for example includes – for listed corporations – the role of directors, the legal setting within which information needs to be handled, and a host of less formalized best practice norms covering such matters as the role of audit committees and non-executive directors.[21]

Stakeholder and other forms of expert panels linked in to the external verification of social and environmental reports are essentially ways of handling inadequacies in the overall approaches to governance taken by individual corporations and the business community as a whole. Many company directors, for example, have neither the credibility nor often the expertise to provide robust oversight for a company's social and environmental performance. Most non-executive directors, at least in the UK, are brought in to strengthen the company's credibility in the eyes of the financial community or major potential customers. Audit committees comprise people with expertise to provide oversight of a company's finances. Few fund managers have the expertise let alone the incentives to seriously factor in social and environmental issues. Even if social and environmental parameters constitute a significant long-term financial risk, this is of little interest to those fund managers who are unlikely to hold the stock for more than a few days or months, as discussed in previous chapters. In short, neither the people principally responsible for the implementation of corporate governance, nor the mandates under which they operate, equip them adequately to cope even with the financial risks associated with social and environmental performance, let alone questions related to the non-financial substantive implications of the performance itself.[22]

Approaches to external verification of social, environmental and sustainability reports must continue to be improved. Furthermore, external verification is a prerequisite for corporations using disclosure as one element of their broader basis of accountability and legitimacy. At the same time, external verification cannot form the pivotal point around which such a broad basis for corporate accountability can be secured. Methodological and institutional limitations noted here and elsewhere will not be effectively or sufficiently overcome such that external verification will ever provide an adequate substitute for establishing a framework of accountability that extends across and beyond the corporate body.

Professionalized, standardized approaches to external verification are useful for securing the robustness of information that fits into well-defined frames of reference. They are not, and are unlikely to be, useful where the boundaries of accountability are contested and dynamic. External verification, at least its more standardized variants, will tend to follow the leading edge of change, and at times some way behind. So, for example, it is becoming increasingly possible to apply standardized approaches to external verification of basic health and safety dimensions of labour standards. On the other hand, the realm of, say, sexual harassment needs to be coped with through more empathetic, dialogic approaches. This does not mean that the latter cannot be 'professional' in the sense of being competent. Rather, that a highly codified approach to this area is less likely to be effective, particularly when implemented by people engaged purely for normal financial gain.

External verification has its rightful place. But this place is, rightly, limited. Engagement with stakeholders, effective learning, and real changes in performance are more likely to count as litmus tests in building trust and credibility. External verification, although certainly necessary, will rarely if ever be sufficient, or even the primary route, for the corporation to gain the credibility to be deemed, or in practice be, civil.

Part 4

Conclusions

CHAPTER 17

How Civil Can Corporations Be?

UNEARTHLY BEINGS

A little known utopian fairy tale written by Carl Ewald during the Weimar period in Germany, *A Fairy Tale About God and Kings*, tells of a group of citizens who, fed up with the kings that rule them, trek to heaven to appeal directly to God. Having talked their way past the heavenly guards, they present their petition. If you are indeed good and all powerful, they plead, you must do something about these kings. God consults extensively with advisers, and goes so far as to commission senior angels to research the matter. Days go by, and the citizens group waits patiently, sure that justice will be done. Eventually, they are called again before God who, flanked by teams of celestial counsellors, gives an answer. Commanding the citizens to return back to earth, God explains, 'Kings were not my idea. They are your own invention, so there's nothing I can do for you; you will have to sort it out yourselves.'[1]

This short, political fable is neither about gods nor kings; nor is it about good, bad or evil. It is about our ability to create the futures that we want, and where necessary to re-mould the institutions that govern our lives to suit the purpose for which they were intended, or for which they are now needed. This is as true for businesses as for any other aspect of our future. Businesses are run by people for people. They are no more or less than a human invention for making things out of other things and getting them into use; using and making money; and for making people variously happy, satisfied or simply able to survive.

Institutions can certainly be changed, but that does not mean it is easy to do so. People in positions of power have vested interests in keeping them as they are. They build and maintain mechanisms that protect and indeed nurture historic patterns. Some of this is laudable and even virtuous; some is destructive and unacceptable, even when it is within the law. Many people quite unknowingly, and sometimes uncaringly, perpetuate institutional bad habits by virtue of their investing or buying patterns. This is rarely because they consciously seek to do others harm. Even the meanest, leanest, short-term investor rarely sets out to support a corporation *because* it undermines human rights or creates environmental havoc. It is simply that they do not take or want to take responsibility for the bigger picture, and therefore are satisfied in taking what they can, given the way things are.

SCEPTICAL OPTIMISM

Sceptical optimism is a productive stance to take in assessing the potential and pitfalls of corporate citizenship. Scepticism is, after all, not only an appropriate foundation on which to base penetrating enquiry, but also guards against today's pervasive, all-too-safe cynicism. Optimism is scepticism's crucial accompaniment in that it offers vision and direction, and so guards against the passivity that comes with its pessimistic alter ego.

This book has taken a sceptically optimistic stance in exploring the critical issue of the role of business in society. It has considered, firstly, the strategic question of what we can and should expect from the business community in addressing the imperatives and aspirations underpinning sustainable development. Secondly, it has delved into the more operational question of whether and how these expectations can in practice be realized. On the first question, the exploration has concluded that there are cautious grounds for optimism. The emerging New Economy does offer corporations greater opportunities for securing significant competitive advantage by addressing social and environmental challenges. The viability of such strategies depends largely on two factors: the economic strength of adopting corporations, and the emergence of institutional arrangements that serve to guide and stabilize progressive market norms as they emerge. For the first, those corporations able to lever markets through their size and agility will be more effective in securing competitive advantage from citizenship strategies. Many are able to force their competitors to follow suit, if necessary through the regulatory route. For the second, the emergence of new governance frameworks involving the business community working with, for example, NGOs and public bodies can over time tend to reinforce and support good corporate citizenship in the New Economy.

On the second question, the book suggests that understanding the real potential contribution of the business community requires a shift away from the aspirational architecture of sustainable development to an approach sensitive to the scope for and nature of change. The *civil corporation* is proposed as one that takes full advantage of opportunities for learning and action in building social and environmental objectives into its core business by effectively developing its internal values and competencies. Such a process-oriented approach is not a retreat from vision, but a means of understanding, encouraging and calibrating progress. Working on the *how* is critically dependent on corporations' adoption of appropriate new approaches, tools, and above all values and attitudes. Those discussed in earlier chapters include new forms of measurement and accounting, stakeholder engagement, the standardization and professionalization of disclosure and external verification, and governance. These dimensions of the business process are all elements of how corporations acquire and use knowledge, and can themselves be impacted and transformed in the process.

Corporations that build such internal competencies can align their business more effectively to those social and environmental issues around which market opportunities based on stakeholder interests, loyalty and commitment can be built. These are the civil corporations that will drive markets in more ethical directions. Others will be followers rather than leaders, tending to emulate best practice by adopting emerging standardized approaches. Then there are and will continue to be those corporations that do not develop such competencies. These will seek other means of securing competitive advantage. In so doing they will either fail to survive, or remain or become part of the problem.

TOMORROW'S WORLD

The civil corporation can exist in the here and now. Their characterization is not based on a predicted financial, nuclear or environmental meltdown. Similarly, there is no reliance on, for example, radical localization or a global citizens' revolution, virtual or otherwise. Finally, the practicality of the civil corporation does not depend on any fundamental change in people's nature as we generally experience it. A 'modern utopia', insisted H G Wells a century ago, 'must have people inherently the same as those in the world'.[2]

Tomorrow has therefore been assumed to be a fundamentally familiar place. But that does not mean that things will stay the same. The unusually public and publicized view of the CIA of the world in 2015 makes salutary reading.[3] It points to what it sees as a wealth of positive potential developments, mainly emerging through the effective application of emerging technological opportunities. However, it also sees an exacerbation of current social and environmental problems as a result of continued population growth, unequal application of new technologies, and constraints in availability of and access to basic resources, notably water. Few people believe, and certainly this includes the host of experts consulted by the CIA, that an extrapolation of current political, social and economic development patterns will deliver the significant improvements needed to underpin a sustainable development pathway.

Not surprisingly, the CIA's public conclusions do not predict any radical shift in the way economic development is guided, whether by governments and international agencies, the business community or other key players. In their future scenario, NGOs become more influential, and national governments in the main become weaker or, for a few, become more powerful transnational players. The CIA is probably correct in its broad view of likely developments for NGOs and governments. Changes in the role of the state over the last two decades are almost certainly little more than a preview of what is to come. NGOs, similarly, are in a period of great change, as they adjust to the extension of the market, the globalization of concerns and opportunities, and the extraordinary rise of their own power into hitherto uncharted waters.

Box 17.1 *Some of the CIA's View of the World in 2015*

Demographics
World population in 2015 will be 7.2 billion, up from 6.1 billion in the year 2000, and in most countries, people will live longer. Ninety-five per cent of the increase will be in developing countries, nearly all in rapidly expanding urban areas. Where political systems are brittle, the combination of population growth and urbanization will foster instability. More than half of the world's population will be urban.

Food
Overall food production will be adequate to feed the world's growing population, but poor infrastructure and distribution, political instability, and chronic poverty will lead to a 20 per cent increase in numbers of malnourished people in parts of sub-Saharan Africa.

Water
Nearly half the world's population – more than 3 billion people – will live in countries that are 'water-stressed' (less than 1700 m^3 of water per capita per year) mostly in Africa, the Middle East, South Asia and northern China.

Environment
Contemporary environmental problems will persist and in many instances grow over the next 15 years. With increasingly intensive land use, significant degradation of arable land will continue as will the loss of tropical forests. . . greenhouse gas emissions will increase substantially. The depletion of tropical forests and other species-rich habitats, such as wetlands and coral reefs, will exacerbate the historically large losses of biological species now occurring.

Health
Disparities in health status between developed and developing countries will persist and widen. In developed countries, major inroads against a variety of maladies will be achieved by 2015 as a result of generous health spending and major medical advances. The revolution in biotechnology holds the promise of even more dramatic improvements in health status. AIDS will reduce economic growth by up to 1 per cent of GDP per year and consume more than 50 per cent of health budgets in the hardest-hit countries.

On business, the CIA and its advisers are strangely silent. The assumption made is, quite simply, business as usual. Yet it is the business community that is changing most rapidly and dramatically, and this is likely only to accelerate over the coming years. The business community is undoubtedly becoming more powerful, notably the small number of global corporations that dominate international trade and investment and have unparalleled access to capital and influence over public policy and the media. At the same time, corporations are not a homogeneous group, and are arguably becoming less so as the nature of competition shifts in ways described in earlier chapters. We are witnessing a global experiment in the evolution of the corporate community. Coming decades will see radical shifts in how they are owned, managed and governed; in what they produce, on what terms, and for whom. Their legal rights and responsibilities will be increasingly fought over; both in the end are likely to grow significantly. As their basis for differentiation becomes increasingly value-based, we may not even call them businesses, but perhaps *value-webs* or simply communities-of-interest. Most of all, perhaps, the relationships between business, the state and private non-profit organizations (of which NGOs are only one variant) will transform over the coming years, as the earlier discussion of the new civil governance suggests.

Today's public concern and often outrage at the growing power and practices of the corporations is, to be frank, unlikely to be sustained into the future in its current forms. Increasing insecurity emanating from civil, environmental and financial instabilities may well make relatively familiar and secure corporations a more attractive proposition to many, particularly in those societies with rapidly ageing populations that place particular value on security and stability. Younger generations, similarly, will be the first to grow up in societies where massive global corporations are the norm. How, or even whether, their particular radical agenda plays itself out remains entirely unclear at this stage. They may well be more comfortable with embracing progressive corporations and setting them against others, rather than challenging the presumptions underlying the corporate community as a whole. This is certainly not a prediction of the 'end of history'. But it is a prediction that the frontlines of our concerns with today's institutions, and also our visions for them, will change in the not too distant future, and dramatically so.

IS BEING CIVIL ENOUGH?

Corporations can be civil. But can they and will they be civil enough? The preceding chapters here posed and sought to answer the practical questions underlying this challenge. Can even the most enlightened business improve its social and environmental performance sufficiently to reach universally accepted standards while remaining a viable business? Even if some could do so by virtue of their visionary leadership and powerful market position, would they remain worthy but isolated examples within what is otherwise a mass of poor social and environmental performers? Finally and most important, will all these developments add up to a coherent response to the third generation (see Chapter 6) question of what roles good corporate citizenship will play in addressing the really big social and environmental challenges of both today's and tomorrow's world?

The recent history of corporate citizenship offers us insights into the answers to these questions.

- *Good practices by some corporations, even those that prove sustainable, will not alone ensure that the wider business community meets basic social and environmental standards.* Market fragmentation, even in those markets where a few players are relatively dominant, will limit the extent to which the wider business community follows corporations leading in improving their social and environmental performance, even where there is a competitive edge gained through such leadership.
- *Powerful dynamics driving the New Economy will tend to undermine good corporate citizenship, as well as those elements that tend to nurture it.* 'Impatient money' will tend to penalize those seeking to enhance their longer-term business success through really significant enhancements in social and environmental performance. Such attempts by most corporations will not be sustainable unless they are rewarded in financial terms through the markets in which they operate, or/and supported by enabling legislation.
- *Private standards could be either part of the solution or the problem, and will in practice be both.* Standards may exist along any of the pathways, even those that extend into ethical wastelands. It should not be assumed that private standards push the change process into the positive innovation cycle (Mecca), even where they are technically good standards.

That is, individual corporations acting alone will rarely be able to sustain *significantly* enhanced social and environmental performance for extended periods of time. Another way of looking at this is that if corporations seeking to achieve this are not emulated by their competitors, it either means that the corporation has failed to achieve any competitive advantage through its good practices, or that its competitive advantage exists only within a restricted market niche that has high barriers to entry and does not threaten the broader market (and so will not have extended impact). From this perspective, corporate citizenship based on leadership practices that are not institutionalized beyond the individual corporation is unlikely to deliver adequate social and environmental goods, and offset bads, to meaningfully address the third generation challenge.

To effectively move beyond the Oasis and steer clear of the Desert pathways, the civil corporation will have to take a lead in creating collective processes, and codifying best practice and building adequate oversight to ensure implementation across the wider business community. Two specific inferences can be drawn from the preceding chapters:

(1) *Alliances of corporations have a far greater chance to sustain significant enhancements in social and environmental performance, and also to influence other market players to follow suit.* Such alliances may form within sectors, or may also be geographically or thematically focused. For this to be worth their while, however, is likely to require multi-stakeholder alliances that bring together public bodies and private non-profit organizations such as NGOs and trade unions.

(2) *Such civil alliances and partnerships will over time seek to codify negotiated agreements into more formalized governance frameworks.* The main reasons for this are to reduce transaction and other costs and increase the potential for replication by others. These new civil governance frameworks will in some instances promote public, statutory regulation and at other times seek to regulate through private standards. Those frameworks that fail to effectively codify agreements will, over time, fail and eventually collapse. Public bodies and private non-profit organizations, and indeed civil corporations, will withdraw their support and so remove a critical source of legitimacy as well as operational competencies.

There is no simple template or magic bullet that will secure a progressive role for the business community in addressing the challenges and aspirations underlying sustainable development. That the business community is so powerful does not offset the fact that even its more dominant members have restricted room for manoeuvre, certainly in the shorter term. It makes no sense to promote virtuous corporations that are, as a result, absorbed by their less angelic competitors. This reality partly reflects on business's more powerful stakeholders. After all, business behaviour and performance embodies, codifies and in many ways reinforces *our own* ambivalence as to how we trade off personal and collective interests, both now and into the future.

The propositions underlying the *civil corporation* do offer a route for getting the most out of economy and business in addressing social and environmental aims and challenges. The book has sought to frame how best to identify and guide corporations in developing viable business strategies and practices that deliver against such aims and challenges. Most important, perhaps, it has sought to answer the more daunting question of how much we can expect from business – and corporate citizenship – in overcoming global poverty, inequality and environmental insecurity. The core answer to this critical question is that corporate citizenship will only be effective if and where it evolves to a point where business becomes active in promoting and institutionalizing new global governance frameworks that effectively secure civil market behaviour. Leading civil corporations will be those that go beyond getting their own house in order, and actively engage in promoting governance frameworks that enable, and if necessary enforce, the wider business community to address, effectively and without contradiction, the aspirations underpinning sustainable development.

Notes

INTRODUCTION – BEYOND THE MAINSTREAM

1 Smith, A (1759) *The Theory of Moral Sentiments*, A Millar, London

2 Paraphrased from a speech he gave at AccountAbility's 'Accountability 21: Reinventing Accountability for the 21st Century' conference in October 2005 (Burgis, T and Zadek, S (2006) *Accountability 21: Reinventing Accountability for the 21st century*, AccountAbility, London).

3 Zadek, S (2006) *The Logic of Collaborative Governance: Corporate Responsibility, Accountability and the Social Contract*, Working Paper 14, CSR Initiative, Centre for Government and Business, J.F Kennedy School for Government, Harvard University, Cambridge, MA

4 Dalberg (2006) *Report of the Task Force on Capacity for Program Delivery: From Talk to Walk: Ideas to Optimize Development Impact*, A Clinton Global Initiative Commitment, Dalberg Global Development Advisors, Washington, DC

5 Zadek, S (2004) 'Paths to corporate responsibility', *Harvard Business Review*, vol 12, December

6 AccountAbility (2003) *AA1000 Assurance Standard*, AccountAbility, London

7 Forstater, M, Oelschaegel, J and Sillanpää, M (2006) *What Assures Consumers?*, AccountAbility in association with the National Consumer Council, London

8 Zadek, S (2006) 'Separating smart from great: Embedding accountability into business practices isn't easy', *Fortune International*, 30 October, pp74–77

9 Radovich, S (2006) *The Global Alliance for Workers and Communities: Lessons Learnt From A Multi-Stakeholder Initiative*, AccountAbility, London

10 Barrientos, S and Smith, S (2006) *The ETI Code of Labour Practice: Do Workers Really Benefit?*, Institute of Development Studies, Brighton

11 Zadek, S, Merme, M and Samans, R (2005) *Mainstreaming Responsible Investment*, World Economic Forum in association with AccountAbility, Geneva

12 Gore, A (2006) *An Inconvenient Truth: The Planetary Emergency of Global Warming and What We Can Do About It*, Bloomsbury, London

13 IPPR (2001) *Building Better Partnerships, the Final Report on the Commission on Private Public Partnerships*, IPPR, London; Radovich, S and Zadek, S (2006) *Governing Partnership Governance: Enhancing Development Outcomes By Improving Partnership Governance and Accountability*, Working Paper 23, CSR Initiative, Centre for Government and Business, J F Kennedy School for Government, Harvard University, Cambridge, MA

14 www.ge.com/en/citizenship/overview/immelt_letter.htm

15 Zadek, S, Merme, M and Samans, R (2005) *Mainstreaming Responsible Investment*, World Economic Forum in association with AccountAbility, Geneva

16 http://technology.guardian.co.uk/ news/story/0,,1842281,00.html
17 Statement of Financial Accounting Concepts No. 2, Qualitative Characteristics of Accounting Information, Financial Accounting Standards Board (FASB).
18 BP US Refineries Independent Safety Review Panel (2007) *The Report of The BP US Refineries Independent Safety Review Panel*, Washington, DC, pxiv
19 Zadek, S and Merme, M (2004) *Redefining Materiality*, AccountAbility, London; Forstater, M, Zadek, S, Evans, D, Knight, A, Sillanpää, M, Tuppen, C and Warris, A-M (2006) *The Materiality Report: Aligning Strategy, Performance and Reporting*, AccountAbility in association with the BT Group and LRQA, London
20 Davis, I (2005) 'The biggest contract', *The Economist*, 6 May
21 My italics for emphasis. Quotation from Annan, K (2000) *Economic Growth About People – Their Health, Education, Security*, opening address to Geneva 2000: World Focus on Social Development, UN General Assembly meeting, 25 June
22 Jaruzelski, B, Dehoff, K and Bordia, R (2006) *Smart Spenders: The Global Innovation 1000*, Booz Allen Hamilton, New York
23 Zadek, S (2004) 'Paths to corporate responsibility', *Harvard Business Review*, vol 12, December; Zadek, S (2006) *The Logic of Collaborative Governance: Corporate Responsibility, Accountability and the Social Contract*, Working Paper 14, CSR Initiative, Centre for Government and Business, J F Kennedy School for Government, Harvard University, Cambridge, MA; Zadek, S, Raynard, P, Oliviero, C, do Nascimento, E and Tello, R (2005) *Responsible Competitiveness: Reshaping Global Markets Through Responsible Business Practices*, AccountAbility, London

24 McGillivray, A, Marten, H, Rüdiger, K, Vilanova, M, Zollo, M, Begley, P and Zadek, S (2007) *Responsible Competitiveness in Europe: Enhancing European Competitiveness through Corporate Responsibility*, AccountAbility, London
25 Zadek, S (2000) *Ethical Trade Futures*, New Economics Foundation, London
26 In discussion with author.
27 Aydin, Z (editor) (2003) *Multi-Stakeholder Partnerships and UN–Civil Society Relationships*, UN, New York
28 Kuhn, T (1962) *The Structure of Scientific Revolutions*, University of Chicago Press, Chicago, IL

CHAPTER 1
CAN CORPORATIONS
BE CIVIL?

1 Social Exclusion Unit (1999) *Social Exclusion Unit's Policy Action Team 3 Report, Enterprise and Social Exclusion*, United Kingdom Government, London
2 Quote drawn from remark made at the annual conference of Business for Social Responsibility in San Francisco in November 1999
3 United Nations (1998) *Human Development Report 1998*, UN, New York
4 *The Economist*, 31 December 1999, p11
5 United Nations (1999) *Human Development Report 1999*, UN, New York, p129–130
6 United Nations (2000) *Human Development Report 2000*, UN, New York, p4
7 Lewnhak, H (1997) *International Labour Organisation Digest*, January
8 United Nations (2000) *Human Development Report 2000*, p4
9 ibid
10 Zadek, S and Tuppen, C (2000) *Adding Values: the Economics*

of Sustainable Business, British Telecommunications Occasional Paper 4, BT, London, p2

11 Hawken, P (1997) 'Natural Capitalism', *Mother Jones Reprints*, San Francisco

12 United Nations (1998), op cit, note 3

13 ibid

14 Speech at Chatham House, London

15 ibidem, italics added

16 Sachs, J, Stone, G and Warner, A (1999) 'Year in Review', in *Global Competitiveness Report*, World Economic Forum, Geneva, p15

17 op cit, note 5, p131

18 Anderson, S and Cavanagh, J (1996) *The Top 200: The Rise of Corporate Global Power*, Institute of Policy Studies, Washington, DC

19 Quoted in Wheeler, D and Sillanpää, M (1997) *The Stakeholder Corporation: A Blueprint for Maximising Stakeholder Value*, Pitman, London

20 Utting, P (2000) *Business Responsibility for Sustainable Development*, United Nations Research Institute on Social Development, Geneva, p5

21 World Bank (1997) *World Development Indicators*, World Bank, Washington, DC

22 Taken from Zarsky, L (1999) *Havens, Halos And Spaghetti: Untangling The Evidence About Foreign Direct Investment And The Environment*, Nautilus Institute for Security and Sustainable Development, California (http://www.nautilus.org/papers/enviro/index.html)

23 United Nations Conference on Trade And Development (1998) *World Investment Report*, quoted from World Development Movement (1998) *Making Investment Work for People: An International Framework for Investment*, WDM Consultation Paper, WDM, London

24 Hawken, P, Lovins, A and Lovins, L H (1999) *Natural Capitalism: Creating the Next Industrial Revolution*, Earthscan, London, p311–312

25 Broad, R and Cavanagh, J (1999) 'The Death of the Washington Consensus?' in *World Policy Journal*, vol XVI, no 3, Fall 1999, p79–88

26 Personal correspondence

27 Business for Social Responsibility's annual conference in San Francisco in November 1999

28 Castells, M (1996–2000) *The Information Age: Economy, Society, and Culture*, Oxford, Blackwell, vols I, II and III

CHAPTER 2
OPENING MINDS

1 Many thanks to the innovative communication company, St Lukes; I have borrowed their mission statement as this chapter's title

2 Max-Neef, M, Elizalde, A and Hopenhayn, M (1991) *Human Scale Development: Conception, Application and Further Reflection*, Apex Press, New York, p1

3 In *New Statesman* 20 December 1999 – 3 January 2000, p7

4 South African Breweries (2000) *Corporate Citizenship Review 1999*, SAB, London (www.sabplc.com)

5 Southern Sun (2000) *Values and Value Adding: Corporate Citizenship Report*, Southern Sun Group, Santon

6 World's Most Respected Companies, FT Survey 2000, www.news.ft.com

7 www.bsr.org

8 The Corporate Citizenship Company (2000) *Monitoring, Measuring and Reporting Corporate Social Responsibility*, The Corporate Citizenship Company, London (www.corporate-citizenship.co.uk)

9 Hines, C (2000) *Localisation: A Global Manifesto*, Earthscan, London

10 Klein, N (2000) *No Logo*, Flamingo, London

11 World Development Movement
(1999) *Making Investment Work for
People*, WDM, London, adapted from
Annex
12 HIS (1999) *Peduli Hak: Caring for
Rights*, Insan Hitawasana Sejahtera,
Jakarta
13 Zadek, S (1999) 'Reflections on a
Factory Visit', in *Global Alliance for
Workers and Communities: Progress
Report*, Fall, p3–4
14 European Commission (1999) *2nd
EU-US Symposium on Codes of Conduct
and International Labour Standards*,
European Commission DGV, March
1999
15 Institute of Social and Ethical
AccountAbility (1999) *AA1000:
Overview of Standard, Guidelines, and
Tools*, ISEA, London
16 CIA (2000) *Global Trends 2015:
A Dialogue About the Future with
Nongovernmental Experts*
www.cia.gov/cia/publications/
globaltrends2015/index.html
17 This section is drawn from
an unpublished paper entitled
'Sustainable (Consumption-
Development)=Factor X' presented
by the author at a conference of the
Society for International Development
(SID) in Santiago de Compostela in
1997
18 Costanza, R, et al (1997) 'The Value
of the World's Ecosystem Services and
Natural Capital', *Nature*, May
19 von Weitsacker, E, Lovins, A
and Lovins, L H (1997) *Factor Four:
Doubling Wealth, Halving Resource Use*,
Earthscan, London
20 Wackernagel, M and Rees, W (1995)
Our Ecological Footprint, New Catalyst,
Philadelphia
21 New Economics Foundation (1997)
Community Works! NEF, London
22 Bloch, E (1986) *The Principle of Hope*,
Blackwell, Oxford
23 Max-Neef, M, Elizalde, A and
Hopenhayn, M (1991) op cit, note 2

CHAPTER 3
ETHICAL FUTURES

1 Cavenagh, T (1999) *Community
Connections: Strategic Partnerships in
the Digital Industries*, Research Report
1254-99-RR, The Conference Board,
New York, p5
2 Joy, B (2000) 'Why the Future
Doesn't Need Us', *Wired Magazine*,
April
3 Earlier versions of this and the
subsequent section appeared in
Zadek, S, Højensgård, N and
Raynard, P (2000) *The New Economy
of Corporate Citizenship*, The
Copenhagen Centre, Copenhagen
(www.copenhagencentre.org)
4 Samuel, J (1999) 'Dotcom Delusions'
(www.ncasindia.org) in Zadek,
S, Højensgård, N and Raynard, P
(eds) (2001) *Perspectives on the New
Economy of Corporate Citizenship*, The
Copenhagen Centre, Copenhagen
(www.copenhagencentre.org)
5 Cavenagh, T (1999) op cit,
note 1
6 In Preface to Zadek, S, Højensgård,
N and Raynard, P (eds) (2001) op cit,
note 4
7 Castells, M (1996–2000) *The
Information Age: Economy, Society, and
Culture*, vols I, II and III, Blackwells,
Oxford
8 European Central Bank (2000)
'Europe, A New Economy?' ECB Press
Office, http://www.ecb.int
9 *The Economist New Economy Survey*,
23 September 2000
10 Zuckerman, M (1999) *Speed:
Linking Innovation, Process, and Time to
Market*, Research Report 1269-00-RR,
Conference Board, New York
11 Thanks to David Vidal of the
Conference Board for offering me this
useful perspective
12 Business Week Online, 28 August
2000

13 Wilsdon, J (2000) *The Capitals Model: A Framework for Sustainability*, Working Paper prepared for SIGMA Project, Forum for the Future, London, p11

14 Clifton, R and Maughan, E (1999) *The Future of Brands: Twenty Five Visions*, Macmillan Business, London

15 Organisation for Economic Co-operation and Development (1999) *The Economic and Social Implications of E-Commerce*, OECD, Paris

16 Johnston, P (2001) 'Corporate Responsibility in Employment Standards in a Global Knowledge Economy', in Zadek, S, Højensgård, N and Raynard, P (eds) *Perspectives on the New Economy of Corporate Citizenship*, The Copenhagen Centre, Copenhagen.

17 Casson, M (1998) 'The Economics of Ethical Leadership' in *The Role of Business Ethics in Economic Performance*, Jones, I and Pollitt, M (eds) Macmillan Press, Basingstoke

18 Forstater, M and Raynard, P (2001) *Key Initiatives in the Development of Corporate Social Responsibility and the New Economy in Europe*, Working Paper prepared for The Copenhagen Centre, TCC, Copenhagen (www. copenhagencentre.org)

19 Reported in *The Economist Technology Quarterly*, 9 December 2000, p6

20 Klein, N (2000) *No Logo*, Flamingo, London

21 www.unglobalcompact.org

22 *FT's Annual Survey of the World's Most Respected Companies* (www.news. ft.com). It is worth noting here that PricewaterhouseCoopers, in designing the methodology, has weighted the responses by the GDP per capita of the countries from which they came. Not surprisingly, this introduces a massive bias in favour of the US, and in some ways leaves one wondering how any non-US companies come to be included in the results

23 United Nations Environment Programme/SustainAbility (2000) *Global Sustainability Reporters: A Benchmark Study*, SustainAbility, London. Score for UK in top 25 includes Anglo-Dutch Shell

24 Sustainability Asset Management (2000) *Biographies of Corporate Sustainability Leaders*, SAM, Zurich (www.sam-group.ch/e/center/c_reports.cfm)

25 www.news.ft.com

26 Quoted in 'A Pragmatic Capitalist and Social Romantic' in the *Financial Times* 27 November 2000, p18

27 These pathways were originally described in Zadek, S (2000) *Ethical Trade Futures*, New Economics Foundation, London. I am indebted to John Elkington, Judith Mullins and Mark Wade for naming and helping me to visualize the pathways

CHAPTER 4
BREAKING THE
TRUST BARRIER

1 Taken from a speech given at a conference on social accountability in Copenhagen in Spring 1999

2 Zadek, S, Lingayah, S and Forstater, M (1998) *Selling Ethics: Understanding How Social Labels Work*, European Commission, Brussels

3 Quoted in Zadek, S (1999) 'The Global Supermarket', in World Business Council for Sustainable Development (ed) *World Development: Aid and Foreign Direct Investment*, Kensington Publications, London, p248–249

4 Green, D (1998) *Views From The South: Conference Report on Ethical Trade*, NGO Labour Rights Network, London

5 Levi Strauss (1998) *Program Overview: An Independent Evaluation of Levi Strauss & Co's. Code of Conduct process: A Pilot Program in the Dominican Republic*, report presented at the annual Business for Social

Responsibility conference in San
Francisco in August 1998
6 Traidcraft plc (1994) *Social Audit
1993*, Traidcraft, Gateshead, UK
7 LaFeber, W (1999) *Michael Jordan
and the New Global Capitalism*, WW
Norton, New York, p137
8 Quoted in LaFeber (1999), op cit,
p134
9 NatWest Group (1999) *Social Impact
Review 1998/1999*, NatWest Group,
London, p24
10 Shell International (1999) *The
Shell Report 1999*, Shell International,
London, p13
11 ibid, p27
12 LaFeber (1999), op cit, p149
13 Extract from open memo sent
by the Maquila Solidarity Network
Canada (perg@web.net) to human
and labour rights activists and
organisations, 10 April 1999
14 NatWest Group (1999), op cit, p24

CHAPTER 5
CIVIL REGULATION

1 Non-attributable statement made on
anti-GAP campaign listserve
2 This study is not publicly available,
but was undertaken as part of a
consultancy by one of the major
accountancy companies for a major
European blue-chip company
3 Arguments and cases presented
in this and the next chapter have
appeared in two publications by the
author: Zadek, S (2000) *Doing Good
and Doing Well: The Business Case for
Corporate Citizenship*, Conference Board,
New York; and Weiser, J and Zadek, S
(2000) *Conversations With Disbelievers:
Persuading Companies to Increase Their
Social Engagement*, Brody & Weiser,
Massachusetts (www.zadek.net)
4 Utting, P (2000) *Business
Responsibility for Sustainable
Development*, Geneva 2000, Occasional
Paper 2, January, United Nations
Research Institute for Social
Development, Geneva, p7
5 Friedman, M (1970) 'The Social
Responsibility Is to Increase Profits', in
New York Times Magazine, 13 September,
p32–33
6 In Nelson, J and Zadek, S
(2000) *Partnership Alchemy: New
Social Partnerships in Europe*, The
Copenhagen Centre, Copenhagen
7 Ford Motor Company (2000)
*Connecting With Society: 1999 Corporate
Citizenship Report*, Ford Motor
Company, Dearborn, Michigan
8 Placer Dome, Inc (2000) *Ensuring
Our Future: Sustainability Report 1999*,
Placer Dome, Vancouver, BC (www.
placerdome.com)
9 British Airports Authority (1999)
*Growing With the Support and Trust of
Our Neighbours*, BAA, London, p2
10 Shell (1999) *The Shell Report 1999:
People, Planet and Profits – An Act
of Commitment*, Shell International,
London. Quote from inside front
cover
11 Quoted in Nelson, J and Zadek, S
(2000) op cit, note 5
12 World Business Council for Social
Development (1999) *Corporate Social
Responsibility*, WBCSD, Geneva, p2
13 Confederation of British Industry
(1999) *Global Social Responsibility*, CBI,
London, p2
14 Korten, D (1997) *When Corporations
Rule the World*, Kumarian, West
Hartford, Connecticut
15 Goyder, M (1998) *The Living
Company*, Gower, Aldershot, UK
16 The idea of lent power was first
advanced in a paper prepared for
the UN Human Development Report
Office, which was subsequently
published as Zadek, S, Lingayah, S
and Murphy, S (1998) *Purchasing
Power: Civil Action for Sustainable
Consumption*, New Economics
Foundation, London
17 A group of largely US-based
corporations committed to opposing

an international agreement on climate control involving business restraints

18 The Body Shop (1998) *Values Report,* The Body Shop, Littlehampton, UK

19 Murphy, D F and Bendell, J (1997) *In the Company of Partners: Business, Environmental Groups and Sustainable Development Post-Rio,* The Polity Press, Bristol

20 Zadek, S and Amalric, F (1998) 'Consumer Works!' in *Development,* vol 41, no 1, March, Special Issue on Consumption, Civil Action, and Sustainable Development, Society for International Development, p7–15

21 International Baby Food Action Network (1998) *Breaking the Rules: Stretching the Rules 1998,* IBFAN, Penang; and Nestlé's most recent externally commissioned report, Emerging Market Economics (2000) *Infant Nutritional Operational Study,* EME, London

22 Zadek, S and Forstater, M 'Making Civil Regulation Work' in Addo, M (ed) (1999) *Human Rights Standards and the Responsibility of Transnational Corporations,* Kluwer, The Hague, p69–75

23 There is a host of studies covering the link between corporate social and environmental, and financial performance. For a good summary of some of the key ones, see Weiser, J and Zadek, S (2000) op cit, note 3

24 Environics International Ltd (1999) *Executive Briefing: The Millennium Poll on Corporate Social Responsibility,* Environics International Ltd, Toronto

25 CSR Europe was formerly the European Business Network for Social Cohesion; the study was carried out by MORI

26 The Conference Board, Inc (1999) *Consumer Expectations on the Social Accountability of Business,* The Conference Board, New York, p9–13

27 Fleishman Hillard (1999) *Consumers Demand Companies with a Conscience,* Fleishman Hillard Europe, London

28 Cowe, R and Williams, S (2000) *Who Are the Ethical Consumers?,* The Co-operative Bank, Manchester

29 Cone Inc (1999) *Cone/Roper Cause Related Trends Report: Evolution of Cause Branding^{SM},* Cone Inc, Boston

30 The Council on Foundations (1996) *Measuring the Value of Corporate Citizenship,* The Council on Foundations, Washington, DC

31 *The Ethical Investor,* September/ October 1998

32 Quoted in Strannegård, L and Wolff, R (1999) 'Discovering Sustainability: A Case Study of Learning Through Environmental Scenarios', *Greener Management International,* Autumn Issue 23, p55

33 See note 2

34 Hopkins, M (1998) *The Planetary Bargain,* HarperCollins, London

35 The actual movement of the curves and their shape may be more complex or just different. For example, the financial market curves may not swivel but shift upwards over time

36 Goyder, M (1998), and Goyder, G (1961) *The Responsible Company,* Blackwell, Oxford

37 Bovet, S (1999) 'The Race to Measure Reputation', *PR Week,* 31 May, p14–15

38 Korten, D (1997) op cit, note 14

CHAPTER 6
FRAMING THE
BUSINESS CASE

1 Chomsky, N (1999) *Profit Over People: Neoliberalism and Global Order,* Seven Stories Press, New York, p8

2 Excerpt from his address to the participants of the Global Compact at the inaugural meeting on 26 July 2000 at the United Nations in New York

3 Adapted from Zadek, S and Scott-Parker, S (2001) *Unlocking the Evidence: the New Disability Case,* Employers' Forum on Disability, London

4 Novo Nordisk (1999) *1998 Social Report*, Novo Nordisk a/s, Bagsværd (www.novo.dk)

5 *The Economist* (1999) 'Business this Week', 11 September, p24. See also Dow Jones Sustainability Group Indexes GmbH (1999) *Guide to the Dow Jones Sustainability Group Indexes – Version 1.0*, September 1999, Dow Jones Sustainability Group Indexes GmbH, Zürich (www.sustainability-index.com)

6 Graves, S and Waddock, S (2002) *Beyond Built to Last: Stakeholder Relations in 'Built-to-Last' Companies* (forthcoming)

7 Social Investment Forum (1999) '1999 Report on Socially Responsible Investing Trends in the United States', SIF Industry Research Program

8 *International Herald Tribune*, Wednesday 22 September 1999, p24

9 Elements of this section are drawn from *Innovation Through Partnership*, a joint initiative between the Institute of Social and Ethical AccountAbility, Business in the Community, and the Local Futures Group with support from the Department of Trade and Industry. More information on this initiative can be found at www. innovation-partnership.org

10 Castells, M (1996) *The Rise of the Network Society*, Blackwell, Oxford, p261

11 Quoted in *Time*, 11 September 2000, p21

12 These questions were first set out in S Zadek's *Third Generation Futures* in *United Utilities Social and Environmental Impact Report 2000*, United Utilities, Warrington (www.unitedutilities.com), and were subsequently developed further in Zadek, S (2001) *Third Generation Corporate Citizenship: How Much Can Corporations Deliver*, Foreign Policy Centre, London. Thanks to Scott Hawkins of Skandia for originally developing this way of thinking about evolving processes

CHAPTER 7
THE FUTURE OF THE CIVIL REGULATORS

1 Quoted in 'Victims of Their Own Success', in *The Guardian Weekly*, 6–12 July 2000, p23

2 'Shell to Consult Pressure Groups' in *Financial Times*, 17 March 1997, p23

3 'Global Chief Thinks Locally', in *Financial Times*, 1 August 2000, p15

4 *The Economist*, 11–17 December 1999, p22

5 Edwards, M (2000) *NGO Rights and Responsibilties*, Foreign Policy Centre, London. See also the volume edited by Lewis, D and Wallace, T (2001) *New Roles and Relevance: Development NGOs and the Challenge of Change*, Kumarian Press, West Hartford, Connecticut

6 Edwards, M 'Victims of their Own Success', *Guardian Weekly*, 6–12 July 2000

7 Slim, H (1999) *Future Imperatives: Quality, Standards and Human Rights*, Prepared for the British Overseas Aid Group, Centre for Development and Emergency Practice, Oxford Brookes University, Oxford

8 Drucker, P (1999) *Management Challenges for the 21st Century*, Butterworth Heinemann, Oxford, p9

9 Taken from Global Compact listserve of the United Nations Association of America, 6 December 2000 (also www.edelman.com)

10 Elkington, J and Fennell, S (1998) 'Partners for Sustainability' in *Greener Management International*, Issue 24 Winter (Special Issue on Business–NGO Relations and Sustainable Development; Guest Editor, J Bendell), p56

11 Asia Monitoring Resource Centre (1998) 'No Illusions: Against the Global Cosmetic SA8000', Unpublished paper by AMRC, Hong Kong

12 See www.cepaa.org for a full response by CEPAA to the concerns raised by AMRC

13 'Pension Funds Catch Charities on Hop' in *The Guardian*, 3 June 2000, p1–2

14 Pilger, J (1999) 'The Siege of Seattle Marked the Rise of a Popular Resistance to the Evils of Globalisation' in *New Statesman*, 13 December 1999, p17 (www.newstatesman.co.uk)

15 See examples of this through an examination of my curriculum vitae on www.zadek.net

16 Mulgan, G (1998) *Connexity: How to Live in a Connected World*, Chatto and Windus, London

17 Extracts from comments made during closed debate dated 7 December 1999

CHAPTER 8
THE NEW CIVIL GOVERNANCE

1 Peter Sutherland address to Amnesty International event in Dublin, September 1997; available at www.bpamoco.com.speeches/sp_9709

2 'A Forum for Improving Globalisation', in *Financial Times*, 1 August 2000

3 This chapter has benefited particularly from the author's early manuscripts for a pamphlet entitled *Third Generation Corporate Citizenship: How Much Can Corporations Deliver*, Foreign Policy Centre, 2001

4 Kelly, G (1999) *The New Partnership Agenda*, Institute for Public Policy Research Commission on Public Private Partnerships, IPPR, London (www.ippr.org.uk)

5 www.bpdweb.org

6 Nelson, J and Zadek, S (1999) *Partnership Alchemy: New Social Partnerships in Europe*, The Copenhagen Centre, Copenhagen

7 Global Reporting Initiative (2000) *Sustainability Reporting Guidelines*, Global Reporting Initiative, Boston (www.globalreporting.org)

8 Reinicke, W and Deng, F (2000) *Critical Choices: The United Nations, Networks, and the Future of Global Governance*, International Development Research Centre, Ottawa, pxiv (www.idrc.org)

9 Provided by the United Nations Association of the US listserve on 24 July 2000 (http://www.un.org/News/)

10 Parts of this section are drawn from an unpublished paper prepared for the UK Government's Department of International Development in late 1998, New Economics Foundation (1999) *The World Trade Organization, Corporate Social Responsibility and Social Audit*, NEF, London (www.zadek.net)

11 *ENDS Report*, 'Procter & Gamble steps up attack on eco-labelling', no 265, 1997

12 http://www.wto.org/wto/environ/eco.htm

13 'Fighting for Workers' Human Rights in the Global Economy', International Confederation of Free Trade Unions, 1998, p45

14 'A Forum for Improving Globalisation', in *Financial Times*, 1 August 2000

15 www.oecd.org/daf/nocorruption/

16 Barnett, A (2000) 'Time to Pay Off the Piper', in *Director*, August, p29

17 Personal communication

CHAPTER 9
FOUNDATIONS OF SUSTAINABILITY

1 www.novo.dk

2 Taken from his keynote address to the 3rd International AccountAbility conference in Copenhagen in November 1999

3 British Telecommunications (1998) *Changing Values: the Role of Business in a*

Sustainable Society, Occasional Paper 2, BT, London, p2 (www.bt.com)

4 www.sustainability.co.uk

5 Bebbington, J and Thomson, I (1996) *Business Conceptions of Sustainability and the Implications for Accountancy*, ACCA Research Report 48, Association of Chartered Certified Accountants, London (www.accaglobal.com)

6 The following quotes are drawn from United Nations (2000) *The Global Compact: Statements from Participants – High-Level Meeting, 26 July 2000, New York*, UN, New York (www.unglobalcompact.org)

7 United Utilities (2000) *Social and Environmental Impact Report*, United Utilities, Warrington, UK, inside front cover

8 Ford Motor Company (2000) *Connecting With Society: 1999 Corporate Citizenship Report*, Ford Motor Company, Dearborn, Michigan, p7

9 Elkington, J (1998) *Cannibals With Forks: The Triple Bottom Line of the 21st Century*, Capstone, Oxford

10 Personal communication

11 Shell International (1999) *The Shell Report 1999*, Shell International, London, p2

12 British Telecommunications (1998) p3, op cit, note 3

13 www.globalreporting.org

14 For an extended discussion about the various definitions of economics and a related bibliography, see Zadek, S (1993) *An Economics of Utopia: the Democratisation of Scarcity*, Avebury, Aldershot, UK

15 This section draws extensively from Zadek, S and C Tuppen (2000) *Adding Values: The Economics of Sustainable Business*, Occasional Paper 4, BT, London

16 This could of course include an interest for example in animals if this is of interest to people and therefore figures in their aims, priorities, decision-making and actions

17 Max-Neef, M, Elizalde, A and Hopenhayn, M (1991) *Human Scale Development: Conception, Application and Further Reflection*, Apex Press, New York

18 Another view is that the environmental lies within the social since we experience the environmental entirely through our senses

19 Zadek and Tuppen (2000) cover page, op cit, note 15

20 http://www.naturalstep.org/what/index_what.html

21 Wilsdon, J (2000) 'The Capitals Model: A Framework for Sustainability', unpublished working paper by Forum for the Future on behalf of SIGMA, SIGMA, London (www.bsi.co.uk/sigma)

22 Perri 6 (1997) *Holistic Government*, DEMOS, London

23 This connection was originally set out in Zadek, S (1999) 'Stalking Sustainability' in *Greener Management International* issue 24 Winter, p1–12

24 Wilsdon (2000), p3, op cit, note 21

25 Which does of course mean that economic outcomes are social outcomes

CHAPTER 10
SUSTAINABILITY AS THE ART OF THE POSSIBLE

1 Sustainability Asset Management (2000) *Biographies of Corporate Sustainability Leaders*, SAM, Zurich, p1

2 United Nations Environmental Program (1998) *What is a Sustainable Enterprise?*, Workshop Report, UNEP, Paris, p4

3 Grossman, G and Krueger, A (1994) 'Economic Growth and the Environment', Working Paper No 4634 of the National Bureau of Economic Research, Cambridge, MA

4 Bhagwati, J, 'The Case for Free Trade', in *Scientific American*, November 1993

5 Cairncross, F (1992) 'The Freedom to be Dirtier Than the Rest', in *The Economist*, 30 May 1995

6 Hawken, P, Lovins, A and Hunter Lovins, L (1999) *Natural Capitalism: Creating the Next Industrial Revolution*, Little Brown, Boston

7 Grossman, G, *New York Times*, 3 January 1992

8 Shell International (1999)*The Shell Report 1999*, Shell, London, p3 (italics added)

9 ibid, p39

10 *Financial Times*, 16 December 1999, p1

11 *Financial Times*, 8 August 2000, p17

12 Traidcraft (2000) *Traidcraft Social Accounts 1999*, Traidcraft, Gateshead, UK, www.traidcraft.co.uk

13 Extracts from transcripts provided courtesy of Business for Social Responsibility

14 ibidem

15 Bronson, D (1999) 'Commerce with Conscience: Options for Business in the Global Economy', Report of Seminar (unpublished), International Centre for Human Rights and Democratic Development, Montreal

16 Sustainability Asset Management (2000), op cit, note 1

17 ibid, p3

18 ibid, p31

19 Hawken, P, Lovins, A and Hunter Lovins, L (1999), p46, op cit, note 6

20 ibid, p89

21 Amnesty International and Prince of Wales Business Leaders Forum (2000) *Human Rights: Is It Any of Your Business?*, Amnesty International, London (www.amnesty.org.uk/business)

22 SustainAbility Ltd (2001) *Politics and Persuasion: Corporate Influence on Sustainable Development Policy*, SustainAbility Ltd, London (www.sustainability.co.uk)

23 Nelson, J and Zadek, S (1999) *Partnership Alchemy: New Social Partnerships in Europe*, Copenhagen Centre, Copenhagen

24 Corporate Europe Observatory (2000) *Global Greenhouse Mania: United Nations Climate Talks Corrupted by Corporate-Pseudo Solutions*, CEO, Amsterdam (www.xs4all.nl/~ceo/greenhouse/corporate.html)

25 Shell International (1999), p34, op cit, note 8

26 Personal communications

27 Gonella, C and Pilling, A and Zadek, S with assistance from Terry, V (1998) *Making Values Count: Contemporary Experience in Social and Ethical Accounting, Auditing and Reporting*, ACCA Research Report 57, Association of Chartered Certified Accountants, London, p1 (www.acca.org.uk)

CHAPTER 11
CIVIL LEARNING

1 Annan, K (2000) *Economic Growth About People – Their Health, Education, Security*, Opening Address to 'Geneva 2000', 25 June 2000

2 www.novo.dk

3 Hadenius, A and Uggla, F (1996) 'Making Civil Society Work, Promoting Democratic Development: What Can States and Donors Do?', *World Development*, vol 24, no 10, p1621–1639

4 Diamond, L (1994) 'Rethinking Civil Society: Toward Democratic Consolidation', *Journal of Democracy* vol 5, no 3 (July), p4–17

5 Korten, D (1999) *The Post-Corporate World: Life After Capitalism*, Kumarian Press and Berrett-Koehler, West Hartford, Connecticut, p139–140

6 ibidem

7 Andersson, G et al (1998) *SANGOCO Response to President Mandela's speech: Civil Society, Politics*

and *Development Organisation*,
SANGOCO, Johannesburg, p1
  8 op cit, note 5
  9 Taken from Bullard, N (2000) *UN
Shows Its True Colours*, Focus on Trade
52 (listserve: 7 August 2000)
10 Workshop was under Chatham
House (non-attribution) rules
11 Co-operative Commission (2000)
*The Future of the Co-operative Movement:
A Round-Table Discussion*, Supplement
to the *New Statesman*, 10 October 2000
12 Galbraith, J (1968) *The New
Industrial State*, Penguin, London
13 Campaign for Labour Rights
(1999) *Update on Nike Vietnam Scandal:
Background* (26 January 1999)
14 Quoted in Amery, C (1999) *Business
and Human Rights in a Time of Change*,
working paper (www.multinationals.
law.eur.nl), p64
15 ibid, p65–66
16 ibidem
17 Schwartz, P and Gibb, B (1999)
When Good Companies Do Bad Things,
Wiley, New York, p60
18 This section has benefited from
Wong, W (2000) *Knowledge and
CSR*, Working Paper prepared for
the Innovation through Partnership
initiative (www.innovation-
partnership.org)
19 Senge, P (1994) *The Fifth Discipline:
The Art & Practice of The Learning
Organization*, Currency Doubleday,
New York
20 Department of Trade and Industry
(2000) *The Future of Corporate Learning*,
DTI, London
21 Probst, G, Raub, S and Romhardt,
K (2000) *Managing Knowledge: Building
Blocks for Success*, John Wiley and Sons,
London, p17
22 ibidem
23 Tissen, R, Andriessen, D and
Lekanne Deprez, F (2000) *The
Knowledge Dividend*, FT Prentice Hall,
London, p34
24 Waddell, S (1999) (1999) 'Business–
Government–Nonprofit Collaborations

as Agents for Social Innovation
and Learning', unpublished paper
presented at the Academy of
Management Annual Meeting, August,
p4
25 Huber, G P (1991) 'Organizational
Learning: The Contributing Processes
and the Literatures', *Organizational
Science*, vol 2, no 1, p88–115: 89.
Quoted in Waddell, S (1999), op cit,
note 24

CHAPTER 12
BUILDING CIVIL
CORPORATIONS

1 Mant, A (1997) *Intelligent Leadership*,
Allen and Unwin, St Leonards
2 Block, P (1991) *The Empowered
Manager*, Jossey-Bass, San Francisco
3 Zohar, D (1997) *Rewiring the
Corporate Brain*, Berrett-Koehler, New
York
4 Handy, C (1999) *The New Alchemists*,
Hutchinson, London
5 Koestler, A (1945) 'The Yogi and the
Commissar', in Koestler, A (ed) *The
Yogi and the Commissar*, p9–20

CHAPTER 13
HOW MUCH IS ENOUGH?

1 Personal communication
2 Question posed to Mark Wade of
Shell International during his plenary
at the Global Reporting Initiative
symposium at Imperial College in
1998
3 I am indebted to Gavin Andersson
for sharing his work and thinking
on the notion of the 'unbounded
organisation' that has informed this
and other parts of the book
4 United Utilities (1999) *Social
Partnership Report 1999: Accounting for
Our Impact on Society*, United Utilities,
Warrington, UK, p5

5 ibid
6 Personal communication
7 Novo Nordisk (1999) *1998 Social Report*, Novo Nordisk a/s, Bagsværd
8 British Telecommunications (1998) *A Question of Balance: Telecommunications Technology – Making a Difference*, BT plc, London, p22
9 Collins, J C and Porras, J I (1995) *Built to Last: Successful Habits of Visionary Companies*, Random House, London
10 See for example the ambitions of the Global Alliance for Workers and Communities at www. theglobalalliance.org
11 United Nations Environment Program (1998) *What is a Sustainable Enterprise?* Workshop Report, UNEP, Paris, p4
12 Zadek, S and Scott-Parker, S (2000) *Unlocking Potential: The New Business Case for Working With Disability*, Employers' Forum on Disability, London
13 Shell International (1998) *Profits and Principles – Does There Have to be a Choice?* Royal Dutch Shell, London
14 The Body Shop (1996) *Values Report*, The Body Shop, Littlehampton, UK

CHAPTER 14
USEFUL MEASURES

1 Quoted in Conference Board (2000) *The 2000 Leadership Conference on Corporate Global Citizenship*, Conference Board, New York (www.conference-board.org)
2 Quoted in Chambers (1993) *Challenging the Professions: Frontiers for Rural Development*, IT Publications, London, p14
3 Ethical Trading Initiative (2000) *Getting to Work on Ethical Trading: Annual Report (1999/2000)*, ETI, London (www.ethicaltrade.org)
4 Prince of Wales Business Leaders Forum (2000) *Measure for Success:*
Assessing the Impact of Partnerships, IBLF, London (www.pwblf.org)
5 Logan, D and Tuffrey, M (2000) *Companies in Communities: Assessing the Impact*, The Corporate Citizenship Company, London
6 Social Venture Network (2000) *Standards for Social Responsibility*, SVN, San Francisco (www.svn.org)
7 Instituto Ethos (2000) *Ethos Indicators on Corporate Social Responsibility*, Instituto Ethos, Sao Paulo (www.ethos.org.br)
8 Global Reporting Initiative (2000) *Sustainability Corporate Reporting Guidelines*, GRI, Boston (www. globalreporting.org)
9 http://www.transparency.de
10 Quoted in MacGillivray, A and Zadek, S (1996) *Accounting for Change: Indicators for Sustainable Development*, New Economics Foundation, London (www.neweconomics.org)
11 Goyder, M (1998) *Living Tomorrow's Company*, Gower, Aldershot, UK
12 Lewis, S (1998) *External Perceptions of Corporate Social Responsibility*, MORI, London
13 For details of this survey, see www. ft.com
14 ibidem
15 Kennedy, A (2000) *The End of Shareholder Value*, Orion Books, London, p167
16 Hawken, P, Lovins, A and Hunter Lovins, L (1999) *Natural Capitalism: Creating the Next Industrial Revolution*, Little Brown, Boston
17 Baxter International (1998) *Environmental, Health and Safety Performance Report*, Baxter International, Deerfield, p3
18 http://indexes.dowjones.com/djsgi/ (accessed 14 August 2000)
19 *International Herald Tribune*, Wednesday, 22 September 1999, p24
20 Ernst & Young (1997) *Measures That Matter*, Ernst and Young Centre for Business Innovation, p7
21 Ampuero, M, Goranson, J and Scott, J (1999) 'Solving the Measurement

Puzzle: How EVA and the Balanced Scorecard Fit Together' in Ernst & Young Centre for Business Innovation (ed) *Measuring Business Performance*, Perspectives on Business Innovation Issue 2, Cambridge, p45–52

22 ibid, p48

23 See for example the 'Merger Briefs' produced by *The Economist* during July–September 2000

24 www.bpamoco.com/live and www.shell.com

25 General Motors (1999) *Environmental, Health and Safety*, General Motors, Detroit (www.gm.com)

26 Ford Motor Company (2000) *Connecting with Society*, Ford Motor Company, Dearborn, Michigan (www.ford.com)

27 International Labour Office (1998) *Governing Body Agenda Item – Overview of Global Developments and Office Activities Concerning Codes of Conduct, Social Labelling and Other Private Sector Activities Addressing Labour Issues*, GB.273/WP/SDL/1. 273 Session, ILO, Geneva

28 This section draws extensively on Zadek, S, Lingayah, S and Forstater, M (1998) *Social Labels: Tools for Ethical Trade*, report by the New Economics Foundation for the European Commission (DGV.D1) (www.zadek.net)

29 Zadek, S and Amalric, F (1998) 'Consumer Works!', in *Development*, vol 41, no 1, on *Consumption, Civil Action and Sustainable Development*, March 1998, Society for International Development

30 Zadek, S, Lingayah, S and Forstater, M (1998) *Purchasing Power: Civil Action for Sustainable Consumption*, New Economics Foundation, London

31 Peter Rogan, CWS, personal communication, March 1998

32 National Consumer's League (1997), op cit

33 Consumer research for the cosmetics manufacturer Yardley found

that the proportion of consumers who rated 'cruelty free' as the most important criterion in choosing cosmetics had risen from 6 per cent to 61 per cent in a nine-month period in 1990 [*Ethical Consumer*, issue 2]

34 Wollman (1916) op cit

35 NCC (1997) op cit

36 Zadek, S, Lingayah, S and Forstater, M (1998), op cit, note 30

37 Zadek, S and Scott-Parker, S (2000) *Unlocking Potential: The New Disability Business Case*, Employers' Forum on Disability, London (www.employers-forum.co.uk)

38 Louis Harris and Associates (1991) *Public Attitudes Towards People with Disabilities*, undertaken for National Organisation on Disability, Louis Harris and Associates, New York

39 Humphries, J and Rubery, J (1995) *The Economics of Equal Opportunities*, Equal Opportunities Commission, Manchester

40 Closed discussion at the UK National Audit Office, 1997

41 Chambers, R (1993) *Challenging the Professions: Frontiers for Rural Development*, IT Publications, London, p3–8

42 Quoted in Chambers (1993), p14

43 Power, M (1995) *The Audit Explosion*, Demos, London

44 Lawson, I (1999) *Leaders for Tomorrow's Society*, The Industrial Society, London, p1

45 Zadek, S and Evans, R (1993) *Auditing the Market: A Practical Approach to Social Auditing*, Traidcraft Exchange and the New Economics Foundation, Gateshead, UK

46 Taken from confidential notes of group discussions held during the company's first social accounting process in 1993/1994

47 Traidcraft plc (1994) *Social Audit 1993*, Traidcraft, Gateshead, UK

48 VanCity (1998) *VanCity's Social Report 1997*, VanCity Savings Credit Union, Vancouver

49 Quote from Mark Lee, then Corporate Social Responsibility Manager, during a plenary presentation at the First International AccountAbility Conference at Nijenrode Business School in September 1997

50 The NEF, Amnesty International UK Business Group, the IBLF and Ashridge Management College (AMC)

51 Council of Economic Priorities Accreditation Agency (1997) *Social Accountability 8000*, CEPAA, New York, p4

52 ibid, p6

53 Global Reporting Initiative (1999) *GRI Sustainability Reporting Guidelines*, GRI/CERES, Boston, p1

54 Global Reporting Initiative (1999), Appendix B: B-1

55 Drafted by a group of NGOs and trade union organizations at the Living Wage Working Summit at the University of California on 17–19 July 1998; material obtained through the Clean Cloths Campaign

56 Asia Monitoring Resource Centre (1998) 'No Illusions: Against the Global Cosmetic SA8000', Unpublished paper by AMRC, Hong Kong, p4

57 New Economics Foundation (1999) *The World Trade Organization, Corporate Social Responsibility and Social Audit*, NEF, London, p8

58 Amery, C (1999) 'Business and Human Rights in a Time of Change', working paper available at www. multinationals.law.eur.nl

CHAPTER 15
CONVERSATIONAL
CORPORATIONS

1 Chambers, R (1993) *Challenging the Professions: Frontiers for Rural Development*, Intermediate Technology Publications ITDG, London, p3–8

2 'Integrated Ethical Auditing: The Body Shop International, UK', in Zadek, S, Pruzan, P and Evans, R (eds) (1997) *Building Corporate AccountAbility*, Earthscan, London, p102–128

3 The Body Shop (1996) *The Body Shop Social Statement 95*, Body Shop, Littlehampton, UK

4 ibid, p9

5 Adapted from The Body Shop (1996), p10, op cit, note 3

6 In the same league, and following broadly the same approach, would be VanCity Savings Credit's and Camelot's first social reports

7 Case material drawn from documentation produced by the World Bank's Business Partners in Development initiative. The text draws on Weiser, J and Zadek, S (2000) *Conversations with Disbelievers*, Brody & Weiser, New York (www.zadek.net)

8 Nelson, J and Zadek, S (1999) *Partnership Alchemy: New Social Partnerships in Europe*, The Copenhagen Centre, Copenhagen

9 The Environment Council (1999) *Guidelines for Stakeholder Dialogue – a Joint Venture*, The Environment Council and Shell International, London, p8

10 The Body Shop (1996) op cit, note 3

11 New Economics Foundation (1998) *Participation Works! 21 Techniques of Community Participation for the 21st Century*, New Economics Foundation, London, p3

12 Pretty, J et al (1995) *Participatory Learning and Action. A Trainer's Guide*, IIED, London

13 Gaventa, J (1998) 'The Scaling-up and Institutionalization of PRA: lessons and challenges', in Blackburn, J and Holland, J (eds) *Who Changes? Institutionalizing participation in development*, IT Press, London

14 Blauert, J and Zadek, S (eds) (1998) *Mediating Sustainability: Making Policy from the Grassroots*, Kumarian, West Hartford, Connecticut

15 Ritchey-Vance, M (1998) 'Widening the Lens on Impact Assessment: The Inter-American Foundation and Its Grassroots Development Framework – The Cone', in Blauert, J and Zadek, S (1998), op cit

16 Estrella, M and Gaventa, J (1998) *Who Counts Reality? Participatory Monitoring and Evaluation: A Literature Review*, Working Paper No. 70, Institute of Development of Sussex, Brighton

17 Zohar, D (1997) *Rewiring the Corporate Brain*, Berrett-Koehler, New York, p136

18 Zadek, S (1999) 'Values, Ethics and Accountability', unpublished working paper prepared for the Committee of Inquiry: A New Vision for Business, New Economics Foundation, London (www.zadek.net)

19 Institute of Social and Ethical AccountAbility (1999) *AA1000 Framework*, ISEA, London

20 ibidem

21 The Environment Council (1999), p17, op cit, note 9

22 Extract from open memo sent by the Maquila Solidarity Network Canada (perg@web.net) to human and labour rights activists and organisations; 10 April 1999

23 The Body Shop (1996) op cit, note 3

24 Morehouse, W (1998) 'Consumption, Civil Action and Corporate Power: Lessons from the Past, Strategies for the Future', in Special Issue of *Development* on *Consumption, Civil Action and Sustainable Development* vol 41, no 1, March, p48–53

CHAPTER 16
PROFESSIONALIZING CREDIBILITY

1 Business for Social Responsibility (2000) *Social and Environmental Internet Reporting Amongst Fortune 100 Companies*, BSR, San Francisco (www.bsr.org)

2 New Economics Foundation (2000) *Corporate Spin: the Troubled Teenage Years of Social Auditing*, NEF, London, p5

3 Shell International (1999) *The Shell Report 1999*, Shell International, London, p2–3

4 SustainAbility Ltd (1999) *The Social Reporting Report*, UNEP/SustainAbility Ltd, London, p10. See also various articles in the Special Issue of *AccountAbility Quarterly* on 'Auditing, Assurance and Challenge', no 13, 2nd Quarter 2000 (www.accountability.org.uk)

5 Novo Nordisk (1999) *Social Report 1999*, Novo Nordisk, Bagsvaerd, p6

6 Quoted in New Economics Foundation (2000), p7, op cit, note 2

7 Taken from a PWC advertisement 'Auditor Independence: It's Time to Change the Rules', in *New York Times*, 10 November 2000

8 Rio Tinto (1999) *1998 Social and Environmental Report*, Rio Tinto, London

9 UDV Polska (1999) *Economic, Social, and Environmental Performance*, UDV Polska, Warsaw

10 ibid, p4

11 Novo Nordisk (1999), p6, op cit, note 5

12 VanCity (2000) *Guided by Values: The VanCity Social Report 1998/98*, VanCity, Vancouver, p10 (www.vancity.com/socialreport)

13 United Utilities (1999) *Social Partnership Report 1999: Accounting for Our Impact on Society*, United Utilities, Warrington, UK

14 British Telecommunications plc (1999) *An Issue of Responsibility: BT's Social Report 1999*, BT, London, p31

15 Gray, R H (2000) 'Social And Environmental Responsibility, Sustainability And Accountability: Can the Corporate Sector Deliver?',

Working Paper, University of Glasgow. Also see Ball, A, Owen, D L and Gray, R H (2000) 'External transparency or internal capture? The role of third party statements in adding value to corporate environmental reports', *Business Strategy and the Environment* 9(1) Jan/Feb, p1–23

16 Business for Social Responsibility (2000) *Designing Social and Environmental Reporting Processes for Verification*, BSR, San Francisco (www.bsr.org)

17 Co-operative Bank (1999) *The Partnership Report: Find Out How Our Principles Measure Up in Practice*, Co-operative Bank, Manchester

18 Novo Nordisk (1999), op cit, note 5

19 Zadek, S and Evans, R (1994) *Auditing the Market: A Practical Approach to Social Auditing*, Traidcraft, Gateshead, UK

20 Taken from unpublished working papers associated with the social audit of The Body Shop by the New Economics Foundation

21 Business for Social Responsibility (2000) *A Summary and Comparison of Selected Corporate Governance Guidelines*, BSR, San Francisco (www.bsr.org)

22 Association of Chartered Certified Accountants and the Institute of Social and Ethical AccountAbility (2000) *Turnbull, Internal Control and Wider Aspects of Risk*, ACCA, London (www.accaglobal.com)

CHAPTER 17
HOW CIVIL CAN
CORPORATIONS BE?

1 Ewald, C (1921) 'A Fairy Tale About God and Kings', in Zipes, J (ed) (1990) *Utopian Tales from Weimar*, Polygon, Edinburgh, p34–35

2 Wells, H G (1976) *A Modern Utopia*, Bison, London

3 Central Intelligence Agency (2000) *Global Trends 2015: A Dialogue About the Future with Nongovernmental Experts* (www.cia.gov/cia/publications/globaltrends2015/index.html)

Bibliography

AccountAbility Quarterly (2000) on 'Auditing, Assurance and Challenge', No. 13, 2nd Quarter

Amery, C (1999) *Business and Human Rights in a Time of Change*, working paper available at website www.multinationals.law.eur.nl.

AccountAbility (2003) *AA1000 Assurance Standard*, AccountAbility, London

Amnesty International and Prince of Wales Business Leaders Forum (2000) *Human Rights: Is It Any of Your Business?*, Amnesty International, London, www.amnesty.org.uk/business

Ampuero, M, Goranson, J and Scott, J (1999) 'Solving the Measurement Puzzle: How EVA and the Balanced Scorecard Fit Together' in Ernst & Young Centre for Business Innovation (1999) *Measuring Business: Performance, Perspectives on Business Innovation* Issue 2, Cambridge: 45–52

Anderson, S and Cavanagh, J (1996) *The Top 200. The Rise of Corporate Global Power*, Institute of Policy Studies, Washington DC

Andersson, G et al (1998) *SANGOCO Response to President Mandela's speech: Civil Society, Politics and Development Organisation*, SANGOCO, Johannesburg

Annan, K (2000) *Economic Growth About People – Their Health, Education, Security*, opening address to 'Geneva 2000', UN General Assembly meeting, 25 June

Asia Monitoring Resource Centre (1998) *No Illusions: Against the Global Cosmetic SA8000*, Unpublished paper by AMRC, Hong Kong

Association of Chartered Certified Accountants and the Institute of Social and Ethical AccountAbility (2000) *Turnbull, Internal Control and Wider Aspects of Risk*, ACCA, London, www.accaglobal.com

Aydin, Z (editor) (2003) *Multi-Stakeholder Partnerships and UN–Civil Society Relationships*, UN, New York

Ball A Owen, D L and Gray, R H (2000) 'External transparency or internal capture? The role of third party statements in adding value to corporate environmental reports', *Business Strategy and the Environment* 9(1) January/February: 1–23

Barnett, A (2000) 'Time to Pay Off the Piper', in *Director*, August 2000: 29

Barrientos, S and Smith, S (2006) *The ETI Code of Labour Practice: Do Workers Really Benefit?*, Institute of Development Studies, Brighton

Baxter International (1998) *Environmental, Health and Safety Performance Report*, Baxter International, Deerfield

Bentley, T Oakley, K Gibson, S and Kilgour, K (1999) *The Real Deal: What Young People Really think About Government, Politics and Social Exclusion*, Demos, London

Bhagwati, J (1993) 'The Case for Free Trade', in *Scientific American*, November

Blauert, J, and Zadek, S (eds) (1998) *Mediating Sustainability: Making Policy from the Grassroots*, Kumarian, West Hartford

Bloch, E (1986) *The Principle of Hope*, Blackwell, Oxford

Block, P (1991) *The Empowered Manager*, Jossey-Bass, San Francisco

The Body Shop (1996) *Social Statement 95*, Body Shop, Littlehampton

The Body Shop (1996) *Values Report*, The Body Shop, Littlehampton

The Body Shop (1998) *Values Report*, The Body Shop, Littlehampton

Bovet, S (1999) 'The Race to Measure Reputation', *PR Week*, 31 May: 14–15.

BP US Refineries Independent Safety Review Panel (2007) *The Report of The BP US Refineries Independent Safety Review Panel*, Washington, DC

British Airports Authority (1999) *Growing With the Support and Trust of Our Neighbours*, British Airports Authority, London

British Petroleum (1998) *What We Stand For: Our Business Policies*, British Petroleum, London

British Telecommunications (1998) *Changing Values: the Role of Business in a Sustainable Society*, Occasional Paper 2, BT plc, London, www.bt.com.

British Telecommunications (1998) *A Question of Balance: Telecommunications Technology Making a Difference*, BT plc, London, www.bt.com

British Telecommunications (1999) *An Issue of Responsibility: BT's Social Report 1999*, BT plc, London, www.bt.com

Broad, R and Cavanagh, J (1999) 'The Death of the Washington Consensus?' in *World Policy Journal* Vol. XVI, No 3, Fall 1999: 79–88

Bronson, D (1999) *Commerce with Conscience: Options for Business in the Global Economy*, Report of Seminar (unpublished), International Centre for Human Rights and Democratic Development, Montreal

Bullard, N (2000) *UN Shows Its True Colours*, Focus on Trade 52 (list serve: 7August 2000)

Burgis, T and Zadek, S (2006) *Accountability 21: Reinventing Accountability for the 21st century*, AccountAbility, London

Business for Social Responsibility (2000) *Social and Environmental Internet Reporting Amongst Fortune 100 Companies*, BSR, San Francisco, www.bsr.org

Business for Social Responsibility (2000) *Designing Social and Environmental Reporting Processes for Verification*, BSR, San Francisco, www.bsr.org

Business for Social Responsibility (2000) *A Summary and Comparison of Selected Corporate Governance Guidelines*, BSR, San Francisco, www.bsr.org

Cairncross, F (1992) 'The freedom to be dirtier than the rest', in *The Economist*, 30 May 1995

Campaign for Labour Rights (1999) *Update on Nike Vietnam Scandal: Background*, (26 January 1999)

Casson, M (1998) 'The Economics of Ethical Leadership' in *The Role of Business Ethics in Economic Performance*, Jones, I and Pollitt, M (Eds.), Macmillan Press Ltd. Basingstoke

Castells, M (1996) *The Rise of the Network Society*, Blackwell

Castells, M (1996–2000), *The Information Age: Economy, Society, and Culture*, Oxford, Blackwell (Vols I, II and III)

Castells, M (1998) 'Information Technology, Globalisation and Social Development', Paper prepared for the United Nations Research Institute for Social Development Conference on Information Technologies and Social Development, Palais des Nations, Geneva, 22–24 June 1998, available online at www.unrisd/infotech/conf.

Cavenagh, T (1999) *Community Connections: Strategic Partnerships in the Digital Industries*, Research Report 1254–99–RR, The Conference Board, New York: 5

Central Intelligence Agency (2000) *Global Trends 2015: A Dialogue About the Future with Nongovernmental Experts*, available online at www.cia.gov/cia/publications/globaltrends2015/index.html.

Chambers, R (1993) *Challenging the Professions: Frontiers for Rural Development*, Intermediate Technology Publications, London

Chomsky, N (1999) *Profit Over People: Neoliberalism and Global Order,* Seven Stories Press, New York: 8

Clifton, R and Maughan E (1999) *The Future of Brands: Twenty Five Visions*, Macmillan Business, London

Collins, J C, and Porras, J I (1995) *Built to Last: Successful Habits of Visionary Companies*, Random House, London

Cone Inc. (1999) *Cone/Roper Cause Related Trends Report: Evolution of Cause Branding^{SM}*,Cone Inc., Boston

Confederation of British Industry (1999) *Global Social Responsibility*, CBI, London

The Conference Board (1997) *Strategic Alliances: Institutionalising Partnering Capabilities*, Research Report Number 1191-97-CH, Conference Board, New York, www.conference-board.org.

The Conference Board, Inc. (1999) *Consumer Expectations on the Social Accountability of Business,* The Conference Board, New York, NY, www.conference-board.org.

The Conference Board, Inc (2000) *The 2000 Leadership Conference on Corporate Global Citizenship*, The Conference Board, New York, www.conference-board.org.

Co-operative Bank (1999) *The Partnership Report: Find Out How Our Principles Measure Up in Practice*, Co-operative Bank, Manchester

Co-operative Commission (2000) *The Future of the Co-operative Movement: A Round-Table Discussion*, Supplement to the *New Statesman*, 10 October 2000

The Corporate Citizenship Company (2000) *Monitoring, Measuring and Reporting Corporate Social Responsibility*, The Corporate Citizenship Company, London, www.corporate-citizenship.co.uk.

Corporate Europe Observatory (2000) *Global Greenhouse Mania: UN Climate Talks Corrupted by Corporate-Pseudo Solutions*, CEO, Amsterdam, available online at www.xs4all.nl/~ceo/greenhouse/corporate.html.

Costanza, R, et. al. (1997) 'The Value of the World's Ecosystem Services and Natural Capital.', *Nature*, May 1997

Council for Economic Priorities Accreditation Agency (1997) *Social Accountability 8000*, CEPAA, New York

The Council on Foundations (1996) *Measuring the Value of Corporate Citizenship*. The Council on Foundations, Washington, DC

Cowe, R, and Williams, S (2000) *Who Are the Ethical Consumers?*, The Co-operative Bank, Manchester

Dalberg (2006) *Report of the Task Force on Capacity for Program Delivery: From Talk to Walk: Ideas to Optimize Development Impact*, A Clinton Global Initiative Commitment, Dalberg Global Development Advisors, Washington, DC

Davis, I (2005) 'The biggest contract', *The Economist*, 6 May

Department of Trade and Industry (2000) *The Future of Corporate Learning*, Dti, London

Diamond, L (1994) 'Rethinking Civil Society: Toward Democratic Consolidation', *Journal of Democracy* Vol 5, No 3, July 1994:4–17

Dow Jones Sustainability Group Indexes GmbH (1999) *Guide to the Dow Jones Sustainability Group Indexes – Version 1.0, September 1999*, Dow Jones Sustainability Group Indexes GmbH, Zürich, www.sustainability-index.com.

Drucker, P (1999) *Management Challenges for the 21st Century*, Butterworth Heineman, Oxford

Edwards, M (2000) *NGO Rights and Responsibilties*, Foreign Policy Centre, London

Edwards, M (2000) *Victims of their Own* Success, in *The Guardian Weekly*, 6–12 July 2000: 23

Elkington, J (1998) *Cannibals With Forks: The Triple Bottom Line of the 21st Century*, Capstone, Oxford

Elkington, J and Fennell, S (1998) 'Partners for Sustainability' in *Greener Management International* Issue 24 Winter 1998

ENDS Report, Procter & Gamble steps up attack on eco-labelling, No 265, 1997

Environics International Ltd (1999) *Executive Briefing: The Millennium Poll on Corporate Social Responsibility*, Environics International Ltd, Toronto

The Environment Council (1999) *Guidelines for Stakeholder Dialogue – a Joint Venture*, The Environment Council and Shell International, London

Ernst & Young (1997) *Measures That Matter*, Ernst and Young Centre for Business Innovation: 7

Estrella, M and Gaventa, J (1998) *Who Counts Reality? Participatory Monitoring and Evaluation: A Literature Review*, Working Paper No. 70, Institute of Development of Sussex, Brighton

Ethical Trading Initiative (1998) *Purpose, Principles, Programme: Membership Information*, Ethical Trading Initiative, London, www.ethicaltrade.org

Ethical Trading Initiative (2000) *Getting to Work on Ethical Trading: Annual Report (1999/2000)*, Ethical Trading Initiative, London, www.ethicaltrade.org

European Central Bank (2000) 'Europe, A New Economy?' ECB Press Office, www.ecb.int.

European Commission (1998) *2nd EU-US Symposium on Codes of Conduct and International Labour Standards*, European Commission DGV: March 1999

Ewald, C (1921) 'A Fairy Tale About God and Kings', in Zipes, J (editor) (1990) *Utopian Tales from Weimar*, Poolygon, Edinburgh: 34–35

Ferguson, D C HaasRaynard, P and Zadek, S (1996) *Dangerous Curves: Does the Environment Improve with Economic Growth*, World Wide Fund for Nature, Gland

Fleishman Hillard (1999) *Consumers Demand Companies with a Conscience*, Fleishman Hillard Europe, London

Ford Motor Company (2000) *Connecting With Society: 1999 Corporate Citizenship Report*, Ford Motor Company, Dearborn

Forstater, M and Raynard, P (2001) *Key Initiatives in the Development of Corporate Social Responsibility and the New Economy in Europe*, Working Paper prepared for The Copenhagen Centre, TCC, Copenhagen, www.copenhagencentre.org.

Forstater, M, Oelschaegel, J and Sillanpää, M (2006) *What Assures Consumers?*, AccountAbility in association with the National Consumer Council, London

Forstater, M, Zadek, S, Evans, D, Knight, A, Sillanpää, M, Tuppen, C and Warris, A-M (2006) *The Materiality Report: Aligning Strategy, Performance and Reporting*, AccountAbility in association with the BT Group and LRQA, London

Friedman, M (1970) 'The Social Responsibility Is to Increase Profits', in *New York Times Magazine*, 13 September: 32–33

Galbraith, J (1968) *The New Industrial State*, Penguin, London

Gaventa, J (1998) 'The Scaling-up and Institutionalisation of PRA: lessons and challenges' in: Blackburn, J and Holland, J (eds): *Who Changes? Institutionalising participation in development*, Intermediate Technology Press, London

General Motors (1999) *General Motors 1998 Environmental Health and Safety Report: Steps Towards Sustainability*, General Motors, Detroit

Gladwin, T (1999) 'A Call for Sustainable Development' in Mastering Strategy: Part Twelve, *Financial Times* 13 December

Global Reporting Initiative (1999) *GRI Sustainability Reporting Guidelines*, GRI/CERES, Boston, www.globalreporting.org.

Global Reporting Initiative (2000) *Sustainability Corporate Reporting Guidelines*, GRI, Boston, www.globalreporting.org.

Global Reporting Iniative (2000) *Sustainability Reporting Guidelines*, Global Reporting Initiative, Boston, www.globalreporting.org

Gonella, C and Pilling, A and Zadek, S with assistance from Terry, V (1998) *Making Values Count: Contemporary Experience in Social and Ethical Accounting, Auditing and Reporting*, Association of Chartered Certified Accountants Research Report 57, ACCA, London

Gore, A (2006) *An Inconvenient Truth: The Planetary Emergency of Global Warming and What We Can Do About It*, Bloomsbury, London

Goyder, M (1998) *Living Tomorrow's Company*, Gower, Aldershot

Goyder, G (1961) *The Responsible Company*, Blackwell, Oxford

Graves, S and Waddock, S (2001) *Beyond Built to Last: Stakeholder Relations in 'Built-to-Last' Companies* (forthcoming)

Gray, J (1998) *False Dawn: the Delusions of Global Capitalism*, Granta, London

Gray, R H (2000) *Social And Environmental Responsibility, Sustainability And Accountability: Can the Corporate Sector Deliver?*, Working Paper, University of Glasgow

Grayson, D (2000) *Business and Community, Dangerous Distraction or Commercial Imperative*, TMP Worldwide, Sydney, available online at www.davidgrayson.net

Green, D (1998) *Views From The South: Conference Report on Ethical Trade*, NGO Labour Rights Network, London

Grossman, G and Krueger A (1994), *Economic Growth and the Environment*, Working Paper No 4634 of the National Bureau of Economic Research, Cambridge MA

Hadenius, A and Uggla, F (1996) 'Making Civil Society Work, Promoting Democratic Development: What Can States and Donors Do?', *World Development*, Vol 24, No 10: 1621–1639

Handy, C (1999) *The New Alchemists*, Hutchinson, London

Hawken, P (1997) 'Natural Capitalism', *Mother Jones Reprints*, San Francisco

Hawken, P, Lovins, A and Hunter Lovins, L (1999) *Natural Capitalism: Creating the Next Industrial Revolution*, Little Brown, Boston

Hines, C (2000) *Localisation: A Global Manifesto*, Earthscan, London

HIS (1999) *Peduli Hak: Caring for Rights*, Insan Hitawasana Sejahtera, Jakarta

Hohnen, P (2000) *NGO Engagement: How Close is Too Close?*, Paper presented at Challenges & Opportunities for Civil Society in the Emerging World Order Conference in Valencia, Spain, 27–28 November, 2000

Hopkins, M (1998) *The Planetary Bargain*, HarperCollins, London

Huber, G P (1991) 'Organizational Learning: The Contributing Processes and the Literatures' *Organizational Science*, 2(1), 88–115: 89

Humphries, J and Rubery, J (1995) *The Economics of Equal Opportunities*, Equal Opportunities Commission, Manchester

Innovation Through Partnership, a joint initiative between the Institute of Social and Ethical AccountAbility, Business in the Community, and the Local Futures Group with support from the Dti. Available at www.innovation-partnership.org.

Instituto Ethos (2000) *Ethos Indicators on Corporate Social Responsibility*, Instituto Ethos, Sao Paulo, www.ethos.org.br.

Interface Inc. (1997) *Interface Sustainability Report*, Interface Corp, La Grange GA
International Baby Food Action Network (1998) *Breaking the Rules: Stretching the Rules 1998*, IBFAN, Penang
International Labour Office (1998) *Governing Body Agenda Item – Overview of Global Developments and Office Activities Concerning Codes of Conduct, Social Labelling and Other Private Sector Activities Addressing Labour Issues*, GB.273/WP/SDL/1. 273rd Session, ILO, Geneva
IPPR (2001) *Building Better Partnerships, the Final Report on the Commission on Private Public Partnerships*, IPPR, London
ISEA (1999) *AA1000 Framework*, ISEA, London
ISEA (1999) *AA1000: Overview of Standard, Guidelines, and Tools*, Institute of Social and Ethical AccountAbility, London
Jaruzelski, B, Dehoff, K and Bordia, R (2006) *Smart Spenders: The Global Innovation 1000*, Booz Allen Hamilton, New York
Johnston, P (2001) 'Corporate Responsibility in Employment Standards in a Global Knowledge Economy', in Zadek, S Højensgård, N and Raynard, P *Perspectives on the New Economy of Corporate Citizenship*, TCC, Copenhagen
Joy, B (2000) 'Why the Future Doesn't Need Us', *Wired Magazine*, April 2000
Kelly, G (1999) *The New Partnership Agenda*, IPPR Commission on Public Private Partnerships, IPPR, London, www.ippr.org.uk.
Kennedy, A (2000) *The End of Shareholder Value*, Orion Books, London
Klein, N (2000) *No Logo*, Flamingo, London
Koestler, A (1945) 'The Yogi and the Commissar', in Koestler, A (1945) *The Yogi and the Commissar*: 9–20
Korten, D (1997) *When Corporations Rule the World*, Kumarian, Hartford
Korten, D (1999) *The Post-Corporate World: Life After Capitalism*, Kumarian Press and Berrett-Koehler, West Hartford
Kuhn, T (1962) *The Structure of Scientific Revolutions*, University of Chicago Press, Chicago, IL
Labour Rights in China (1999) *No Illusions: Against the Global Cosmetic SA8000*, AMRC, Hong Kong
LaFeber, W (1999) *Michael Jordan and the New Global Capitalism*, WW Norton, New York
Lawson, I (1999) *Leaders for Tomorrow's Society*, The Industrial Society, London
Levi Strauss (1998) *Program Overview: An Independent Evaluation of Levi Strauss & Co's Code of Conduct process: A Pilot Program in the Dominican Republic*, report presented at the annual Business for Social Responsibility conference in San Francisco in August 1998.
Lewis, D and Wallace, T (2001) *New Roles and Relevance: Development NGOs and the Challenge of Change*, Kumarian Press, Harts
Lewis, S (1998) *External Perceptions of Corporate Social Responsibility*, MORI, London
Lewnhak, H (1997) *International Labour Organization Digest*, January 1997
Logan, D and Tuffrey, M (2000) *Companies in Communities: Assessing the Impact*, The Corporate Citizenship Company, London
Louis Harris and Associates (1991) *Public Attitudes Towards People with Disabilities*, undertaken for National Organisation on Disability, Louis Harris and Associates, New York
MacGillivray, A and Zadek, S (1996) *Accounting for Change: Indicators for Sustainable Development*, New Economics Foundation, London, www.neweconomics.org

Mant, A (1997) *Intelligent Leadership*, Allen and Unwin, St Leonards

Max-Neef, M, Elizalde, A and Hopenhayn, M (1991) *Human Scale Development: Conception, Application and Further Reflection*, Apex Press, New York

McGillivray, A, Marten, H, Rüdiger, K, Vilanova, M, Zollo, M, Begley, P and Zadek, S (2007) *Responsible Competitiveness in Europe: Enhancing European Competitiveness through Corporate Responsibility*, AccountAbility, London

Morehouse, W (1998) 'Consumption, Civil Action and Corporate Power: Lessons from the Past, Strategies for the Future', in Special Issue of *Development Consumption, Civil Action and Sustainable Development* Vol 41 No 1 March: 48–53

Mulgan, G (1998) *Connexity: How to Live in a Connected World*, Chatto and Windus, London

Murphy, D F, and Bendell, J (1997) *In the Company of Partners: Business, Environmental Groups and Sustainable Development Post-Rio*, The Polity Press, Bristol

NatWest Group (1999) *Social Impact Review 1998/1999*, NatWest Group, London

Nelson, J and Zadek, S (2000) *Partnership Alchemy: New Social Partnerships in Europe*, The Copenhagen Centre, Copenhagen

Nestlé report, Emerging Market Economics (2000) *Infant Nutritional Operational Study*, EME, London

New Economics Foundation (1997) *Community Works!*, NEF, London, www.neweconomics.org

New Economics Foundation/Catholic Institute for International Relations (1997) *Open Trading: Effective Options for Monitoring Corporate Codes of Conduct*, NEF/CIIR, London, www.neweconomics.org

New Economics Foundation (1998) *Participation Works! 21 Techniques of Community Participation for the 21st Century*, NEF,London, www.neweconomics.org

New Economics Foundation (2000) *Corporate Spin: the Troubled Teenage Years of Social Auditing*, NEF, London: 5

Novo Nordisk (1999) *1998 Social Report*, Novo Nordisk a/s, Bagsværd

Organisation for Economic Co-Operation and Development (1999) *The Economic and Social Implications of E-Commerce*, OECD, Paris

Perri 6 (1997) *Holistic Government*, DEMOS, London

Pilger, J (1999) 'The Siege of Seattle Marked the Rise of a Popular Resistance to the Evils of Globalisation', *New Statesman*

Placer Dome, Inc (2000) *Ensuring Our Future: Sustainability Report 1999*, Placer Dome, Vancouver BC, available online at www.placerdome.com.

Power, M (1995) *The Audit Explosion*, Demos, London

Pretty, J et al (1995) *Participatory Learning and Action. A Trainer's Guide*, International Institute for Environment and Development, London

Prince of Wales Business Leader Forum (2000) *Measure for Success: Assessing the Impact of Partnerships*, IBLF, London, www.pwblf.org.

Probst, G, Raub, S and Romhardt, K (2000) *Managing Knowledge: Building Blocks for Success*, John Wiley and Sons, London

Radovich, S (2006) *The Global Alliance for Workers and Communities: Lessons Learnt From A Multi-Stakeholder Initiative*, AccountAbility, London

Radovich, S and Zadek, S (2006) *Governing Partnership Governance: Enhancing Development Outcomes By Improving Partnership Governance and Accountability*, Working Paper 23, CSR Initiative, Centre for Government and Business, J. F. Kennedy School for Government, Harvard University, Cambridge, MA

Reinicke, W, and Deng, F (2000) *Critical Choices: The United Nations, Networks, and the Future of Global Governance*, IDRC, Ottowa: xiv, www.idrc.org.

Rio Tinto (1999) *1998 Social and Environmental Report*, Rio Tinto, London

Ritchey-Vance, M (1998) 'Widening the Lens on Impact Assessment: The Inter-American Foundation and Its Grassroots Development Framework – The Cone', in: Blauert, J and Zadek, S (1998*)*, *Mediating Sustainability: Growing Policy from the Grassroots*, Kumarian Press, West Hartford, CT

Sachs, J, Stone, G and Warner, A (1999) 'Year in Review', in *Global Competitiveness Report*, World Economic Forum, Geneva: 15

Samuel, J (1999) 'Dotcom Delusions' www.ncasindia.org in Zadek, S, Hojengard, N and Raynard, P (eds) (2001) *Perspectives on the New Economy of Corporate Citizenship*, The Copenhagen Centre

Schwartz, P and Gibb, B (1999) *When Good Companies Do Bad Things*, Wiley, New York

Senge, P, (1994) *The Fifth Discipline: The Art & Practice of The Learning Organization*, Currency Doubleday, New York

Shell International (1998) *Profits and Principles – Does There Have to be a Choice?*, Royal Dutch Shell, London

Shell International (1999) *The Shell Report 1999: People, Planet and Profits – An Act of Commitment*, Shell International, London

Slim, H (1999) *Future Imperatives: Quality, Standards and Human Rights*, Prepared for the British Overseas Aid Group, Centre for Development and Emergency Practice, Oxford Brookes University, Oxford

Smith, A (1759) *The Theory of Moral Sentiments*, A Millar, London

Social Exclusion Unit (1999) *Social Exclusion Unit's Policy Action Team 3 Report, Enterprise and Social Exclusion*, UK Government, London

Social Investment Forum (1999) '1999 Report on Socially Responsible Investing Trends in the United States', SIF Industry Research Program

Social Venture Network (2000) *Standards for Social Responsibility*, SVN, San Francisco, www.svn.org.

Sogge, D with Biekart, K and Saxby, J (1996) *Compassion and Calculation: the Business of Private Foreign Aid*, Pluto Press, London

South African Breweries (2000) *Corporate Citizenship Review 1999*, SAB, London, www.sabplc.com.

Southern Sun (2000) *Values and Value Adding: Corporate Citizenship Report*, Southern Sun Group, Santon

Strannegård, L and Wolff, R (1999) 'Discovering Sustainability: A Case Study of Learning Through Environmental Scenarios', *Greener Management International*, Autumn Issue 23

SustainAbility Ltd (1999) *The Social Reporting Report*, UNEP/SustainAbility Ltd, London, www.sustainability.co.uk

SustainAbility Ltd (2001) *Politics and Persuasion: Corporate Influence on Sustainable Development Policy*, SustainAbility Ltd, London, www.sustainability.co.uk

Sustainability Asset Management (2000) *Biographies of Corporate Sustainability Leaders*, SAM, Zurich, available on line at www.sam-group.ch/e/center/c_reports.cfm.

Terry, V (1998) *Making Values Count: Contemporary Experience in Social and Ethical Accounting, Auditing and Reporting*, ACCA Research Report 57, Association of Chartered Certified Accountants, London, www.acca.org.uk

Tissen, R, Andriessen, D and Lekanne Deprez, F (2000) *The Knowledge Dividend*, FT Prentice-Hall, London: 34

Traidcraft plc (1994) *Social Audit 1993*, Traidcraft, Gateshead
UDV Polska (1999) *Economic, Social, and Environmental Performance*, UDV Polska, Warsaw
UNCTAD (1998) *World Investment Report*, UNCTAD, Geneva
UNEP/SustainAbility (2000) *Global Sustainability Reporters: A Benchmark Study*, SustainAbility, London
United Nations (1998) *Human Development Report 1998*, UN, New York
United Nations (1999) *Human Development Report 1999*, UN, New York
United Nations (2000) *Human Development Report 2000*, UN, New York
United Nations (2000) *The Global Compact: Statements from Participants* – High-Level Meeting, 26 July 2000, New York, UN, New York, www.unglobalcompact. org.
United Nations Environmental Program (1998) *What is a Sustainable Enterprise?*, Workshop Report, UNEP, Paris
United Utilities (1999) *Social Partnership Report 1999: Accounting for Our Impact on Society*, United Utilities, Warrington
United Utilities (2000) *Social and Environmental Impact Report*, United Utilities, Warrington
Utting, P (2000) *Business Responsibility for Sustainable Development*, UNRISD, Geneva
VanCity (1998) *VanCity's Social Report 1997*, VanCity Savings Credit Union, Vancouver
VanCity (2000) *Guided by Values: The VanCity Social Report 1998/98*, VanCity, Vancouver: 10, available online at www.vancity.com/socialreport
von Weitsacker, E Lovins, A and Lovins, H (1997) *Factor Four: Doubling Wealth, Halving Resource Use*, Earthscan, London
Wackernagel, M and Rees, W (1995) *Our Ecological Footprint*, New Catalyst, Philadelphia
Wells, H G (1976) *A Modern Utopia*, Bison, London
Wheeler, D, and Sillanpää, M (1997) *The Stakeholder Corporation: A Blueprint for Maximising Stakeholder Value*, Pitman, London
Wilsdon, J (2000) *The Capitals Model: A Framework for Sustainability*, Working Paper prepared for SIGMA Project, Forum for the Future, London
Wong, W, (2000) *Knowledge and CSR*, Working Paper prepared for the Innovation through Partnership initiative, www.innovation-partnership.org
World Bank (1997) *World Development Indicators*, Washington DC: World Bank
World Business Council for Sustainable Development (1998) *Exploring Sustainable Development: Global Scenarios 2000–2050, Summary Brochure*, WBCSD, London
World Business Council for Sustainable Development (1999) *Corporate Social Responsibility*, WBCSD, Geneva
World Development Movement (1998) *Making Investment Work for People: An International Framework for Investment*, WDM Consultation Paper, WDM, London
World Development Movement (1999) *Making Investment Work for People*, WDM, London
World's Most Respected Companies, FT Survey 2000, www.ft.com
Zadek, S (1993) *An Economics of Utopia: the Democratisation of Scarcity*, Avebury, Aldershot
Zadek, S (1996) 'Looking Back from 2010' in Sogge, D (1996), *Compassion & Calculation: the Business of Private Foreign Aid*, Pluto Press, London

Zadek, S (1999) 'Looking Back from 2050' in *European Review of Business Ethics*, July 1999 – Vol. 8 No 3

Zadek, S (1999) *Ethical Trade Futures*, New Economics Foundation, London

Zadek, S (1999) 'Reflections on a Factory Visit', in *Global Alliance for Workers and Communities: Progress Report*, Fall 1999: 3–4

Zadek, S (1999) 'Stalking Sustainability' in *Greener Management International* issue 24 Winter 1999: 1–12

Zadek, S (1999) 'The Global Supermarket' in World Business Council for Sustainable Development (1999) *World Development: Aid and Foreign Direct Investment*, Kensington Publications, London: 248–249

Zadek, S (2000) *Doing Good and Doing Well: The Business Case for Corporate Citizenship*, Conference Board, New York

Zadek, S (2000) *Conversations With Disbelievers: Persuading Companies to Increase Their Social Engagement*, Brody & Weiser, Mass.

Zadek, S (2000) '*Third Generation Futures*' in *United Utilities Social and Environmental Impact Report 2000*, United Utilities, Warrington

Zadek, S (2001) *Third Generation Corporate Citizenship: How Much Can Corporations Deliver*, Foreign Policy Centre, London

Zadek, S (2004) 'Paths to corporate responsibility', *Harvard Business Review*, vol 12, December

Zadek, S (2006) 'Separating smart from great: Embedding accountability into business practices isn't easy', *Fortune International*, 30 October, pp74–77

Zadek, S (2006) *The Logic of Collaborative Governance: Corporate Responsibility, Accountability and the Social Contract*, Working Paper 14, CSR Initiative, Centre for Government and Business, J.F Kennedy School for Government, Harvard University, Cambridge, MA

Zadek, S. (2007) *The New Competitiveness*, Harvard Business School Press, Boston, MA

Zadek, S, and Amalric, F (1998) 'Consumer Works!' in *Development* Vol 41 No 1 March 1998, Special Issue on Consumption, Civil Action, and Sustainable Development, Society for International Development: 7–15

Zadek, S, and Evans, R (1993) *Auditing the Market: A Practical Approach to Social Auditing*, Traidcraft Exchange and the New Economics Foundation, Gateshead

Zadek, S and Forstater, M 'Making Civil Regulation Work' in Addo, M (ed.) (1999) *Human Rights Standards and the Responsibility of Transnational Corporations*, Kluwer, Hague: 69–75

Zadek, S and Merme, M (2004) *Redefining Materiality*, AccountAbility, London

Zadek, S, Hojengard, N and Raynard, P (2000) *The New Economy of Corporate Citizenship*, The Copenhagen Centre, Copenhagen

Zadek, S, Lingayah, S, and Forstater, M (1998) *Social Labels: Tools for Ethical Trade*, report by the New Economics Foundation for the European Commission (DGV.D1)

Zadek, S, Lingayah, S and Murphy, S (1998) *Purchasing Power: Civil Action for Sustainable Consumption*, New Economics Foundation. London

Zadek, S, Merme, M and Samans, R (2005) *Mainstreaming Responsible Investment*, World Economic Forum in association with AccountAbility, Geneva

Zadek, S, Pruzan, P and Evans, R (editors) (1997) *Building Corporate AccountAbility*, Earthscan, London

Zadek, S, Raynard, P, Oliviero, C, do Nascimento, E and Tello, R (2005) *Responsible Competitiveness: Reshaping Global Markets Through Responsible Business Practices*, AccountAbility, London

Zadek, S and Scott-Parker, S (2000) *Unlocking Potential: The New Disability Business Case*, Employers' Forum on Disability, London, www.employers-forum.co.uk.

Zadek, S and Scott-Parker, S (2001) *Unlocking the Evidence: the New Disability Case*, Employers' Forum on Disability, London, www.employers-forum.co.uk

Zadek, S, and Szabo, S (1996) *Valuing Organisation: The Case of Sarvodaya*, New Economics Foundation, London

Zadek, S and Tuppen, C (2000) *Adding Values: the Economics of Sustainable Business*, British Telecommunications Occasional Paper 4, BT, London

Zarsky, (1999) *Havens, Halos And Spaghetti: Untangling The Evidence About Foreign Direct Investment And The Environment*, Nautilus Institute for Security and Sustainable Development, California, www.nautilus.org/papers/enviro/index.html

Zohar, D (1997) *Rewiring the Corporate Brain*, Berrett-Koehler, New York

Zuckerman, M (1999) *Speed: Linking Innovation, Process, and Time to Market*, Research Report 1269-00-RR, Conference Board, New York

Index

AA1000 accountability standard 182,
    227–228, 238, 239
accountability 2, 15, 18–19, 20, 23, 25,
    104, 110–111
accounting entities 186–189, 194
ActionAid 72
activism 109, 110, 154, 239
Adriano, Dino 107
advertising 67, 75, 108
Ahold 77, 221–222
AIP see Apparel Industry Partnership
Amery, Christopher 167, 217
Amnesty Business Group 72, 73, 112
AMRC *see* Asia Monitoring Resource
    Centre
Andersson, Gavin 163
Angiers, Phil 152
Anglian Water 134
Anglo-American corporate model
    55–58, 98
Annan, Kofi 17, 44, 115, 127, 164
Apparel Industry Partnership (AIP)
    63, 65
Atlanta Agreement 7
Ashridge Centre for Business and
    Society 234
Asia Monitoring Resource Centre
    (AMRC) 107–108, 216
audits 4, 14, 209, 212, 219, 228, 232–241
automobiles 47, 98, 99, 189, 201

B&Q 96, 157
Balanced Scorecards 40, 179
basic livelihoods 213–217
BAT *see* British American Tobacco
Baxter International 199
behavioural change 167–171
Ben & Jerry's 6, 69, 73–74, 152
benchmarks 162–164
Bhagwati, J 150
Bhopal 81, 168, 229

Bloch, Ernst 49
Block, Peter 181
BMW 155, 158
Body Shop
    fair trade 69
    financial performance 79
    Formal Stakeholder Dialogue
        220
    market remould 160
    media campaign against 69, 191
    NEF association 73
    niche dominance 58
    Oasis pathway 60, 61
    social assessment 74
    Social Statement 4, 95 219–220
    Values Report 4, 195
Bofors 168
Books-for-Schools 125
boundaries 41, 184–195, 230, 235–236,
    237, 238
BP 6, 14–15, 16, 79, 111, 151, 154
brand switching 84–85
Branson, Richard 11, 12, 69–70
British American Tobacco (BAT) 98
British Standards Institute (BSI) 143
Brown, Gordon 180
Brundtland, Gro Harlem 45
Brundtland Report 131
Bryer, David 66
BSI *see* British Standards Institute
BSR *see* Business for Social
        Responsibility
BT 95, 108, 131, 135, 234
Bullard, Nicola 164
business level
    boundaries 189–190, 237–238
    case 17–18, 25, 90–101
    cultures 146
    engagement 7–8
    reputation 81–82
    tools 39–40, 179, 180

Business in the Community 74, 124, 205, 208
Business Partners in Development program 116–117
Business for Social Responsibility (BSR) 42–43, 58, 152, 212
Butterfield, Herbert 180

Cafédirect 203
Cairncross, Frances 150
capital 143–146
Cardoso Panel 22
Care International (UK) 71
cash-flow 141–142, 146
Casson, Mark 53–54
Castells, Professor Manuel 35, 52, 95
Cavenagh, Tom 51–52
Central Intelligence Agency (CIA) 45, 247–248
Centre for Tomorrow's Company 78, 197, 235
CEPAA see Council on Economic Priorities Accreditation Agency
CEP see Council on Economic Priorities
CERES see Coalition of Environmentally Responsible Economies
Chambers, Robert 208, 219
Chandler, Sir Geoffrey 172
Changing Values report, BT 135
characterizing organizations 186–189
child labour 40, 64, 79
China 9–10, 13, 65
Christian Aid 73, 108
Christie, Alan 63
CIA see Central Intelligence Agency
citizenship cultures 55–58
CIVICUS 117
Civil Learning Cycle 168–171
climate change 10, 20, 24
Co-operative Bank 58, 84, 235
Co-operative Wholesale Society 203
Coalition of Environmentally Responsible Economies (CERES) 71, 193, 216
Coca-Cola 12, 16, 85, 103
codes of conduct 5, 42, 44, 99, 214, 191–192, 158
see also standards

coffee 203
cognitive visualizations 138–139
Cohen, Ben 69
committed boundaries 194–195
Committee on Trade and Environment (CTE) 120
company-specific degrees of freedom 155–156
competence 16, 73, 104, 112, 117–118, 235
competitiveness 32
computers 37
confidence see trust
'connexity' 109
consumerism 5, 84, 203
consumption 30–32
contingent boundaries 189–190
conversational performance 206
Cook, David 235
COP see Corporate Europe Observatory
core standards 44
Corporación Venezolana de Guayana (CVG) 221
Corporate Europe Observatory (COP) 160
corporate social responsibility 1–25, 77, 82–83, 197, 198
corruption 8–9
cost-benefit see traditional business case
Costanza, Robert 47
Council on Economic Priorities Accreditation Agency (CEPAA) 108, 197, 216
Council on Economic Priorities (CEP) 79
credibility 111, 232–241
see also trust
Credit Swiss First Boston 37
CTE see Committee on Trade and Environment

Daft, Douglas 103
Data–Knowledge Continuum 169
Davis, Ian 16
Day Chocolate Company 67
Day, Will 71
defensive business case see pain alleviation business case

definitions
  civil society 12–13, 163–164
  dialogue 225
  stakeholder dialogue 223
  sustainability 145
degrees of freedom 13, 37, 39, 155–156, 158, 159, 161, 183, 224
demonstrations 34, 35, 111
Deng, Francis 118
Desert pathway 59–60, 61, 88, 160, 161
dialogue 219–231
Diamond, Larry 163
disabled people 91, 96, 157, 206–207
disadvantaged groups 54
discrimination 54, 120, 207–208
divergent relevance 200–201
DJSI see Dow Jones Sustainability Index
'dolphin' strategy 106
Domini Social 400 Index 93
Dow Jones Sustainability Index (DJSI) 93, 95, 199
Duisenburg, Wim 52

ECB see European Central Bank
e-commerce 54
economic level 31, 32, 135–141, 150
economic value added (EVA) 200
The Economist 16, 93, 103, 108
Edwards, Michael 104
Electrolux 86
Elkington, John 73, 106, 131–132, 151, 229–230
Elton, Ben 67, 69
EMAS standard 181, 237
Employers' Forum on Disability 206–207
endorsements 71–74, 107, 234, 235, 236
engagement 7–8, 23, 107, 195
Entine, Jon 73, 191, 220
Environment Council 222–223, 227–228
environmental level
  capital 144, 145
  economics 139, 140, 141
  labelling 120
  sustainability 131–133, 136–139, 148–161
Environmental Kuznets Curve 150
Equal Opportunities Commission 207
Ericsson 42

Ernst and Young's Centre for Business Innovation 199
Ethical Trading Initiative (ETI) 7, 20, 64, 65, 107, 120, 126, 196, 216
ethical level 5, 51–62, 63–65, 78, 108, 203
Ethics Etc 235
ETI see Ethical Trading Initiative
Europe 6, 83
European Central Bank (ECB) 52
EVA see economic value added
Evans, Richard 235, 236
Ewald, Carl 245
expert panels 236–237, 239, 240
'expert views' 208
extensively accountable 18, 19
external verification 232–241
ExxonMobil 79, 151, 193, 195

Factor Four 47, 49
Factor Ten proposition 45, 49
factory ownership 153
Fair Labor Association (FLA) 20, 65, 66, 112–113, 160
fairness 154, 210–212
Fairtrade Foundation (FTF) 104, 106
fatalism 48
financial level
  audits 14, 209
  capital 143–146
  public opinion effects 85–87
  returns 164–166
  sustainability 132–133
  twinning 198–200, 205, 207
Financial Times 42, 55, 198, 151, 103
Fisher, Robert 152–153
Five Capital Model 143–144
FLA see Fair Labor Association
Fleishman Hillard 84
Focus on the Global South 119, 164
footprints 4, 33, 36, 49, 135, 180
Ford Motor Corporation 6, 98, 132, 201
'foreign corrupt practices' 7, 123
foreign direct investment 33
Foreign Policy Centre 104
Forest Stewardship Council labels 205
Fortune 100 companies 232
Forum for the Future 68, 143

Four-level Business Case 90
fourth generation responsibility 21–25
freedom, degrees of 154–161, 224
Friedman, Milton 1, 17, 36, 76–80, 90
Friends of the Earth 68, 108
FTF *see* Fairtrade Foundation
Fukuda-Parr, Sakiko 32
future trends 247–251

Galbraith, John Kenneth 166
GAP 76, 82, 99, 152–153, 185
Gates, Jeff 166
GDP *see* gross domestic product
General Electric 198
General Motors 33, 71, 201
generations of corporate responsibility
    11–25
generational waves 110
Global Alliance for Workers and
    Communities 7, 43–44
global balance sheet 30–35, 78
Global Climate Coalition 79, 160
Global Compact, UN 55, 58, 115–116,
    119, 122, 127, 132
Global Exchange 73
Global Public Policy Networks 118
Global Reporting Initiative (GRI)
    accountability/performance 58
    description 117
    evolution 216
    perspectives 136
    reporting 214–215, 237
    standard 15, 193–194
Global Sullivan Principles 71
GNP *see* gross national product
good practices 59–60, 95
Google 13
Gore, Al 9, 13
governance 21, 23,30, 37–39, 115–127
government partnerships 117, 124
Goyder effect 87–88, 161
Goyder, Mark 78, 197, 235
Grajew, Oded 29, 34
Gray, Professor Rob 234
Greenpeace 66, 86, 110, 112
'greens' 34
GRI *see* Global Reporting Initiative
gross domestic product (GDP) 32, 33
gross national product (GNP) 197
Grossman, G 150

Hadenius, Axel 163
Hanson, Professor Kirk 74
HarperCollins 124–125
Harvey, Pharis 112–113
Hawken, Paul 31, 34, 74, 108, 156–157,
    192, 199
HDI *see* human development index
Henriques, Adrian 234
Hines, Colin 43
Hopkins, Michael 86
Ha, Joseph 167, 172, 173
human capital 143, 144
Human Development Index (HDI) 31,
    32
Human Development Report 31, 202
human needs 137, 139–140, 142
human rights 4, 65, 73–74, 110, 167
Human Rights Watch 13, 72, 110
Huntingdon Life Sciences Laboratories
    86
hybrid verification 235–237

IAF *see* Inter-American Foundation
IBLF *see* International Business
    Leaders Forum
ICFTU *see* International Confederation
    of Free Trades Unions
ICHRDD *see* International Centre for
    Human Rights and Democratic
    Development
ILO *see* International Labour
    Organization
ILRF *see* International Labor Rights
    Fund
Immelt, Jeff 11
in-market effects 159
inaction, reasons for 45–49
income *see* wage levels
independence dilemmas 235
indicators *see* performance indicators
Industrial Society 209
inertia 45–49
information 12, 170, 171, 188, 202–205
initiatives
    Books-for-Schools 125
    emerging 111
    lack of 45–49
    voluntary 120–124
innovation 12, 43, 45, 52–53, 92–93, 181
Institute of Development Studies 208

Institute of Social and Ethical
    AccountAbility (ISEA) 143, 182,
    212, 227, 232–233
institutional level 68–69, 70–72, 245
Instituto Ethos (Brazil) 34, 197
intensively accountable 18
Inter-American Foundation (IAF) 224
interconnectivity 108, 109
International Business Leaders Forum
    (IBLF) 58, 83, 196
International Centre for Human Rights
    and Democratic Development
    (ICHRDD) 153
International Confederation of Free
    Trades Unions (ICFTU) 43
International Institute for Environment
    and Development 223
International Labour Organization
    (ILO) 42, 44
International Labour Rights Fund
    (ILRF) 112–113
International Organization for
    Standardization (ISO) 40, 179, 181,
    237
International Textiles and Garments
    Workers Union (ITGWU) 153, 216
International Youth Foundation 44, 117
investment 8, 11, 108, 157, 158–159, 199,
    200
Iraq 9
ISEA see Institute of Social and Ethical
    AccountAbility
ISO see International Organization for
    Standardization
ITGWU see International Textiles and
    Garment Workers Union

Jennings, John 102, 113
job losses 151–152
Jones, Melissa 233
Jordan, Michael 67–68, 69, 71
Joy, Bill 51

Kay, Professor John 63
Kearney, Neil 73, 153–154
Kennedy, Allan 198
Kennedy, John F 197
Kernaghan, Charlie 73
Khor, Martin 114
Klein, Naomi 43

Knight, Phil 115, 122, 173
knowledge 24, 170, 171, 188
Knowledge Dividend 170
Koestler, Arthur 182–183
Korten, David 78, 108, 163
Korten effect 88–89, 161
KPMG 44, 187, 206, 233–234
Kruger 150
Kuhn, Thomas 24
Kuszewski, Judy 71
Kuznets Curve 150

Label Behind the Label 34
labelling 120, 202–205
labour rights 7, 73–74, 112
labour standards
    evolving boundaries 192
    GAP 152–153
    Nike 72, 73, 167
    Patagonia 153, 154
    rewards 158
    voluntary 120, 122
ladder of participation 223–224
LaFeber, Walter 67–68
Las Cristinas gold deposits 221
Latin America 9
learning 40, 92, 95–97, 225
Lee, Mark 212
legislation, statutory 118
legitimizing engagement 105
Levi Strauss 63–65, 79, 95, 152, 201
literal visualizations 138
livelihoods, basic 213–217
Liz Claiborne 63, 79, 160
Logan, David 43
London Benchmarking Group 205,
    237
Lovins, Amory and L Hunter 34, 47,
    150, 156–157, 192, 199

management tools 179, 180
manufactured capital 143–144
Maquila Solidarity Network Canada
    73, 228
market remould 160
Marks & Spencer 63–64, 65, 173
Max-Neef, Manfred 42, 49–50, 140
materiality 14, 15
McDonald's 42, 81
measurement 14–15, 196–231

Mecca pathway 60–61, 100–101, 124, 152, 160, 250
mediating indicators 211–213
Mellor, Chris 134
metaphoric visualizations 131–133, 137–138
metrics 15, 199
MFA *see* Multi Fibre Arrangements
Microsoft 13–14
Millennium Poll 82–83, 84
mining activities 221
modelling, sustainable development 146–147
Monks, Bob 166
Monsanto 12, 73, 82, 85, 168, 173, 189–190, 208, 229–230
Moody-Stuart, Mark 134–135, 150–151, 161
Moore's Law 52
Morris, Phillip 42, 98, 162
Mulgan, Geoff 109
Multi Fibre Arrangements (MFA) 20–21
multilateral partnerships 107
Murray, Rick 14

National Consumer Council 5, 203–204
National Organization on Disability 207
natural capital 143–144
Natural Step 40, 141, 142, 145, 179, 235
NatWest 68, 69, 74
navigation, civil 39–41
NEF *see* New Economics Foundation
negotiated boundaries 190–191
Nestlé 7, 37, 81, 86, 99, 104, 109
Neuberger, Rabbi Julia 68, 74
New Economics Foundation (NEF) 19–20, 48, 203, 206
News International 86, 124, 125
'new social partnerships' 117, 118, 127
New Statesman 108
Nguyen, Thuyen 167
Nigeria 8–9
nihilism 48
Nike
  Apparel Industry Partnership 63
  campaign against 7, 79, 82, 85, 109
  Ha, Joseph 172
  Jordan, Michael 67

Knight, Phil 122
labour code 42, 99
Nguyen, Thuyen 167
trusting 72
non-measures 186, 198–200
non-governmental organizations (NGOs)
  CIA 247
  emergence of 22, 37–38
  future of 102–114
  Global Compact 127
  labour standards 201
  'show me' myth 66–67
  trust in 70–72
  UK corporate citizenship 57
Novo Nordisk 92, 99, 122–123, 131, 162, 186, 233, 234, 235–236

Oasis pathway 59, 60–61, 100, 101
OECD *see* Organisation for Economic Co-operation and Development
operational characteristics 186
opinion polls 9, 57, 82–83, 105
OPS *see* Overleg Platform Stedelijk Vernieuwing
optimism 3, 34, 46, 47, 246–7
organic stakeholder dialogue 220–2
Organisation for Economic Co-operation and Development (OECD) 7, 53, 123
organizational level 1–2, 39–40, 167–73, 184–195
  see also non-governmental organizations
outcome quality 228–230
Overleg Platform Stedelijk Vernieuwing (OPS) 222
Øvlisen, Mads 122, 131
Oxfam
  Bryer, David 66
  fair trade 174
  labels 202
  Levi Strauss 64
  Sainsbury's 71, 107, 108–109
  UK corporate citizenship 57

pain alleviation business case 91, 99, 101
participatory development 208, 220–230

partnerships
   accountability 23, 109
   disabled people 96
   drawbacks 116–125
   new civil governance 125–127
   private–public 115–116
   tri-sectoral 117
Patagonia 153, 154
performance benchmarks 162–164
performance indicators 198–218
perplexity, state of 42, 49–50
Perrier 85
Philip Morris 42, 98, 162
Pilger, John 108
Pineda, Magaly 64
Placer Dome De Venezuela 77, 221
Plan International 110
polarization of debate 33–34
Porritt, Sir Jonathon, CBE 68–69, 74
poverty, global 19, 24, 41, 251
Power, Professor Michael 209
prejudice 207–208
Premier Oil 42, 67
PricewaterhouseCoopers 187, 233
Prisoner's Dilemma 46, 48
private–public partnerships 115–116
Probst 169
procedural quality, dialogue 226–228
product labels 202–205
professional 'expert view' 208
professionalism 206–208
professionalization 237, 239
profits 78, 79, 139, 164–166,
public opinion 48–49, 57, 66, 197
public level
   policy 2, 118, 160
   pressure engagement 104, 106
   private partnerships 9, 23
   protest 34, 109, 111
   purposes of business 164–166
Putnam, Robert 144

quality 226–230

Rabobank 222
ranking, tools 224
'reds' 34
Reebok 43, 101, 154
regulation, civil 38, 76–89, 103–104,
   123

Reinicke, Wolfgang 118
relevance, divergent 220–221
renewables 158, 161
reporting 192, 193, 214–215, 232–241
   see also Global Reporting Initiative
reputation 13, 68–72, 81–82, 85–89
responsibility boundaries 184–195
responsiveness 156–8, 229–230
rewards 21, 171
Ringger, Reto 94–95
Rio Tinto 66, 159, 233
risk management 92, 95–97, 155–159
'Road Map' 167
Roddick, Anita 44
Rogan, Peter 175
Royal Dutch Shell 125
Royal Institute of International Affairs
   (RIIA) 85, 86
Rugmark 177
rule-based systems 10, 101, 153–154

S&P 500 Index 68
SA8000 standard 4, 40, 73, 108, 179, 181,
   214–215, 216, 237–238
Sainsbury's 71, 95, 107, 160, 201
SAM see Sustainability Asset
   Management
Sarah Lee 63
Saro-Wiwa, Ken 195
Save the Children Fund 7, 66, 202
sceptical optimism 3, 246–247
Schiro, James 233
scientific management 24, 53
Scott-Parker, Susan 192
Sears Roebuck 33
Seattle 103, 108, 109
second generation of corporate
   responsibility 12–17
sector indicators 201
'Seeing is Believing' programme 208
selfishness 46–47, 48
Senge, Peter 169
sexual harassment 241
shareholders 93–95
Shell International
   campaign against 81, 82, 85
   company statement 77
   corporate prejudice 208
   credibility 71
   divergent relevance 200

engagement/transparency 10, 195
Jennings, John 102
Moody-Stuart, Mark 150–151, 161
niche dominance 58
renewables investment 158
'show me' myth 66
'triple bottom line' reporting 79
UK NGOs 57
UN Declaration of Human Rights
    111
shifting proximity 53
shopping decisions 202
Short, Clare 64
'show me' myth 66–67
Siemens 56
SIGMA *see* Sustainability Integrated
    Guidelines for Management
Slim, Hugo 104
SMART (simple, measurable, accurate,
    relevant and timely) 5, 196, 198
smoking habit 46–48, 162
Social Accountability International *see*
    Council on Economic Priorities
    Accreditation Agency
social level,
    accounting 210–211
    sustainability 131–133, 136–141
    audits 4, 212, 219, 228, 233
    capital 143–145
    contract 56, 57
    credibility 232–241
    exclusion 55
    labels 203–205
    norms 78
    performance 39–41
    responsibility 198
Social Venture Network 197
Solstice Consulting 234
sourcing strategies 65–66
South African Breweries 37, 42
speed of change 52
spending habits 18–19
stakeholders
    The Body Shop 195, 220
    corporate citizenship 54
    dialogue 219–230
    engagement 14–15, 23
    indicator selection 217–218
    proof required by 79
    taking into account 36

standards
    AA1000 standard 182, 227–228, 238,
        239
    boundaries 192–194
    core standards 44
    credibility 237–239
    development 15
    measures 213–217
    see also Global Reporting Initiative;
        labour standards; SA8000
        standard
Starbucks 42
stock markets 53, 86, 93, 142, 143,
        187–188, 198
strategic level
    business case 90, 91–92, 94, 101
    characterization 187
    opportunities 155, 156
strong sustainability principle 146
Suez 57, 77, 160
sustainability 36–37, 131–161, 238
Sustainability Asset Management
        (SAM) 56, 94–95, 148, 155–156, 199
Sustainability Integrated Guidelines
        for Management (SIGMA)
        143–144
SustainAbility Ltd 5, 73, 151, 229, 238
Sutherland, Peter 115
Sweeny, Kevin 153, 154

Taylor, Frederick Winslow 53
Teijin Ltd 155–156
tele-working 53
Tepper-Marlin, Alice 78
Tesco 98
there is no alternative (TINA) 48
third generation corporate
        responsibility 17–21
Third World Network 114
Three Generations of corporate
        citizenship 11, 98–100
TINA *see* there is no alternative
Tobin tax 49
Todd, Susan 234
Total Quality Management 40, 179
trade-offs 150, 153, 161
trade unions 107, 120
traditional business case 91, 92, 93, 94
Traidcraft 152, 210
tramline debate 33–34, 35, 43

transparency 5, 8, 56, 58, 104, 195,
    232–233
tri-sectoral partnerships 117
'triple bottom line' 131–133
trust 8, 53, 63–75, 232–241
Tutu, Archbishop Desmond 74
twinning, financial 198–200, 205,
    207

Uggla, Fredrik 163
UK see United Kingdom
UN see United Nations
United Kingdom (UK)
    climate change 20
    Company Law Review 120–121
    corporate model 6–7, 55, 56
    disability 206–207
    Environment Council 222–223
    'foreign corrupt practices' 123
    Industrial Society 209
    utilities 132, 184–185, 234
UNDHR see United Nations,
    Declaration of Human Rights
unemployment, global 3
UNEP see United Nations,
    Environment Program
unethical investments 36, 55
Unilever 33
Union Carbide 81, 168, 229
United Nations (UN)
    Declaration of Human Rights
        (UNDHR) 213–216
    Environment Program (UNEP)
        55–56, 149, 191, 238
    Human Development Index (HDI)
        31, 32
    Human Development Report 31,
        202
    see also Global Compact
United Utilities 132, 184, 234
United States of America (USA)
    apparel industry 112
    corporate activity 63, 64–65
    corporate model 55, 56
    'foreign corrupt practices' 123
    National Organization on Disability
        207
    opinion polls 82, 83, 84
USA see United States of America
utility companies 184–185, 189

value-chains 154, 158, 188
van Riemsdijk, Patrice 232–233
VanCity Savings and Credit Union 212,
    234
verification 63–65, 232–241
Viederman, Stephen 161
Vietnam Labour Watch 167
Virgin 11, 12, 69–70
visualizations 137–139
voluntary initiatives 120–124
von Pierer, Heinrich 56

wage levels 154, 210, 215
Walkers 124, 125
Wal-Mart 7, 13, 58–59, 201
Washington Consensus 34
WB see World Bank
WBSCD see World Business Council
        for Sustainable Development
WDM see World Development
        Movement
weak sustainability principle 145–146
wealth 30–31
web companies 13–14
'whites' 34
Wilson, Andrew 74, 234
win–win strategies 10, 76, 78–79
'windows and mirrors' concept
    202–205
Wolf, Martin 1
Wolfensen, Jim 52
World Bank (WB) 34, 52, 116–117, 123
World Business Council for
        Sustainable Development
        (WBCSD) 77, 92, 193, 216
World Development Movement
        (WDM) 43, 104
World Economic Forum 32
World Trade Organization (WTO) 34,
        92, 103, 109, 115, 120, 135, 229
World Wide Fund for Nature (WWF)
        70, 105
WTO see World Trade Organization
Wuppertal Institute 45
WWF see World Wide Fund for Nature

Yanz, Lynda 34
Young, Andrew 72–73

Zohah, Donar 225

Dr Simon Zadek is Chief Executive of AccountAbility, a Senior Fellow at the Centre for Government and Business of Harvard University's Kennedy School, and an Honorary Professor at the University of South Africa's Centre for Corporate Citizenship. He sits on the International Advisory Board of Instituto Ethos, the Advisory Board of Generation Investment Management, and the boards of the Employers' Forum on Disability and GAN-NET. In 2003 he was named one of the World Economic Forum's 'Global Leaders for Tomorrow'.

Simon's previous roles include Visiting Professor at the Copenhagen Business School, the Development Director of the New Economics Foundation, and founding Chair of the Ethical Trading Initiative. He has served on numerous boards and advisory councils, including the State of the World's Commission on Globalization, the International Labour Organization's World Commission on the Social Dimensions of Globalization, the UN Commission for Social Development Expert Group on CSR, and the founding Steering Committee of the Global Reporting Initiative.

Simon has supported many businesses' efforts around the world in driving accountability innovations into their strategies and practices. His work has increasingly focused on facilitating businesses and their stakeholders in developing mutual understanding and collaborative initiatives. His work in this regard has been both at company level (for example, for Gap Inc in their work around labour standards, and GE in its development of its approach to human rights) through to his convening role of the MFA Forum, a large-scale collaboration involving leading textiles and apparel companies, civil society and labour organizations, international development agencies and financing institutions, and national governments and business associations.

He has authored, co-authored and co-edited numerous publications, including, most recently, two Harvard Working Papers on the role of multi-stakeholder partnerships in development and governance, *Governing Partnership Governance* (2006) and *The Logic of Collaborative Governance* (2005). He has written extensively on the impact of corporate responsibility on the competitiveness of nations *Responsible Competitiveness* (2005). His PhD thesis was published as *The Economics of Utopia* (1994), and an anthology of his writings was published under the title *Tomorrow's History* (2004). *The Civil Corporation: the New Economy of Corporate Citizenship* has become a classic in the field since it was first published in 2001, and has been recognized by the Academy of Management by being honoured with the Social Issues in Management Book Award for 2006. He is currently completing his next book, *The New Competitiveness*, which will be published during 2007 (Harvard Business School Press).